X-MEN LEGACY

SINS OF THE FATHER

X-MEN: LEGACY — SINS OF THE FATHER. Contains material originally published in magazine form as X-MEN: LEGACY #213-216, X-MEN: THE UNLIKELY SAGA OF XAVIER, MAGNETO AND STAN and X-MEN: ODD MEN OUT. First printing 2008. ISBN# 978-0-7851-3002-4. Published by MARVEL PUBLISHING, INC., a subsidiary of MARVEL ENTERTAINMENT, INC. OFFICE OF PUBLICATION: 417 5th Avenue, New York, NY 10016. Copyright © 2006 and 2008 Marvel Characters, Inc. All rights reserved. $24.99 per copy in the U.S. and $26.50 in Canada (GST #R127032852); Canadian Agreement #40668537. All characters featured in this issue and the distinctive names and likenesses thereof, and all related indicia are trademarks of Marvel Characters, Inc. No similarity between any of the names, characters, persons, and/or institutions in this magazine with those of any living or dead person or institution is intended, and any such similarity which may exist is purely coincidental. **Printed in the U.S.A** ALAN FINE, CEO Marvel Toys & Publishing Divisions and CMO Marvel Characters, Inc.; DAVID GABRIEL, SVP of Publishing Sales & Circulation; DAVID BOGART, SVP of Business Affairs & Talent Management; MICHAEL PASCIULLO, VP of Merchandising & Communications; JIM O'KEEFE, VP of Operations & Logistics; DAN CARR, Executive Director of Publishing Technology; JUSTIN F. GABRIE, Director of Editorial Operations; SUSAN CRESPI, Editorial Operations Manager; OMAR OTIEKU, Production Manager; STAN LEE, Chairman Emeritus. For information regarding advertising in Marvel Comics or on Marvel.com, please contact Mitch Dane, Advertising Director, at mdane@marvel.com. For Marvel subscription inquiries, please call 800-217-9158.

10 9 8 7 6 5 4 3 2 1

X-MEN LEGACY

SINS OF THE FATHER

WRITER: Mike Carey

ISSUE #213:
PENCILER: Scot Eaton
INKER: Drew Hennessey
COLORIST: Frank D'Armata

ISSUE #214:
PENCILER: Scot Eaton
INKER: Drew Hennessey
COLORIST: Frank D'Armata
MINDSCAPE SEQUENCES:
PENCILER: Ken Lashley
INKER: Paul Neary
COLORIST: Edgar Delgado

ISSUE #215:
PENCILER: Scot Eaton
INKER: Drew Hennessey
COLORIST: Frank D'Armata
ROGUE AND HELLFIRE SEQUENCES:
ARTIST: Marco Checchetto
COLORIST: Jean-Francois Beaulieu

ISSUE #216:
PENCILER: Phil Briones
INKER: Scott Hanna
COLORIST: Brian Reber

LETTERER: Cory Petit
COVER ART: Alan Davis, Ken Lashley & Salvador Larroca
ASSISTANT EDITORS: Will Panzo & Daniel Ketchum
EDITOR: Nick Lowe
EXECUTIVE EDITOR: Axel Alonso

X-MEN: ODD MEN OUT ONE-SHOT

"ODD MEN OUT"
WRITER: Roger Stern
PENCILER: Dave Cockrum
INKER: Joe Rubinstein
COLORIST: Andrew Crossley
LETTERER: Dave Sharpe

"THE NEW MUTANTS THINK AGAIN"
WRITER: Mike Higgins
PENCILER: Dave Cockrum
INKER: Joe Rubinstein
COLORIST: Andrew Crossley
LETTERER: Joe Rosen

COVER ART: Eric Nguyen
ASSISTANT EDITOR: Suzanne Gaffney
EDITOR: Bob Harras

X-MEN: THE UNLIKELY SAGA OF XAVIER, MAGNETO & STAN
WRITER: Stan Lee
PENCILERS: Ron Lim, Ben Oliver, Ron Frenz, Klaus Janson, Sean Chen, John Romita Jr., Pasqual Ferry, Leinil Francis Yu & Howard Chaykin
INKERS: Mostafa Moussa, Ben Oliver, Tom Palmer, Klaus Janson, Sandu Florea, Scott Hanna, Pasqual Ferry, Leinil Francis Yu & Howard Chaykin
COLORIST: Guru eFX
LETTERER: Virtual Calligraphy's Joe Caramagna
COVER: Brandon Peterson
ASSOCIATE EDITORS: John Barber & Nicole Boose
EDITOR: Ralph Macchio

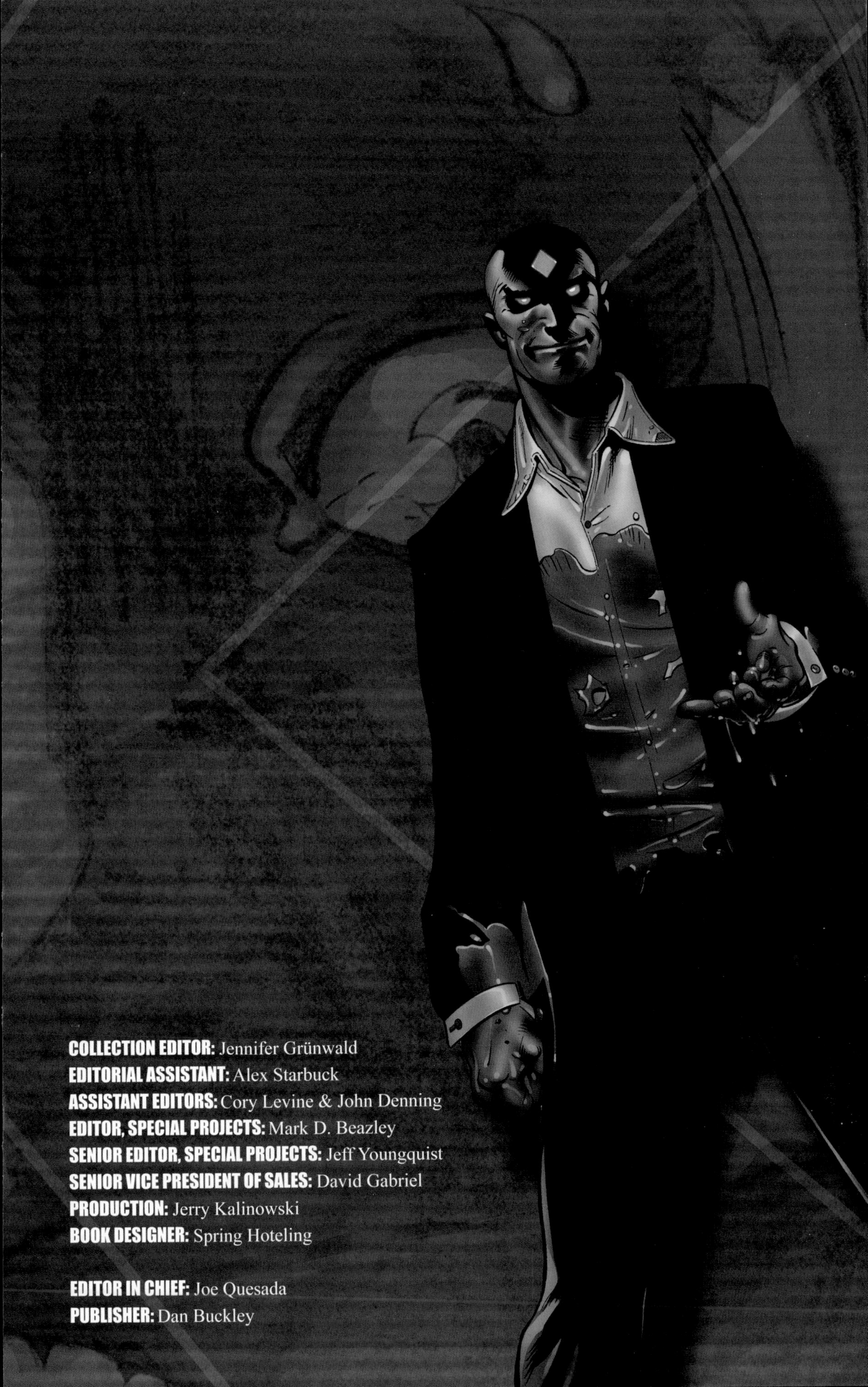

COLLECTION EDITOR: Jennifer Grünwald
EDITORIAL ASSISTANT: Alex Starbuck
ASSISTANT EDITORS: Cory Levine & John Denning
EDITOR, SPECIAL PROJECTS: Mark D. Beazley
SENIOR EDITOR, SPECIAL PROJECTS: Jeff Youngquist
SENIOR VICE PRESIDENT OF SALES: David Gabriel
PRODUCTION: Jerry Kalinowski
BOOK DESIGNER: Spring Hoteling

EDITOR IN CHIEF: Joe Quesada
PUBLISHER: Dan Buckley

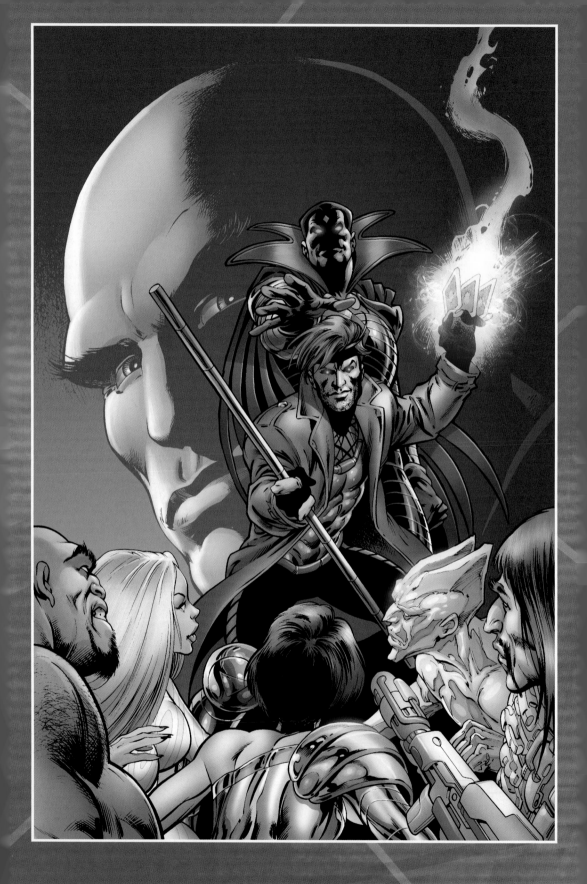

#213

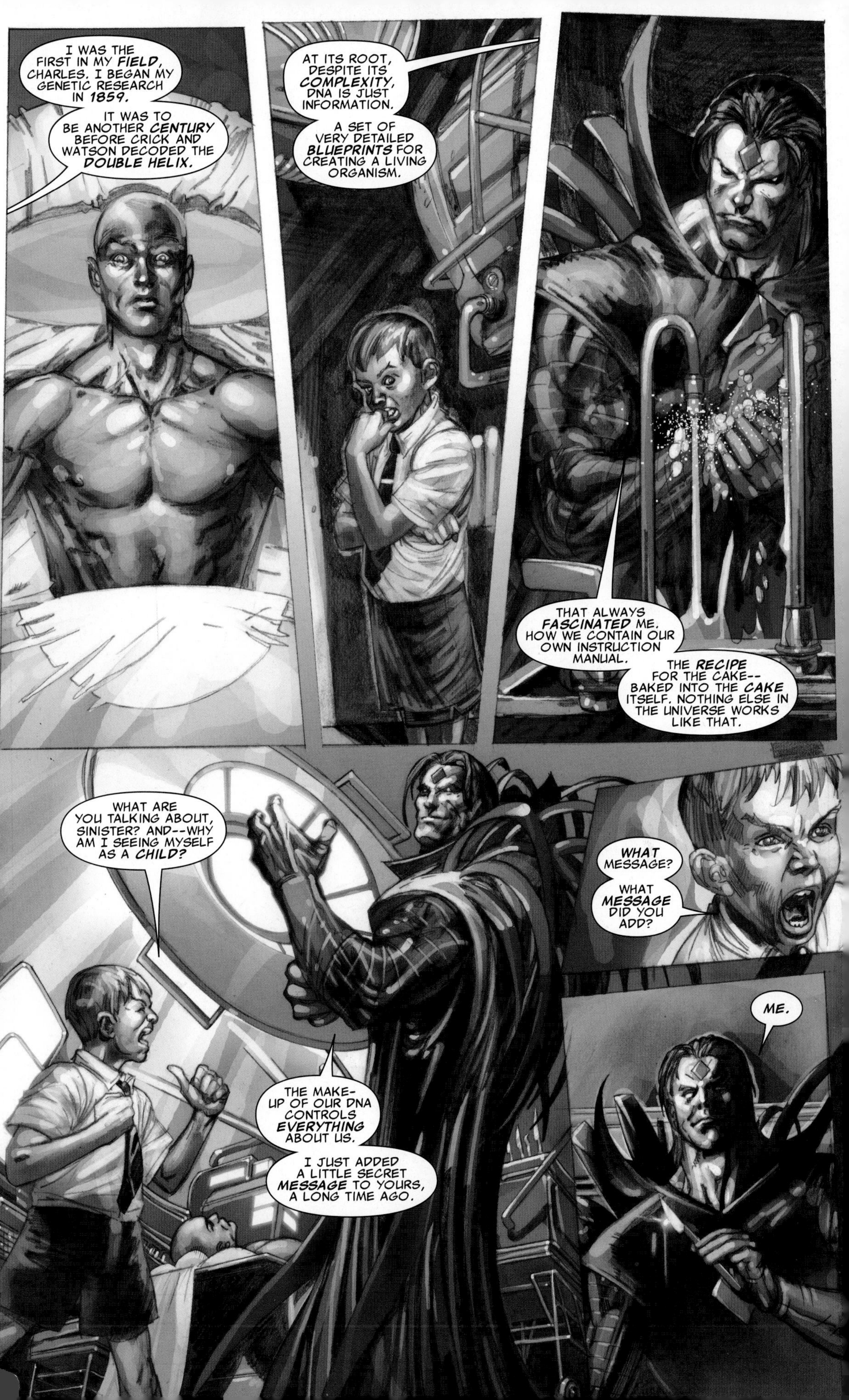
I WAS THE FIRST IN MY FIELD, CHARLES. I BEGAN MY GENETIC RESEARCH IN 1859.
IT WAS TO BE ANOTHER CENTURY BEFORE CRICK AND WATSON DECODED THE DOUBLE HELIX.
AT ITS ROOT, DESPITE ITS COMPLEXITY, DNA IS JUST INFORMATION.
A SET OF VERY DETAILED BLUEPRINTS FOR CREATING A LIVING ORGANISM.
THAT ALWAYS FASCINATED ME. HOW WE CONTAIN OUR OWN INSTRUCTION MANUAL.
THE RECIPE FOR THE CAKE-- BAKED INTO THE CAKE ITSELF. NOTHING ELSE IN THE UNIVERSE WORKS LIKE THAT.
WHAT ARE YOU TALKING ABOUT, SINISTER? AND--WHY AM I SEEING MYSELF AS A CHILD?
THE MAKE-UP OF OUR DNA CONTROLS EVERYTHING ABOUT US.
I JUST ADDED A LITTLE SECRET MESSAGE TO YOURS, A LONG TIME AGO.
WHAT MESSAGE?
WHAT MESSAGE DID YOU ADD?
ME.

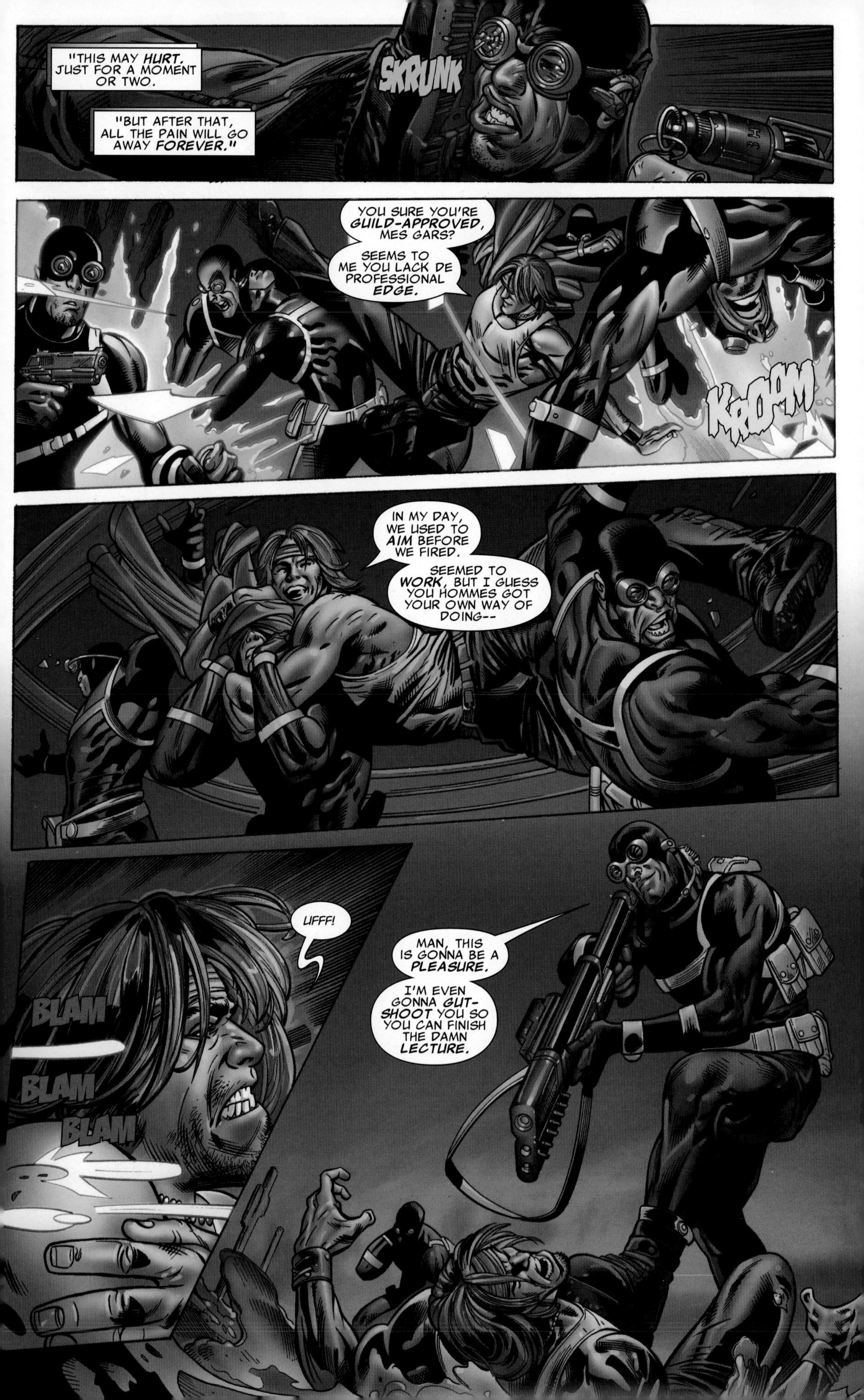
"THIS MAY HURT. JUST FOR A MOMENT OR TWO.
"BUT AFTER THAT, ALL THE PAIN WILL GO AWAY FOREVER."
SKRUNK
YOU SURE YOU'RE GUILD-APPROVED, MES GARS?
SEEMS TO ME YOU LACK DE PROFESSIONAL EDGE.
KROOM
IN MY DAY, WE USED TO AIM BEFORE WE FIRED.
SEEMED TO WORK, BUT I GUESS YOU HOMMES GOT YOUR OWN WAY OF DOING--
BLAM
BLAM
BLAM
UFFF!
MAN, THIS IS GONNA BE A PLEASURE.
I'M EVEN GONNA GUT-SHOOT YOU SO YOU CAN FINISH THE DAMN LECTURE.

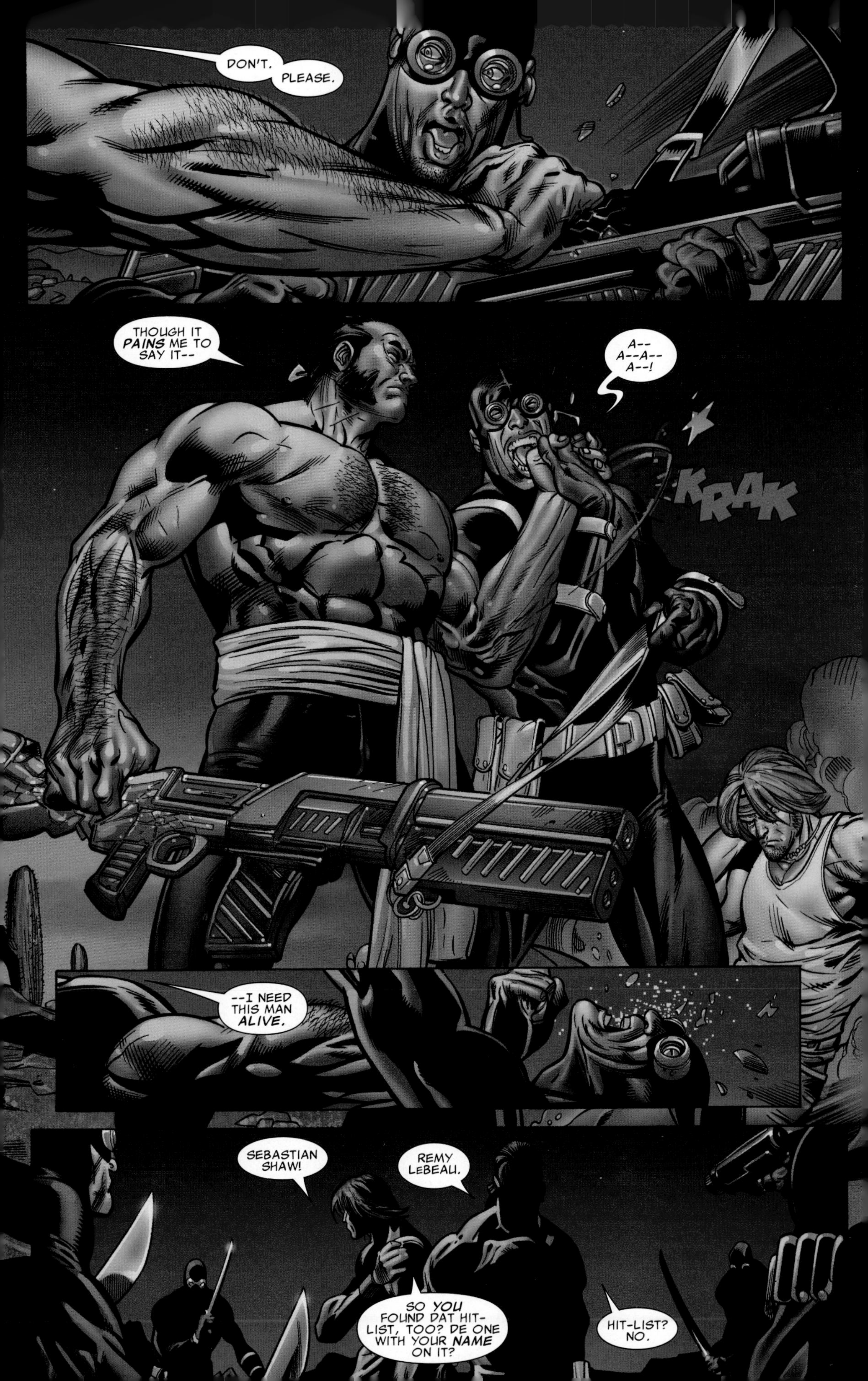
DON'T.
PLEASE.
THOUGH IT PAINS ME TO SAY IT--
A-- A--A-- A--!
KRAK
--I NEED THIS MAN ALIVE.
SEBASTIAN SHAW!
REMY LEBEAU.
SO YOU FOUND DAT HIT-LIST, TOO? DE ONE WITH YOUR NAME ON IT?
HIT-LIST? NO.

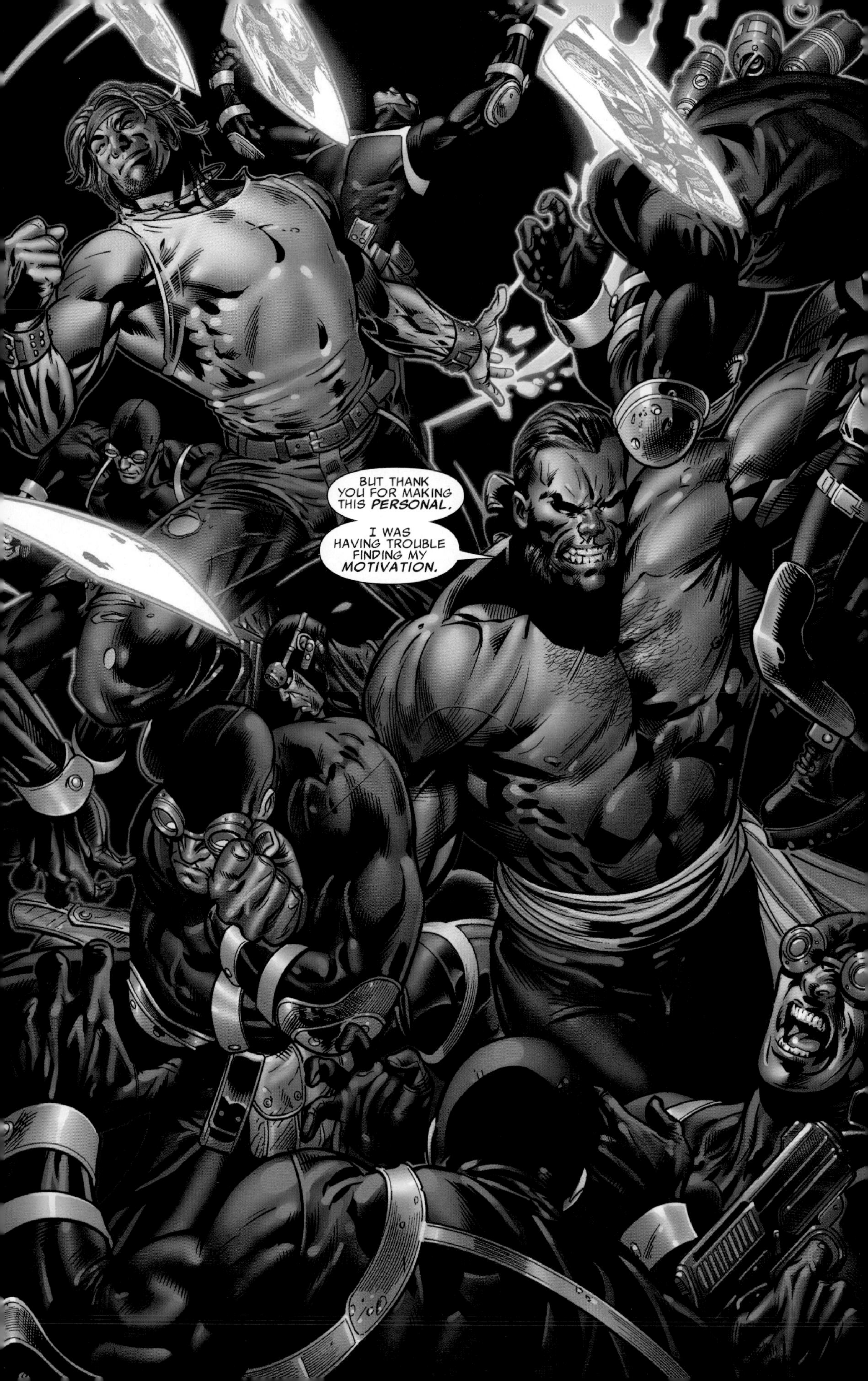
BUT THANK YOU FOR MAKING THIS PERSONAL.
I WAS HAVING TROUBLE FINDING MY MOTIVATION.

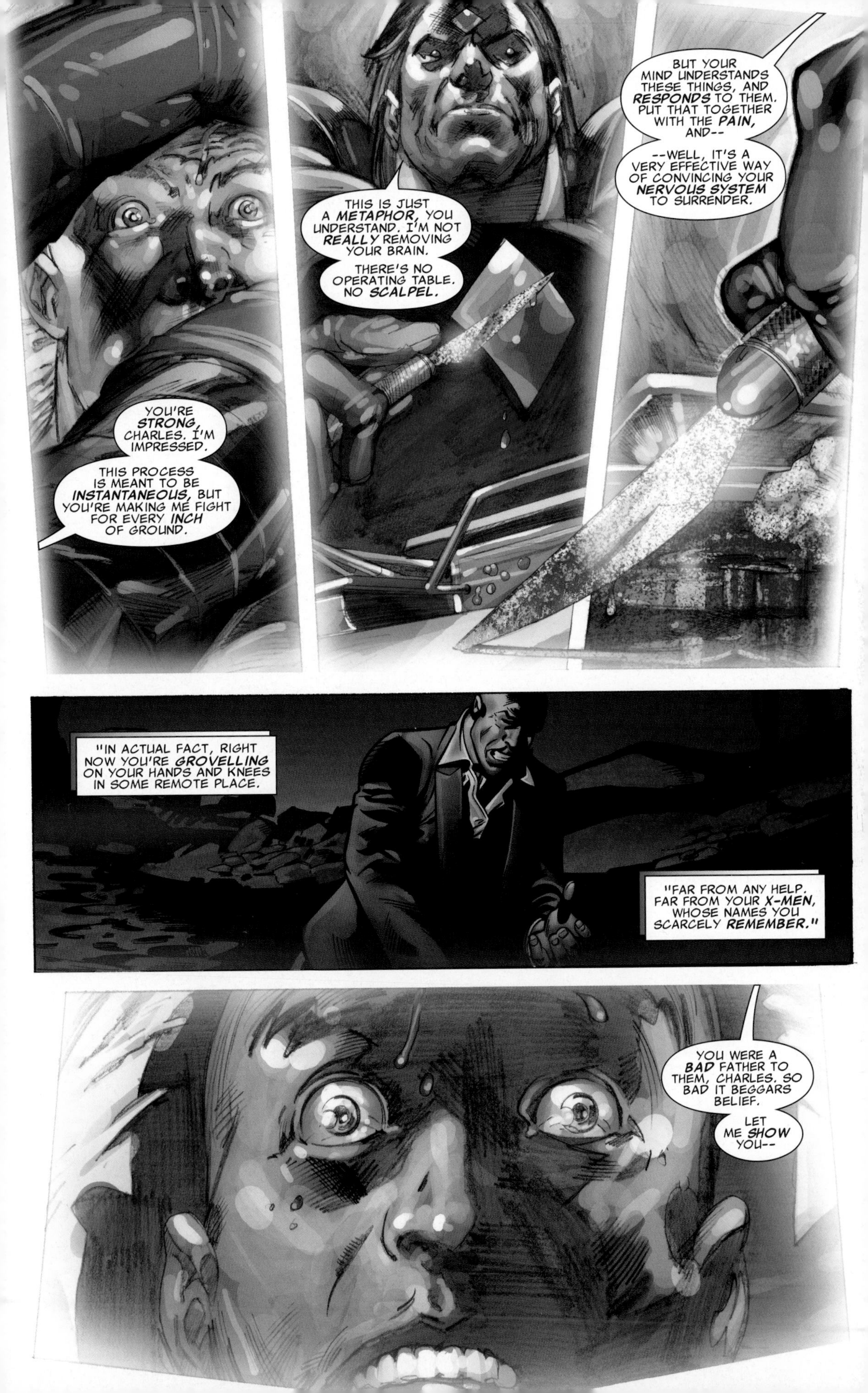
YOU'RE STRONG, CHARLES. I'M IMPRESSED.
THIS PROCESS IS MEANT TO BE INSTANTANEOUS, BUT YOU'RE MAKING ME FIGHT FOR EVERY INCH OF GROUND.
THIS IS JUST A METAPHOR, YOU UNDERSTAND. I'M NOT REALLY REMOVING YOUR BRAIN.
THERE'S NO OPERATING TABLE. NO SCALPEL.
BUT YOUR MIND UNDERSTANDS THESE THINGS, AND RESPONDS TO THEM. PUT THAT TOGETHER WITH THE PAIN, AND--
--WELL, IT'S A VERY EFFECTIVE WAY OF CONVINCING YOUR NERVOUS SYSTEM TO SURRENDER.
"IN ACTUAL FACT, RIGHT NOW YOU'RE GROVELLING ON YOUR HANDS AND KNEES IN SOME REMOTE PLACE.
"FAR FROM ANY HELP. FAR FROM YOUR X-MEN, WHOSE NAMES YOU SCARCELY REMEMBER."
YOU WERE A BAD FATHER TO THEM, CHARLES. SO BAD IT BEGGARS BELIEF.
LET ME SHOW YOU--

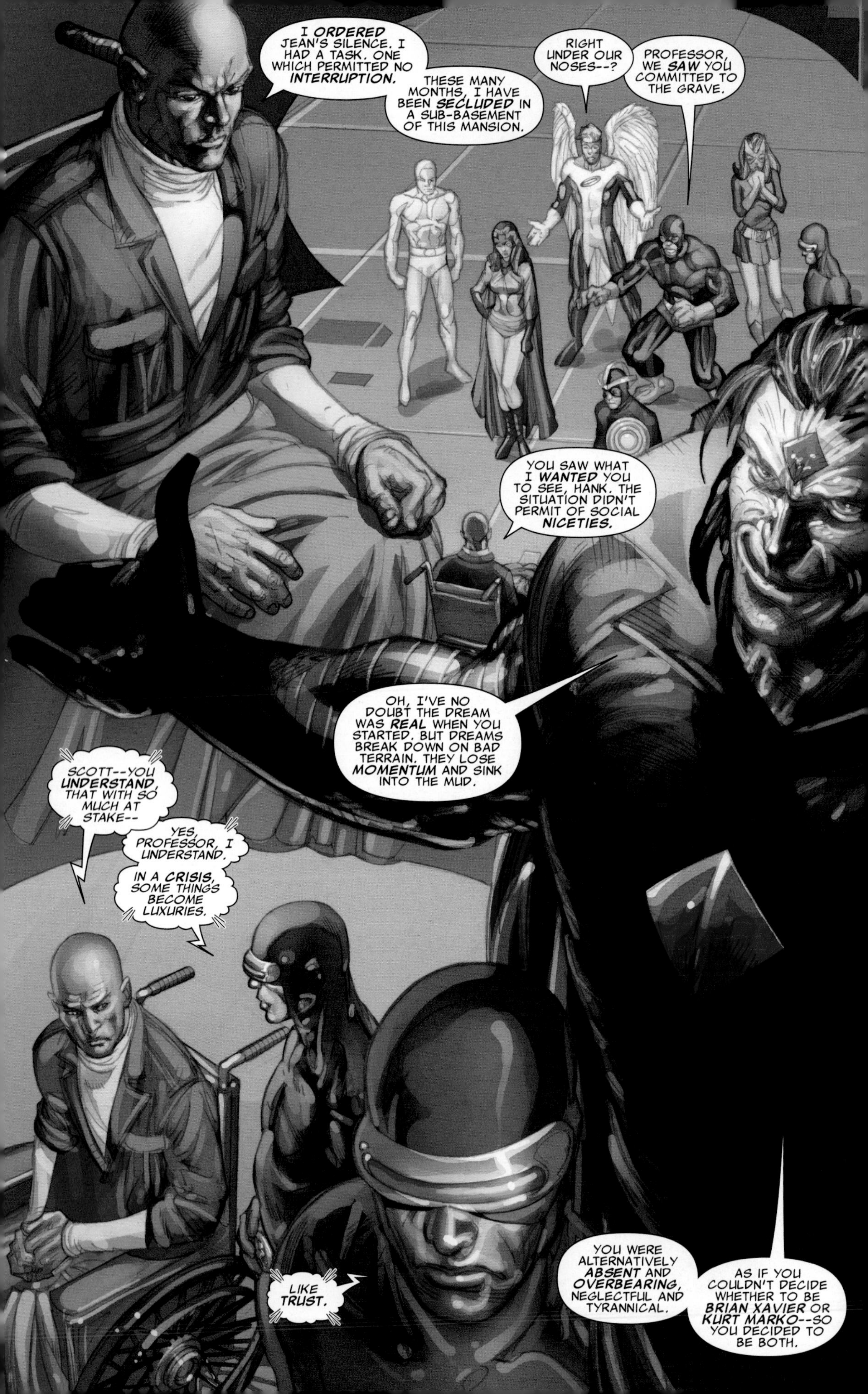
I ORDERED JEAN'S SILENCE. I HAD A TASK. ONE WHICH PERMITTED NO INTERRUPTION.
THESE MANY MONTHS, I HAVE BEEN SECLUDED IN A SUB-BASEMENT OF THIS MANSION.
RIGHT UNDER OUR NOSES--?
PROFESSOR, WE SAW YOU COMMITTED TO THE GRAVE.
YOU SAW WHAT I WANTED YOU TO SEE, HANK. THE SITUATION DIDN'T PERMIT OF SOCIAL NICETIES.
OH, I'VE NO DOUBT THE DREAM WAS REAL WHEN YOU STARTED. BUT DREAMS BREAK DOWN ON BAD TERRAIN. THEY LOSE MOMENTUM AND SINK INTO THE MUD.
SCOTT--YOU UNDERSTAND, THAT WITH SO MUCH AT STAKE--
YES, PROFESSOR, I UNDERSTAND.
IN A CRISIS, SOME THINGS BECOME LUXURIES.
LIKE TRUST.
YOU WERE ALTERNATIVELY ABSENT AND OVERBEARING, NEGLECTFUL AND TYRANNICAL.
AS IF YOU COULDN'T DECIDE WHETHER TO BE BRIAN XAVIER OR KURT MARKO--SO YOU DECIDED TO BE BOTH.

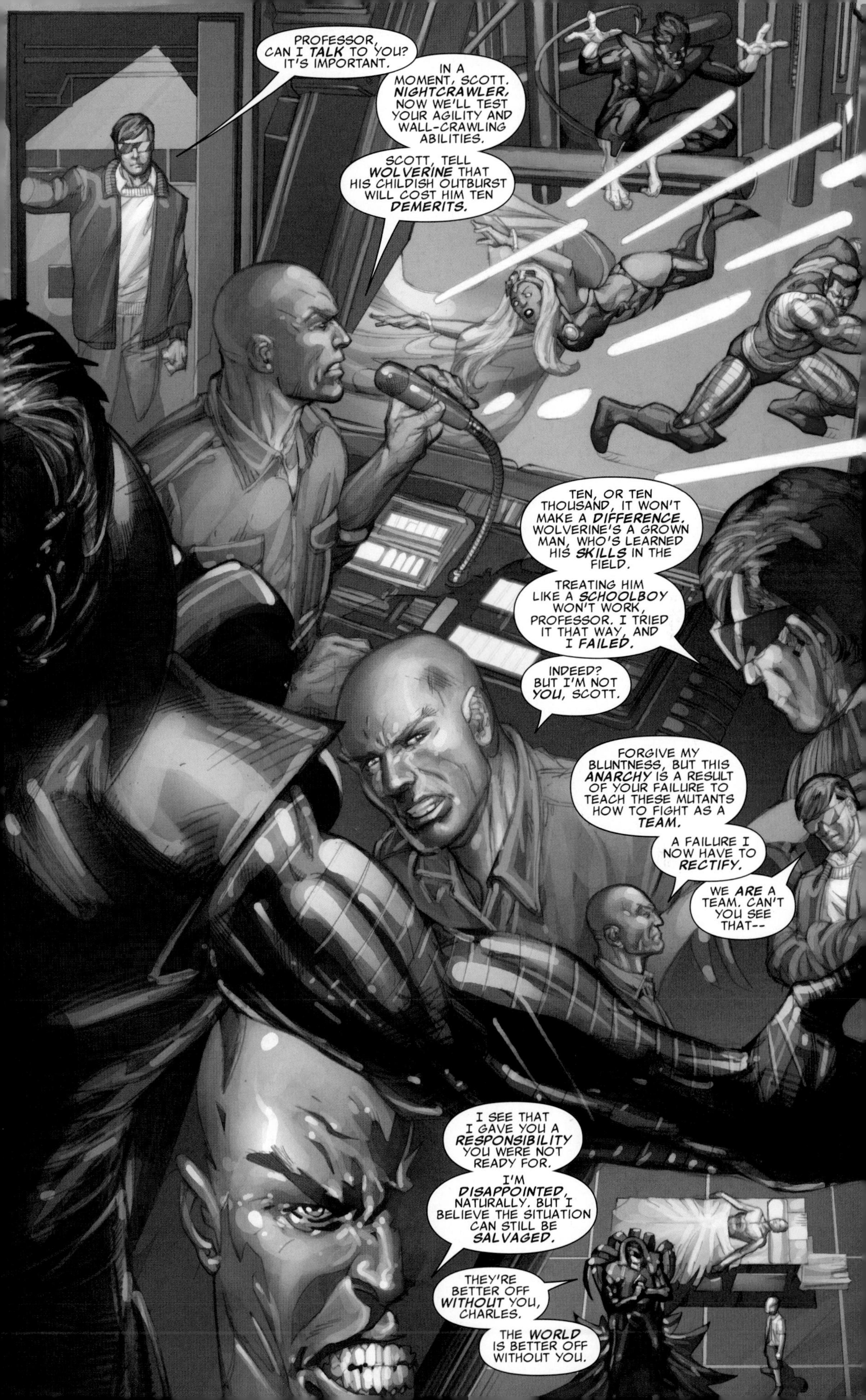

PROFESSOR, CAN I TALK TO YOU? IT'S IMPORTANT.
IN A MOMENT, SCOTT. NIGHTCRAWLER, NOW WE'LL TEST YOUR AGILITY AND WALL-CRAWLING ABILITIES.
SCOTT, TELL WOLVERINE THAT HIS CHILDISH OUTBURST WILL COST HIM TEN DEMERITS.
TEN, OR TEN THOUSAND, IT WON'T MAKE A DIFFERENCE. WOLVERINE'S A GROWN MAN, WHO'S LEARNED HIS SKILLS IN THE FIELD.
TREATING HIM LIKE A SCHOOLBOY WON'T WORK, PROFESSOR. I TRIED IT THAT WAY, AND I FAILED.
INDEED? BUT I'M NOT YOU, SCOTT.
FORGIVE MY BLUNTNESS, BUT THIS ANARCHY IS A RESULT OF YOUR FAILURE TO TEACH THESE MUTANTS HOW TO FIGHT AS A TEAM.
A FAILURE I NOW HAVE TO RECTIFY.
WE ARE A TEAM. CAN'T YOU SEE THAT--
I SEE THAT I GAVE YOU A RESPONSIBILITY YOU WERE NOT READY FOR.
I'M DISAPPOINTED, NATURALLY. BUT I BELIEVE THE SITUATION CAN STILL BE SALVAGED.
THEY'RE BETTER OFF WITHOUT YOU, CHARLES.
THE WORLD IS BETTER OFF WITHOUT YOU.

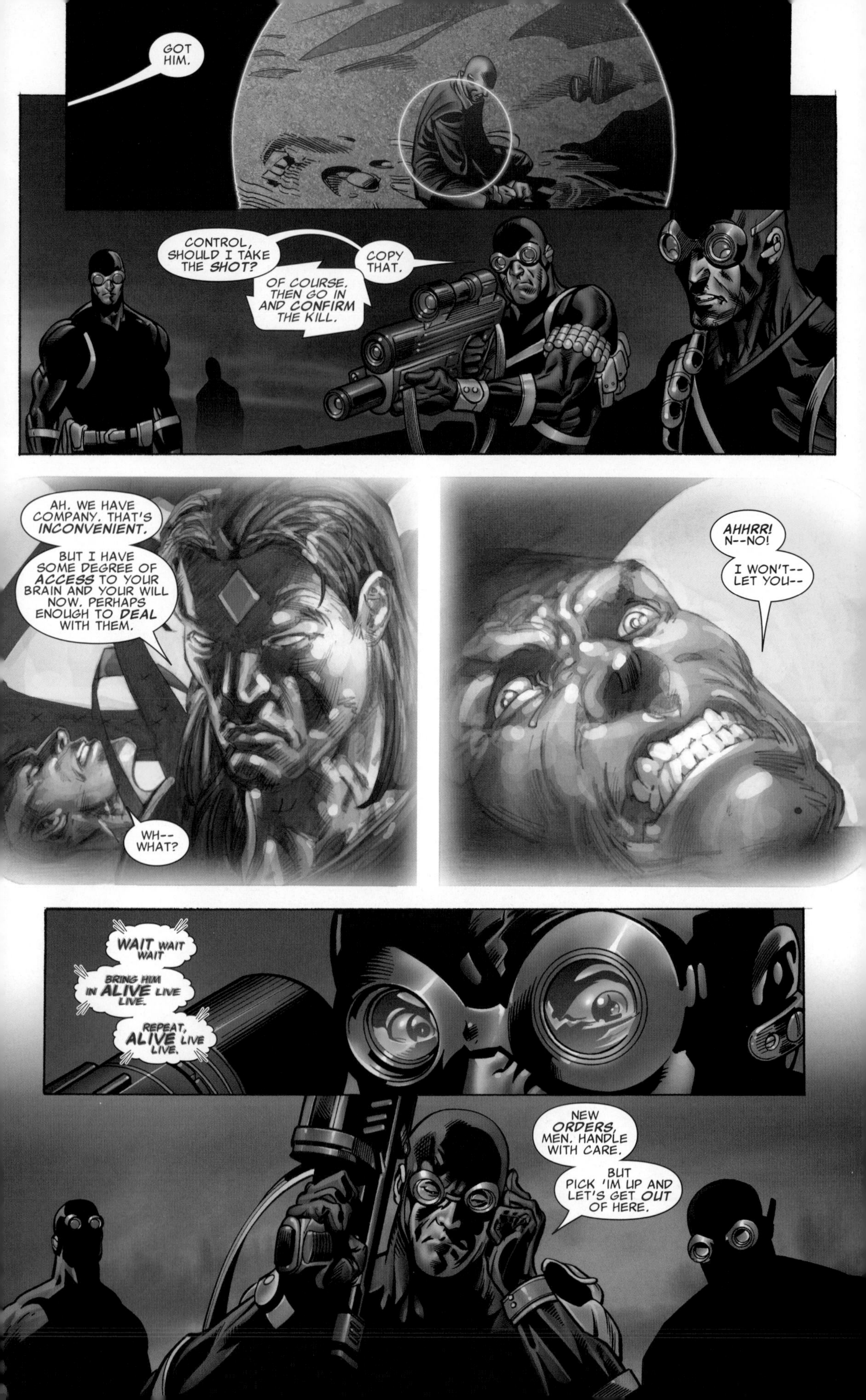
GOT HIM.
CONTROL, SHOULD I TAKE THE SHOT?
OF COURSE. THEN GO IN AND CONFIRM THE KILL.
COPY THAT.
AH. WE HAVE COMPANY. THAT'S INCONVENIENT.
BUT I HAVE SOME DEGREE OF ACCESS TO YOUR BRAIN AND YOUR WILL NOW. PERHAPS ENOUGH TO DEAL WITH THEM.
WH-- WHAT?
AHHRR! N--NO!
I WON'T-- LET YOU--
WAIT WAIT WAIT
BRING HIM IN ALIVE LIVE LIVE.
REPEAT, ALIVE LIVE LIVE.
NEW ORDERS, MEN. HANDLE WITH CARE.
BUT PICK 'IM UP AND LET'S GET OUT OF HERE.

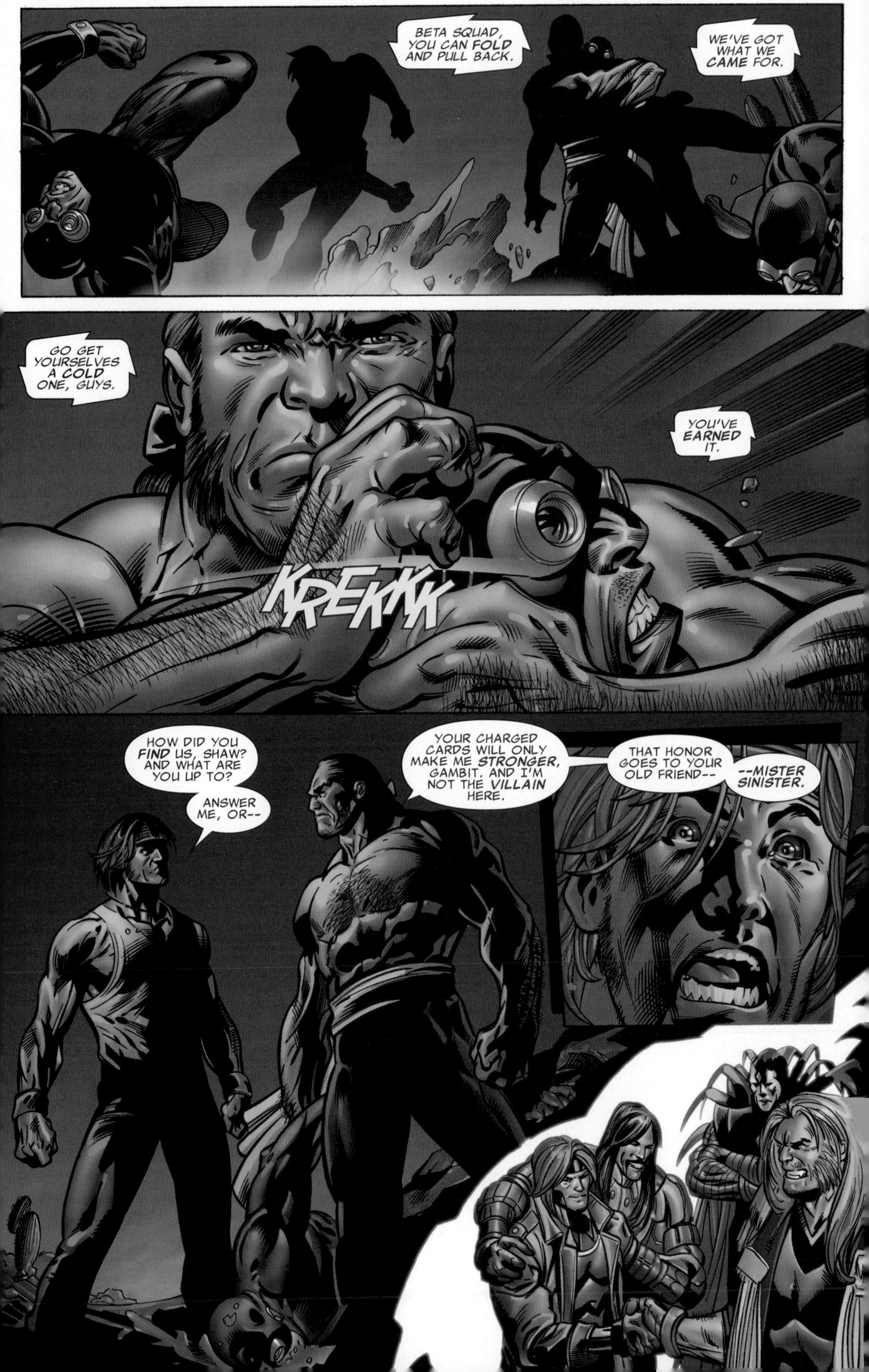
BETA SQUAD, YOU CAN FOLD AND PULL BACK.
WE'VE GOT WHAT WE CAME FOR.
GO GET YOURSELVES A COLD ONE, GUYS.
YOU'VE EARNED IT.
KREKKK
HOW DID YOU FIND US, SHAW? AND WHAT ARE YOU UP TO?
ANSWER ME, OR--
YOUR CHARGED CARDS WILL ONLY MAKE ME STRONGER, GAMBIT. AND I'M NOT THE VILLAIN HERE.
THAT HONOR GOES TO YOUR OLD FRIEND--
--MISTER SINISTER.

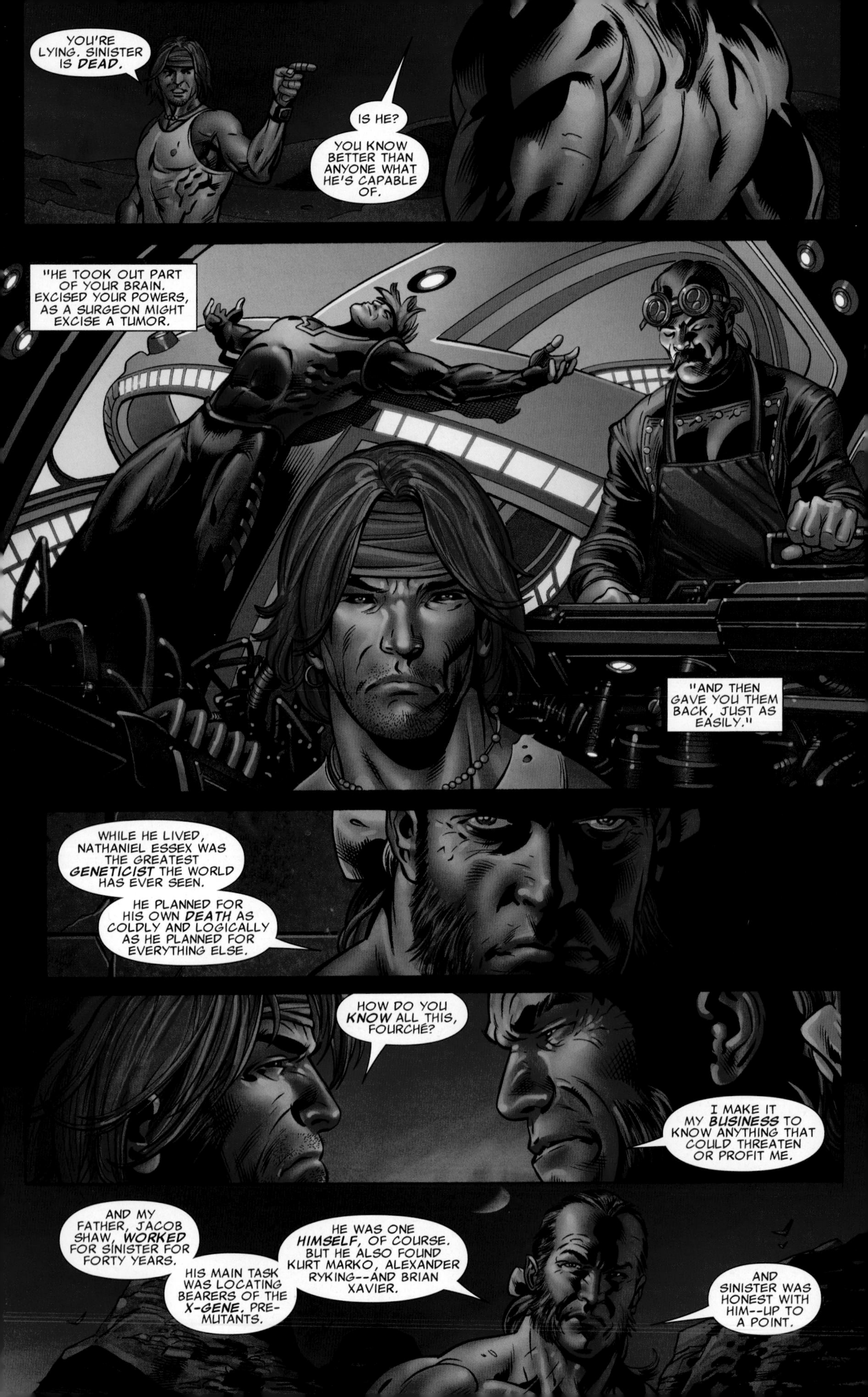
YOU'RE LYING. SINISTER IS DEAD.
IS HE?
YOU KNOW BETTER THAN ANYONE WHAT HE'S CAPABLE OF.
"HE TOOK OUT PART OF YOUR BRAIN. EXCISED YOUR POWERS, AS A SURGEON MIGHT EXCISE A TUMOR.
"AND THEN GAVE YOU THEM BACK, JUST AS EASILY."
WHILE HE LIVED, NATHANIEL ESSEX WAS THE GREATEST GENETICIST THE WORLD HAS EVER SEEN.
HE PLANNED FOR HIS OWN DEATH AS COLDLY AND LOGICALLY AS HE PLANNED FOR EVERYTHING ELSE.
HOW DO YOU KNOW ALL THIS, FOURCHÉ?
I MAKE IT MY BUSINESS TO KNOW ANYTHING THAT COULD THREATEN OR PROFIT ME.
AND MY FATHER, JACOB SHAW, WORKED FOR SINISTER FOR FORTY YEARS.
HIS MAIN TASK WAS LOCATING BEARERS OF THE X-GENE. PRE-MUTANTS.
HE WAS ONE HIMSELF, OF COURSE. BUT HE ALSO FOUND KURT MARKO, ALEXANDER RYKING--AND BRIAN XAVIER.
AND SINISTER WAS HONEST WITH HIM--UP TO A POINT.

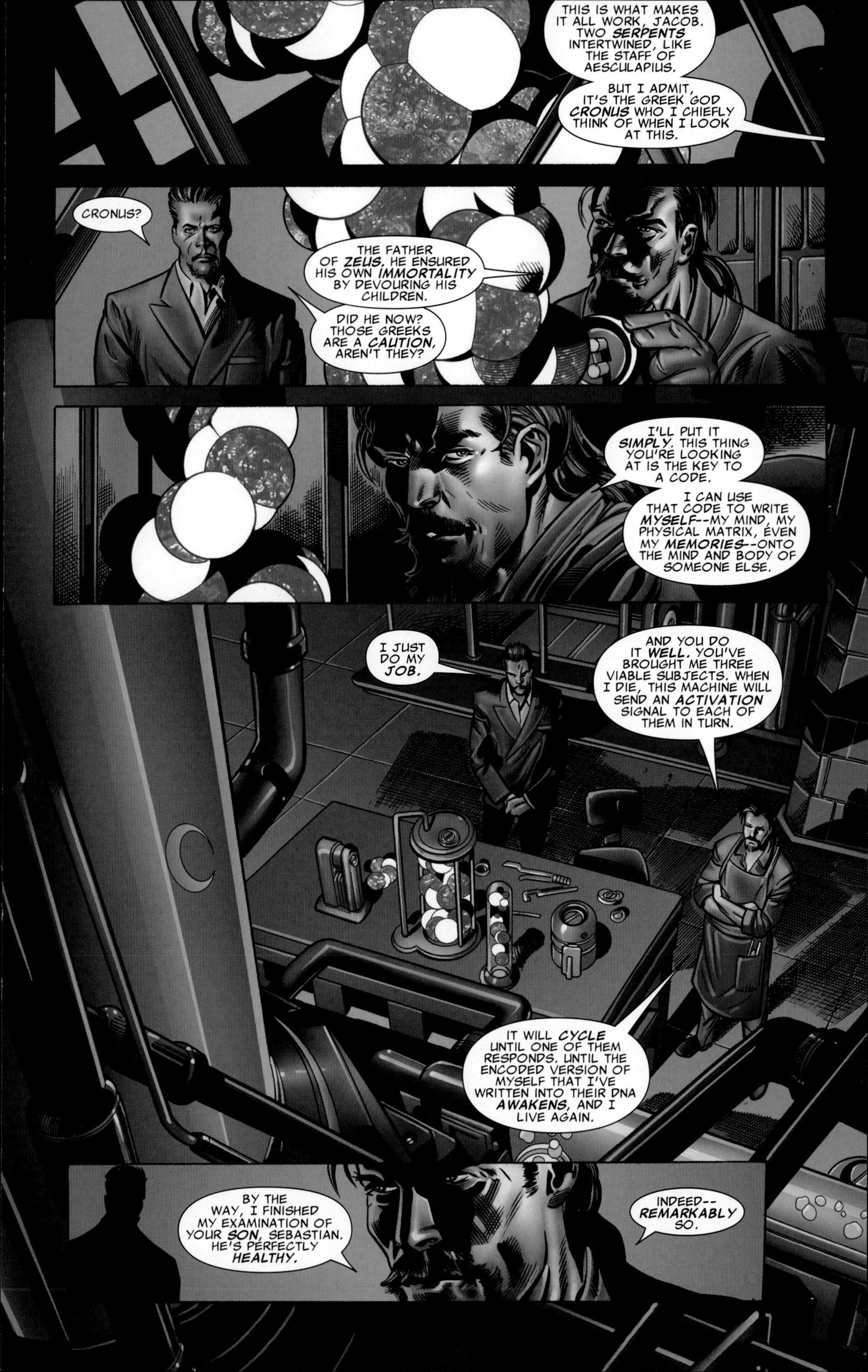
THIS IS WHAT MAKES IT ALL WORK, JACOB. TWO SERPENTS INTERTWINED, LIKE THE STAFF OF AESCULAPIUS.
BUT I ADMIT, IT'S THE GREEK GOD CRONUS WHO I CHIEFLY THINK OF WHEN I LOOK AT THIS.
CRONUS?
THE FATHER OF ZEUS, HE ENSURED HIS OWN IMMORTALITY BY DEVOURING HIS CHILDREN.
DID HE NOW? THOSE GREEKS ARE A CAUTION, AREN'T THEY?
I'LL PUT IT SIMPLY. THIS THING YOU'RE LOOKING AT IS THE KEY TO A CODE.
I CAN USE THAT CODE TO WRITE MYSELF--MY MIND, MY PHYSICAL MATRIX, EVEN MY MEMORIES--ONTO THE MIND AND BODY OF SOMEONE ELSE.
I JUST DO MY JOB.
AND YOU DO IT WELL. YOU'VE BROUGHT ME THREE VIABLE SUBJECTS. WHEN I DIE, THIS MACHINE WILL SEND AN ACTIVATION SIGNAL TO EACH OF THEM IN TURN.
IT WILL CYCLE UNTIL ONE OF THEM RESPONDS. UNTIL THE ENCODED VERSION OF MYSELF THAT I'VE WRITTEN INTO THEIR DNA AWAKENS, AND I LIVE AGAIN.
BY THE WAY, I FINISHED MY EXAMINATION OF YOUR SON, SEBASTIAN. HE'S PERFECTLY HEALTHY.
INDEED--REMARKABLY SO.

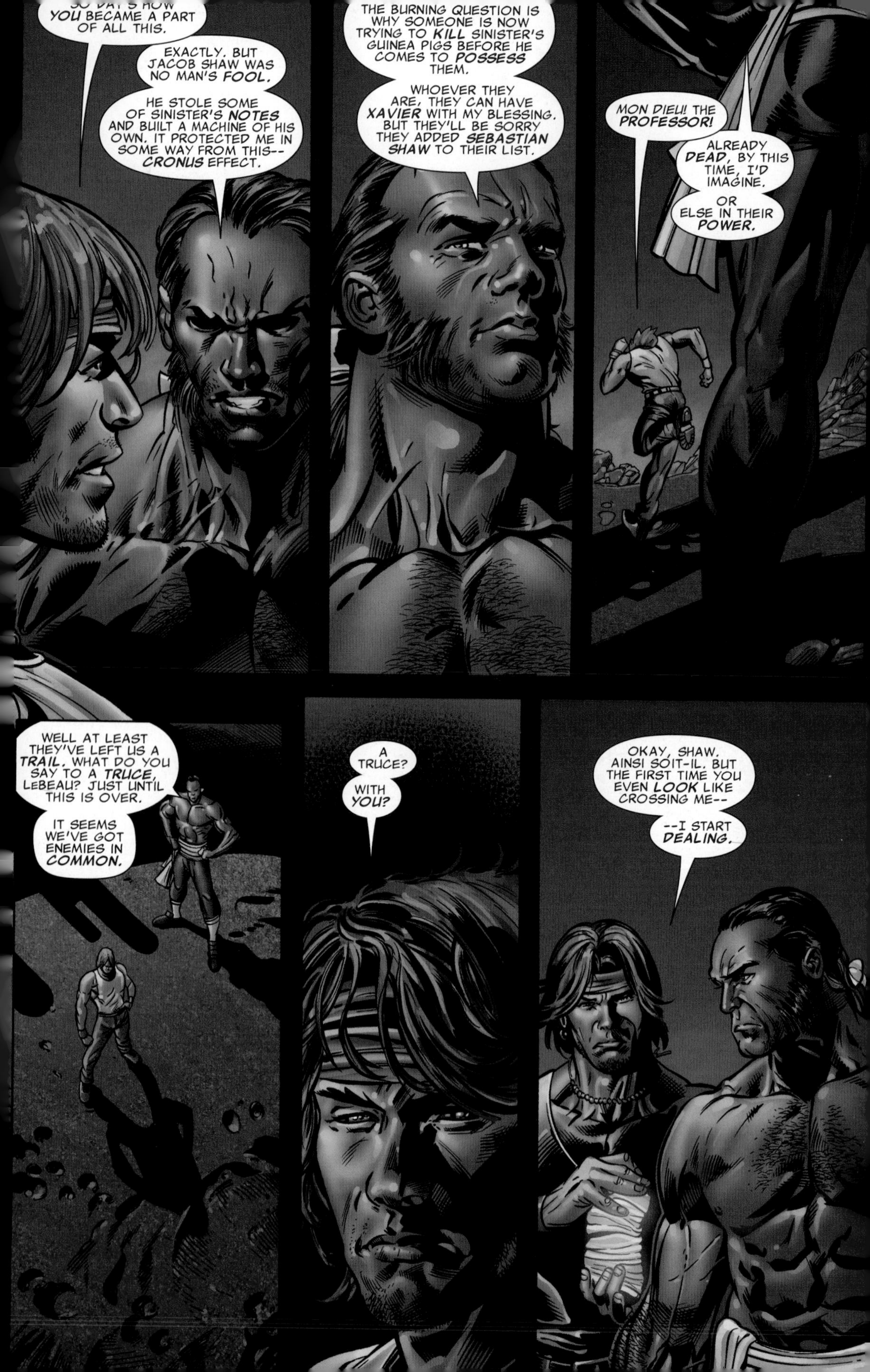
SO DAT'S HOW YOU BECAME A PART OF ALL THIS.
EXACTLY. BUT JACOB SHAW WAS NO MAN'S FOOL.
HE STOLE SOME OF SINISTER'S NOTES AND BUILT A MACHINE OF HIS OWN. IT PROTECTED ME IN SOME WAY FROM THIS-- CRONUS EFFECT.
THE BURNING QUESTION IS WHY SOMEONE IS NOW TRYING TO KILL SINISTER'S GUINEA PIGS BEFORE HE COMES TO POSSESS THEM.
WHOEVER THEY ARE, THEY CAN HAVE XAVIER WITH MY BLESSING. BUT THEY'LL BE SORRY THEY ADDED SEBASTIAN SHAW TO THEIR LIST.
MON DIEU! THE PROFESSOR!
ALREADY DEAD, BY THIS TIME, I'D IMAGINE.
OR ELSE IN THEIR POWER.
WELL AT LEAST THEY'VE LEFT US A TRAIL. WHAT DO YOU SAY TO A TRUCE, LEBEAU? JUST UNTIL THIS IS OVER.
IT SEEMS WE'VE GOT ENEMIES IN COMMON.
A TRUCE?
WITH YOU?
OKAY, SHAW. AINSI SOIT-IL. BUT THE FIRST TIME YOU EVEN LOOK LIKE CROSSING ME--
--I START DEALING.

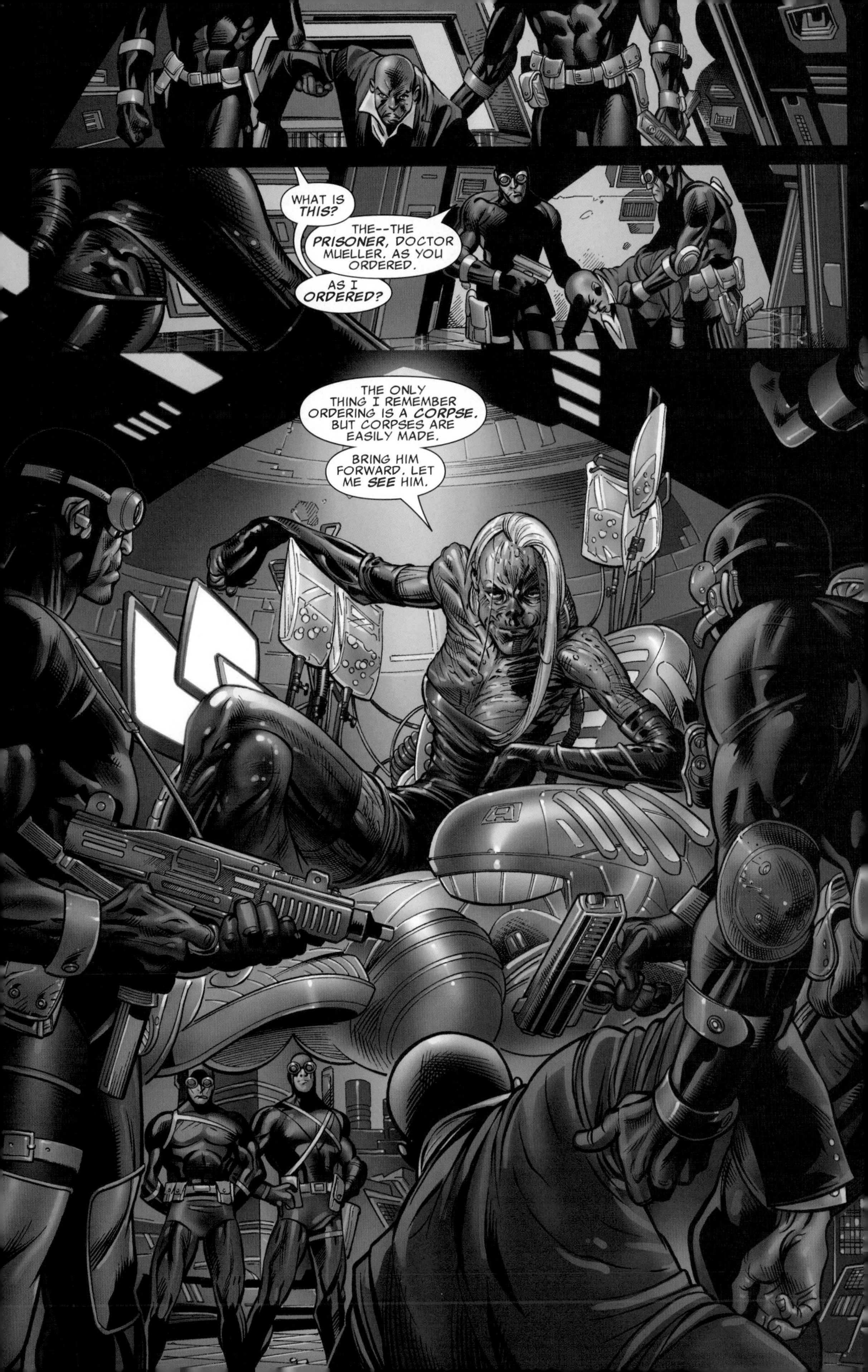

WHAT IS THIS?
THE--THE PRISONER, DOCTOR MUELLER. AS YOU ORDERED.
AS I ORDERED?
THE ONLY THING I REMEMBER ORDERING IS A CORPSE. BUT CORPSES ARE EASILY MADE.
BRING HIM FORWARD. LET ME SEE HIM.

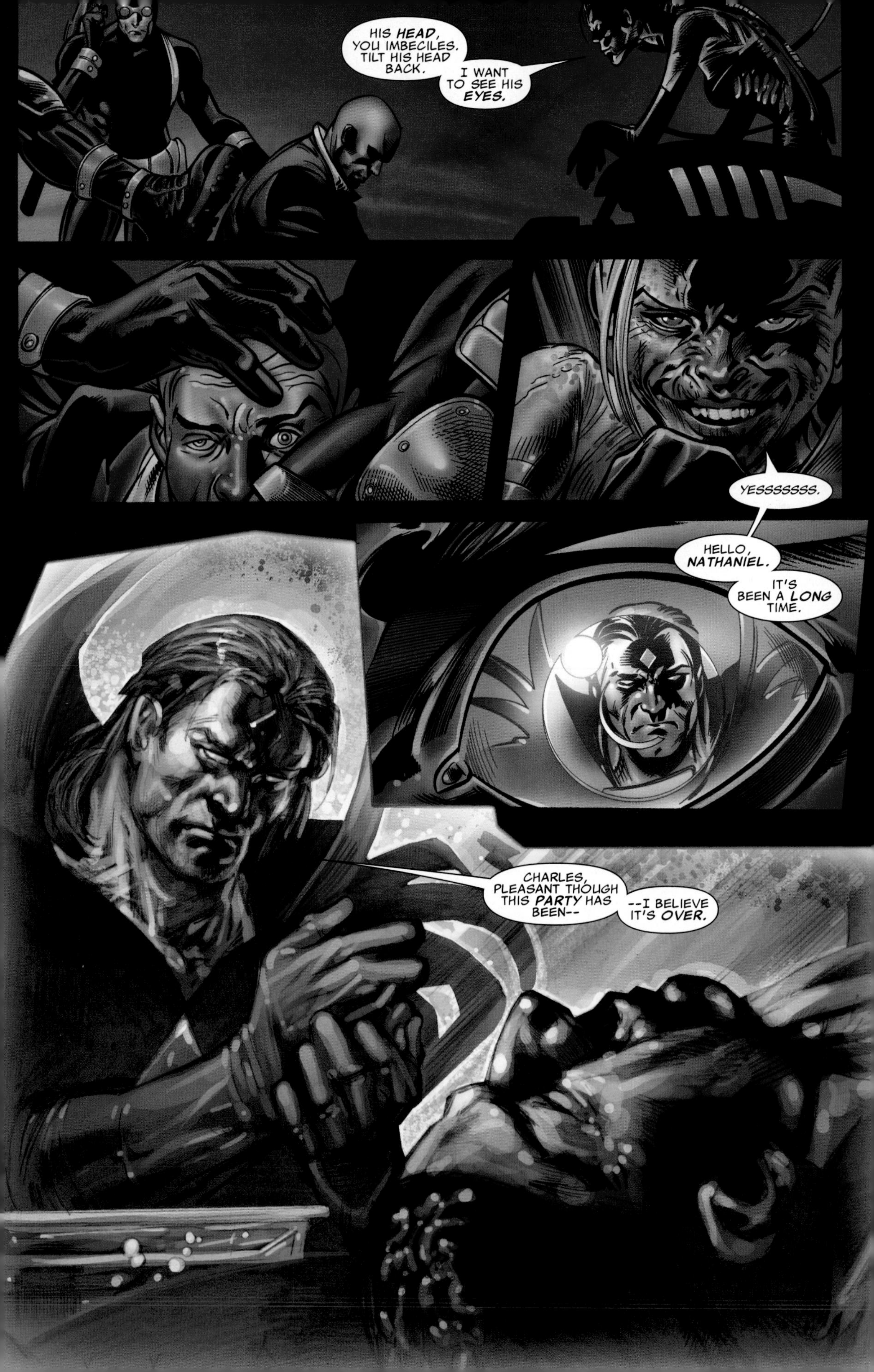
HIS HEAD, YOU IMBECILES. TILT HIS HEAD BACK.
I WANT TO SEE HIS EYES.
YESSSSSSS.
HELLO, NATHANIEL.
IT'S BEEN A LONG TIME.
CHARLES, PLEASANT THOUGH THIS PARTY HAS BEEN--
--I BELIEVE IT'S OVER.

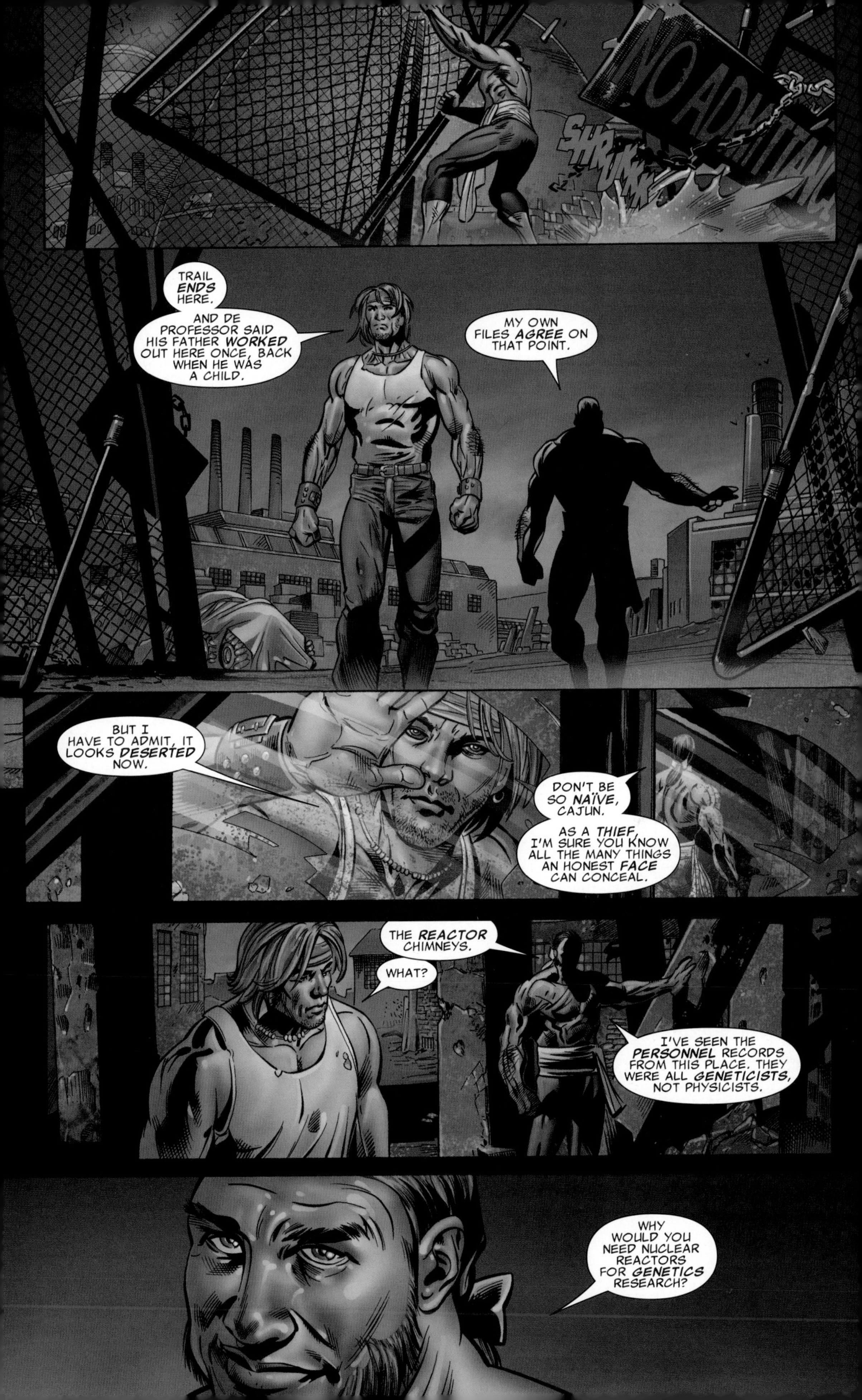
NO ADMITTANC
SHRUNKK
TRAIL ENDS HERE.
AND DE PROFESSOR SAID HIS FATHER WORKED OUT HERE ONCE, BACK WHEN HE WAS A CHILD.
MY OWN FILES AGREE ON THAT POINT.
BUT I HAVE TO ADMIT, IT LOOKS DESERTED NOW.
DON'T BE SO NAÏVE, CAJUN.
AS A THIEF, I'M SURE YOU KNOW ALL THE MANY THINGS AN HONEST FACE CAN CONCEAL.
THE REACTOR CHIMNEYS.
WHAT?
I'VE SEEN THE PERSONNEL RECORDS FROM THIS PLACE. THEY WERE ALL GENETICISTS, NOT PHYSICISTS.
WHY WOULD YOU NEED NUCLEAR REACTORS FOR GENETICS RESEARCH?

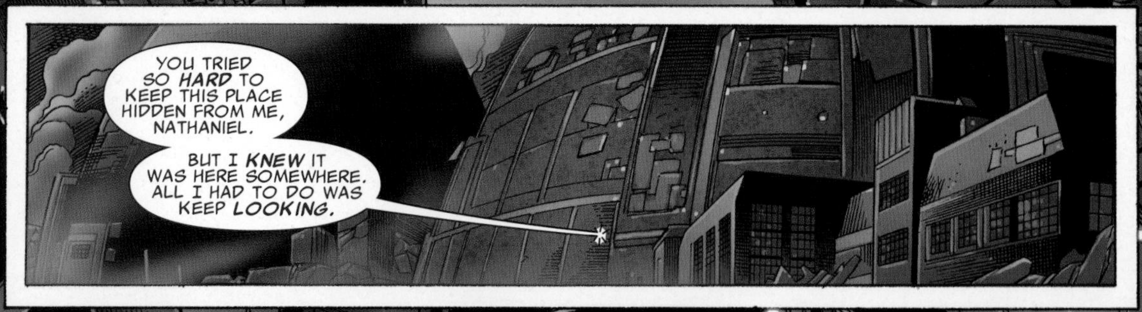
YOU TRIED SO HARD TO KEEP THIS PLACE HIDDEN FROM ME, NATHANIEL.
BUT I KNEW IT WAS HERE SOMEWHERE. ALL I HAD TO DO WAS KEEP LOOKING.

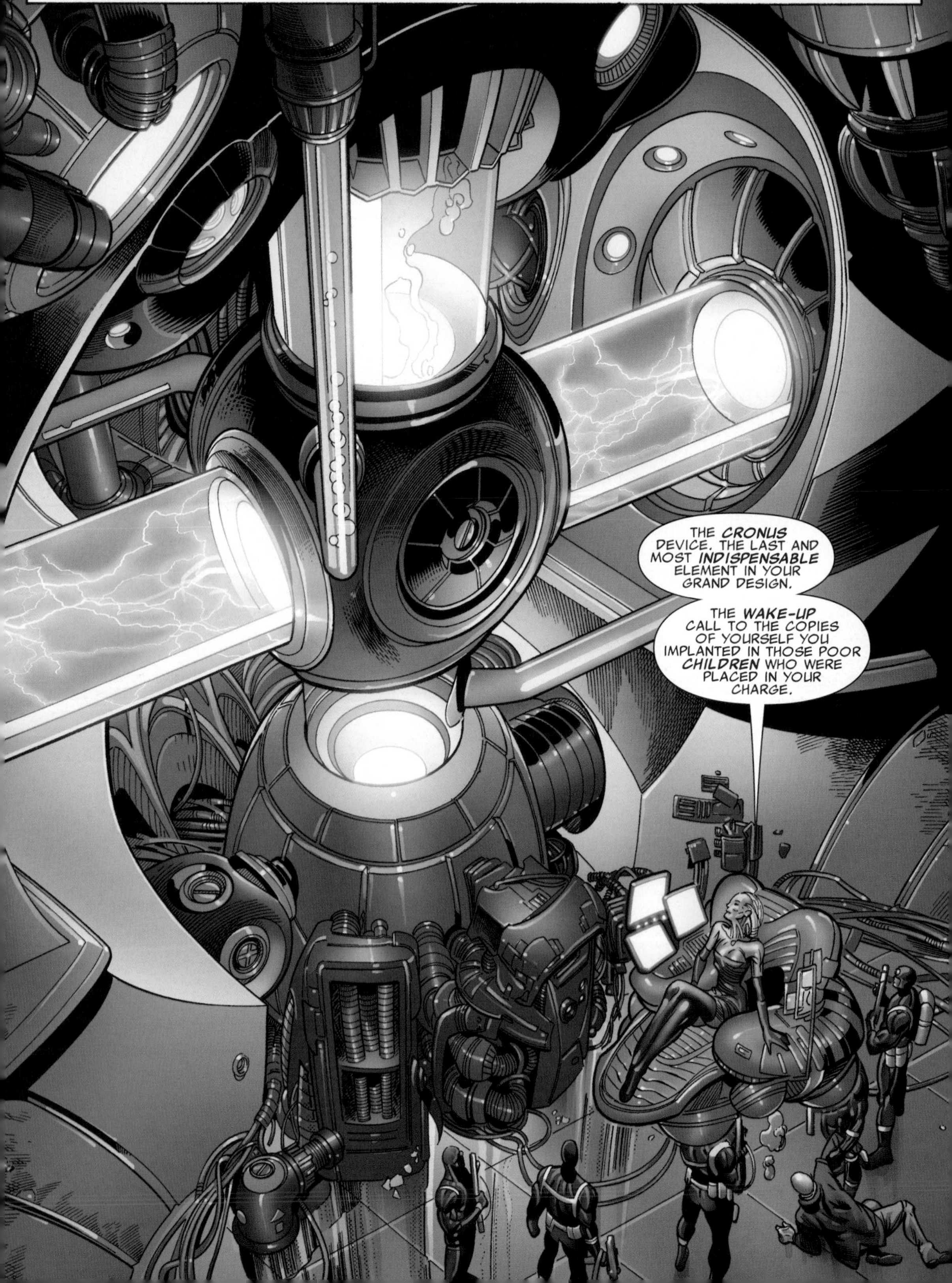
THE CRONUS DEVICE. THE LAST AND MOST INDISPENSABLE ELEMENT IN YOUR GRAND DESIGN.
THE WAKE-UP CALL TO THE COPIES OF YOURSELF YOU IMPLANTED IN THOSE POOR CHILDREN WHO WERE PLACED IN YOUR CHARGE.

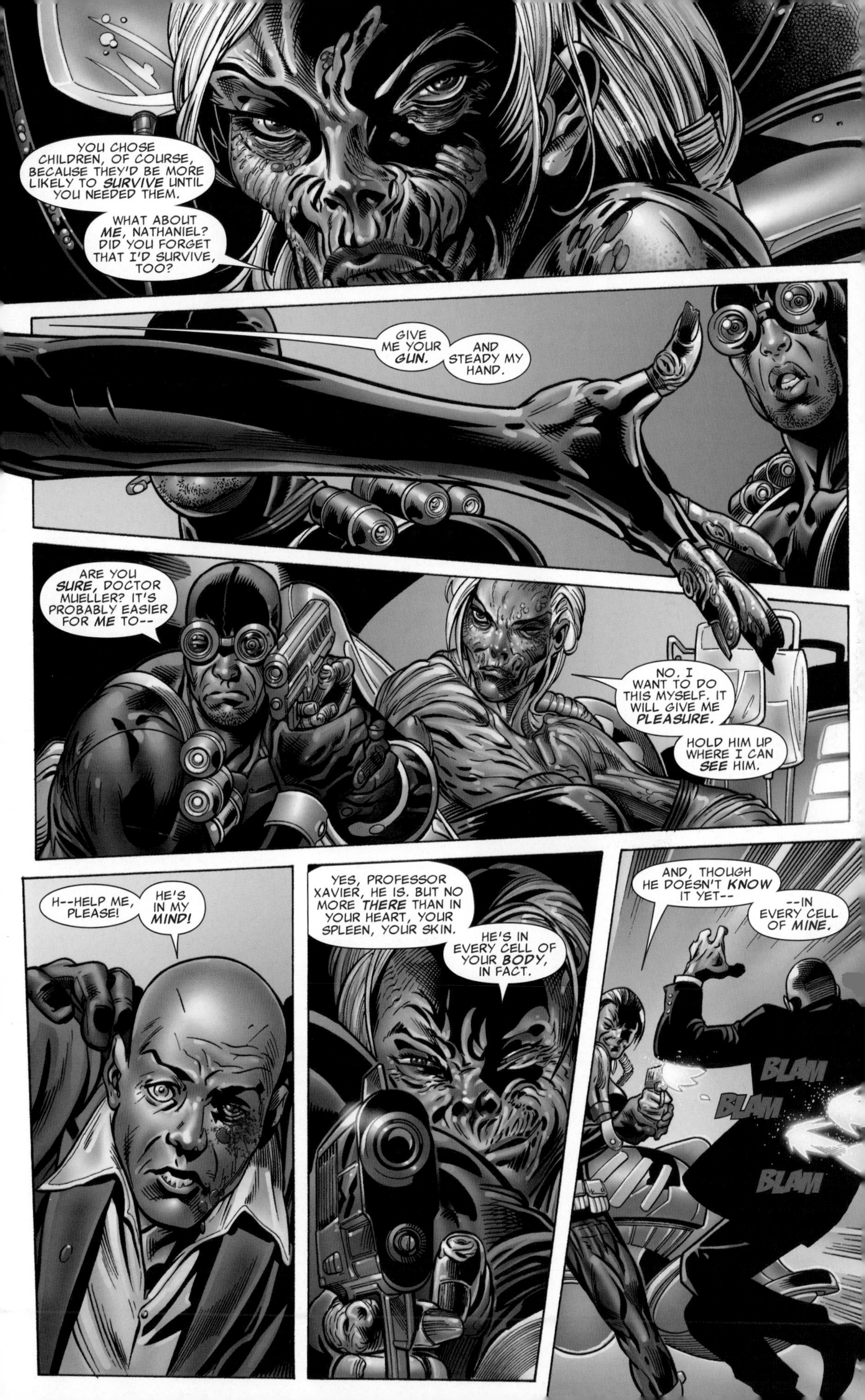
YOU CHOSE CHILDREN, OF COURSE, BECAUSE THEY'D BE MORE LIKELY TO SURVIVE UNTIL YOU NEEDED THEM.
WHAT ABOUT ME, NATHANIEL? DID YOU FORGET THAT I'D SURVIVE, TOO?
GIVE ME YOUR GUN.
AND STEADY MY HAND.
ARE YOU SURE, DOCTOR MUELLER? IT'S PROBABLY EASIER FOR ME TO--
NO. I WANT TO DO THIS MYSELF. IT WILL GIVE ME PLEASURE.
HOLD HIM UP WHERE I CAN SEE HIM.
H--HELP ME, PLEASE!
HE'S IN MY MIND!
YES, PROFESSOR XAVIER, HE IS. BUT NO MORE THERE THAN IN YOUR HEART, YOUR SPLEEN, YOUR SKIN.
HE'S IN EVERY CELL OF YOUR BODY, IN FACT.
AND, THOUGH HE DOESN'T KNOW IT YET--
--IN EVERY CELL OF MINE.
BLAM
BLAM
BLAM

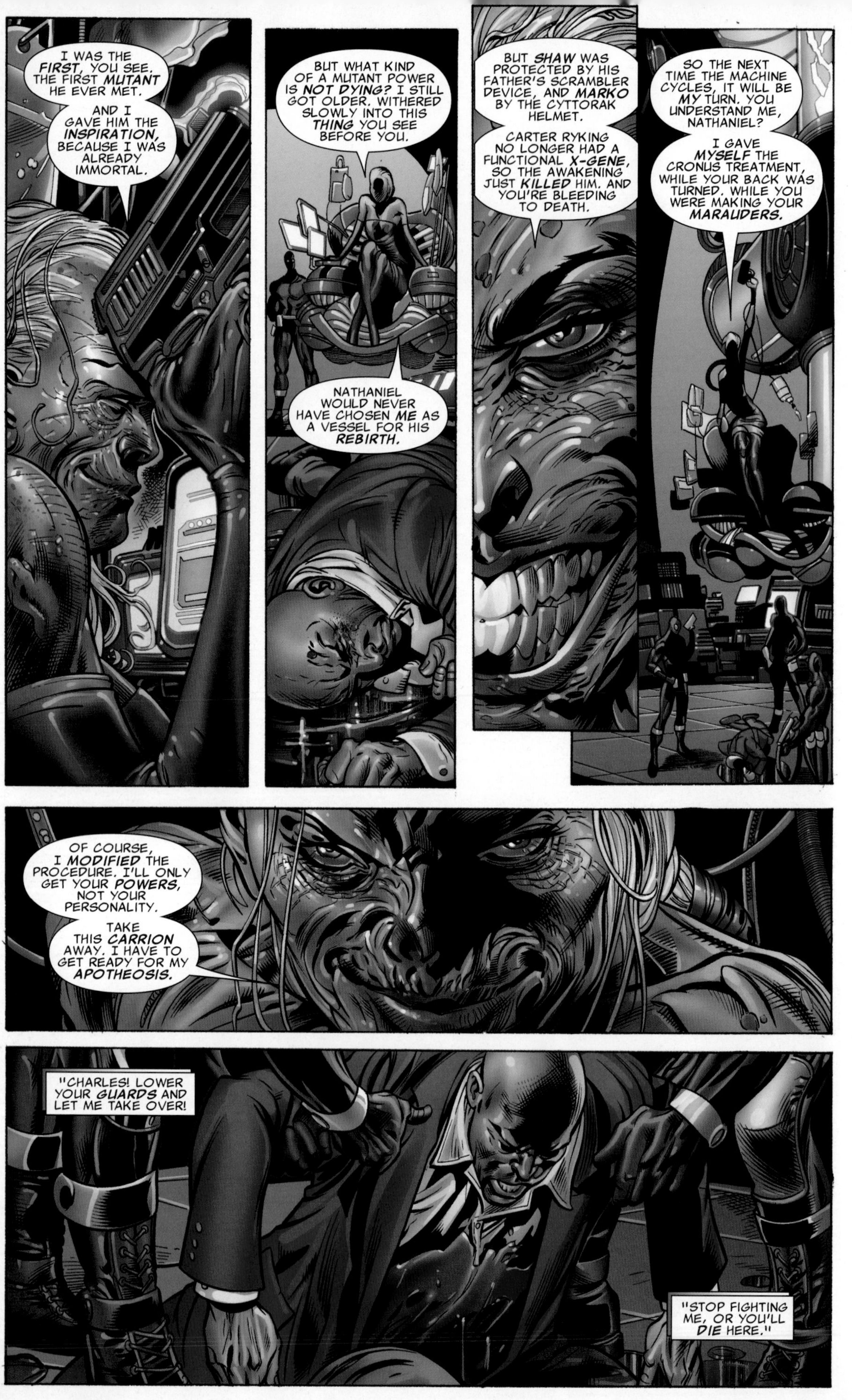
I WAS THE FIRST, YOU SEE. THE FIRST MUTANT HE EVER MET.
AND I GAVE HIM THE INSPIRATION, BECAUSE I WAS ALREADY IMMORTAL.
BUT WHAT KIND OF A MUTANT POWER IS NOT DYING? I STILL GOT OLDER. WITHERED SLOWLY INTO THIS THING YOU SEE BEFORE YOU.
NATHANIEL WOULD NEVER HAVE CHOSEN ME AS A VESSEL FOR HIS REBIRTH.
BUT SHAW WAS PROTECTED BY HIS FATHER'S SCRAMBLER DEVICE, AND MARKO BY THE CYTTORAK HELMET.
CARTER RYKING NO LONGER HAD A FUNCTIONAL X-GENE, SO THE AWAKENING JUST KILLED HIM. AND YOU'RE BLEEDING TO DEATH.
SO THE NEXT TIME THE MACHINE CYCLES, IT WILL BE MY TURN. YOU UNDERSTAND ME, NATHANIEL?
I GAVE MYSELF THE CRONUS TREATMENT, WHILE YOUR BACK WAS TURNED. WHILE YOU WERE MAKING YOUR MARAUDERS.
OF COURSE, I MODIFIED THE PROCEDURE. I'LL ONLY GET YOUR POWERS, NOT YOUR PERSONALITY.
TAKE THIS CARRION AWAY. I HAVE TO GET READY FOR MY APOTHEOSIS.
"CHARLES! LOWER YOUR GUARDS AND LET ME TAKE OVER!
"STOP FIGHTING ME, OR YOU'LL DIE HERE."

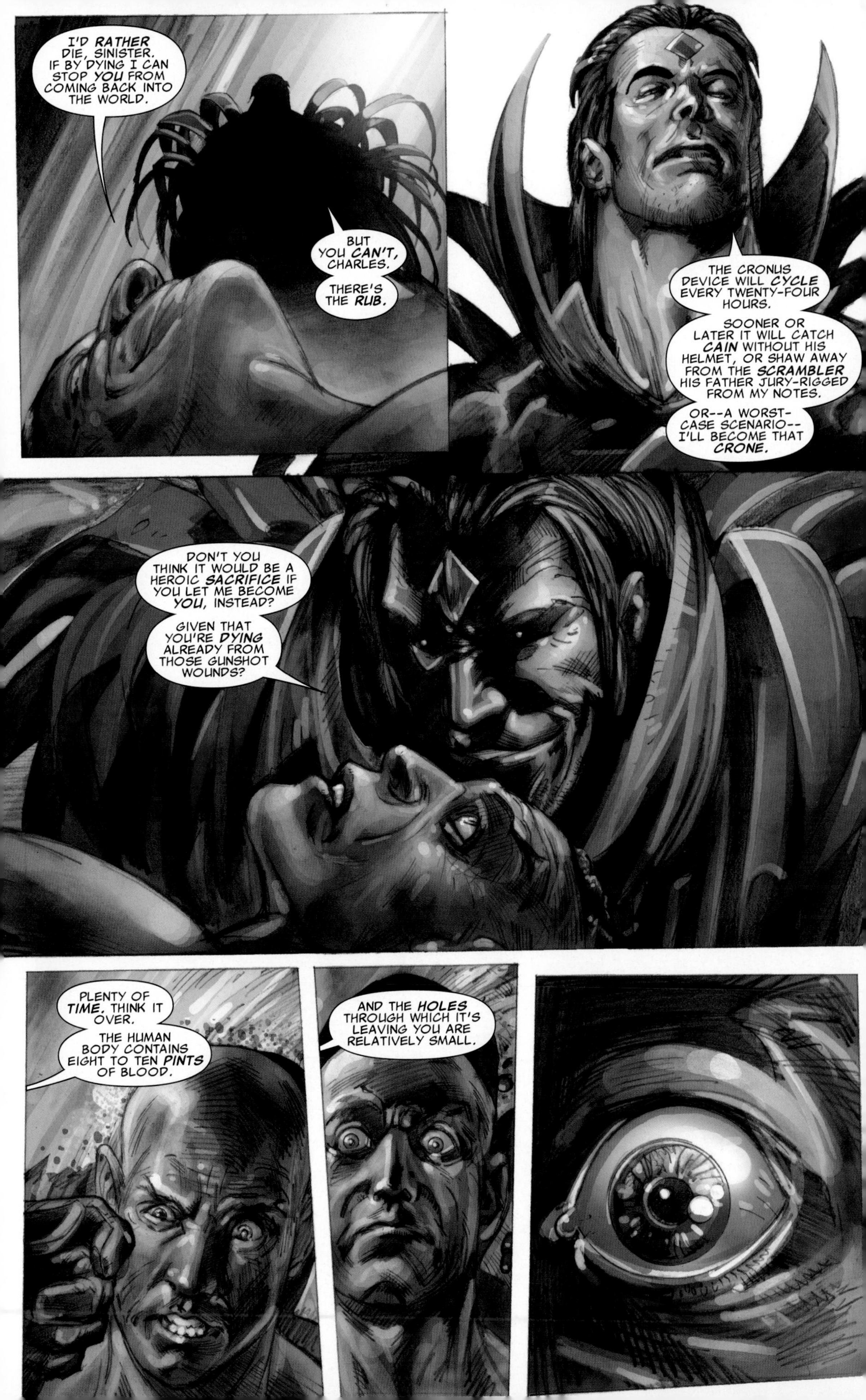
I'D RATHER DIE, SINISTER. IF BY DYING I CAN STOP YOU FROM COMING BACK INTO THE WORLD.
BUT YOU CAN'T, CHARLES.
THERE'S THE RUB.
THE CRONUS DEVICE WILL CYCLE EVERY TWENTY-FOUR HOURS.
SOONER OR LATER IT WILL CATCH CAIN WITHOUT HIS HELMET, OR SHAW AWAY FROM THE SCRAMBLER HIS FATHER JURY-RIGGED FROM MY NOTES.
OR--A WORST-CASE SCENARIO--I'LL BECOME THAT CRONE.
DON'T YOU THINK IT WOULD BE A HEROIC SACRIFICE IF YOU LET ME BECOME YOU, INSTEAD?
GIVEN THAT YOU'RE DYING ALREADY FROM THOSE GUNSHOT WOUNDS?
PLENTY OF TIME. THINK IT OVER.
THE HUMAN BODY CONTAINS EIGHT TO TEN PINTS OF BLOOD.
AND THE HOLES THROUGH WHICH IT'S LEAVING YOU ARE RELATIVELY SMALL.

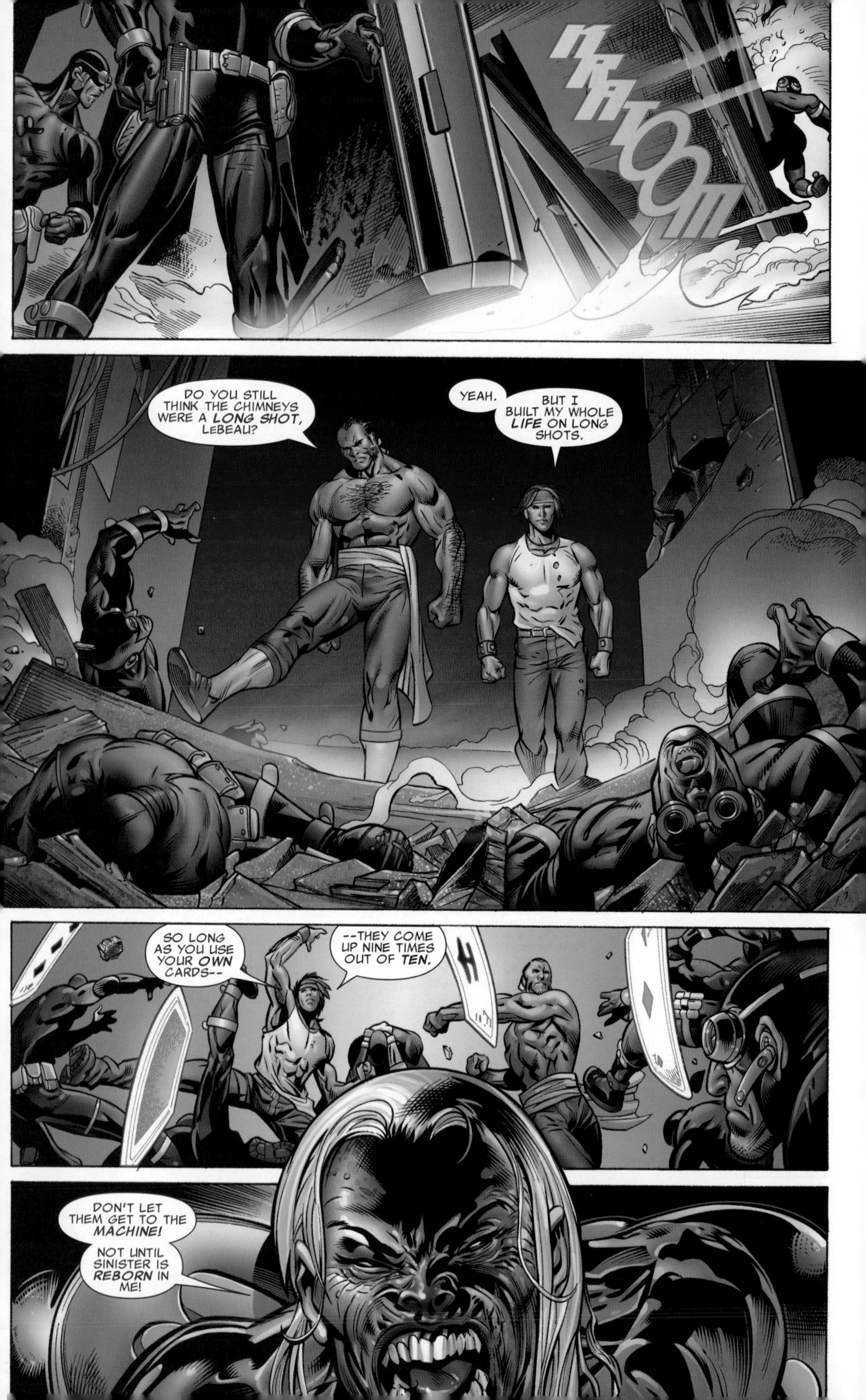
KRATOOM
DO YOU STILL THINK THE CHIMNEYS WERE A LONG SHOT, LEBEAU?
YEAH.
BUT I BUILT MY WHOLE LIFE ON LONG SHOTS.
SO LONG AS YOU USE YOUR OWN CARDS--
--THEY COME UP NINE TIMES OUT OF TEN.
DON'T LET THEM GET TO THE MACHINE!
NOT UNTIL SINISTER IS REBORN IN ME!

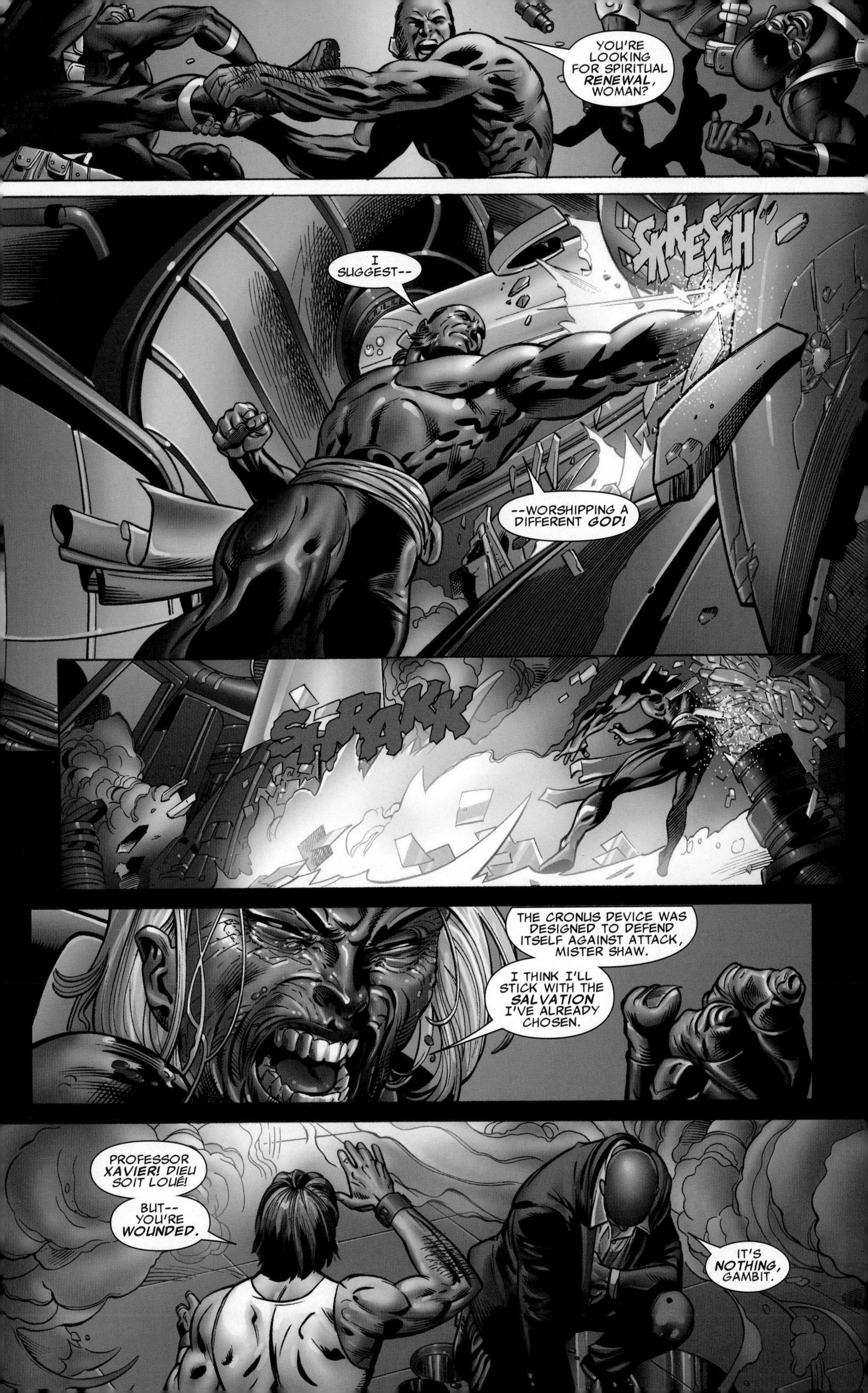
YOU'RE LOOKING FOR SPIRITUAL RENEWAL, WOMAN?
I SUGGEST--
SKRESCH
--WORSHIPPING A DIFFERENT GOD!
SHRAKK
THE CRONUS DEVICE WAS DESIGNED TO DEFEND ITSELF AGAINST ATTACK, MISTER SHAW.
I THINK I'LL STICK WITH THE SALVATION I'VE ALREADY CHOSEN.
PROFESSOR XAVIER! DIEU SOIT LOUÉ!
BUT-- YOU'RE WOUNDED.
IT'S NOTHING, GAMBIT.

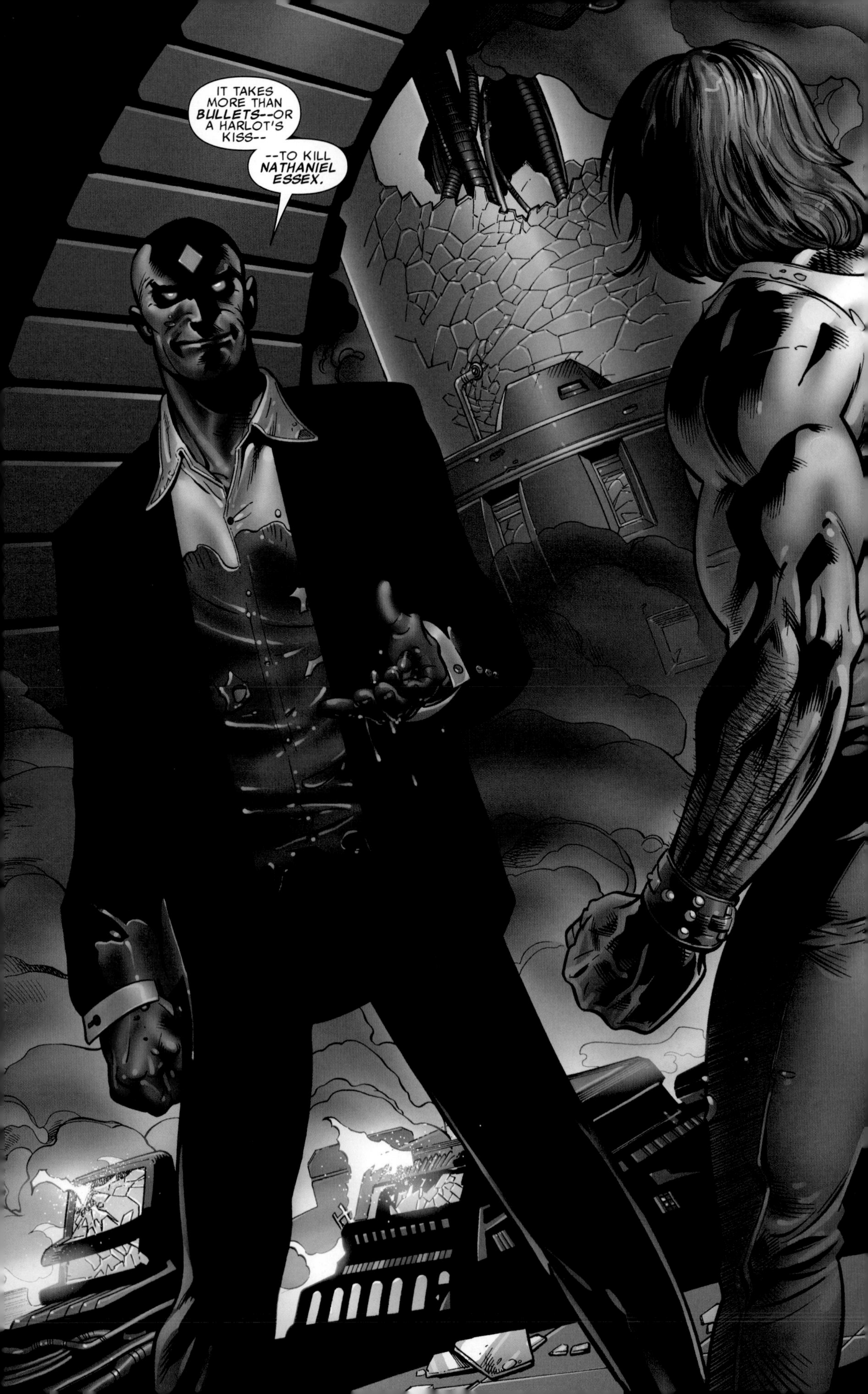
IT TAKES MORE THAN BULLETS--OR A HARLOT'S KISS--
--TO KILL NATHANIEL ESSEX.

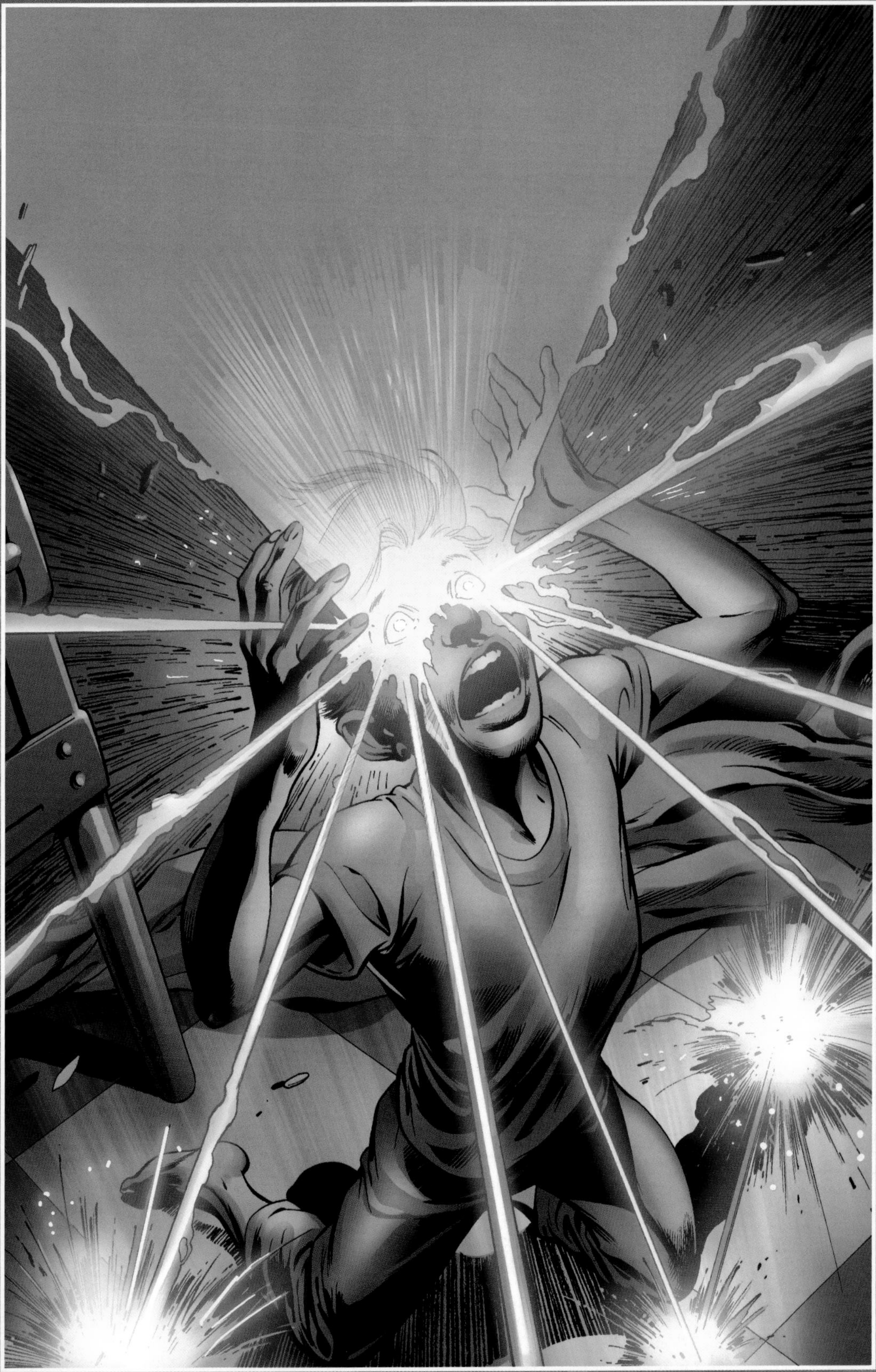

#214

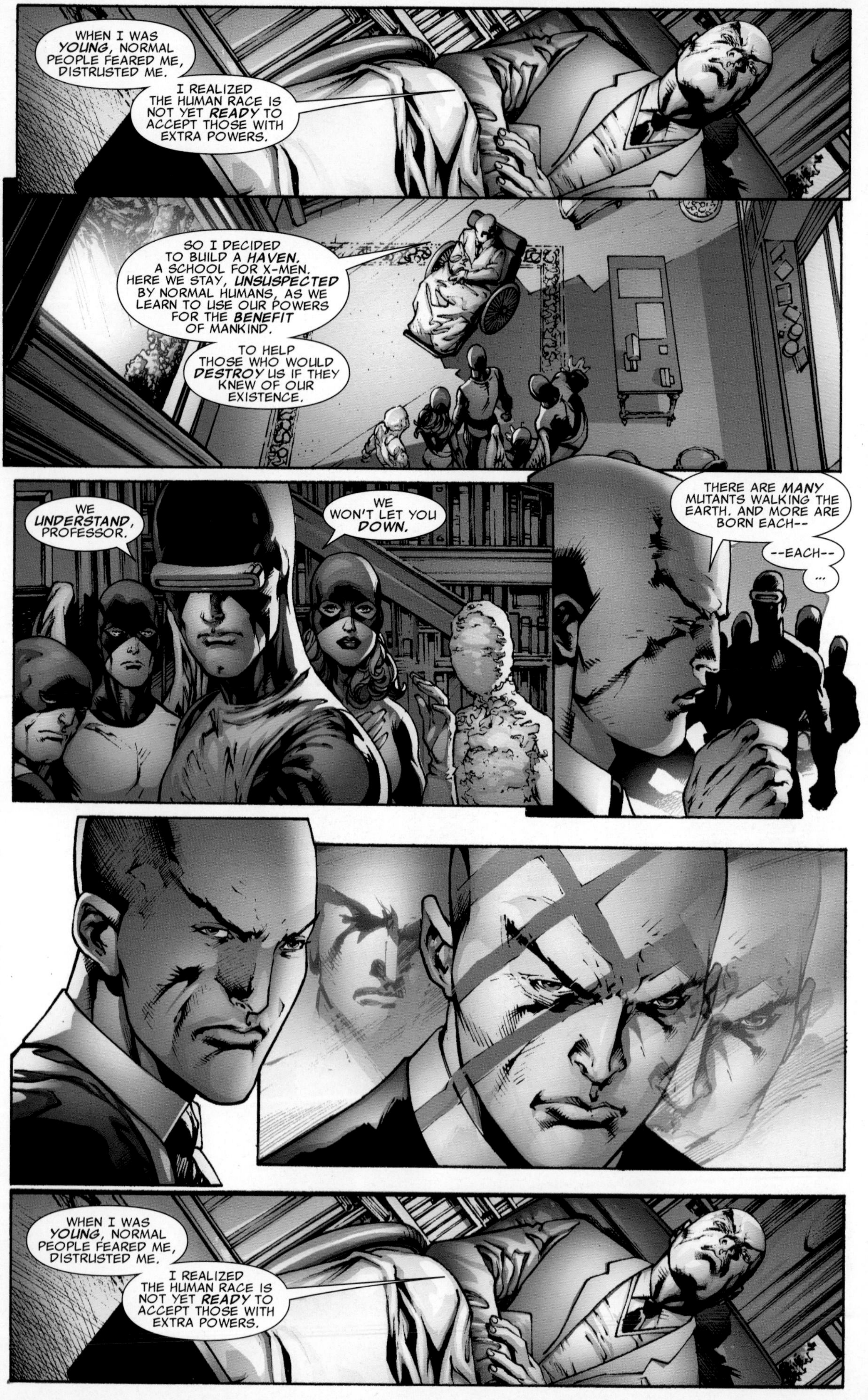
WHEN I WAS YOUNG, NORMAL PEOPLE FEARED ME, DISTRUSTED ME.
I REALIZED THE HUMAN RACE IS NOT YET READY TO ACCEPT THOSE WITH EXTRA POWERS.
SO I DECIDED TO BUILD A HAVEN. A SCHOOL FOR X-MEN. HERE WE STAY, UNSUSPECTED BY NORMAL HUMANS, AS WE LEARN TO USE OUR POWERS FOR THE BENEFIT OF MANKIND.
TO HELP THOSE WHO WOULD DESTROY US IF THEY KNEW OF OUR EXISTENCE.
WE UNDERSTAND, PROFESSOR.
WE WON'T LET YOU DOWN.
THERE ARE MANY MUTANTS WALKING THE EARTH. AND MORE ARE BORN EACH--
--EACH--
...
WHEN I WAS YOUNG, NORMAL PEOPLE FEARED ME, DISTRUSTED ME.
I REALIZED THE HUMAN RACE IS NOT YET READY TO ACCEPT THOSE WITH EXTRA POWERS.

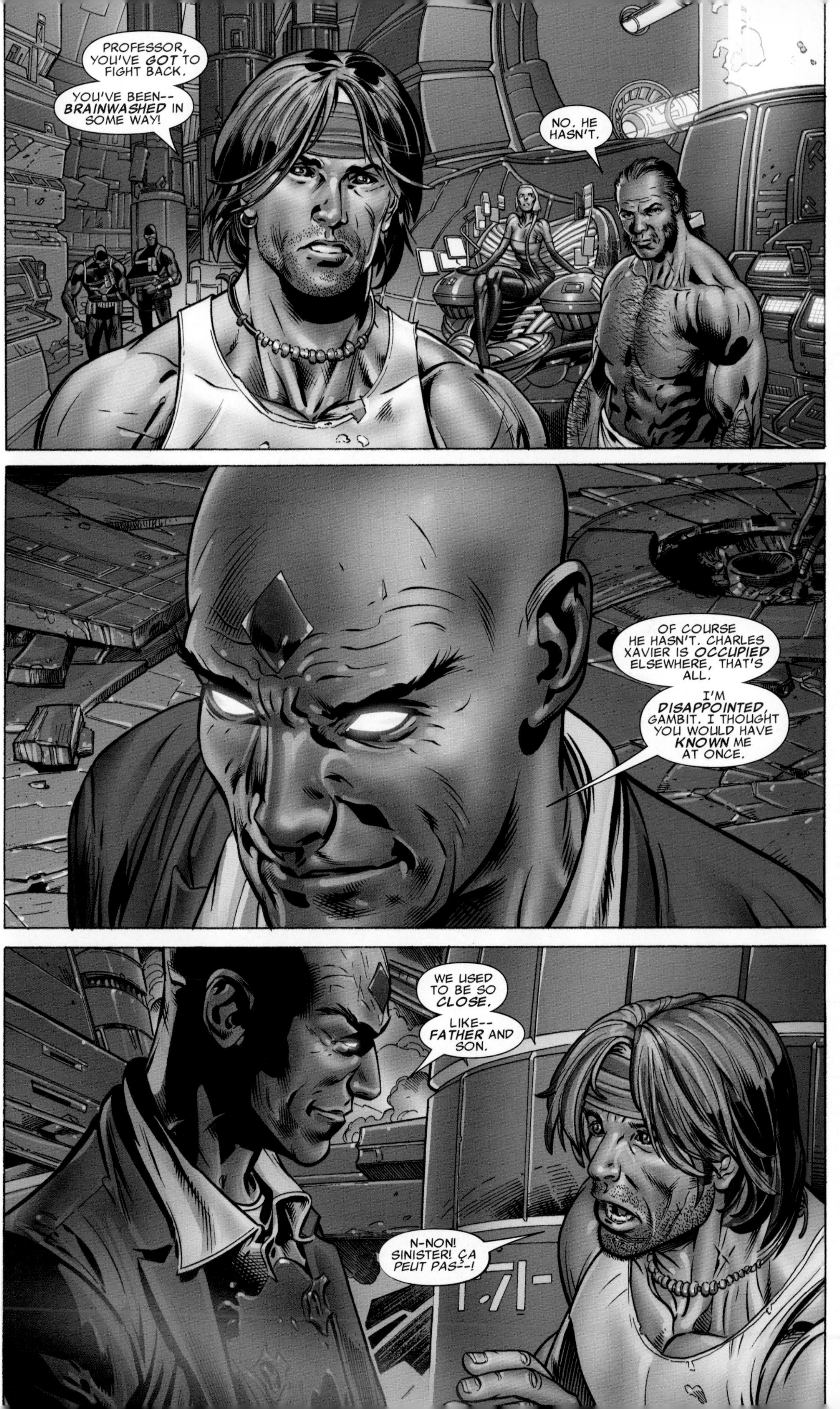
PROFESSOR, YOU'VE GOT TO FIGHT BACK.
YOU'VE BEEN-- BRAINWASHED IN SOME WAY!
NO. HE HASN'T.
OF COURSE HE HASN'T. CHARLES XAVIER IS OCCUPIED ELSEWHERE, THAT'S ALL.
I'M DISAPPOINTED, GAMBIT. I THOUGHT YOU WOULD HAVE KNOWN ME AT ONCE.
WE USED TO BE SO CLOSE.
LIKE-- FATHER AND SON.
N-NON! SINISTER! ÇA PEUT PAS--!

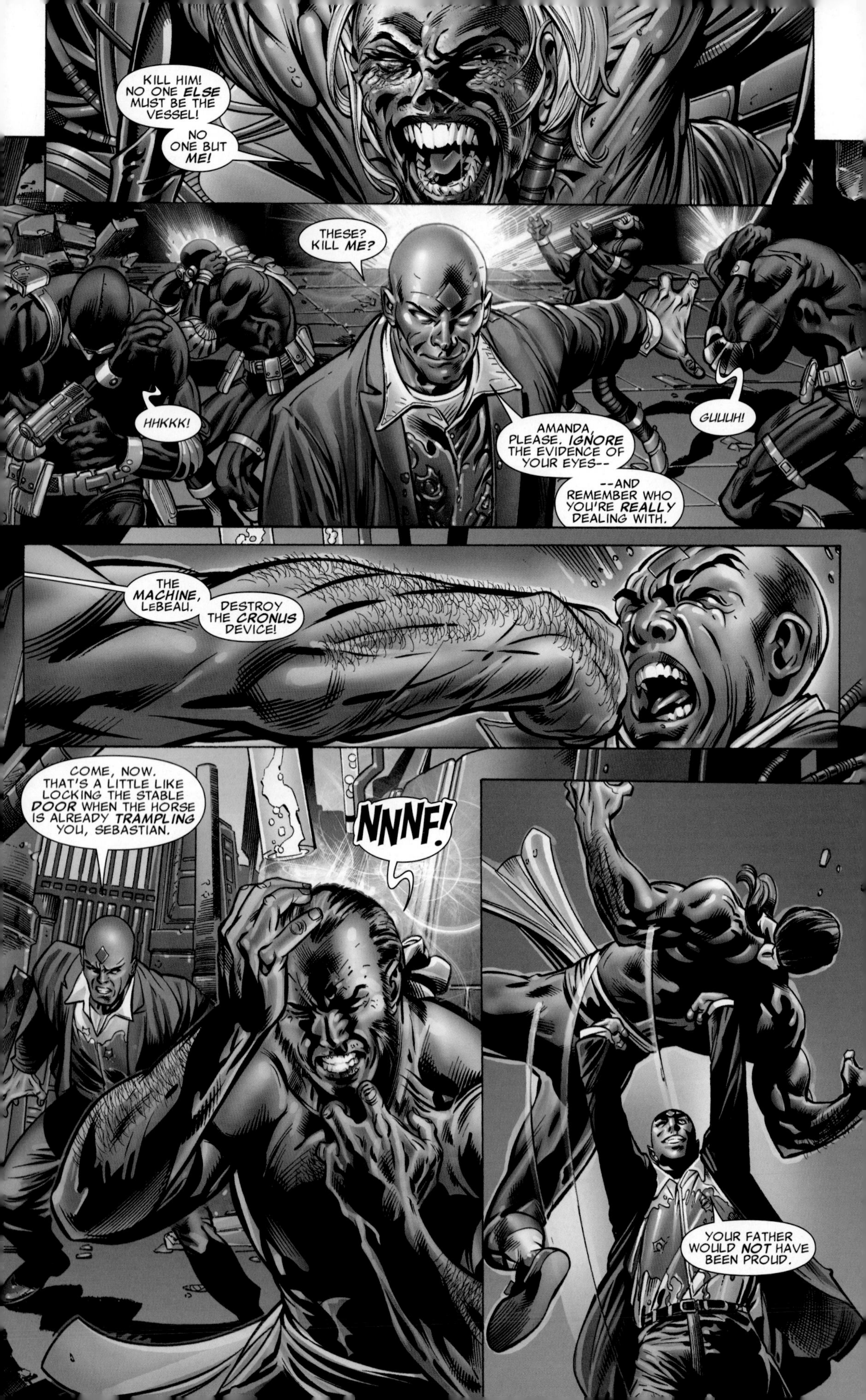
KILL HIM! NO ONE ELSE MUST BE THE VESSEL!
NO ONE BUT ME!
THESE? KILL ME?
HHKKK!
AMANDA, PLEASE. IGNORE THE EVIDENCE OF YOUR EYES--
--AND REMEMBER WHO YOU'RE REALLY DEALING WITH.
GUUUH!
THE MACHINE, LEBEAU.
DESTROY THE CRONUS DEVICE!
COME, NOW. THAT'S A LITTLE LIKE LOCKING THE STABLE DOOR WHEN THE HORSE IS ALREADY TRAMPLING YOU, SEBASTIAN.
NNNF!
YOUR FATHER WOULD NOT HAVE BEEN PROUD.

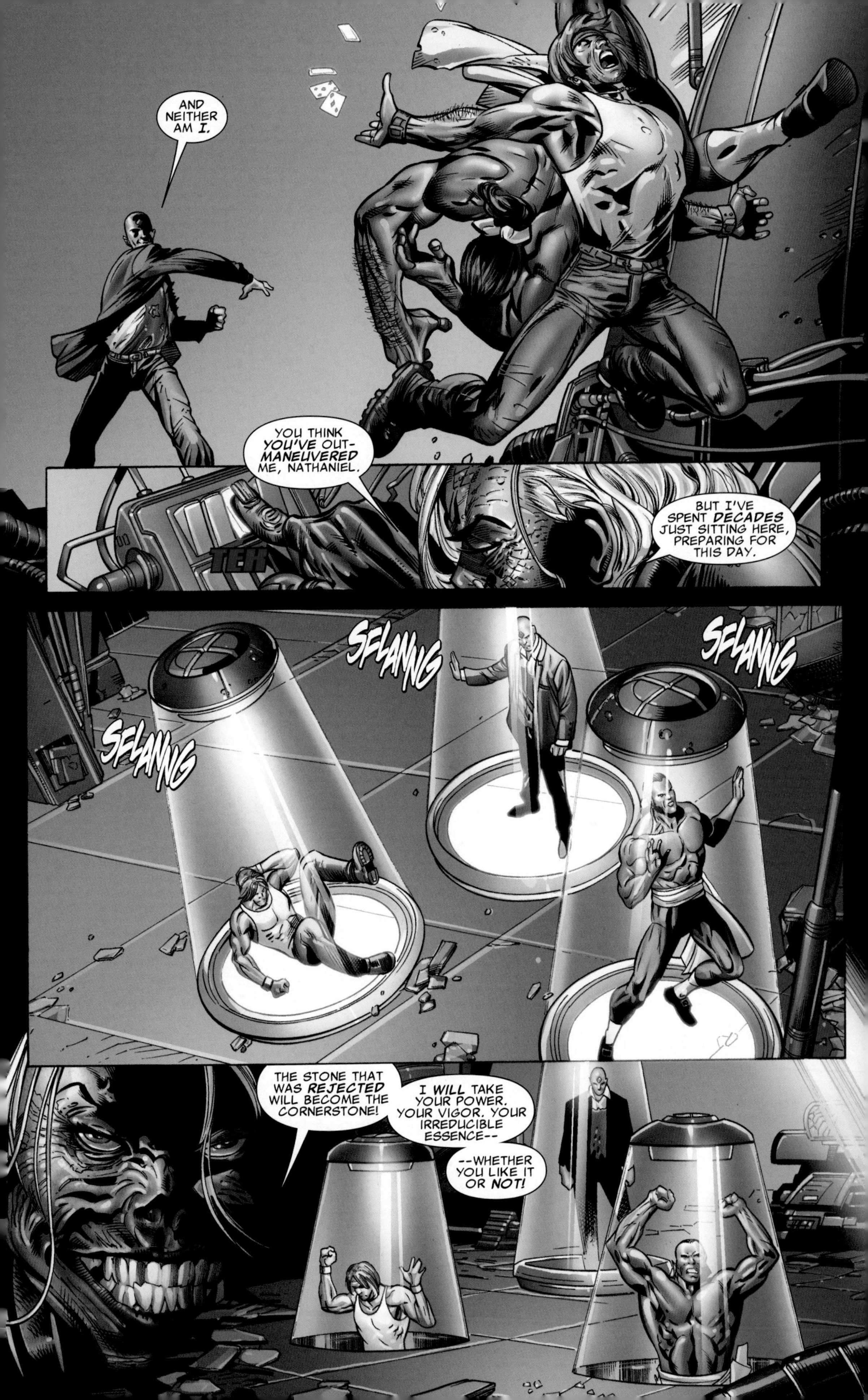
AND NEITHER AM I.
YOU THINK YOU'VE OUT-MANEUVERED ME, NATHANIEL.
TEK
BUT I'VE SPENT DECADES JUST SITTING HERE, PREPARING FOR THIS DAY.
SFLANNG
SFLANNG
SFLANNG
THE STONE THAT WAS REJECTED WILL BECOME THE CORNERSTONE!
I WILL TAKE YOUR POWER. YOUR VIGOR. YOUR IRREDUCIBLE ESSENCE--
--WHETHER YOU LIKE IT OR NOT!

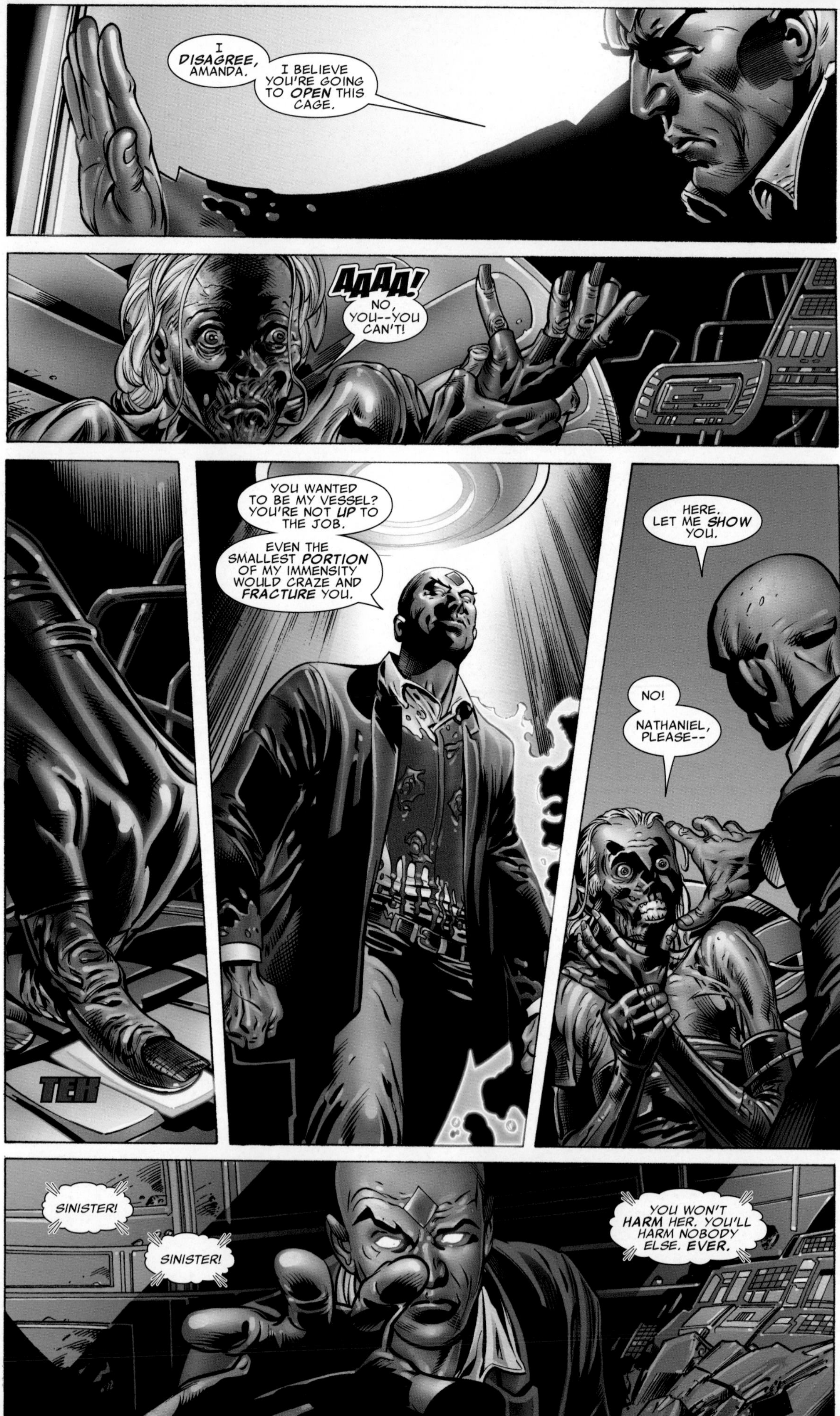
I DISAGREE, AMANDA.
I BELIEVE YOU'RE GOING TO OPEN THIS CAGE.
AAAA!
NO, YOU--YOU CAN'T!
YOU WANTED TO BE MY VESSEL? YOU'RE NOT UP TO THE JOB.
EVEN THE SMALLEST PORTION OF MY IMMENSITY WOULD CRAZE AND FRACTURE YOU.
HERE. LET ME SHOW YOU.
NO!
NATHANIEL, PLEASE--
TEH
SINISTER!
SINISTER!
YOU WON'T HARM HER. YOU'LL HARM NOBODY ELSE. EVER.

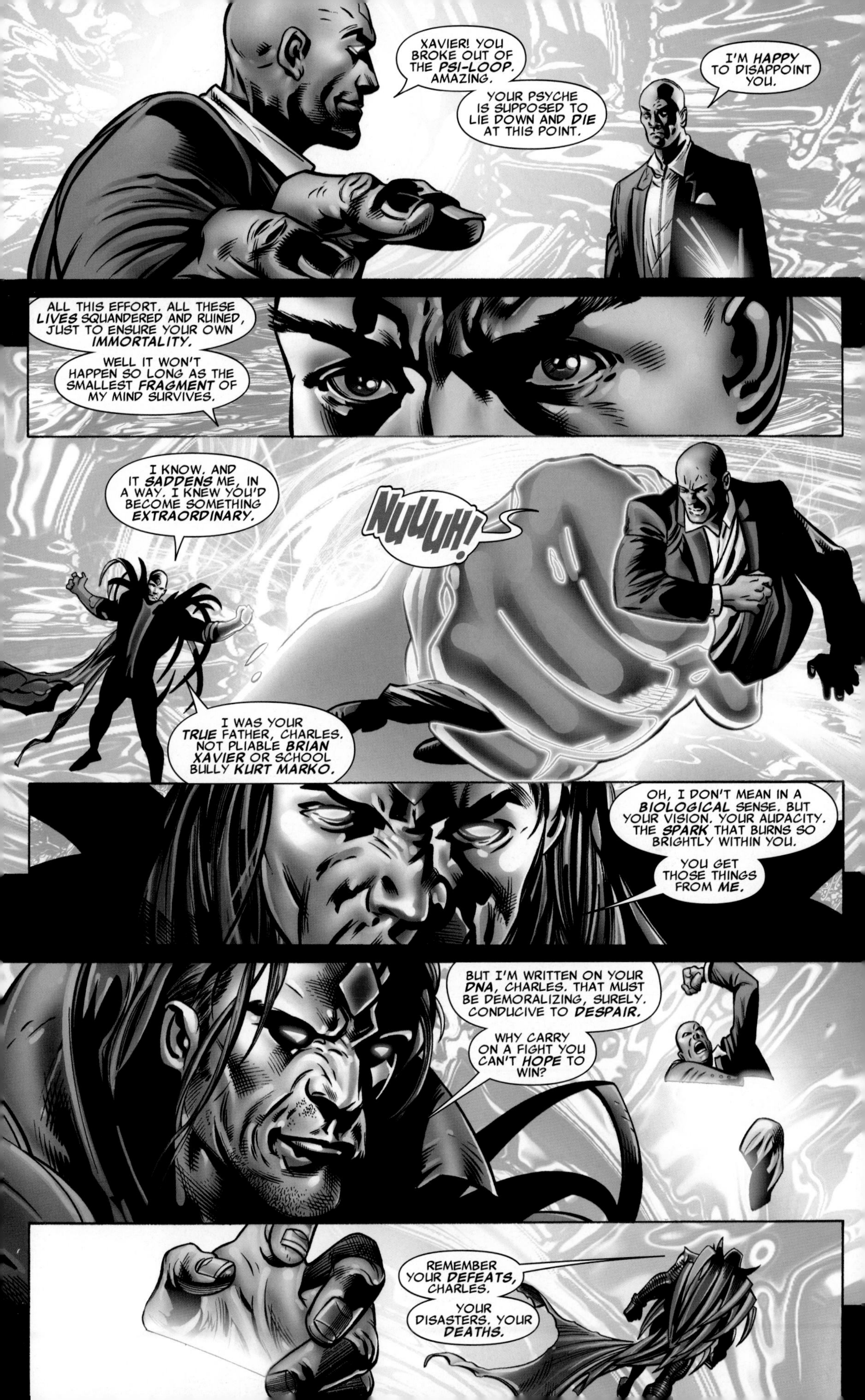
XAVIER! YOU BROKE OUT OF THE PSI-LOOP. AMAZING.
YOUR PSYCHE IS SUPPOSED TO LIE DOWN AND DIE AT THIS POINT.
I'M HAPPY TO DISAPPOINT YOU.
ALL THIS EFFORT. ALL THESE LIVES SQUANDERED AND RUINED, JUST TO ENSURE YOUR OWN IMMORTALITY.
WELL IT WON'T HAPPEN SO LONG AS THE SMALLEST FRAGMENT OF MY MIND SURVIVES.
I KNOW. AND IT SADDENS ME, IN A WAY. I KNEW YOU'D BECOME SOMETHING EXTRAORDINARY.
NUUUH!
I WAS YOUR TRUE FATHER, CHARLES. NOT PLIABLE BRIAN XAVIER OR SCHOOL BULLY KURT MARKO.
OH, I DON'T MEAN IN A BIOLOGICAL SENSE. BUT YOUR VISION. YOUR AUDACITY. THE SPARK THAT BURNS SO BRIGHTLY WITHIN YOU.
YOU GET THOSE THINGS FROM ME.
BUT I'M WRITTEN ON YOUR DNA, CHARLES. THAT MUST BE DEMORALIZING, SURELY. CONDUCIVE TO DESPAIR.
WHY CARRY ON A FIGHT YOU CAN'T HOPE TO WIN?
REMEMBER YOUR DEFEATS, CHARLES.
YOUR DISASTERS. YOUR DEATHS.

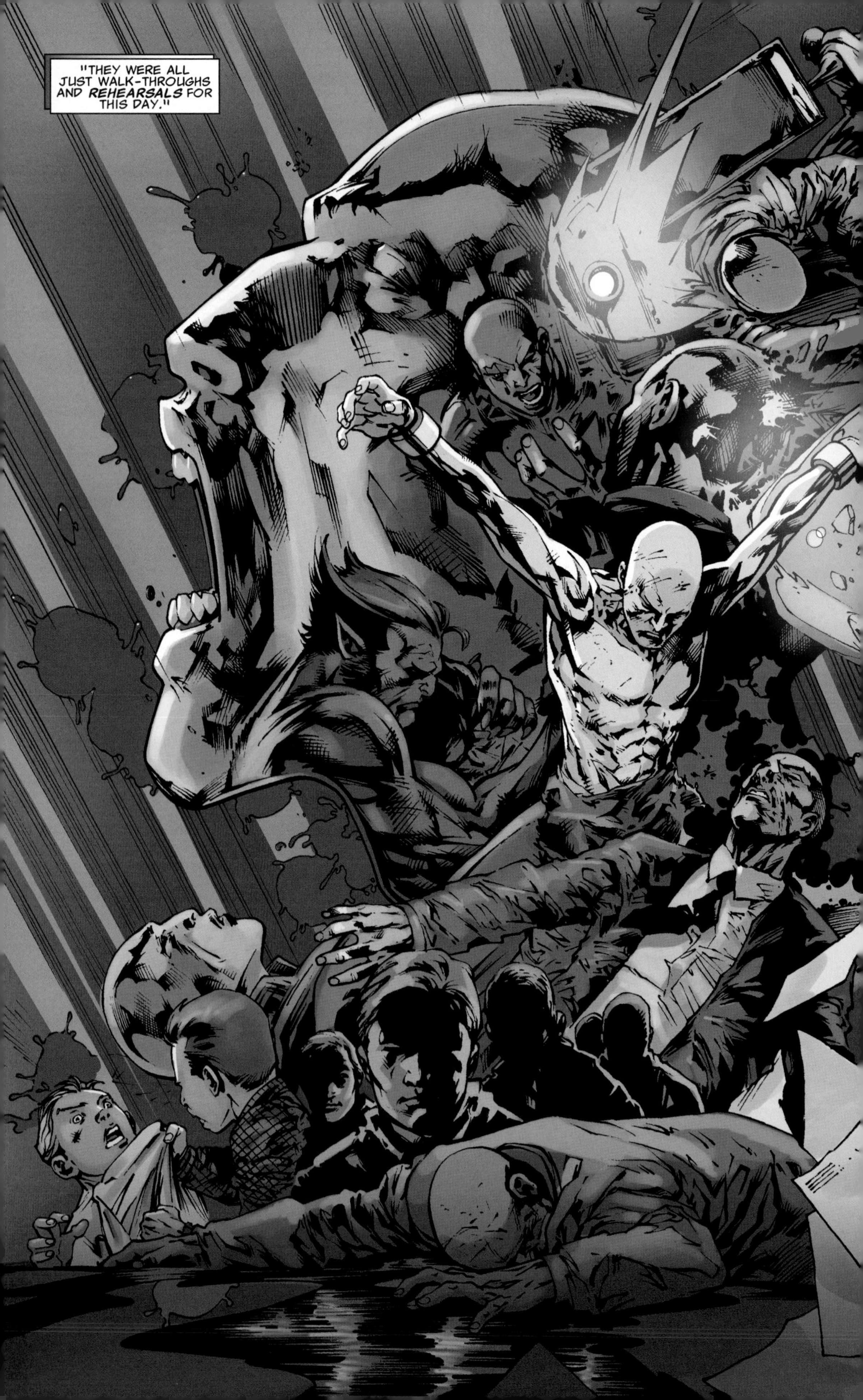
"THEY WERE ALL JUST WALK-THROUGHS AND REHEARSALS FOR THIS DAY."

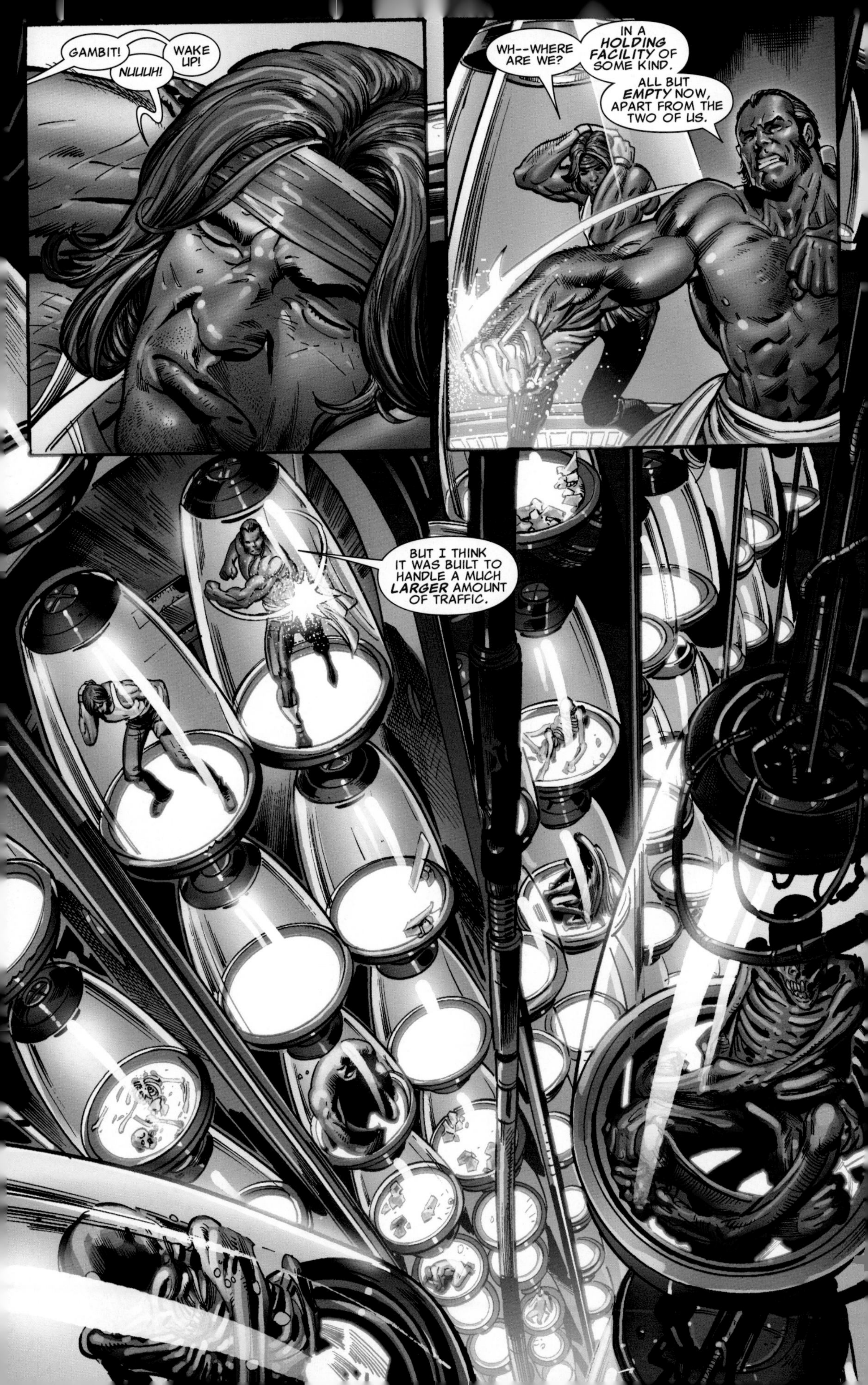
GAMBIT!
NUUUH!
WAKE UP!
WH--WHERE ARE WE?
IN A HOLDING FACILITY OF SOME KIND.
ALL BUT EMPTY NOW, APART FROM THE TWO OF US.
BUT I THINK IT WAS BUILT TO HANDLE A MUCH LARGER AMOUNT OF TRAFFIC.

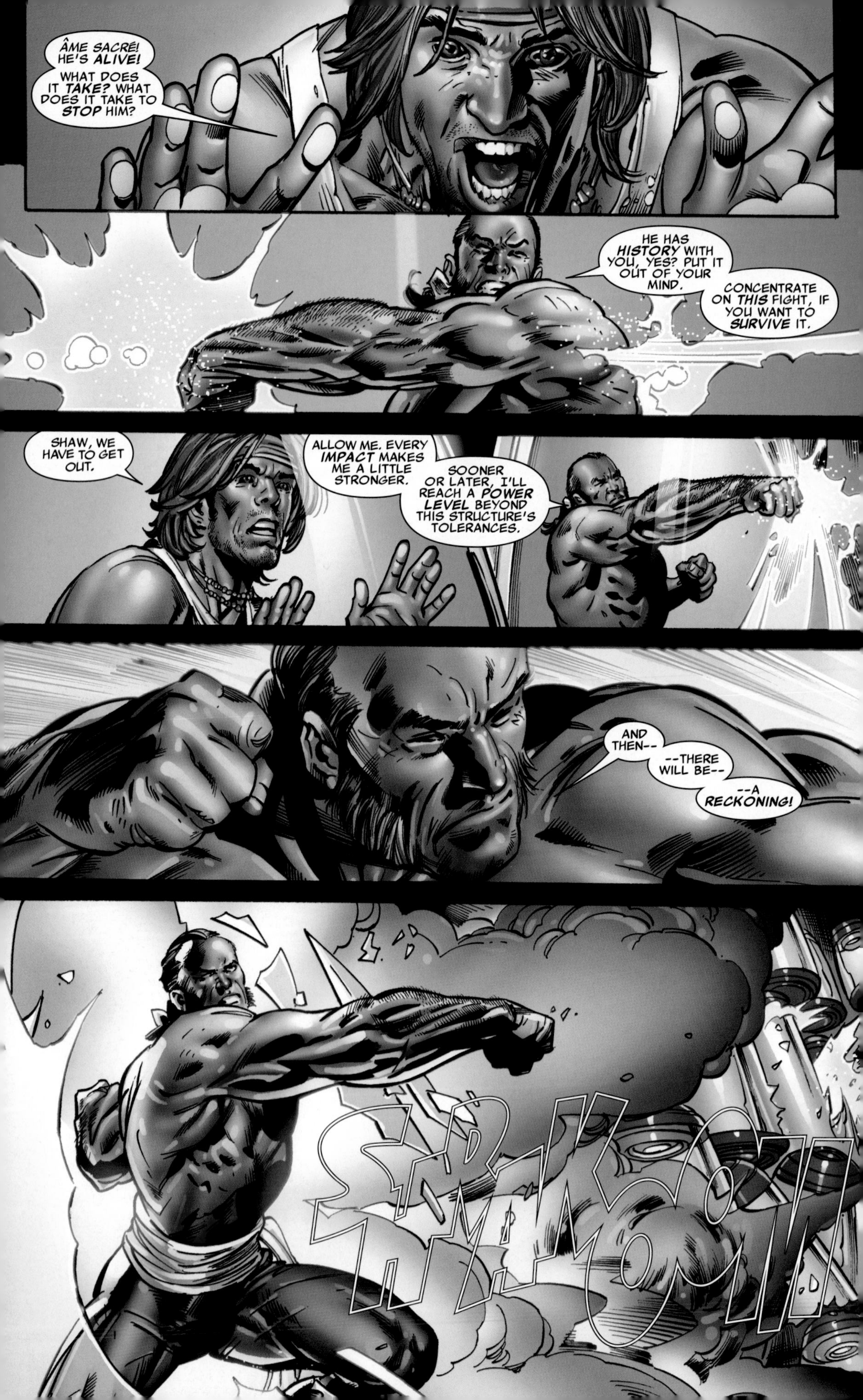
ÂME SACRÉ! HE'S ALIVE!
WHAT DOES IT TAKE? WHAT DOES IT TAKE TO STOP HIM?
HE HAS HISTORY WITH YOU, YES? PUT IT OUT OF YOUR MIND.
CONCENTRATE ON THIS FIGHT, IF YOU WANT TO SURVIVE IT.
SHAW, WE HAVE TO GET OUT.
ALLOW ME. EVERY IMPACT MAKES ME A LITTLE STRONGER.
SOONER OR LATER, I'LL REACH A POWER LEVEL BEYOND THIS STRUCTURE'S TOLERANCES.
AND THEN--
--THERE WILL BE--
--A RECKONING!

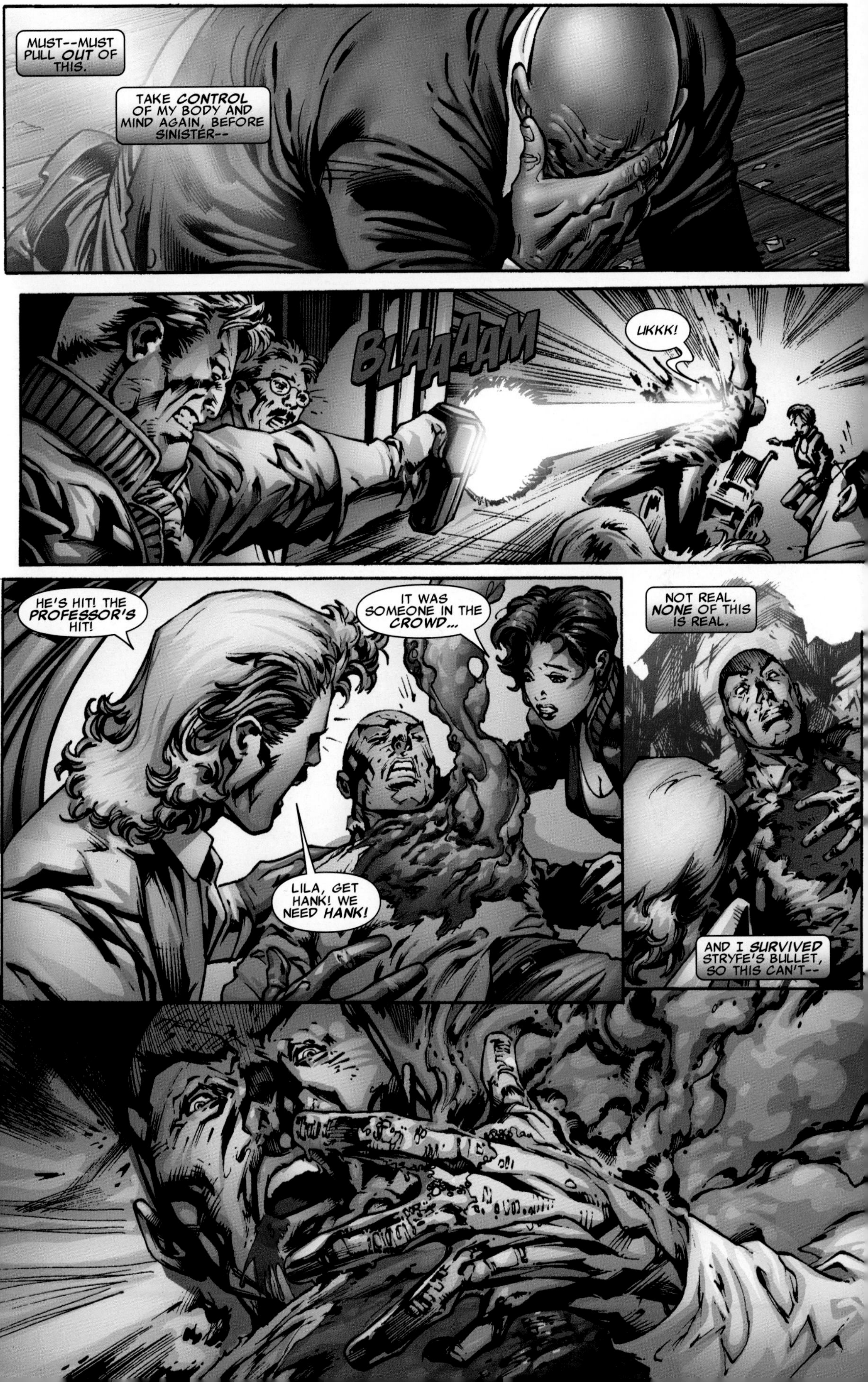
MUST--MUST PULL OUT OF THIS.
TAKE CONTROL OF MY BODY AND MIND AGAIN, BEFORE SINISTER--
BLAAAAAM
UKKK!
HE'S HIT! THE PROFESSOR'S HIT!
IT WAS SOMEONE IN THE CROWD...
LILA, GET HANK! WE NEED HANK!
NOT REAL. NONE OF THIS IS REAL.
AND I SURVIVED STRYFE'S BULLET, SO THIS CAN'T--

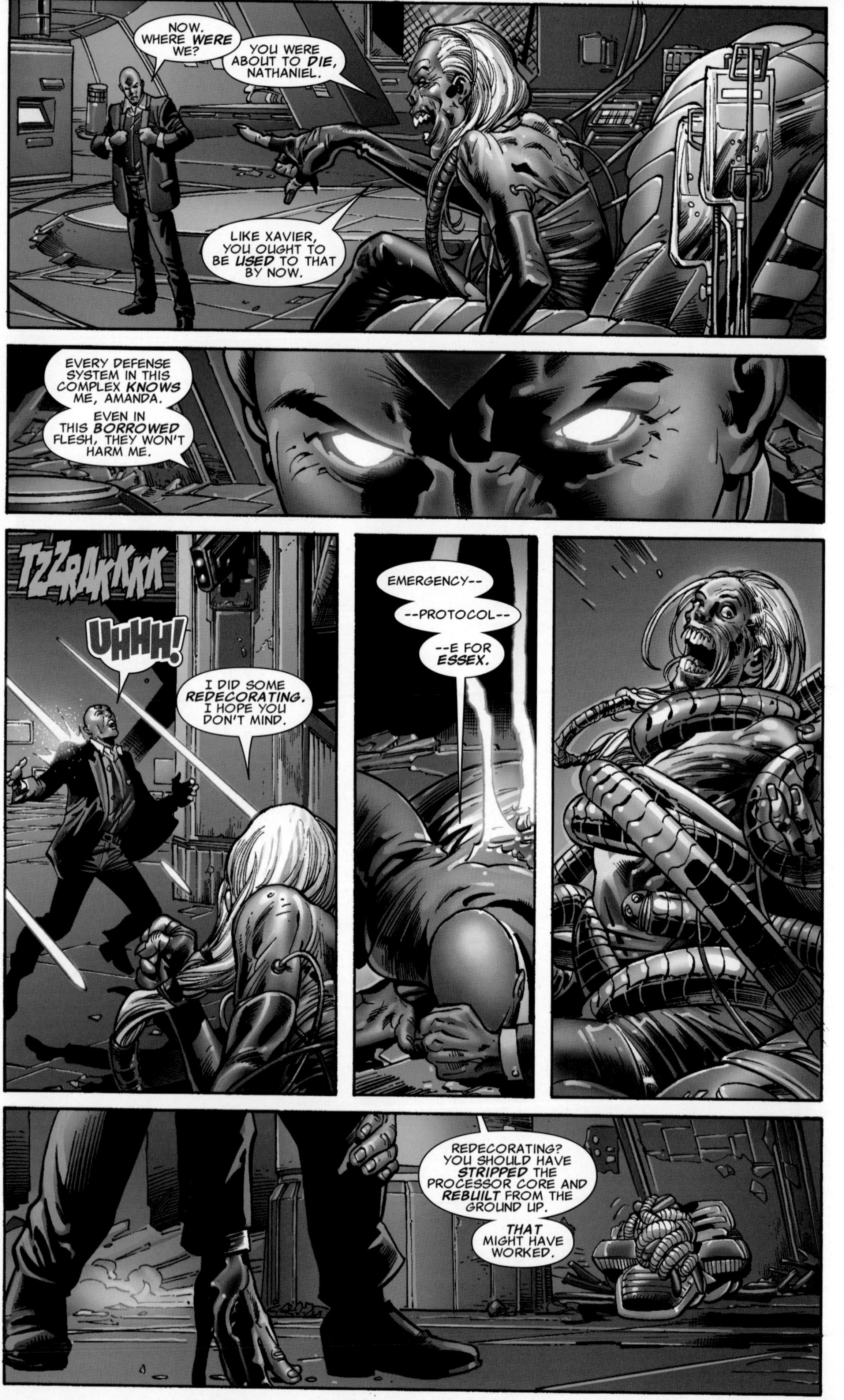
NOW. WHERE WERE WE?
YOU WERE ABOUT TO DIE, NATHANIEL.
LIKE XAVIER, YOU OUGHT TO BE USED TO THAT BY NOW.
EVERY DEFENSE SYSTEM IN THIS COMPLEX KNOWS ME, AMANDA.
EVEN IN THIS BORROWED FLESH, THEY WON'T HARM ME.
TZZRAKKKK
UHHH!
I DID SOME REDECORATING. I HOPE YOU DON'T MIND.
EMERGENCY--
--PROTOCOL--
--E FOR ESSEX.
REDECORATING? YOU SHOULD HAVE STRIPPED THE PROCESSOR CORE AND REBUILT FROM THE GROUND UP.
THAT MIGHT HAVE WORKED.

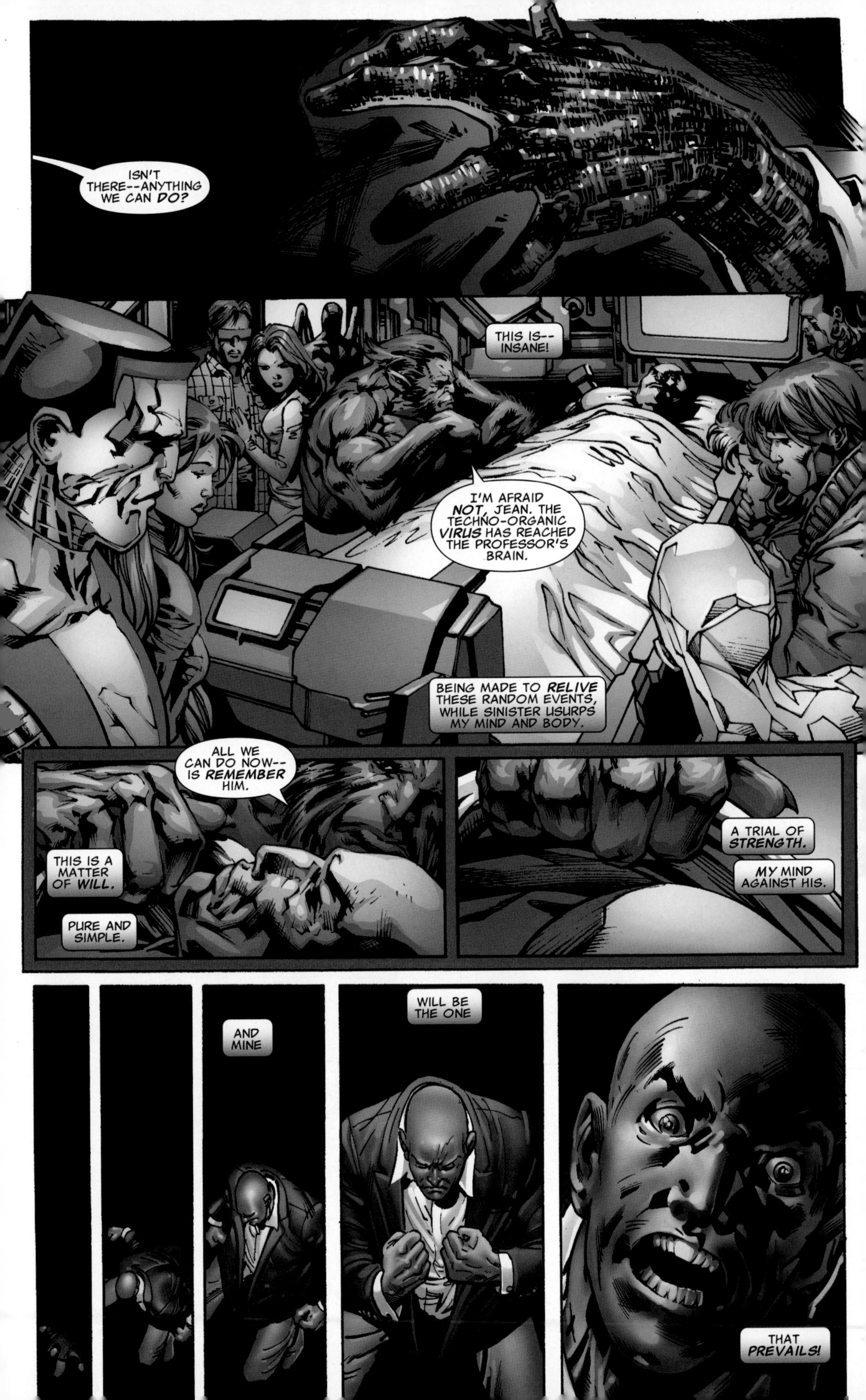
ISN'T THERE--ANYTHING WE CAN DO?
THIS IS-- INSANE!
I'M AFRAID NOT, JEAN. THE TECHNO-ORGANIC VIRUS HAS REACHED THE PROFESSOR'S BRAIN.
BEING MADE TO RELIVE THESE RANDOM EVENTS, WHILE SINISTER USURPS MY MIND AND BODY.
ALL WE CAN DO NOW-- IS REMEMBER HIM.
THIS IS A MATTER OF WILL.
PURE AND SIMPLE.
A TRIAL OF STRENGTH.
MY MIND AGAINST HIS.
AND MINE
WILL BE THE ONE
THAT PREVAILS!

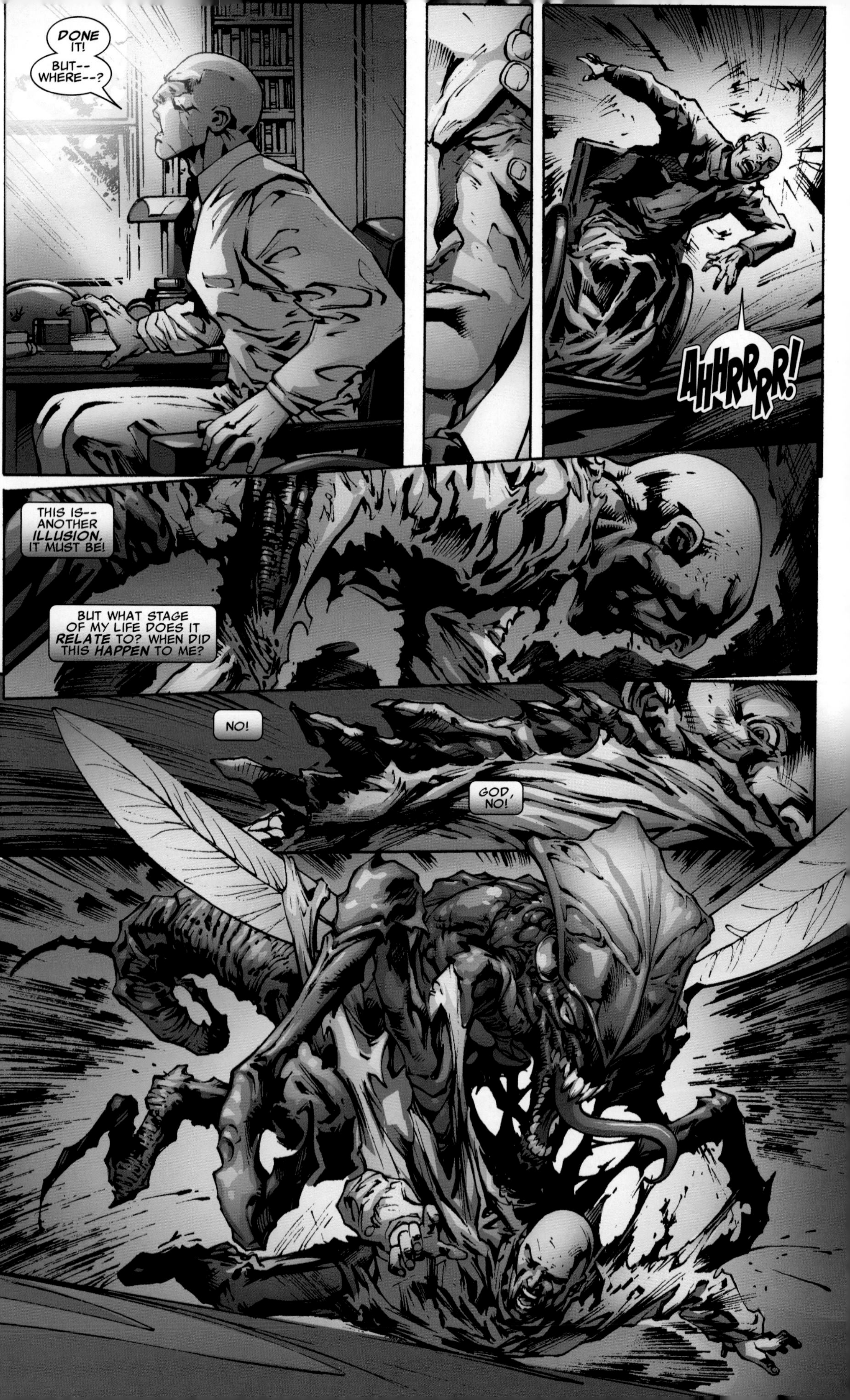
DONE IT! BUT-- WHERE--?
AHHRRRR!
THIS IS-- ANOTHER ILLUSION. IT MUST BE!
BUT WHAT STAGE OF MY LIFE DOES IT RELATE TO? WHEN DID THIS HAPPEN TO ME?
NO!
GOD, NO!

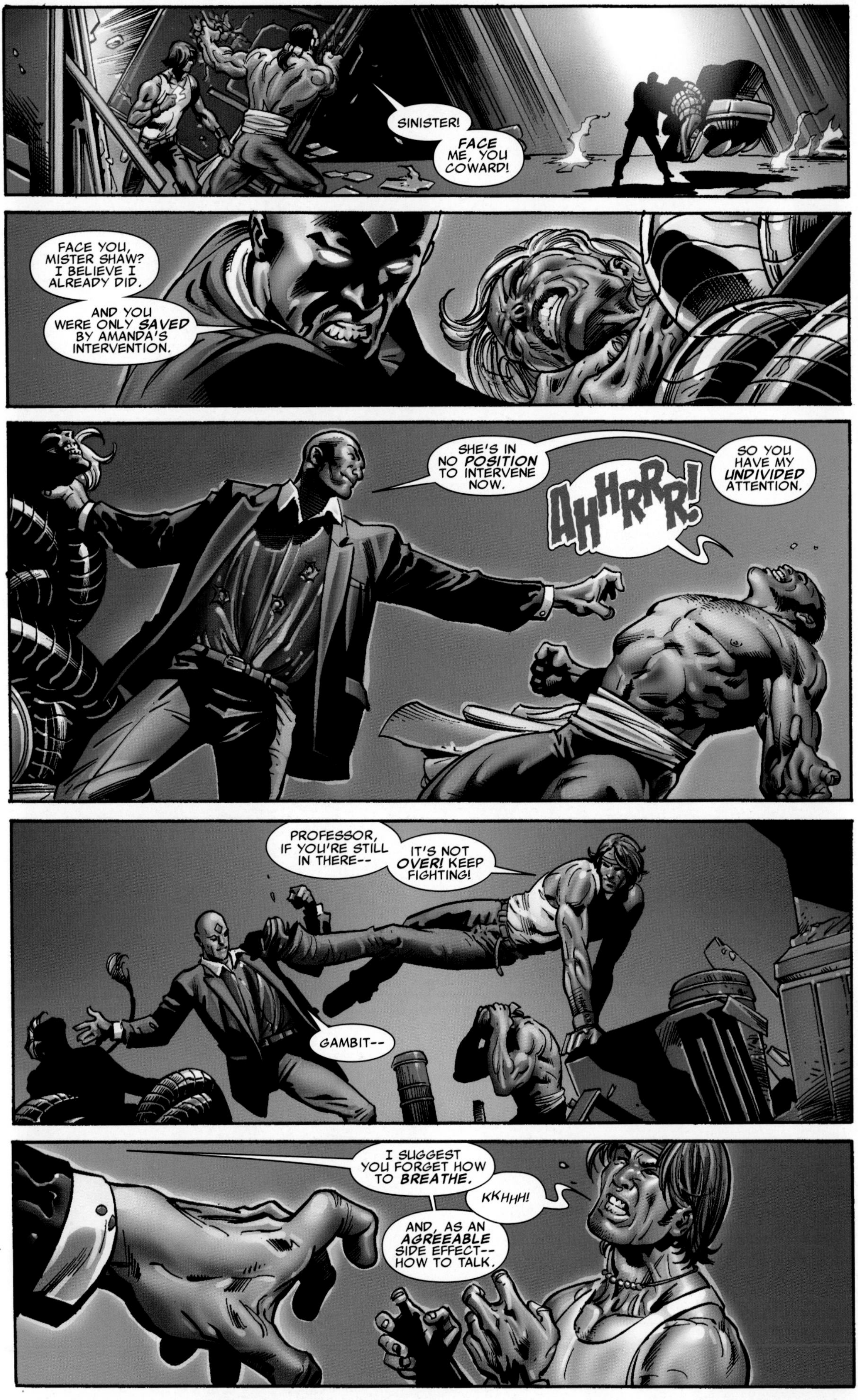

SINISTER! FACE ME, YOU COWARD!
FACE YOU, MISTER SHAW? I BELIEVE I ALREADY DID.
AND YOU WERE ONLY SAVED BY AMANDA'S INTERVENTION.
SHE'S IN NO POSITION TO INTERVENE NOW.
SO YOU HAVE MY UNDIVIDED ATTENTION.
AHHRRR!
PROFESSOR, IF YOU'RE STILL IN THERE--
IT'S NOT OVER! KEEP FIGHTING!
GAMBIT--
I SUGGEST YOU FORGET HOW TO BREATHE.
KKHHH!
AND, AS AN AGREEABLE SIDE EFFECT-- HOW TO TALK.

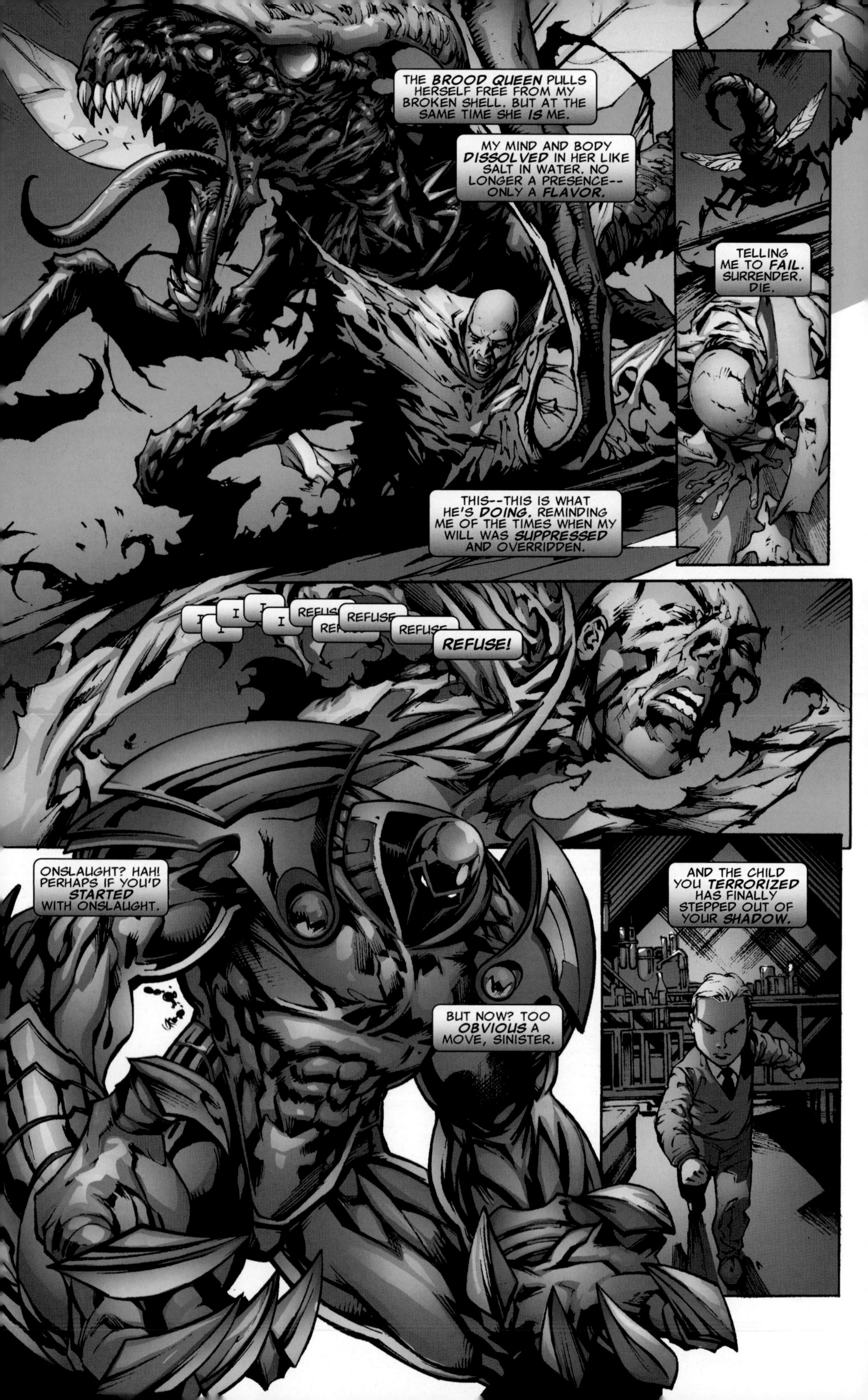
THE BROOD QUEEN PULLS HERSELF FREE FROM MY BROKEN SHELL. BUT AT THE SAME TIME SHE IS ME.
MY MIND AND BODY DISSOLVED IN HER LIKE SALT IN WATER. NO LONGER A PRESENCE-- ONLY A FLAVOR.
TELLING ME TO FAIL. SURRENDER. DIE.
THIS--THIS IS WHAT HE'S DOING. REMINDING ME OF THE TIMES WHEN MY WILL WAS SUPPRESSED AND OVERRIDDEN.
I I I I REFUSE REFUSE REFUSE REFUSE!
ONSLAUGHT? HAH! PERHAPS IF YOU'D STARTED WITH ONSLAUGHT.
BUT NOW? TOO OBVIOUS A MOVE, SINISTER.
AND THE CHILD YOU TERRORIZED HAS FINALLY STEPPED OUT OF YOUR SHADOW.

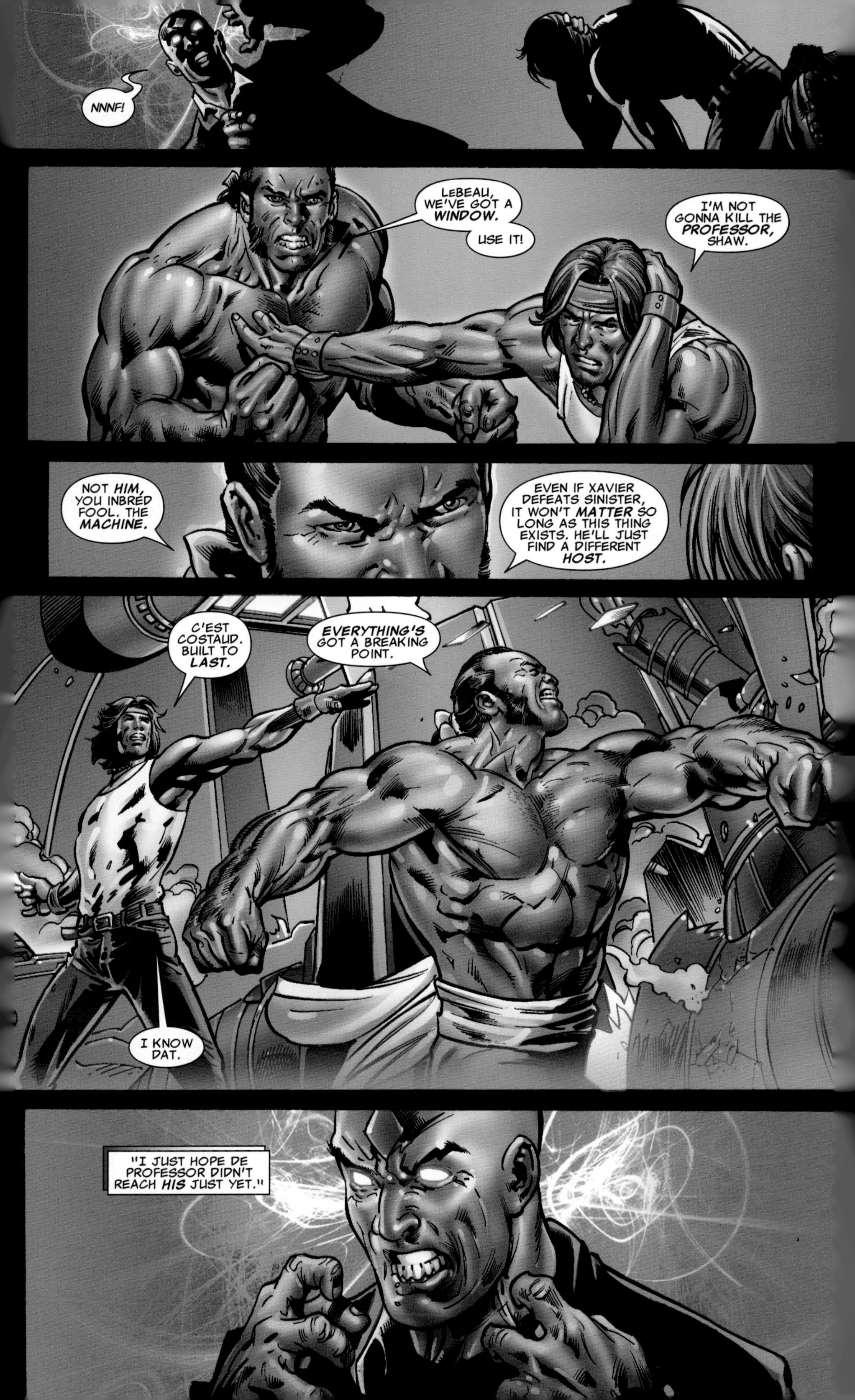
NNNF!
LEBEAU, WE'VE GOT A WINDOW.
USE IT!
I'M NOT GONNA KILL THE PROFESSOR, SHAW.
NOT HIM, YOU INBRED FOOL. THE MACHINE.
EVEN IF XAVIER DEFEATS SINISTER, IT WON'T MATTER SO LONG AS THIS THING EXISTS. HE'LL JUST FIND A DIFFERENT HOST.
C'EST COSTAUD. BUILT TO LAST.
EVERYTHING'S GOT A BREAKING POINT.
I KNOW DAT.
"I JUST HOPE DE PROFESSOR DIDN'T REACH HIS JUST YET."

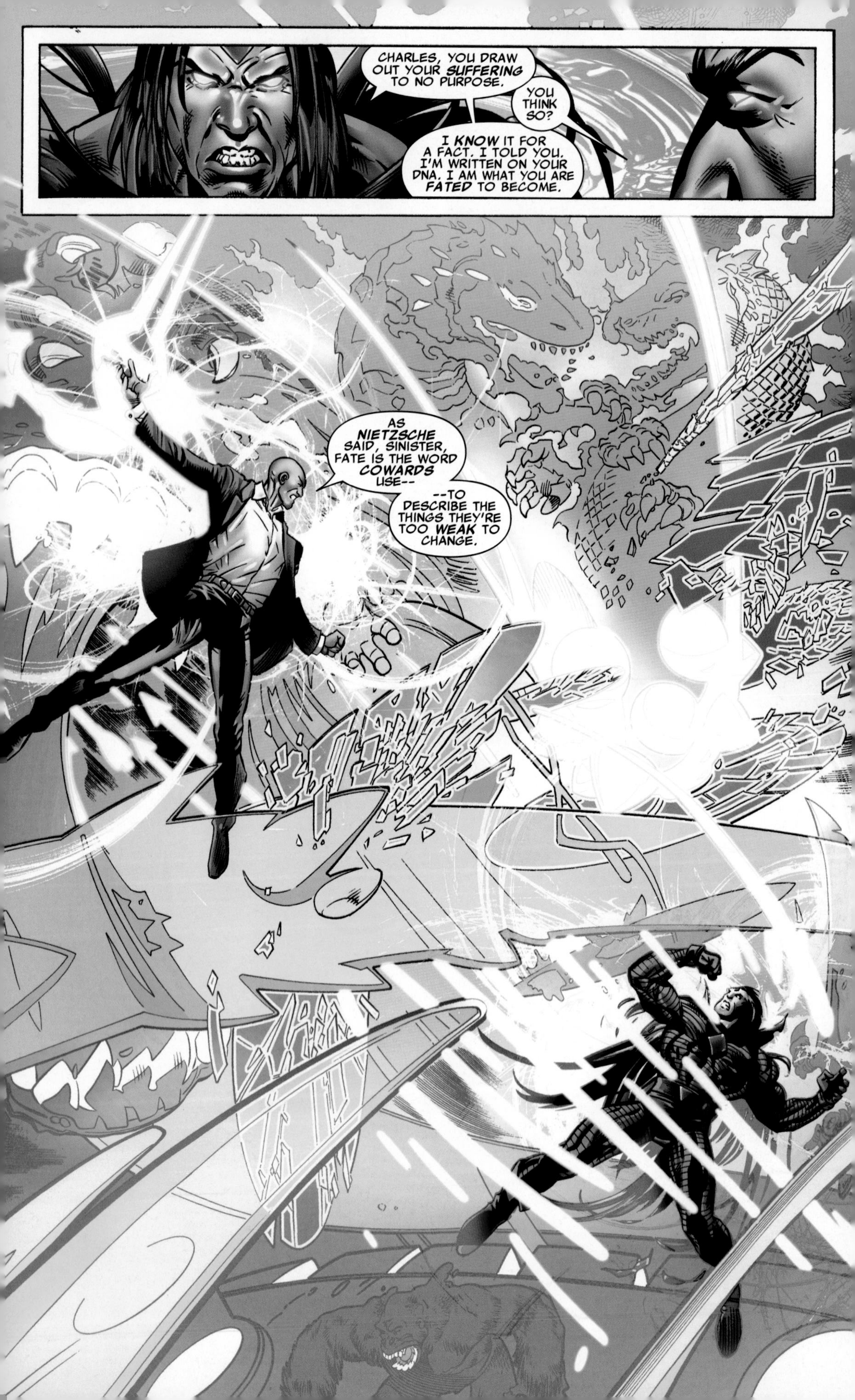
CHARLES, YOU DRAW OUT YOUR SUFFERING TO NO PURPOSE.
YOU THINK SO?
I KNOW IT FOR A FACT. I TOLD YOU. I'M WRITTEN ON YOUR DNA. I AM WHAT YOU ARE FATED TO BECOME.
AS NIETZSCHE SAID, SINISTER, FATE IS THE WORD COWARDS USE--
--TO DESCRIBE THE THINGS THEY'RE TOO WEAK TO CHANGE.

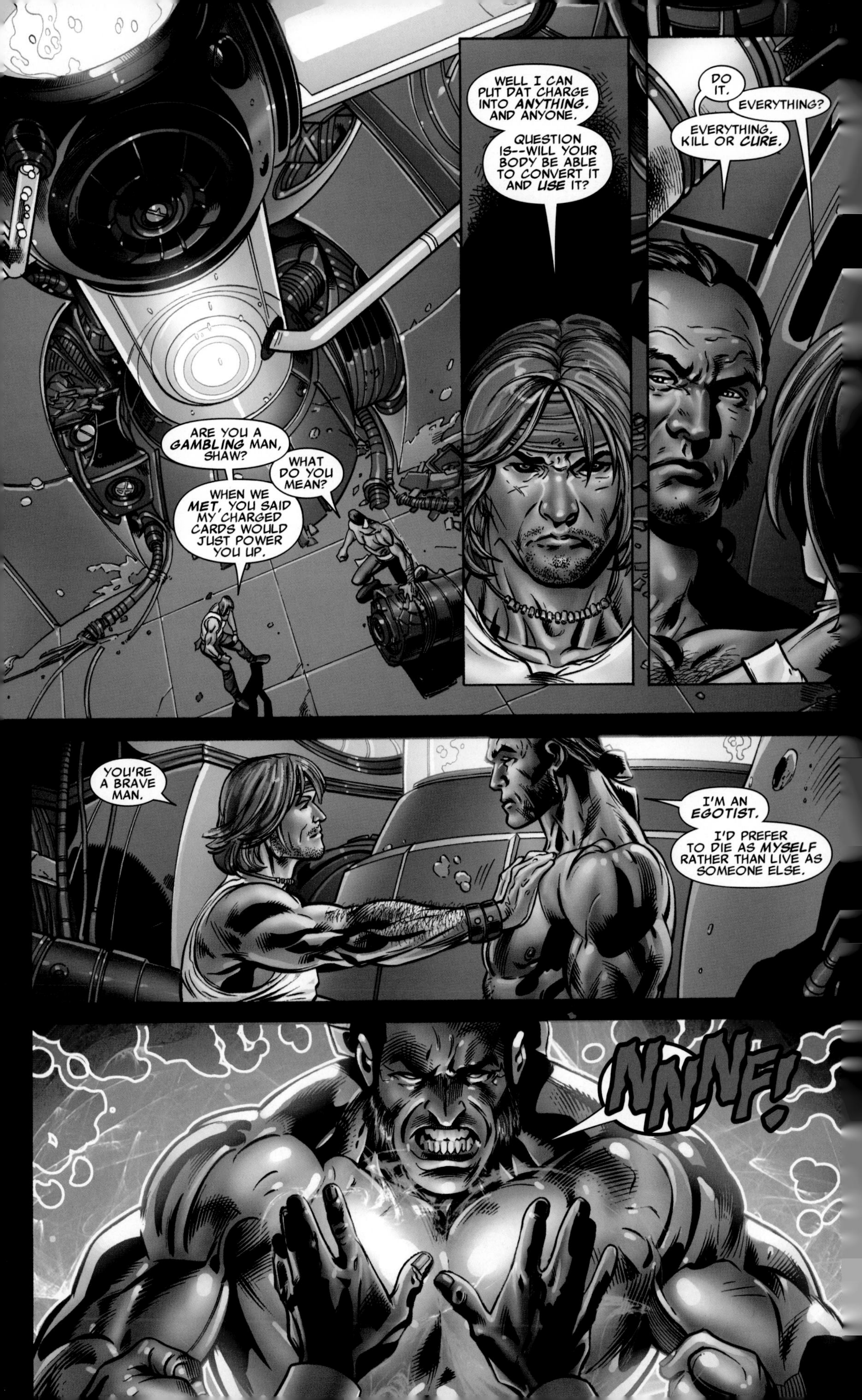

ARE YOU A GAMBLING MAN, SHAW?
WHAT DO YOU MEAN?
WHEN WE MET, YOU SAID MY CHARGED CARDS WOULD JUST POWER YOU UP.
WELL I CAN PUT DAT CHARGE INTO ANYTHING. AND ANYONE.
QUESTION IS--WILL YOUR BODY BE ABLE TO CONVERT IT AND USE IT?
DO IT.
EVERYTHING?
EVERYTHING. KILL OR CURE.
YOU'RE A BRAVE MAN.
I'M AN EGOTIST.
I'D PREFER TO DIE AS MYSELF RATHER THAN LIVE AS SOMEONE ELSE.
NNNF!

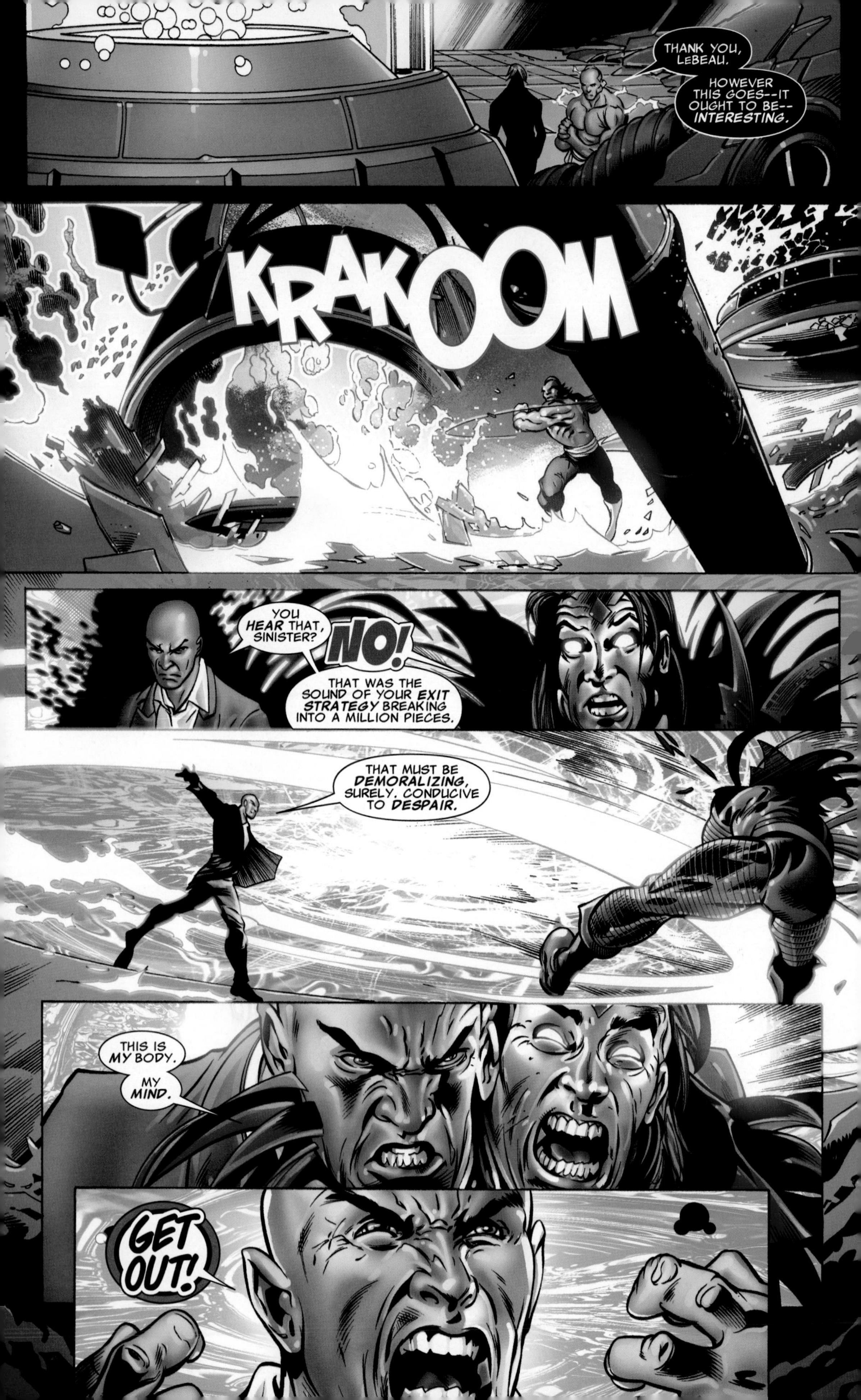
THANK YOU, LEBEAU.
HOWEVER THIS GOES--IT OUGHT TO BE--INTERESTING.
KRAKOOM
YOU HEAR THAT, SINISTER?
NO!
THAT WAS THE SOUND OF YOUR EXIT STRATEGY BREAKING INTO A MILLION PIECES.
THAT MUST BE DEMORALIZING, SURELY. CONDUCIVE TO DESPAIR.
THIS IS MY BODY.
MY MIND.
GET OUT!

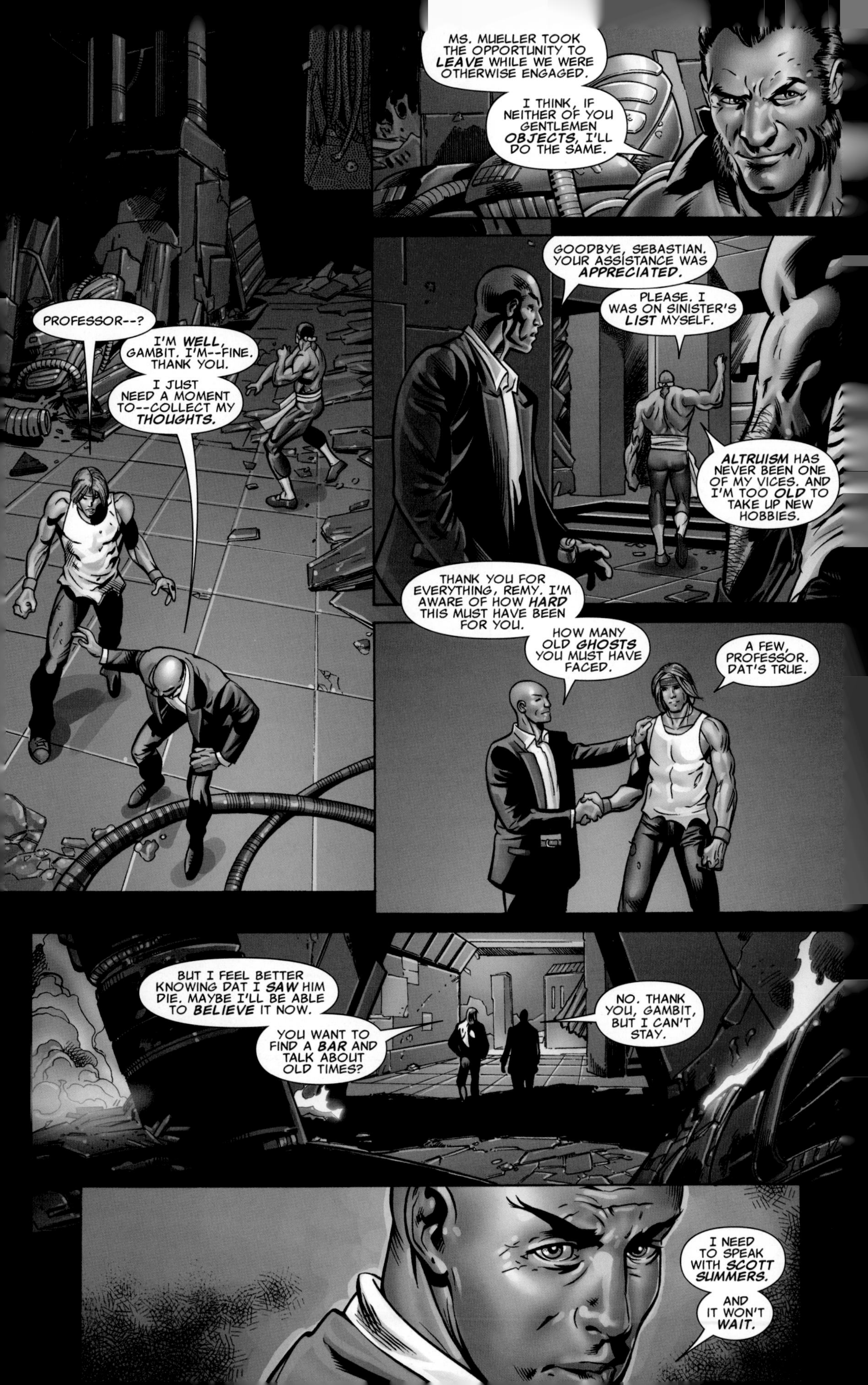
MS. MUELLER TOOK THE OPPORTUNITY TO LEAVE WHILE WE WERE OTHERWISE ENGAGED.
I THINK, IF NEITHER OF YOU GENTLEMEN OBJECTS, I'LL DO THE SAME.
PROFESSOR--?
I'M WELL, GAMBIT. I'M--FINE. THANK YOU.
I JUST NEED A MOMENT TO--COLLECT MY THOUGHTS.
GOODBYE, SEBASTIAN. YOUR ASSISTANCE WAS APPRECIATED.
PLEASE. I WAS ON SINISTER'S LIST MYSELF.
ALTRUISM HAS NEVER BEEN ONE OF MY VICES. AND I'M TOO OLD TO TAKE UP NEW HOBBIES.
THANK YOU FOR EVERYTHING, REMY. I'M AWARE OF HOW HARD THIS MUST HAVE BEEN FOR YOU.
HOW MANY OLD GHOSTS YOU MUST HAVE FACED.
A FEW, PROFESSOR. DAT'S TRUE.
BUT I FEEL BETTER KNOWING DAT I SAW HIM DIE. MAYBE I'LL BE ABLE TO BELIEVE IT NOW.
YOU WANT TO FIND A BAR AND TALK ABOUT OLD TIMES?
NO. THANK YOU, GAMBIT, BUT I CAN'T STAY.
I NEED TO SPEAK WITH SCOTT SUMMERS.
AND IT WON'T WAIT.

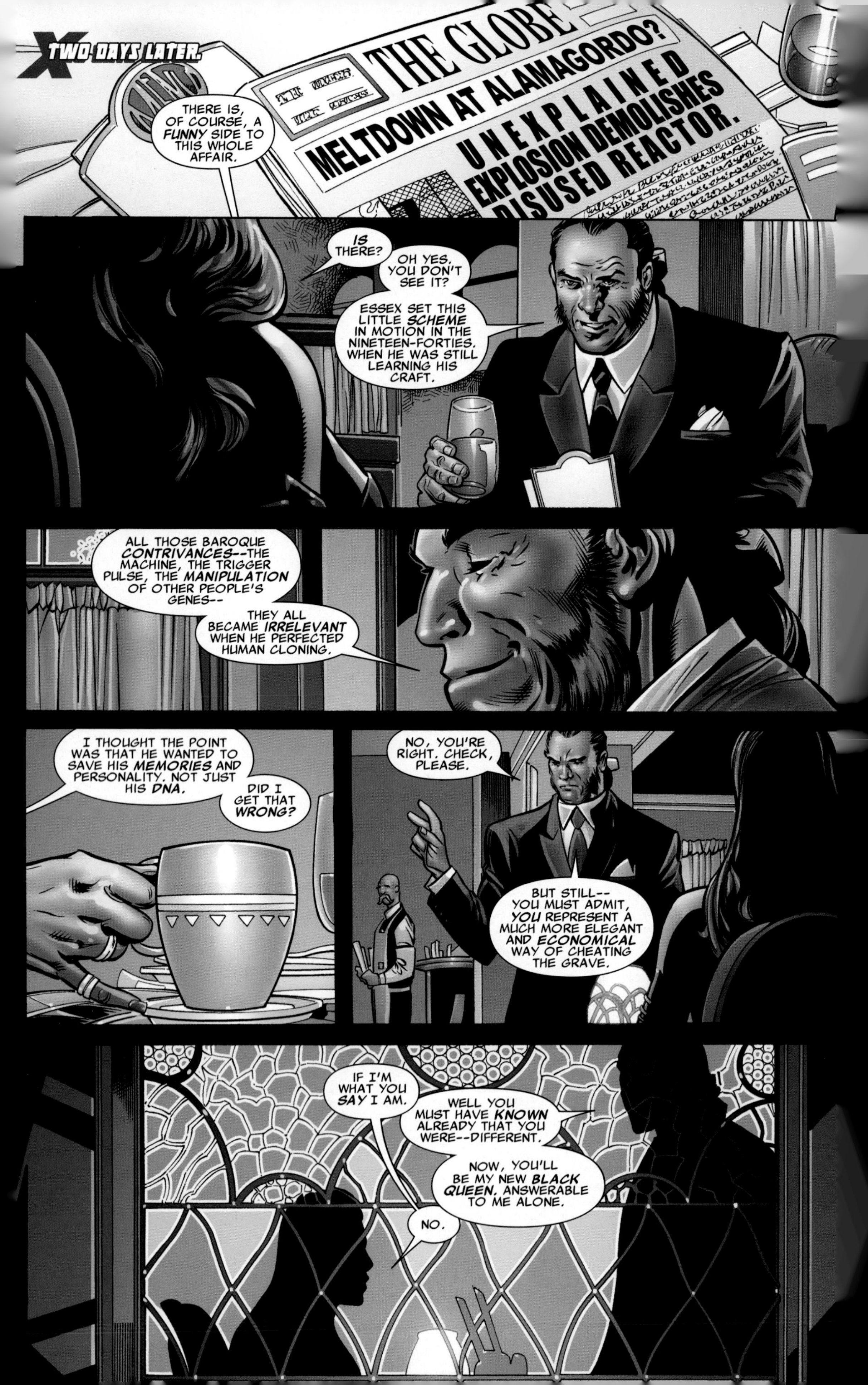
TWO DAYS LATER.
THE GLOBE
MELTDOWN AT ALAMAGORDO?
UNEXPLAINED EXPLOSION DEMOLISHES DISUSED REACTOR.
THERE IS, OF COURSE, A FUNNY SIDE TO THIS WHOLE AFFAIR.
IS THERE?
OH YES. YOU DON'T SEE IT?
ESSEX SET THIS LITTLE SCHEME IN MOTION IN THE NINETEEN-FORTIES, WHEN HE WAS STILL LEARNING HIS CRAFT.
ALL THOSE BAROQUE CONTRIVANCES--THE MACHINE, THE TRIGGER PULSE, THE MANIPULATION OF OTHER PEOPLE'S GENES--
THEY ALL BECAME IRRELEVANT WHEN HE PERFECTED HUMAN CLONING.
I THOUGHT THE POINT WAS THAT HE WANTED TO SAVE HIS MEMORIES AND PERSONALITY. NOT JUST HIS DNA.
DID I GET THAT WRONG?
NO, YOU'RE RIGHT. CHECK, PLEASE.
BUT STILL-- YOU MUST ADMIT, YOU REPRESENT A MUCH MORE ELEGANT AND ECONOMICAL WAY OF CHEATING THE GRAVE.
IF I'M WHAT YOU SAY I AM.
WELL YOU MUST HAVE KNOWN ALREADY THAT YOU WERE--DIFFERENT.
NOW, YOU'LL BE MY NEW BLACK QUEEN, ANSWERABLE TO ME ALONE.
NO.

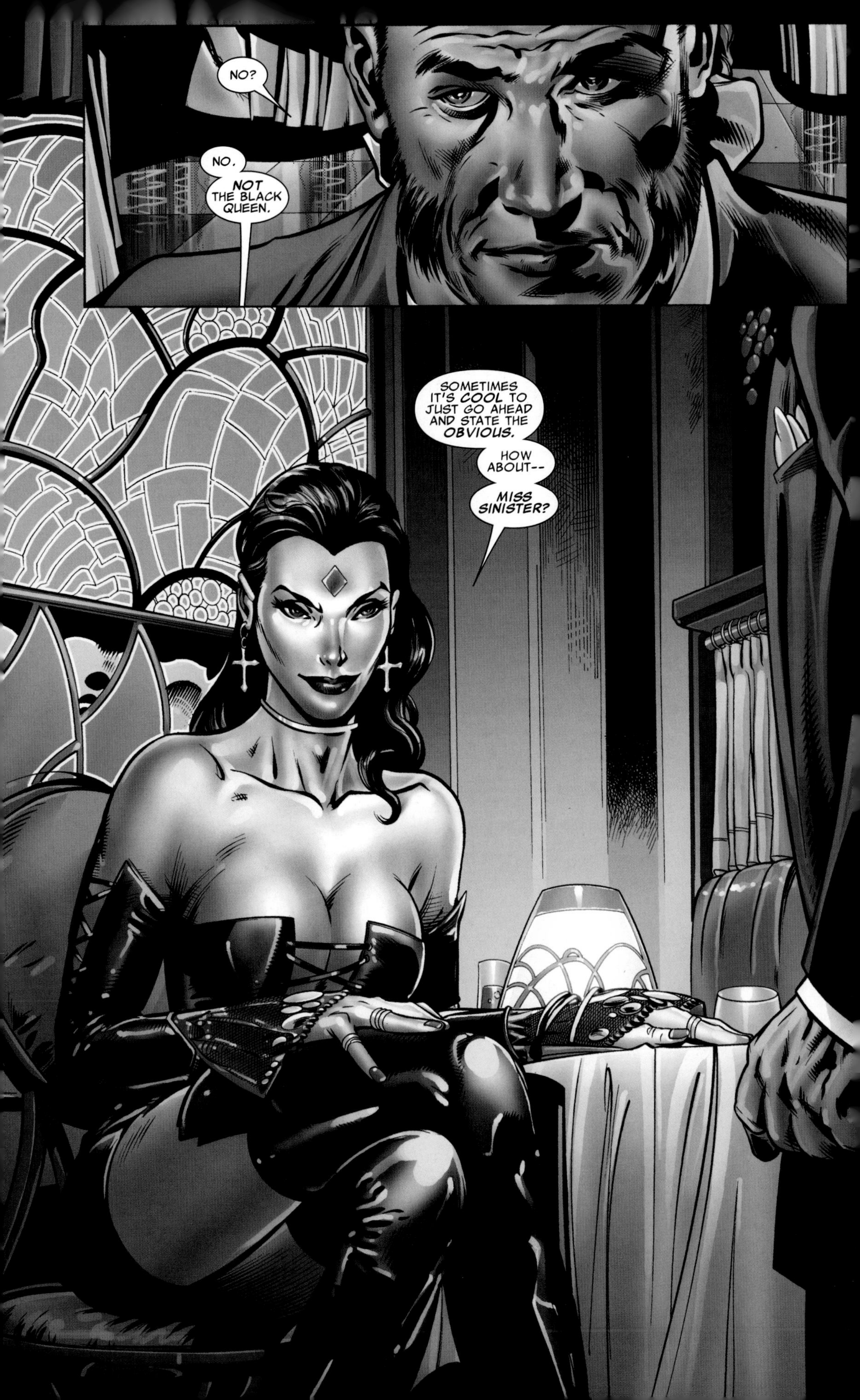
NO?
NO. NOT THE BLACK QUEEN.
SOMETIMES IT'S COOL TO JUST GO AHEAD AND STATE THE OBVIOUS.
HOW ABOUT--
MISS SINISTER?

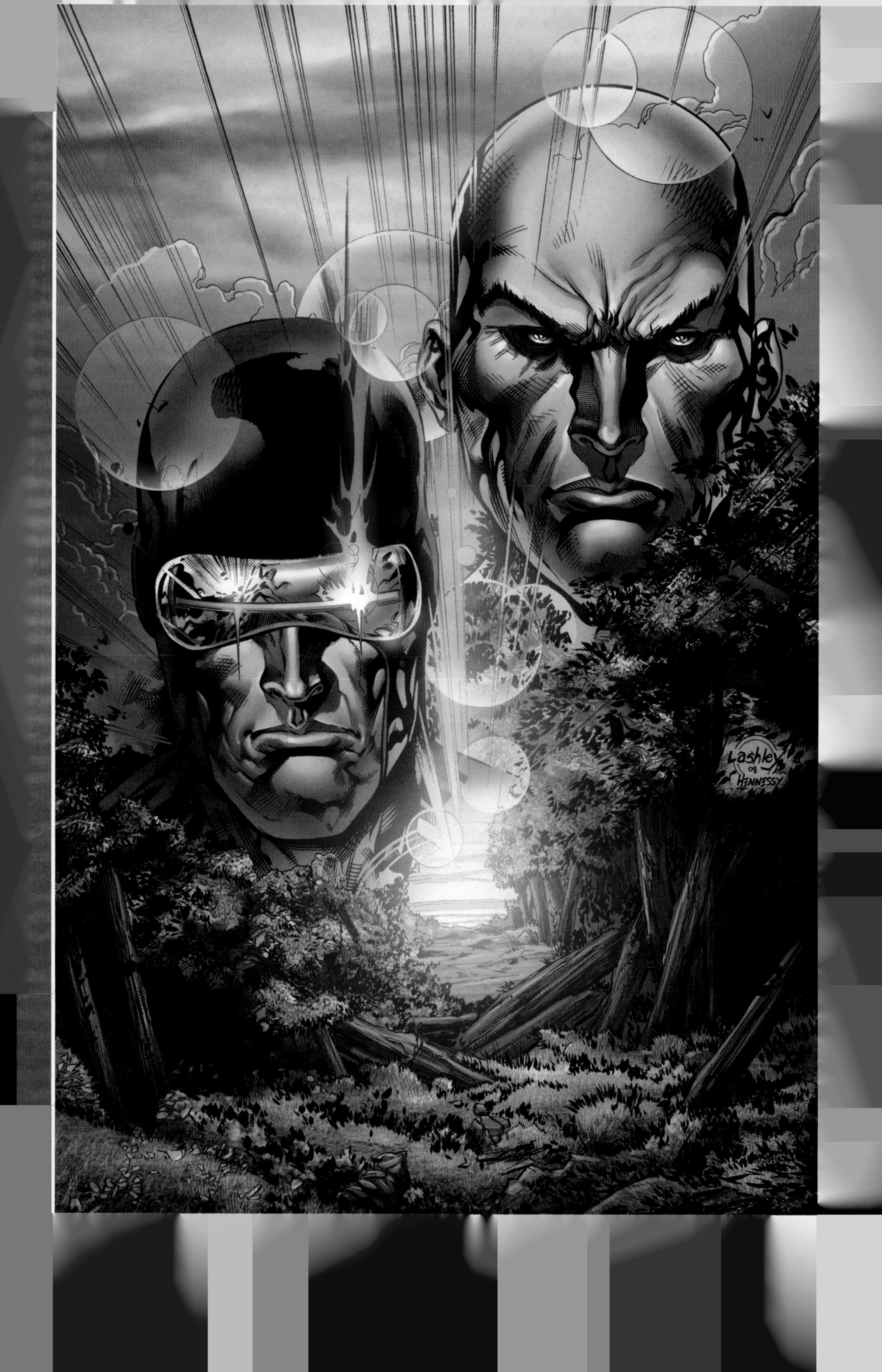
Lashley 08
Hennessy

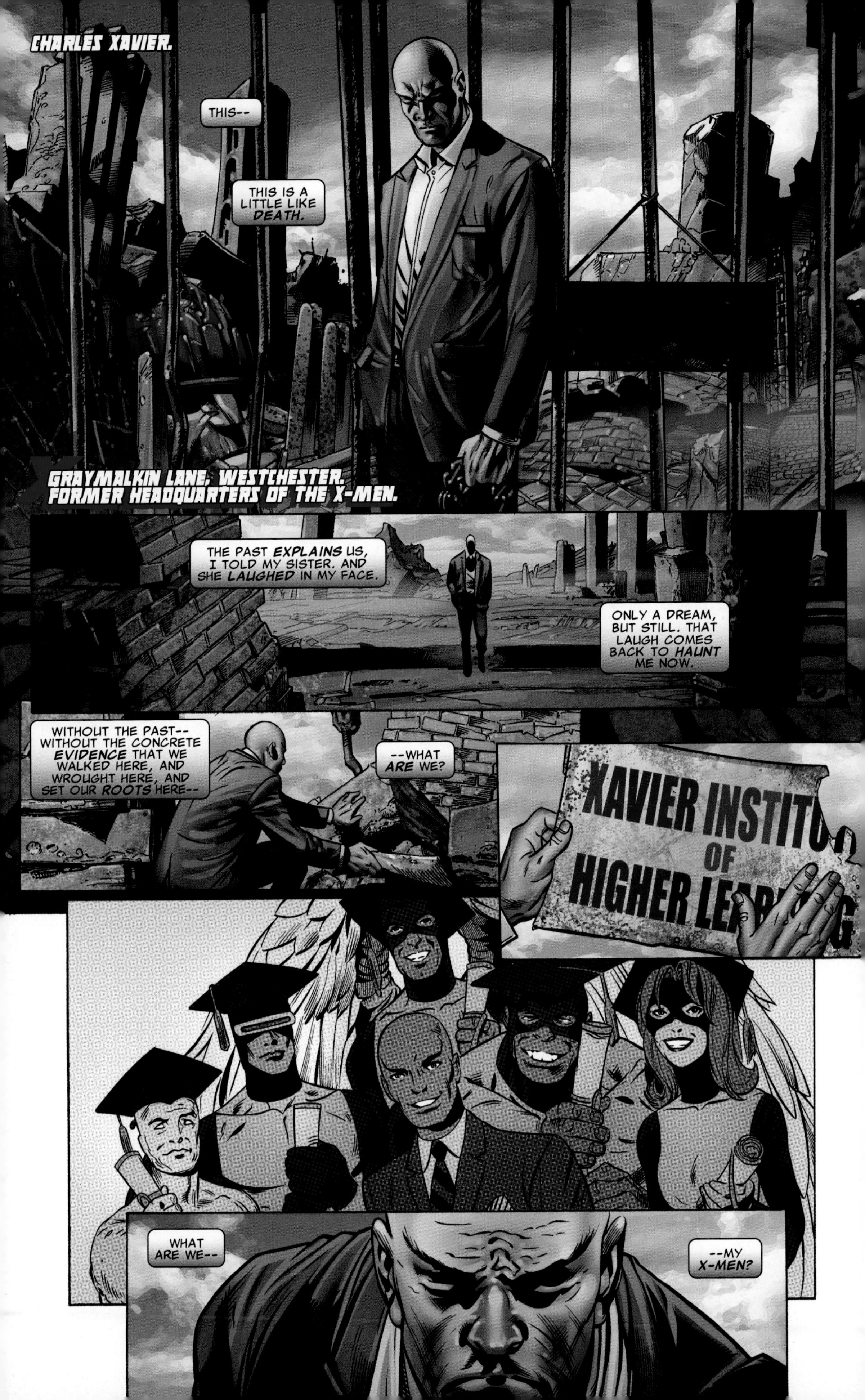
CHARLES XAVIER.
THIS--
THIS IS A LITTLE LIKE DEATH.
GRAYMALKIN LANE, WESTCHESTER. FORMER HEADQUARTERS OF THE X-MEN.
THE PAST EXPLAINS US, I TOLD MY SISTER. AND SHE LAUGHED IN MY FACE.
ONLY A DREAM, BUT STILL. THAT LAUGH COMES BACK TO HAUNT ME NOW.
WITHOUT THE PAST-- WITHOUT THE CONCRETE EVIDENCE THAT WE WALKED HERE, AND WROUGHT HERE, AND SET OUR ROOTS HERE--
--WHAT ARE WE?
XAVIER INSTITU
OF
HIGHER LEA
WHAT ARE WE--
--MY X-MEN?

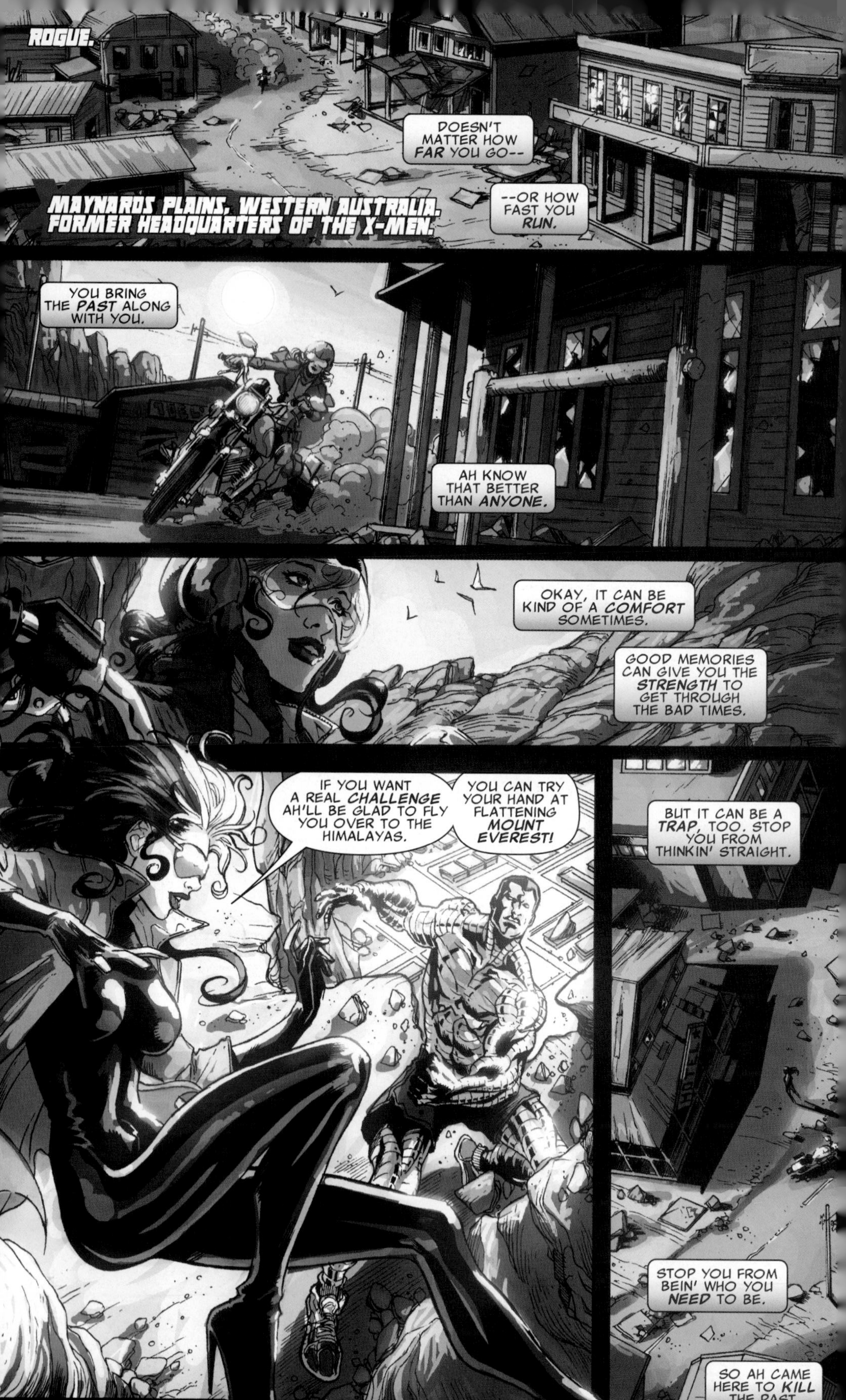
ROGUE.
DOESN'T MATTER HOW FAR YOU GO--
MAYNARDS PLAINS, WESTERN AUSTRALIA. FORMER HEADQUARTERS OF THE X-MEN.
--OR HOW FAST YOU RUN.
YOU BRING THE PAST ALONG WITH YOU.
AH KNOW THAT BETTER THAN ANYONE.
OKAY, IT CAN BE KIND OF A COMFORT SOMETIMES.
GOOD MEMORIES CAN GIVE YOU THE STRENGTH TO GET THROUGH THE BAD TIMES.
IF YOU WANT A REAL CHALLENGE AH'LL BE GLAD TO FLY YOU OVER TO THE HIMALAYAS.
YOU CAN TRY YOUR HAND AT FLATTENING MOUNT EVEREST!
BUT IT CAN BE A TRAP, TOO. STOP YOU FROM THINKIN' STRAIGHT.
STOP YOU FROM BEIN' WHO YOU NEED TO BE.
SO AH CAME HERE TO KILL THE PAST.

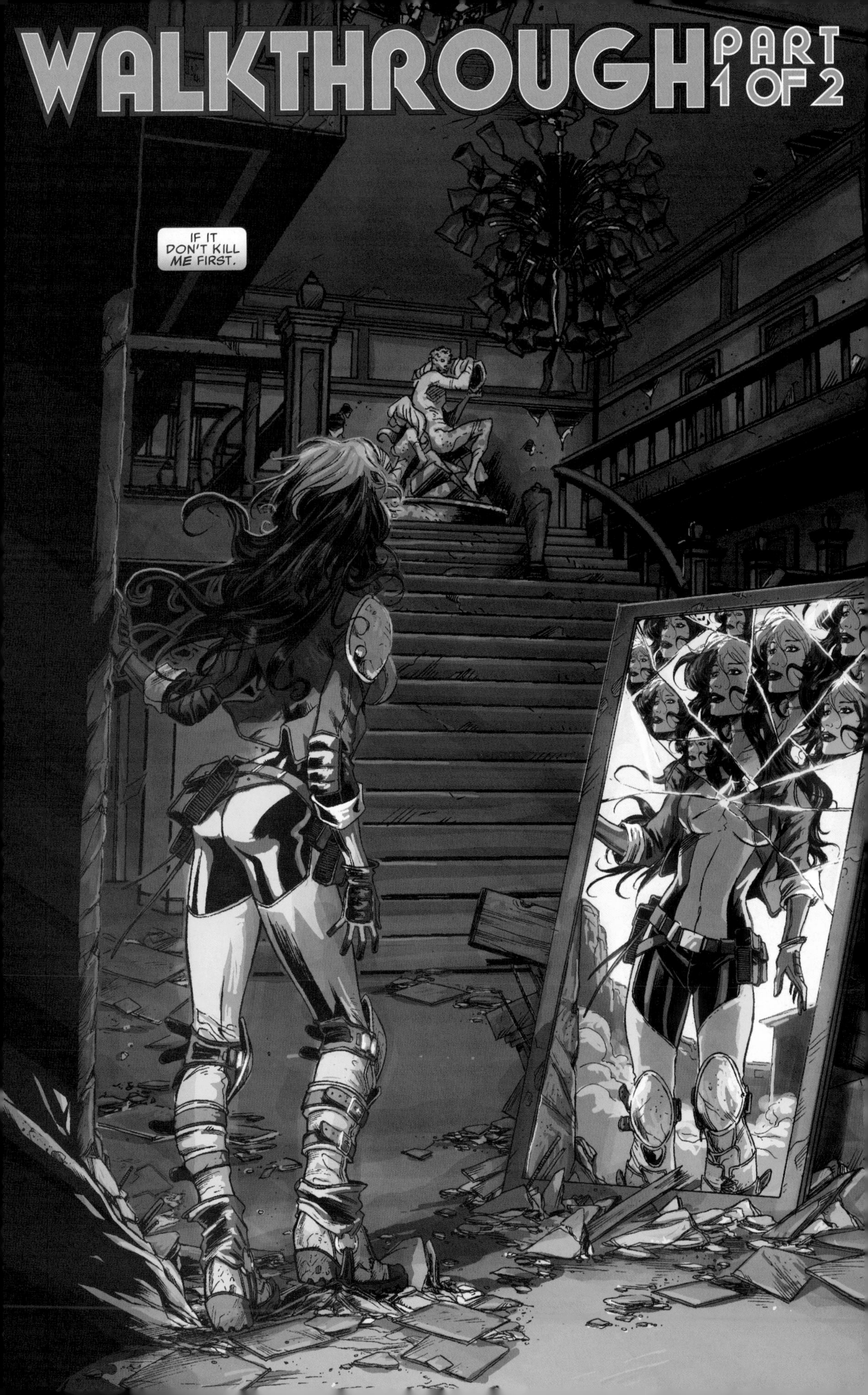
WALKTHROUGH PART 1 OF 2
IF IT DON'T KILL ME FIRST.

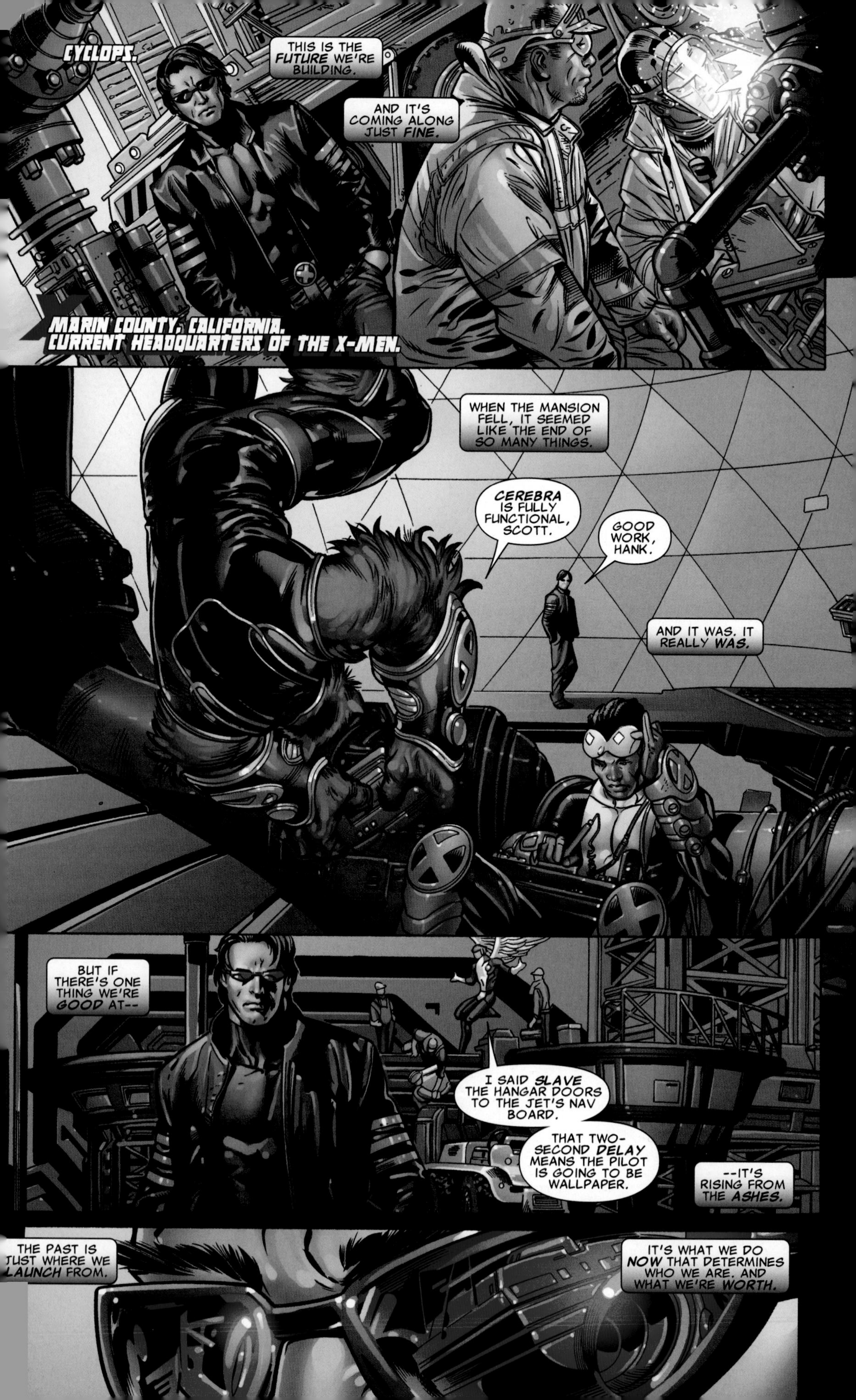
CYCLOPS.
THIS IS THE FUTURE WE'RE BUILDING.
AND IT'S COMING ALONG JUST FINE.
MARIN COUNTY, CALIFORNIA. CURRENT HEADQUARTERS OF THE X-MEN.
WHEN THE MANSION FELL, IT SEEMED LIKE THE END OF SO MANY THINGS.
CEREBRA IS FULLY FUNCTIONAL, SCOTT.
GOOD WORK, HANK.
AND IT WAS. IT REALLY WAS.
BUT IF THERE'S ONE THING WE'RE GOOD AT--
I SAID SLAVE THE HANGAR DOORS TO THE JET'S NAV BOARD.
THAT TWO-SECOND DELAY MEANS THE PILOT IS GOING TO BE WALLPAPER.
--IT'S RISING FROM THE ASHES.
THE PAST IS JUST WHERE WE LAUNCH FROM.
IT'S WHAT WE DO NOW THAT DETERMINES WHO WE ARE. AND WHAT WE'RE WORTH.

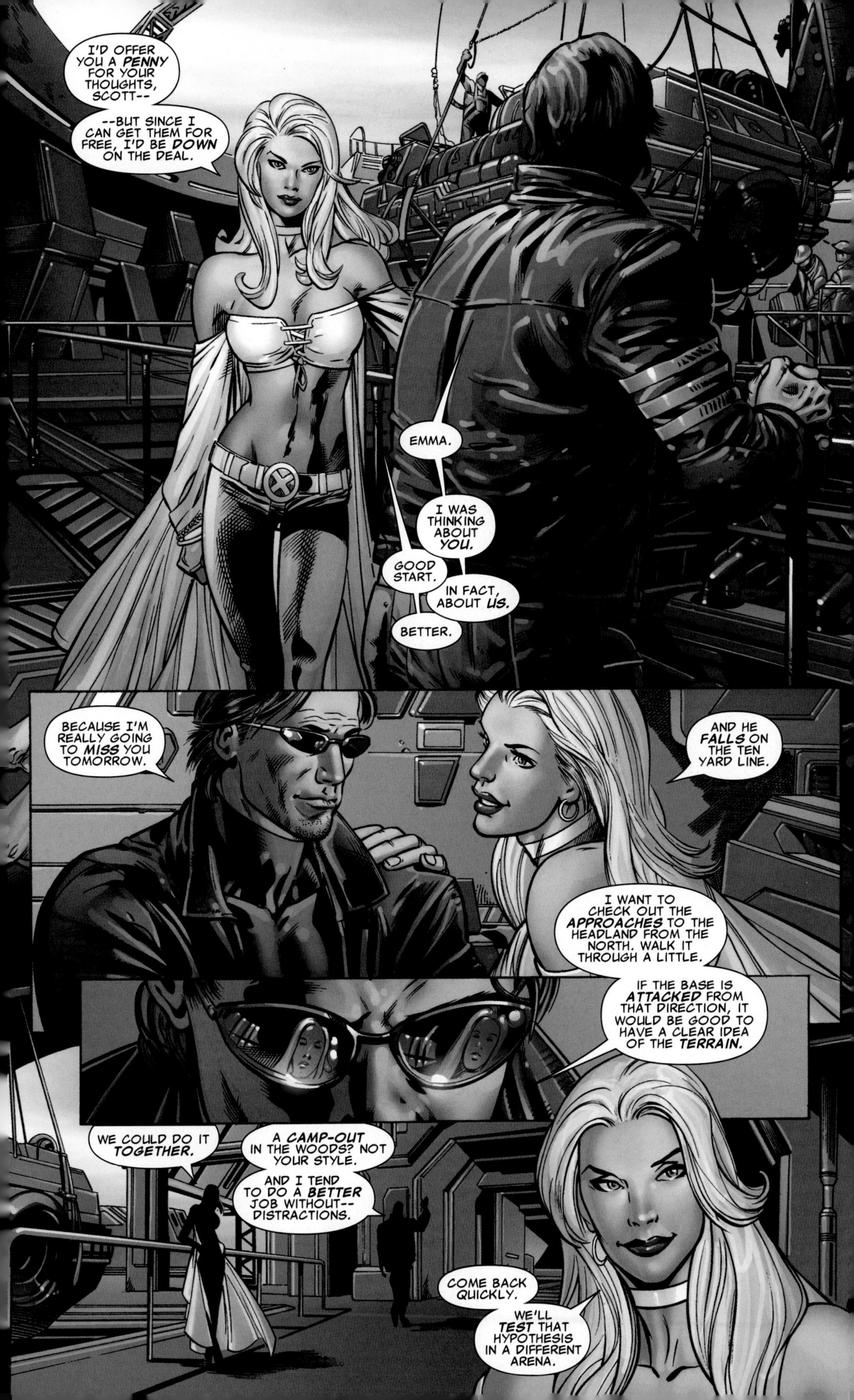
I'D OFFER YOU A PENNY FOR YOUR THOUGHTS, SCOTT--
--BUT SINCE I CAN GET THEM FOR FREE, I'D BE DOWN ON THE DEAL.
EMMA.
I WAS THINKING ABOUT YOU.
GOOD START.
IN FACT, ABOUT US.
BETTER.
BECAUSE I'M REALLY GOING TO MISS YOU TOMORROW.
AND HE FALLS ON THE TEN YARD LINE.
I WANT TO CHECK OUT THE APPROACHES TO THE HEADLAND FROM THE NORTH. WALK IT THROUGH A LITTLE.
IF THE BASE IS ATTACKED FROM THAT DIRECTION, IT WOULD BE GOOD TO HAVE A CLEAR IDEA OF THE TERRAIN.
WE COULD DO IT TOGETHER.
A CAMP-OUT IN THE WOODS? NOT YOUR STYLE.
AND I TEND TO DO A BETTER JOB WITHOUT--DISTRACTIONS.
COME BACK QUICKLY.
WE'LL TEST THAT HYPOTHESIS IN A DIFFERENT ARENA.

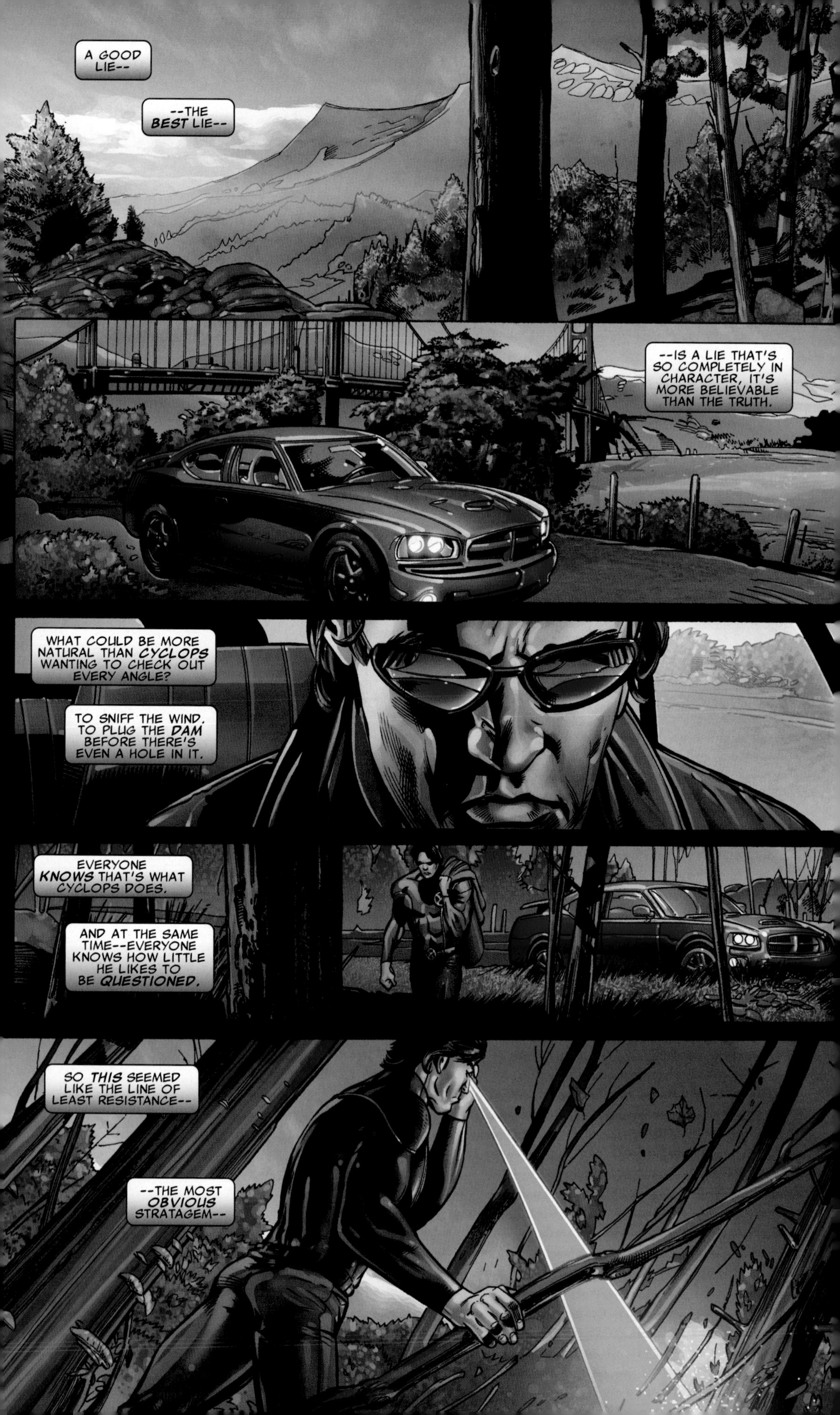
A GOOD LIE--
--THE BEST LIE--
--IS A LIE THAT'S SO COMPLETELY IN CHARACTER, IT'S MORE BELIEVABLE THAN THE TRUTH.
WHAT COULD BE MORE NATURAL THAN CYCLOPS WANTING TO CHECK OUT EVERY ANGLE?
TO SNIFF THE WIND. TO PLUG THE DAM BEFORE THERE'S EVEN A HOLE IN IT.
EVERYONE KNOWS THAT'S WHAT CYCLOPS DOES.
AND AT THE SAME TIME--EVERYONE KNOWS HOW LITTLE HE LIKES TO BE QUESTIONED.
SO THIS SEEMED LIKE THE LINE OF LEAST RESISTANCE--
--THE MOST OBVIOUS STRATAGEM--

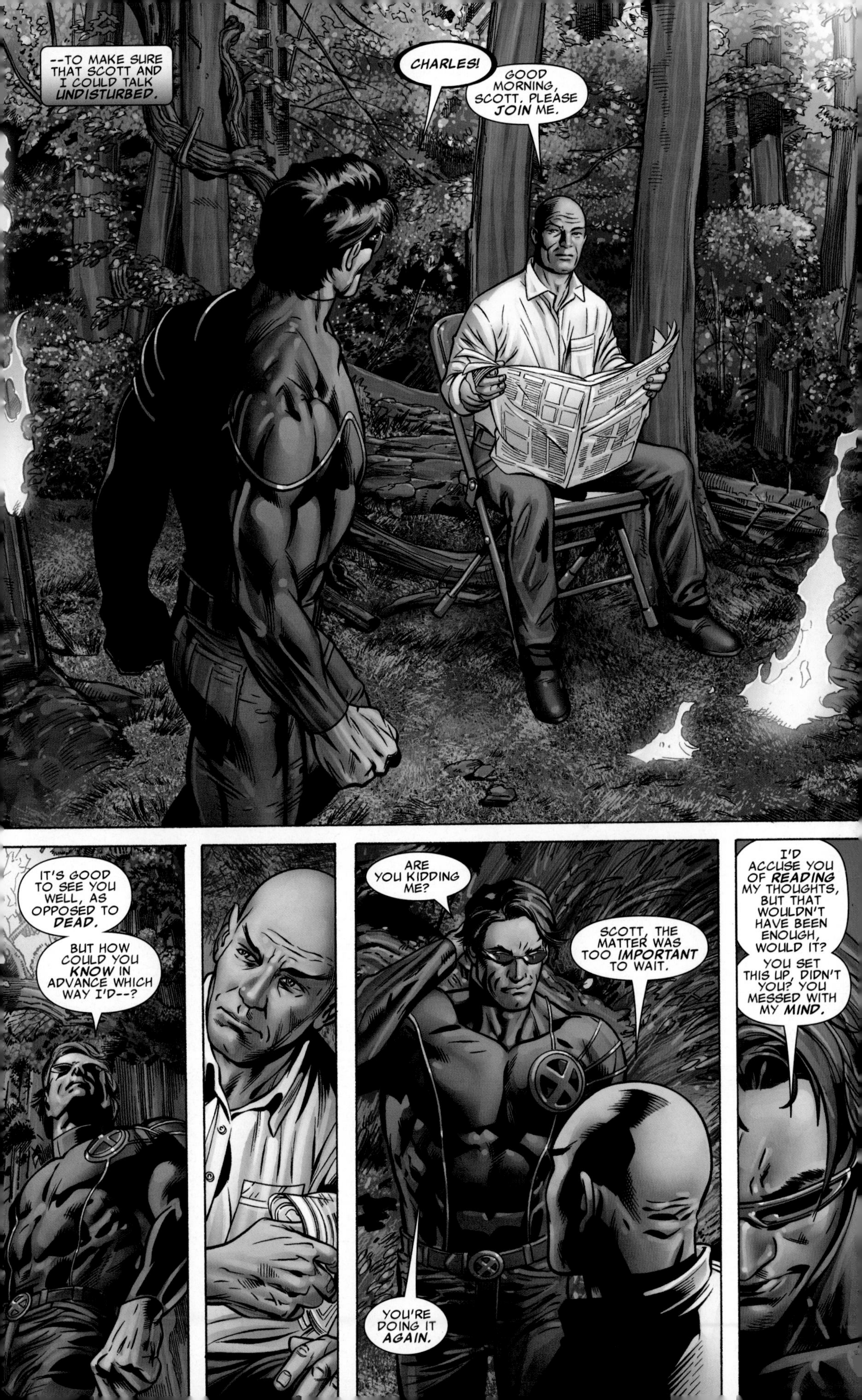
--TO MAKE SURE THAT SCOTT AND I COULD TALK UNDISTURBED.
CHARLES!
GOOD MORNING, SCOTT. PLEASE JOIN ME.
IT'S GOOD TO SEE YOU WELL, AS OPPOSED TO DEAD.
BUT HOW COULD YOU KNOW IN ADVANCE WHICH WAY I'D--?
ARE YOU KIDDING ME?
SCOTT, THE MATTER WAS TOO IMPORTANT TO WAIT.
YOU'RE DOING IT AGAIN.
I'D ACCUSE YOU OF READING MY THOUGHTS, BUT THAT WOULDN'T HAVE BEEN ENOUGH, WOULD IT?
YOU SET THIS UP, DIDN'T YOU? YOU MESSED WITH MY MIND.

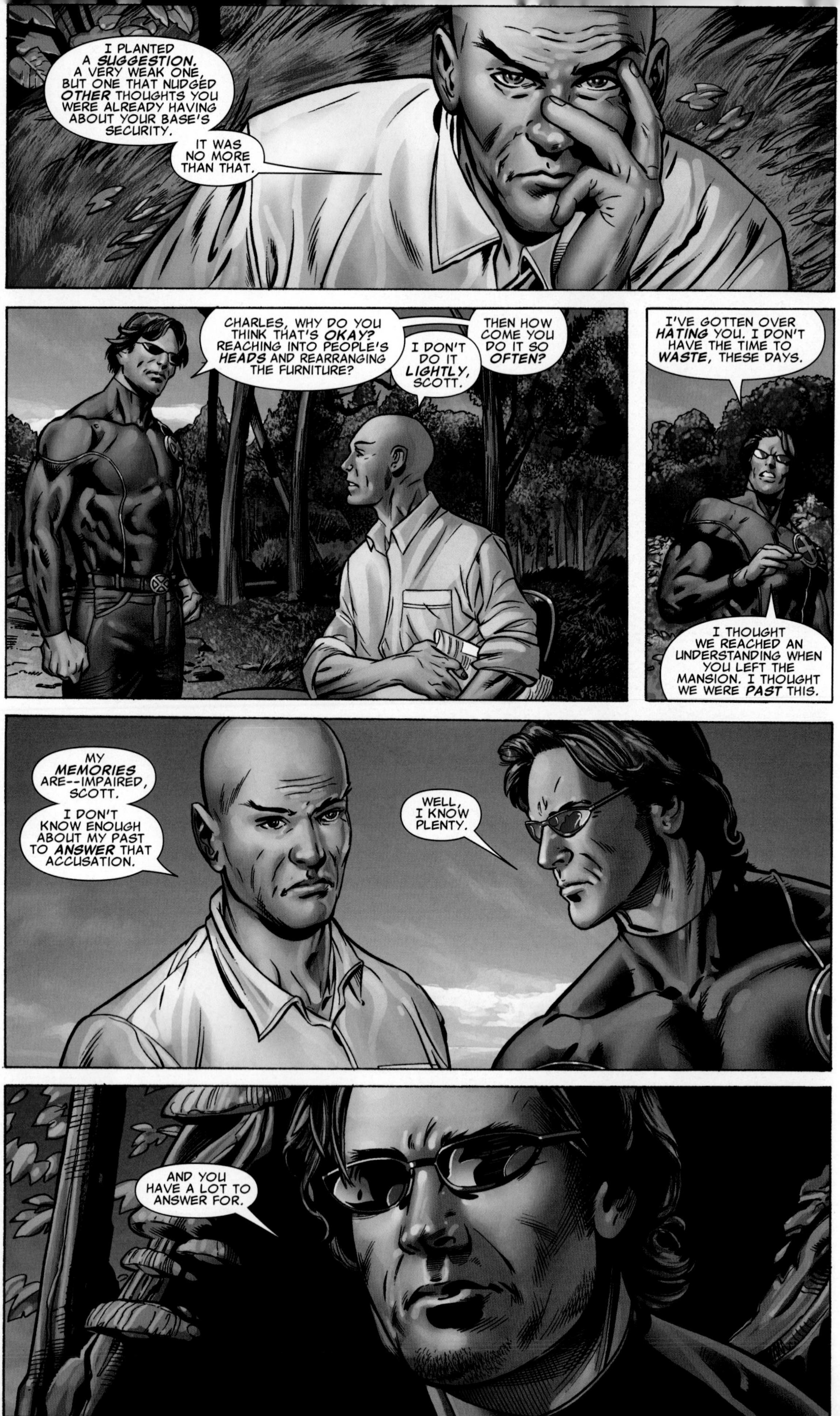
I PLANTED A SUGGESTION. A VERY WEAK ONE, BUT ONE THAT NUDGED OTHER THOUGHTS YOU WERE ALREADY HAVING ABOUT YOUR BASE'S SECURITY.
IT WAS NO MORE THAN THAT.
CHARLES, WHY DO YOU THINK THAT'S OKAY? REACHING INTO PEOPLE'S HEADS AND REARRANGING THE FURNITURE?
I DON'T DO IT LIGHTLY, SCOTT.
THEN HOW COME YOU DO IT SO OFTEN?
I'VE GOTTEN OVER HATING YOU. I DON'T HAVE THE TIME TO WASTE, THESE DAYS.
I THOUGHT WE REACHED AN UNDERSTANDING WHEN YOU LEFT THE MANSION. I THOUGHT WE WERE PAST THIS.
MY MEMORIES ARE--IMPAIRED, SCOTT.
I DON'T KNOW ENOUGH ABOUT MY PAST TO ANSWER THAT ACCUSATION.
WELL, I KNOW PLENTY.
AND YOU HAVE A LOT TO ANSWER FOR.

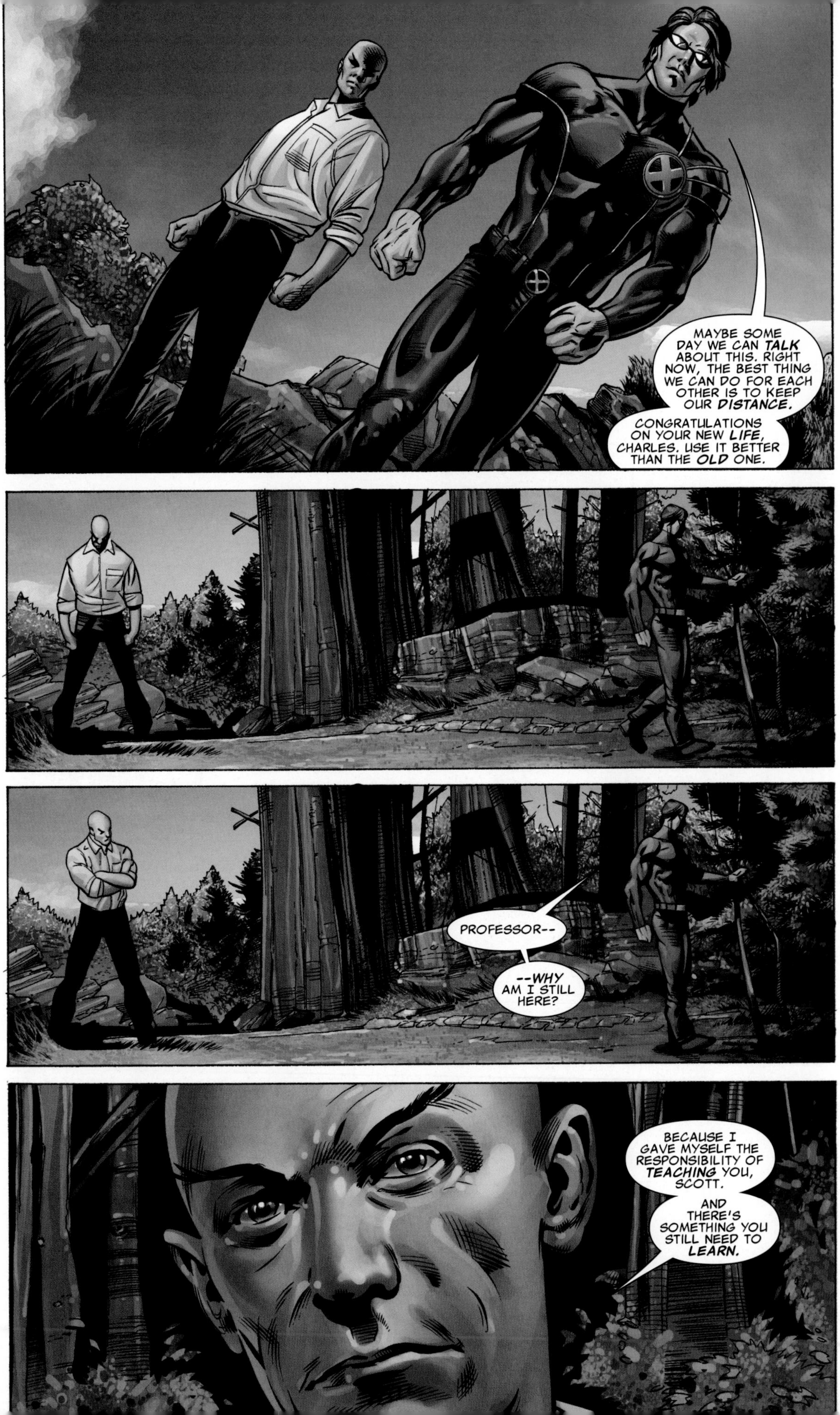
MAYBE SOME DAY WE CAN TALK ABOUT THIS. RIGHT NOW, THE BEST THING WE CAN DO FOR EACH OTHER IS TO KEEP OUR DISTANCE.
CONGRATULATIONS ON YOUR NEW LIFE, CHARLES. USE IT BETTER THAN THE OLD ONE.
PROFESSOR--
--WHY AM I STILL HERE?
BECAUSE I GAVE MYSELF THE RESPONSIBILITY OF TEACHING YOU, SCOTT.
AND THERE'S SOMETHING YOU STILL NEED TO LEARN.

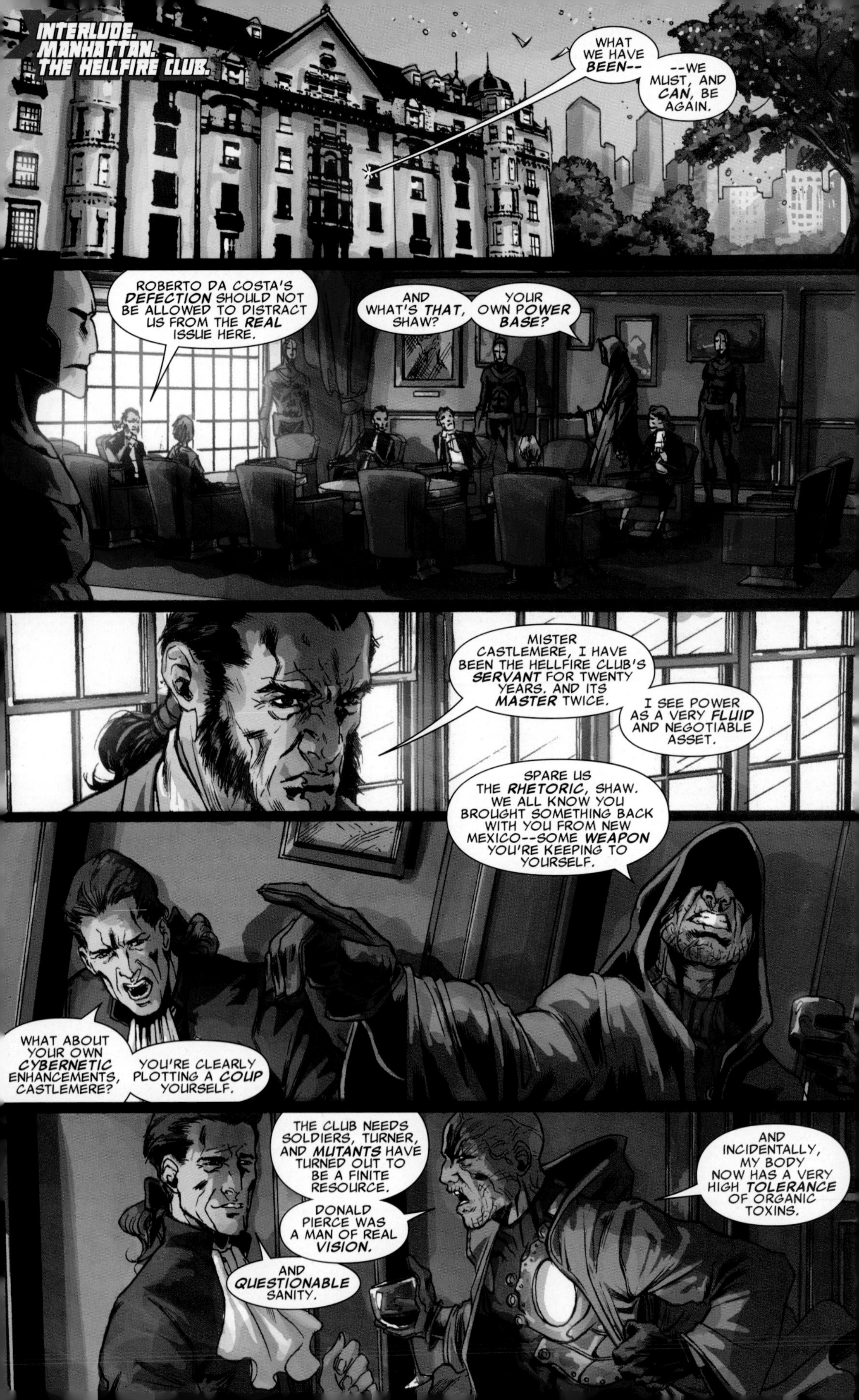
INTERLUDE. MANHATTAN. THE HELLFIRE CLUB.
WHAT WE HAVE BEEN--
--WE MUST, AND CAN, BE AGAIN.
ROBERTO DA COSTA'S DEFECTION SHOULD NOT BE ALLOWED TO DISTRACT US FROM THE REAL ISSUE HERE.
AND WHAT'S THAT, SHAW?
YOUR OWN POWER BASE?
MISTER CASTLEMERE, I HAVE BEEN THE HELLFIRE CLUB'S SERVANT FOR TWENTY YEARS. AND ITS MASTER TWICE.
I SEE POWER AS A VERY FLUID AND NEGOTIABLE ASSET.
SPARE US THE RHETORIC, SHAW. WE ALL KNOW YOU BROUGHT SOMETHING BACK WITH YOU FROM NEW MEXICO--SOME WEAPON YOU'RE KEEPING TO YOURSELF.
WHAT ABOUT YOUR OWN CYBERNETIC ENHANCEMENTS, CASTLEMERE?
YOU'RE CLEARLY PLOTTING A COUP YOURSELF.
THE CLUB NEEDS SOLDIERS, TURNER, AND MUTANTS HAVE TURNED OUT TO BE A FINITE RESOURCE.
DONALD PIERCE WAS A MAN OF REAL VISION.
AND QUESTIONABLE SANITY.
AND INCIDENTALLY, MY BODY NOW HAS A VERY HIGH TOLERANCE OF ORGANIC TOXINS.

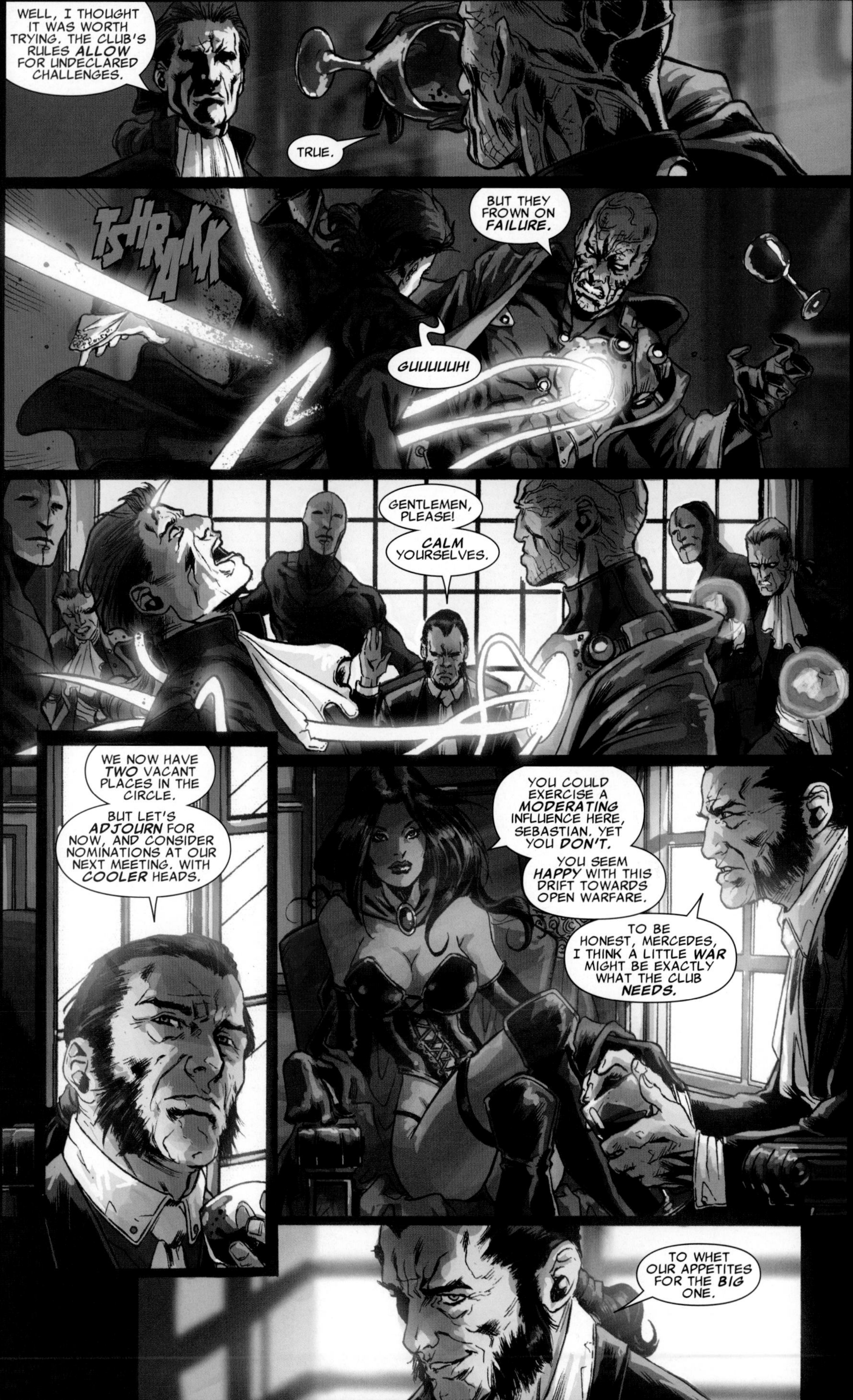
WELL, I THOUGHT IT WAS WORTH TRYING. THE CLUB'S RULES ALLOW FOR UNDECLARED CHALLENGES.
TRUE.
TSHRAKK
BUT THEY FROWN ON FAILURE.
GUUUUUH!
GENTLEMEN, PLEASE!
CALM YOURSELVES.
WE NOW HAVE TWO VACANT PLACES IN THE CIRCLE.
BUT LET'S ADJOURN FOR NOW, AND CONSIDER NOMINATIONS AT OUR NEXT MEETING. WITH COOLER HEADS.
YOU COULD EXERCISE A MODERATING INFLUENCE HERE, SEBASTIAN. YET YOU DON'T.
YOU SEEM HAPPY WITH THIS DRIFT TOWARDS OPEN WARFARE.
TO BE HONEST, MERCEDES, I THINK A LITTLE WAR MIGHT BE EXACTLY WHAT THE CLUB NEEDS.
TO WHET OUR APPETITES FOR THE BIG ONE.

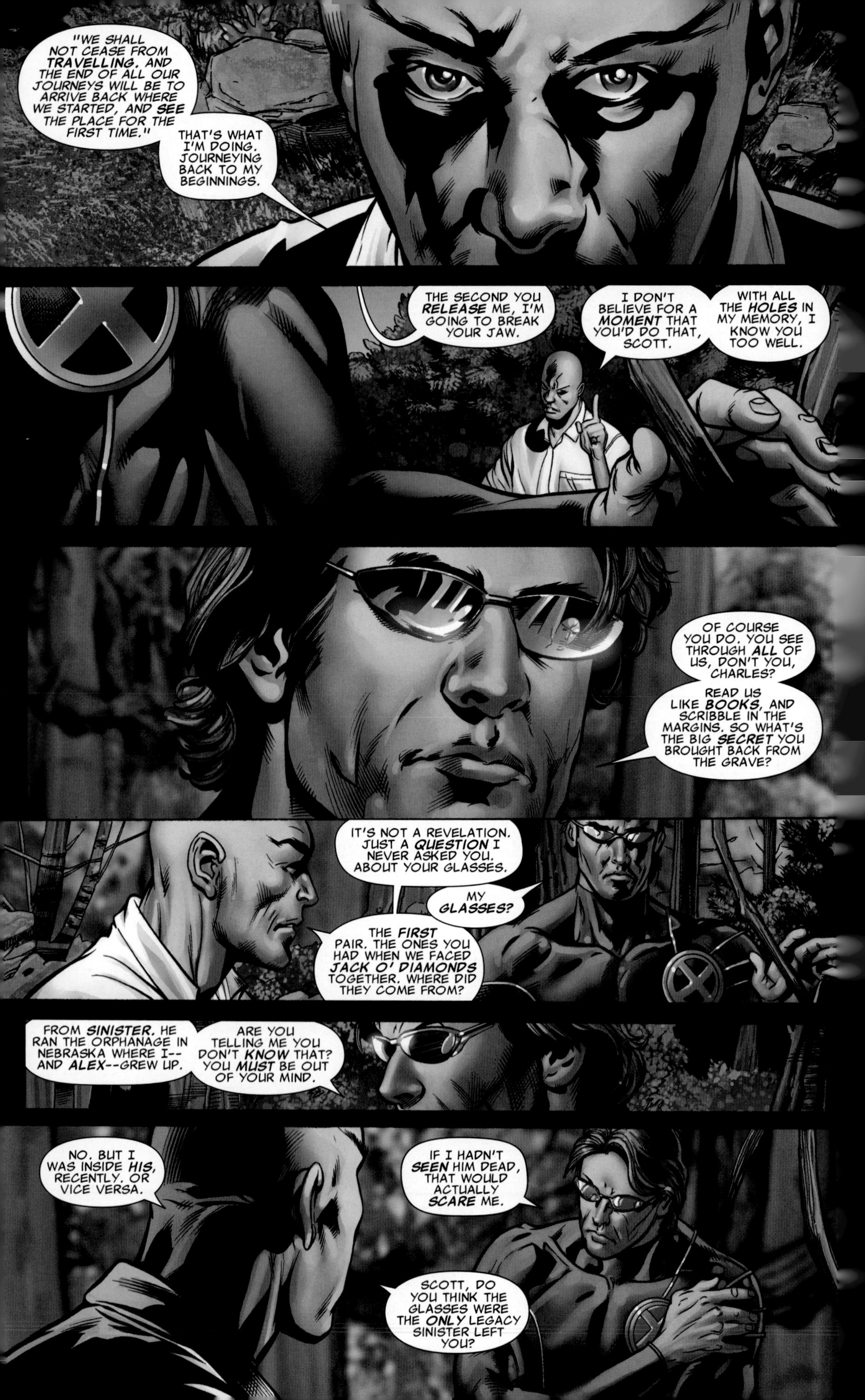
"WE SHALL NOT CEASE FROM TRAVELLING, AND THE END OF ALL OUR JOURNEYS WILL BE TO ARRIVE BACK WHERE WE STARTED, AND SEE THE PLACE FOR THE FIRST TIME."
THAT'S WHAT I'M DOING. JOURNEYING BACK TO MY BEGINNINGS.
THE SECOND YOU RELEASE ME, I'M GOING TO BREAK YOUR JAW.
I DON'T BELIEVE FOR A MOMENT THAT YOU'D DO THAT, SCOTT.
WITH ALL THE HOLES IN MY MEMORY, I KNOW YOU TOO WELL.
OF COURSE YOU DO. YOU SEE THROUGH ALL OF US, DON'T YOU, CHARLES?
READ US LIKE BOOKS, AND SCRIBBLE IN THE MARGINS. SO WHAT'S THE BIG SECRET YOU BROUGHT BACK FROM THE GRAVE?
IT'S NOT A REVELATION. JUST A QUESTION I NEVER ASKED YOU. ABOUT YOUR GLASSES.
MY GLASSES?
THE FIRST PAIR. THE ONES YOU HAD WHEN WE FACED JACK O' DIAMONDS TOGETHER. WHERE DID THEY COME FROM?
FROM SINISTER. HE RAN THE ORPHANAGE IN NEBRASKA WHERE I-- AND ALEX--GREW UP.
ARE YOU TELLING ME YOU DON'T KNOW THAT? YOU MUST BE OUT OF YOUR MIND.
NO. BUT I WAS INSIDE HIS, RECENTLY. OR VICE VERSA.
IF I HADN'T SEEN HIM DEAD, THAT WOULD ACTUALLY SCARE ME.
SCOTT, DO YOU THINK THE GLASSES WERE THE ONLY LEGACY SINISTER LEFT YOU?

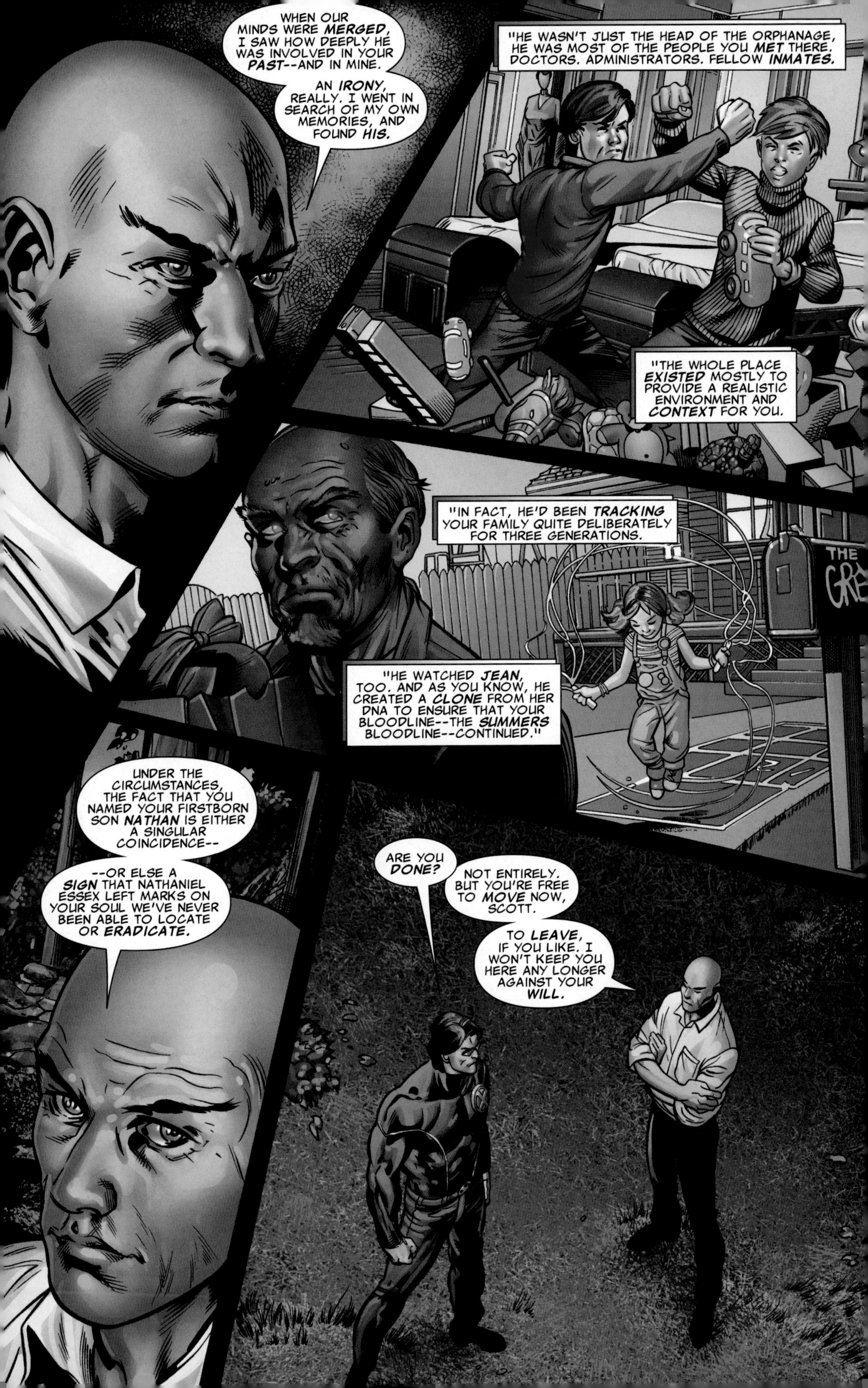
WHEN OUR MINDS WERE MERGED, I SAW HOW DEEPLY HE WAS INVOLVED IN YOUR PAST--AND IN MINE.
AN IRONY, REALLY. I WENT IN SEARCH OF MY OWN MEMORIES, AND FOUND HIS.
"HE WASN'T JUST THE HEAD OF THE ORPHANAGE, HE WAS MOST OF THE PEOPLE YOU MET THERE. DOCTORS. ADMINISTRATORS. FELLOW INMATES.
"THE WHOLE PLACE EXISTED MOSTLY TO PROVIDE A REALISTIC ENVIRONMENT AND CONTEXT FOR YOU.
"IN FACT, HE'D BEEN TRACKING YOUR FAMILY QUITE DELIBERATELY FOR THREE GENERATIONS.
"HE WATCHED JEAN, TOO. AND AS YOU KNOW, HE CREATED A CLONE FROM HER DNA TO ENSURE THAT YOUR BLOODLINE--THE SUMMERS BLOODLINE--CONTINUED."
UNDER THE CIRCUMSTANCES, THE FACT THAT YOU NAMED YOUR FIRSTBORN SON NATHAN IS EITHER A SINGULAR COINCIDENCE--
--OR ELSE A SIGN THAT NATHANIEL ESSEX LEFT MARKS ON YOUR SOUL WE'VE NEVER BEEN ABLE TO LOCATE OR ERADICATE.
ARE YOU DONE?
NOT ENTIRELY. BUT YOU'RE FREE TO MOVE NOW, SCOTT.
TO LEAVE, IF YOU LIKE. I WON'T KEEP YOU HERE ANY LONGER AGAINST YOUR WILL.

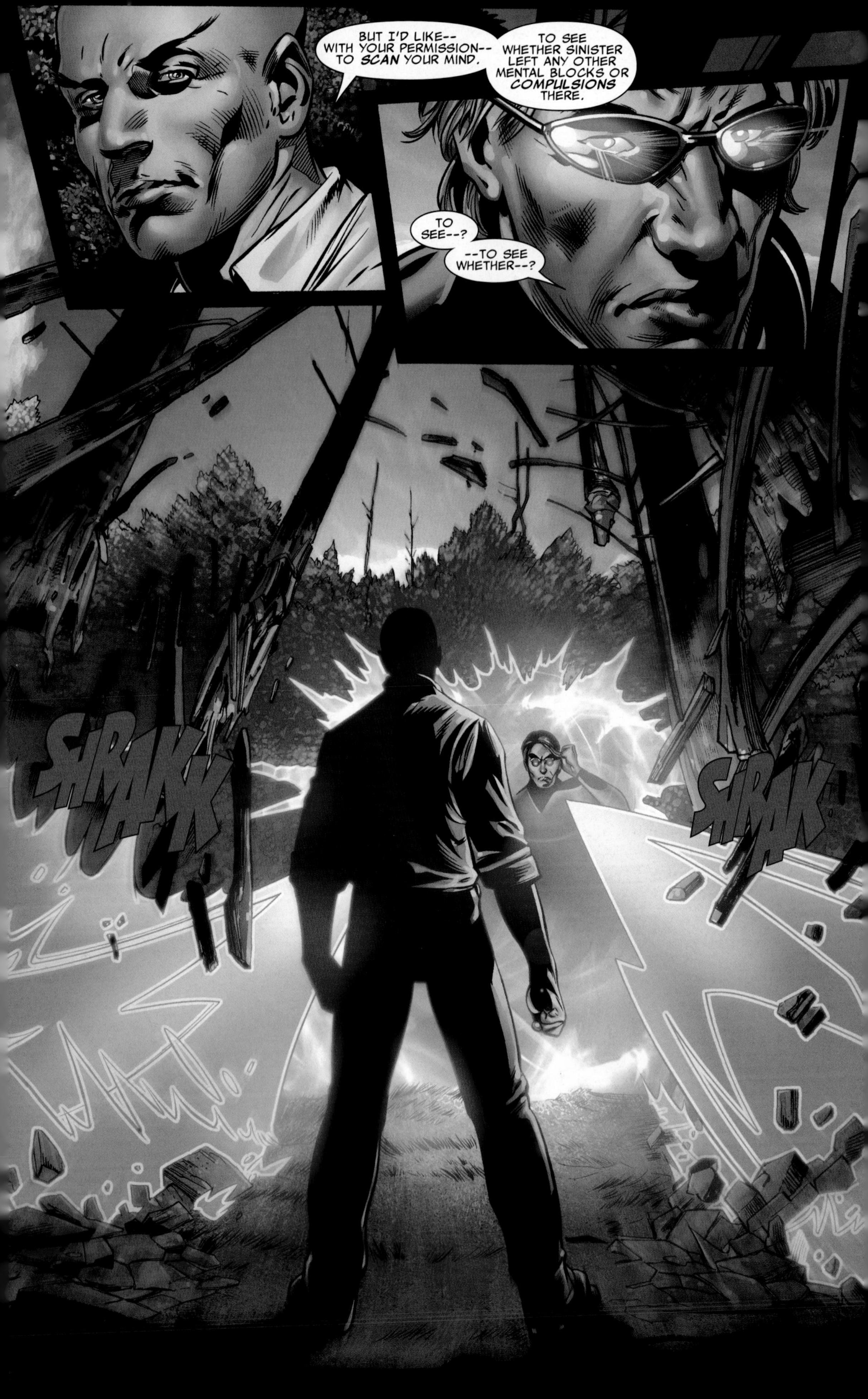
BUT I'D LIKE-- WITH YOUR PERMISSION-- TO SCAN YOUR MIND.
TO SEE WHETHER SINISTER LEFT ANY OTHER MENTAL BLOCKS OR COMPULSIONS THERE.
TO SEE--?
--TO SEE WHETHER--?
SHRAKK
SHRAK

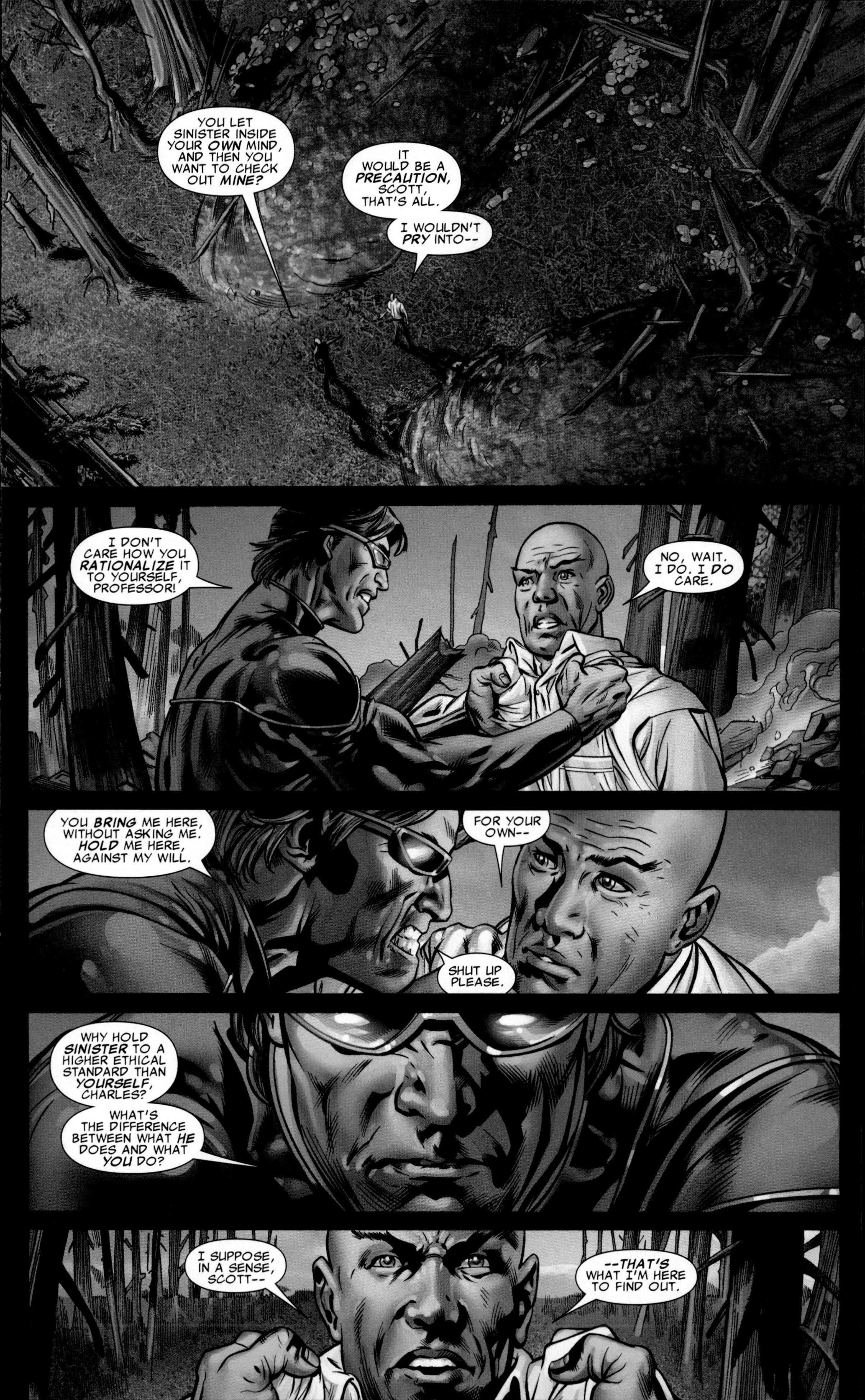
YOU LET SINISTER INSIDE YOUR OWN MIND, AND THEN YOU WANT TO CHECK OUT MINE?
IT WOULD BE A PRECAUTION, SCOTT, THAT'S ALL.
I WOULDN'T PRY INTO--
I DON'T CARE HOW YOU RATIONALIZE IT TO YOURSELF, PROFESSOR!
NO, WAIT. I DO. I DO CARE.
YOU BRING ME HERE, WITHOUT ASKING ME. HOLD ME HERE, AGAINST MY WILL.
FOR YOUR OWN--
SHUT UP PLEASE.
WHY HOLD SINISTER TO A HIGHER ETHICAL STANDARD THAN YOURSELF, CHARLES?
WHAT'S THE DIFFERENCE BETWEEN WHAT HE DOES AND WHAT YOU DO?
I SUPPOSE, IN A SENSE, SCOTT--
--THAT'S WHAT I'M HERE TO FIND OUT.

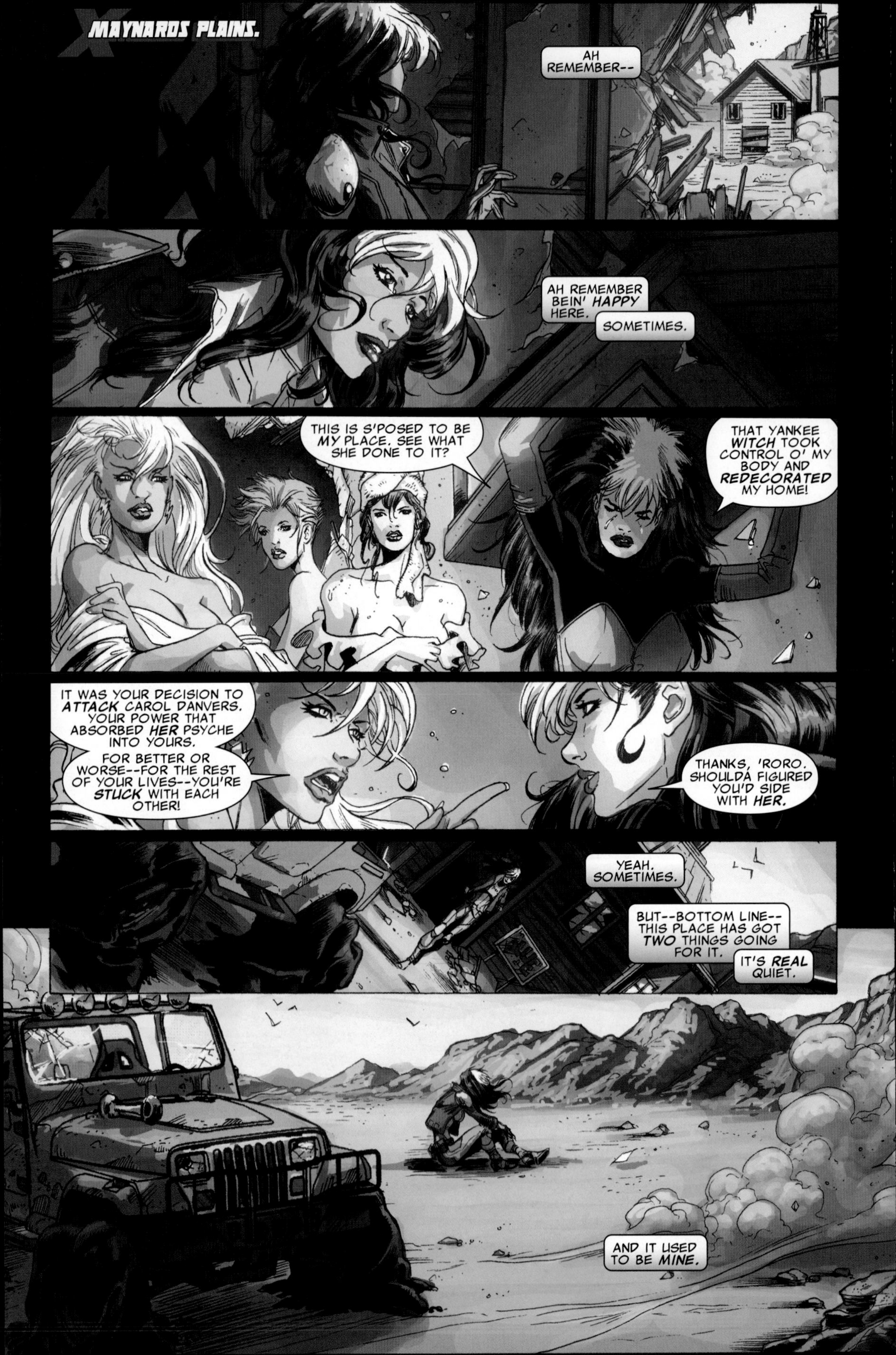
MAYNARDS PLAINS.
AH REMEMBER--
AH REMEMBER BEIN' HAPPY HERE.
SOMETIMES.
THIS IS S'POSED TO BE MY PLACE. SEE WHAT SHE DONE TO IT?
THAT YANKEE WITCH TOOK CONTROL O' MY BODY AND REDECORATED MY HOME!
IT WAS YOUR DECISION TO ATTACK CAROL DANVERS. YOUR POWER THAT ABSORBED HER PSYCHE INTO YOURS.
FOR BETTER OR WORSE--FOR THE REST OF YOUR LIVES--YOU'RE STUCK WITH EACH OTHER!
THANKS, 'RORO. SHOULDA FIGURED YOU'D SIDE WITH HER.
YEAH. SOMETIMES.
BUT--BOTTOM LINE--THIS PLACE HAS GOT TWO THINGS GOING FOR IT.
IT'S REAL QUIET.
AND IT USED TO BE MINE.

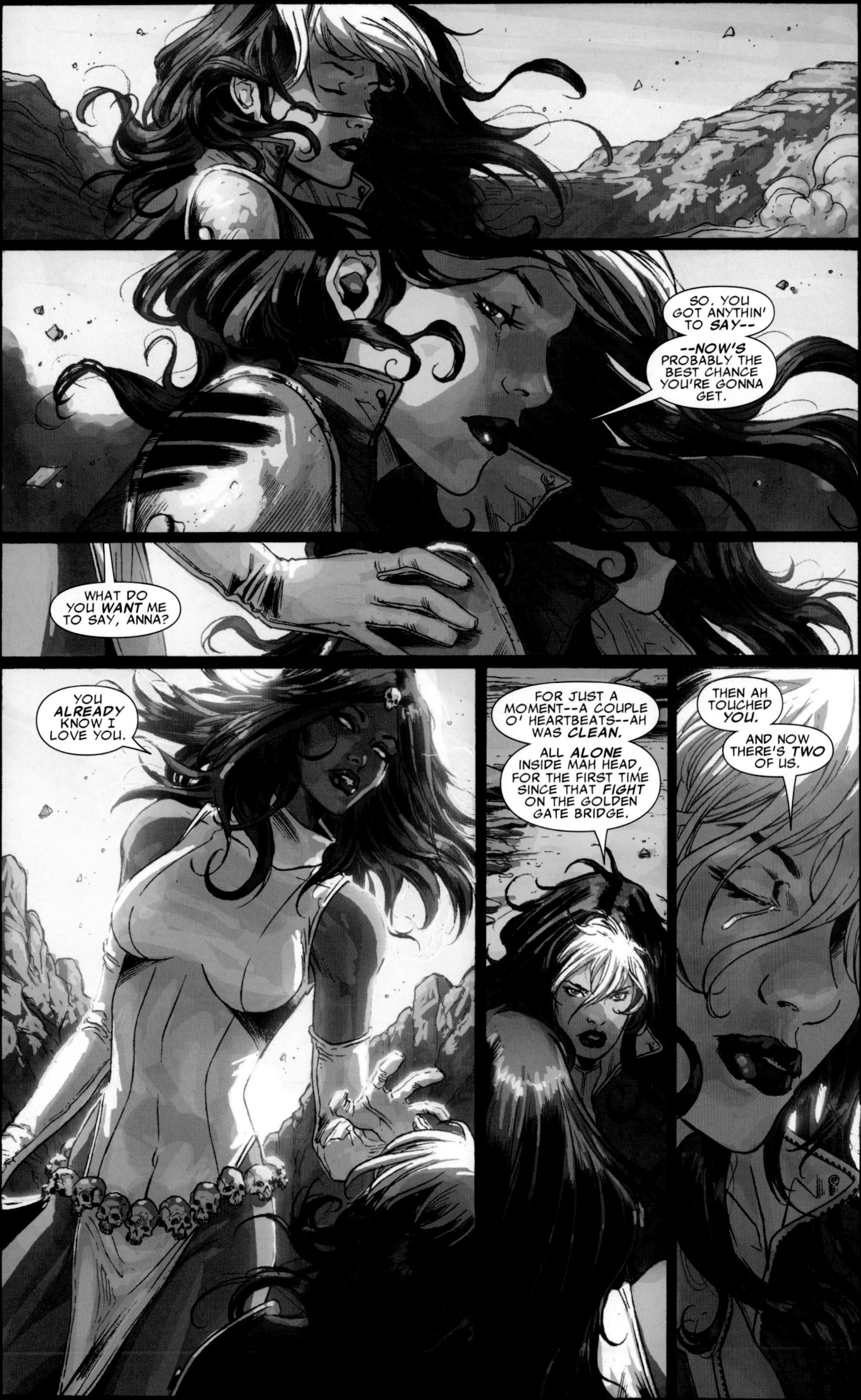
SO, YOU GOT ANYTHIN' TO SAY--
--NOW'S PROBABLY THE BEST CHANCE YOU'RE GONNA GET.
WHAT DO YOU WANT ME TO SAY, ANNA?
YOU ALREADY KNOW I LOVE YOU.
FOR JUST A MOMENT--A COUPLE O' HEARTBEATS--AH WAS CLEAN.
ALL ALONE INSIDE MAH HEAD, FOR THE FIRST TIME SINCE THAT FIGHT ON THE GOLDEN GATE BRIDGE.
THEN AH TOUCHED YOU.
AND NOW THERE'S TWO OF US.

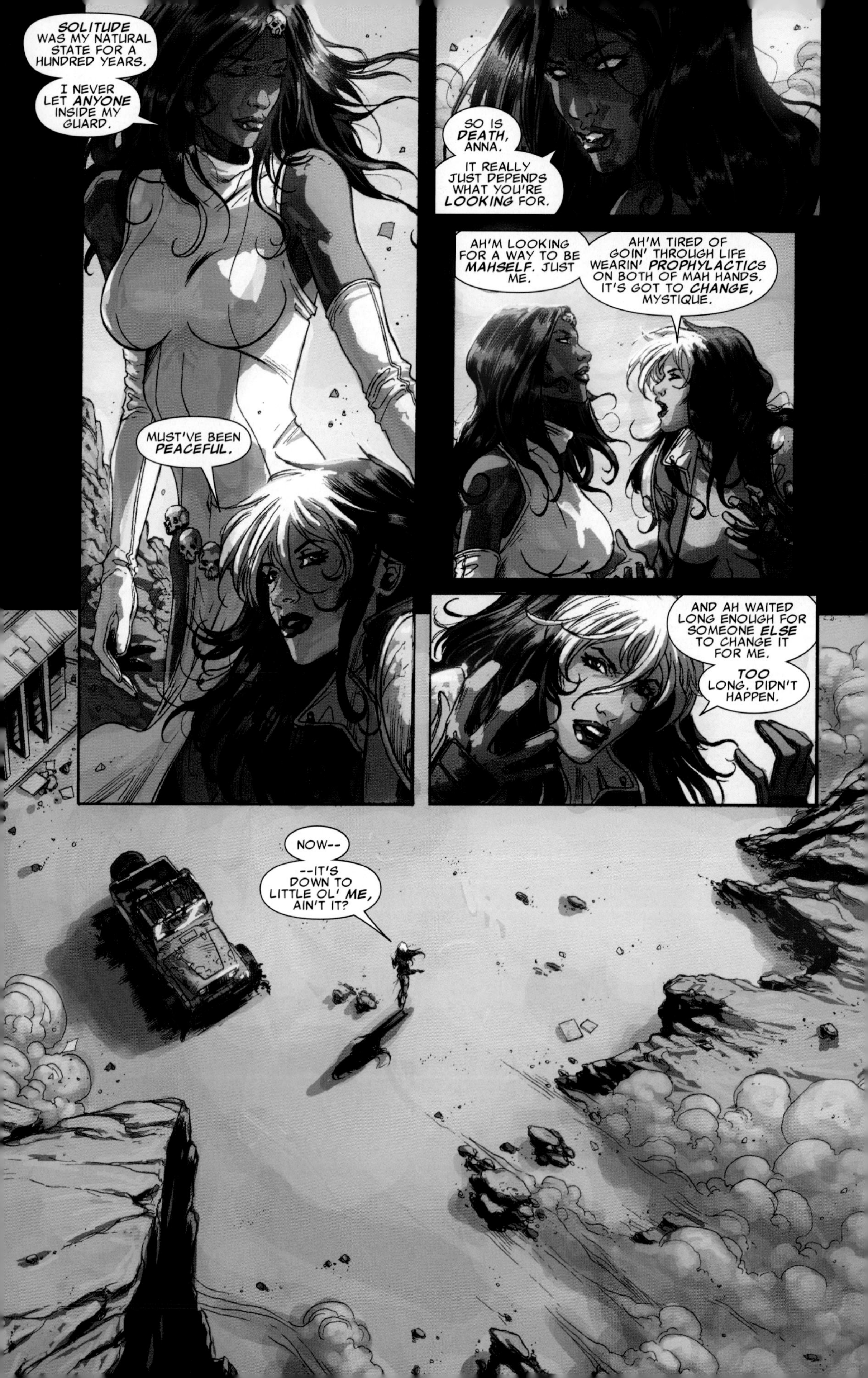
SOLITUDE WAS MY NATURAL STATE FOR A HUNDRED YEARS.
I NEVER LET ANYONE INSIDE MY GUARD.
SO IS DEATH, ANNA.
IT REALLY JUST DEPENDS WHAT YOU'RE LOOKING FOR.
MUST'VE BEEN PEACEFUL.
AH'M LOOKING FOR A WAY TO BE MAHSELF. JUST ME.
AH'M TIRED OF GOIN' THROUGH LIFE WEARIN' PROPHYLACTICS ON BOTH OF MAH HANDS. IT'S GOT TO CHANGE, MYSTIQUE.
AND AH WAITED LONG ENOUGH FOR SOMEONE ELSE TO CHANGE IT FOR ME.
TOO LONG. DIDN'T HAPPEN.
NOW--
--IT'S DOWN TO LITTLE OL' ME, AIN'T IT?

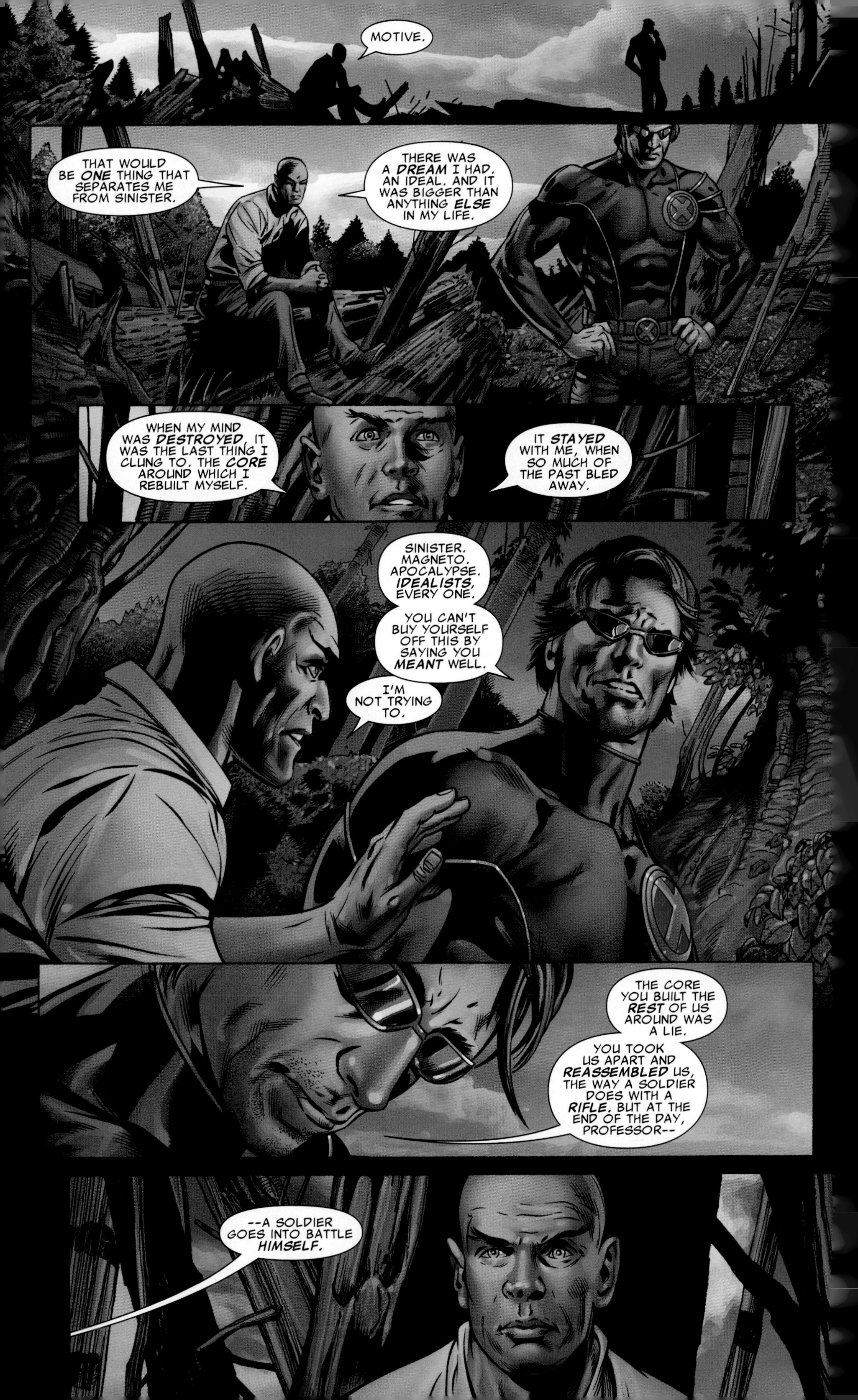
MOTIVE.
THAT WOULD BE ONE THING THAT SEPARATES ME FROM SINISTER.
THERE WAS A DREAM I HAD. AN IDEAL. AND IT WAS BIGGER THAN ANYTHING ELSE IN MY LIFE.
WHEN MY MIND WAS DESTROYED, IT WAS THE LAST THING I CLUNG TO. THE CORE AROUND WHICH I REBUILT MYSELF.
IT STAYED WITH ME, WHEN SO MUCH OF THE PAST BLED AWAY.
SINISTER. MAGNETO. APOCALYPSE. IDEALISTS, EVERY ONE.
YOU CAN'T BUY YOURSELF OFF THIS BY SAYING YOU MEANT WELL.
I'M NOT TRYING TO.
THE CORE YOU BUILT THE REST OF US AROUND WAS A LIE.
YOU TOOK US APART AND REASSEMBLED US, THE WAY A SOLDIER DOES WITH A RIFLE. BUT AT THE END OF THE DAY, PROFESSOR--
--A SOLDIER GOES INTO BATTLE HIMSELF.

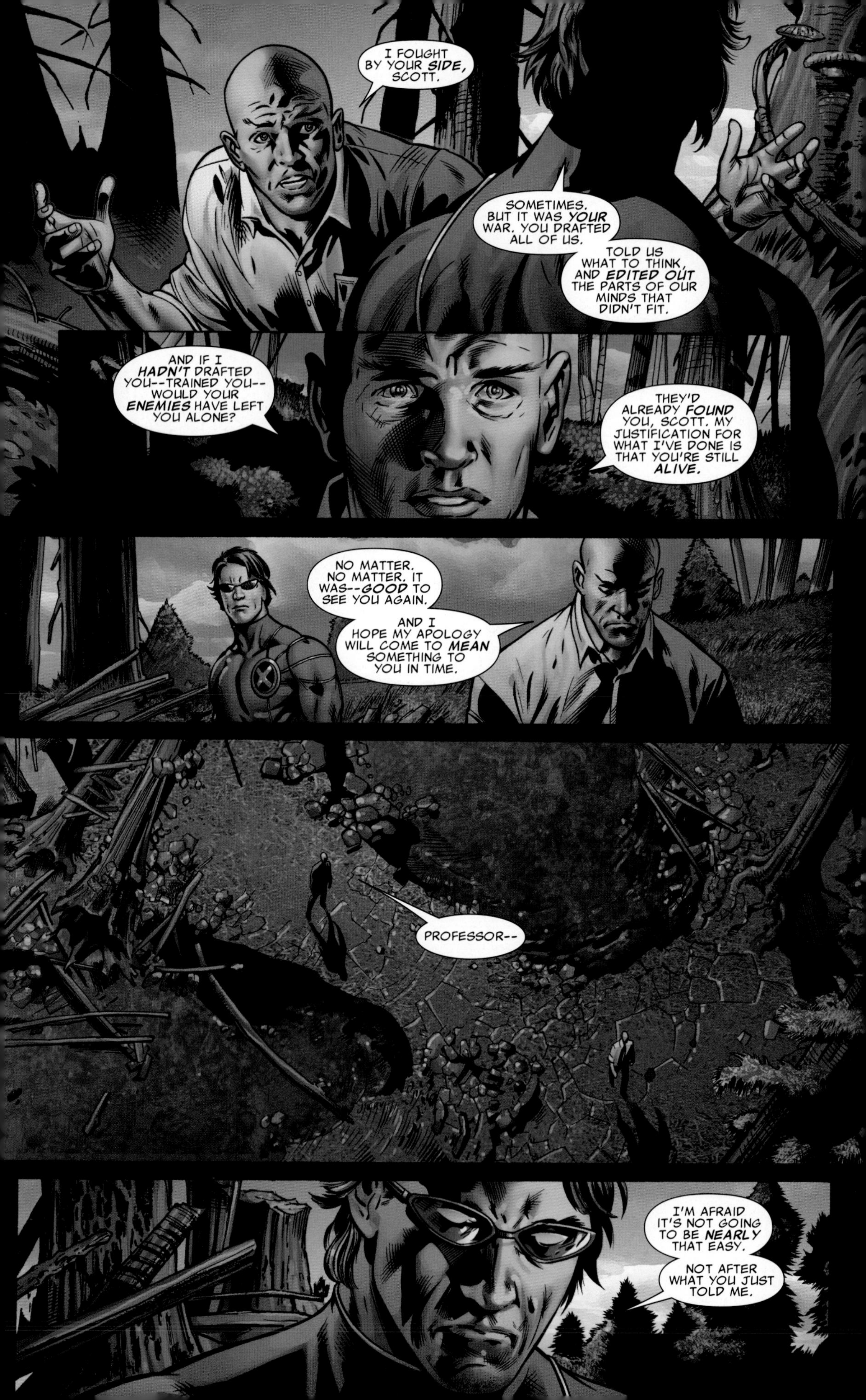
I FOUGHT BY YOUR SIDE, SCOTT.
SOMETIMES. BUT IT WAS YOUR WAR. YOU DRAFTED ALL OF US.
TOLD US WHAT TO THINK, AND EDITED OUT THE PARTS OF OUR MINDS THAT DIDN'T FIT.
AND IF I HADN'T DRAFTED YOU--TRAINED YOU--WOULD YOUR ENEMIES HAVE LEFT YOU ALONE?
THEY'D ALREADY FOUND YOU, SCOTT. MY JUSTIFICATION FOR WHAT I'VE DONE IS THAT YOU'RE STILL ALIVE.
NO MATTER. NO MATTER. IT WAS--GOOD TO SEE YOU AGAIN.
AND I HOPE MY APOLOGY WILL COME TO MEAN SOMETHING TO YOU IN TIME.
PROFESSOR--
I'M AFRAID IT'S NOT GOING TO BE NEARLY THAT EASY.
NOT AFTER WHAT YOU JUST TOLD ME.

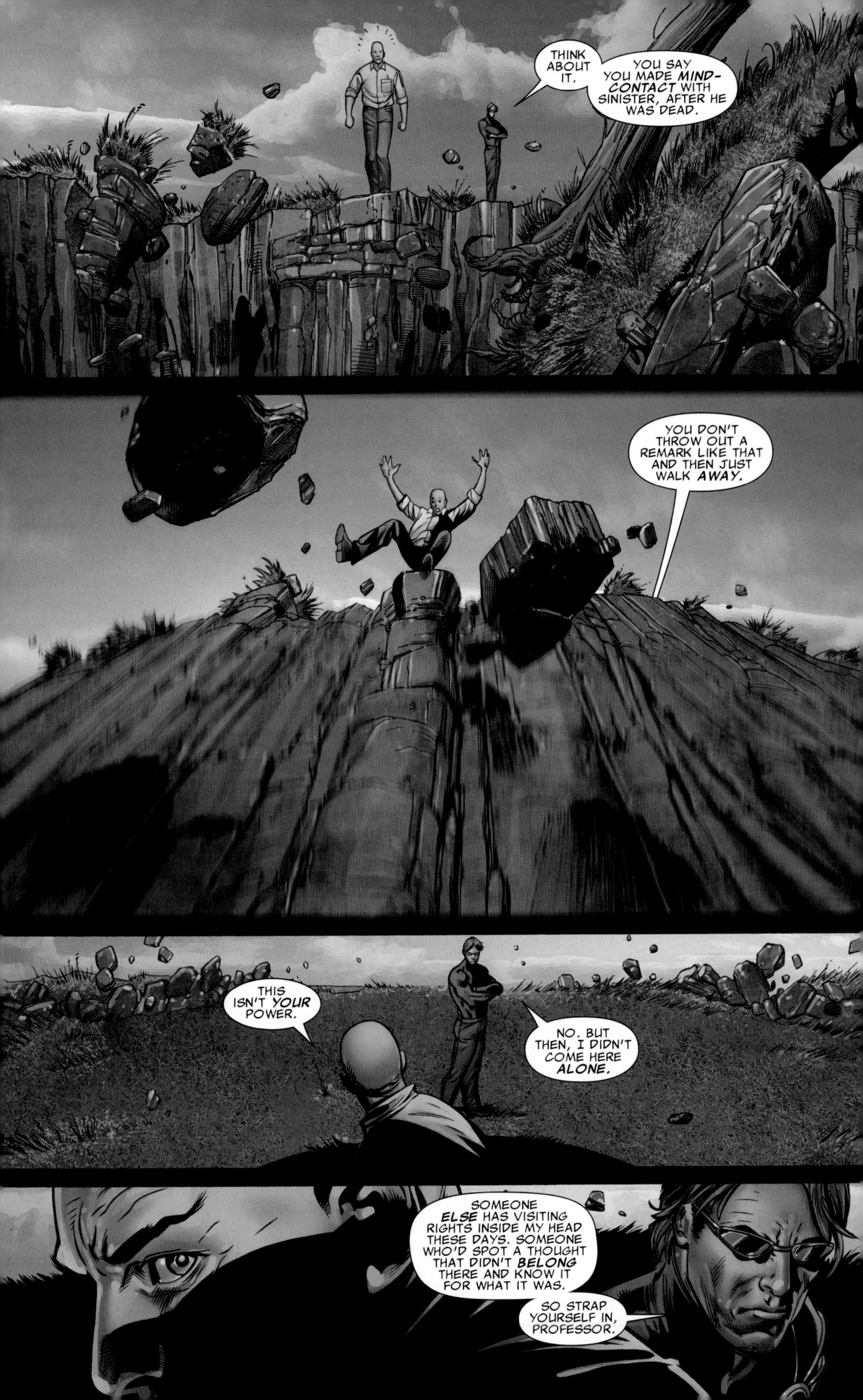
THINK ABOUT IT.
YOU SAY YOU MADE MIND-CONTACT WITH SINISTER, AFTER HE WAS DEAD.
YOU DON'T THROW OUT A REMARK LIKE THAT AND THEN JUST WALK AWAY.
THIS ISN'T YOUR POWER.
NO. BUT THEN, I DIDN'T COME HERE ALONE.
SOMEONE ELSE HAS VISITING RIGHTS INSIDE MY HEAD THESE DAYS. SOMEONE WHO'D SPOT A THOUGHT THAT DIDN'T BELONG THERE AND KNOW IT FOR WHAT IT WAS.
SO STRAP YOURSELF IN, PROFESSOR.

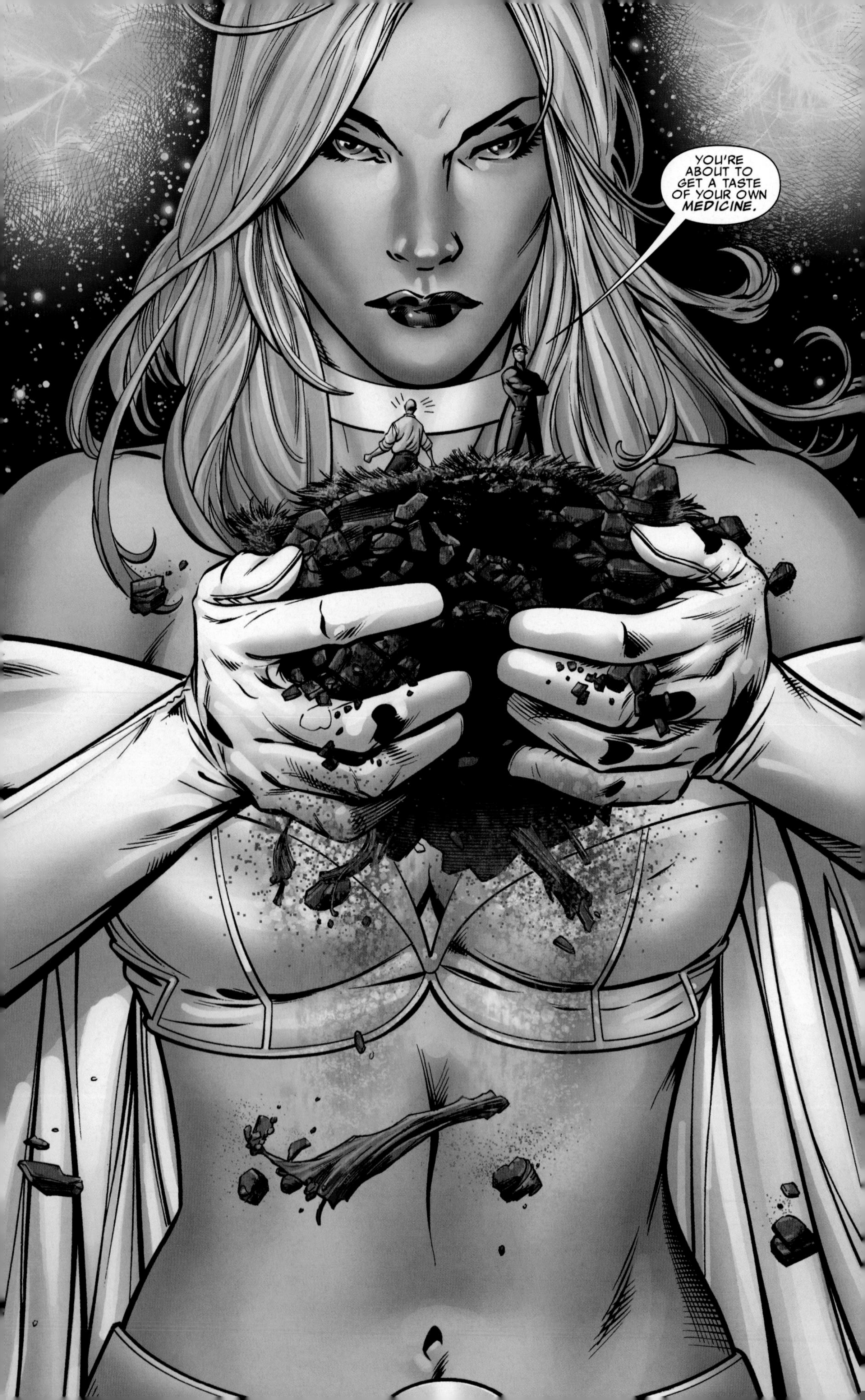
YOU'RE ABOUT TO GET A TASTE OF YOUR OWN MEDICINE.

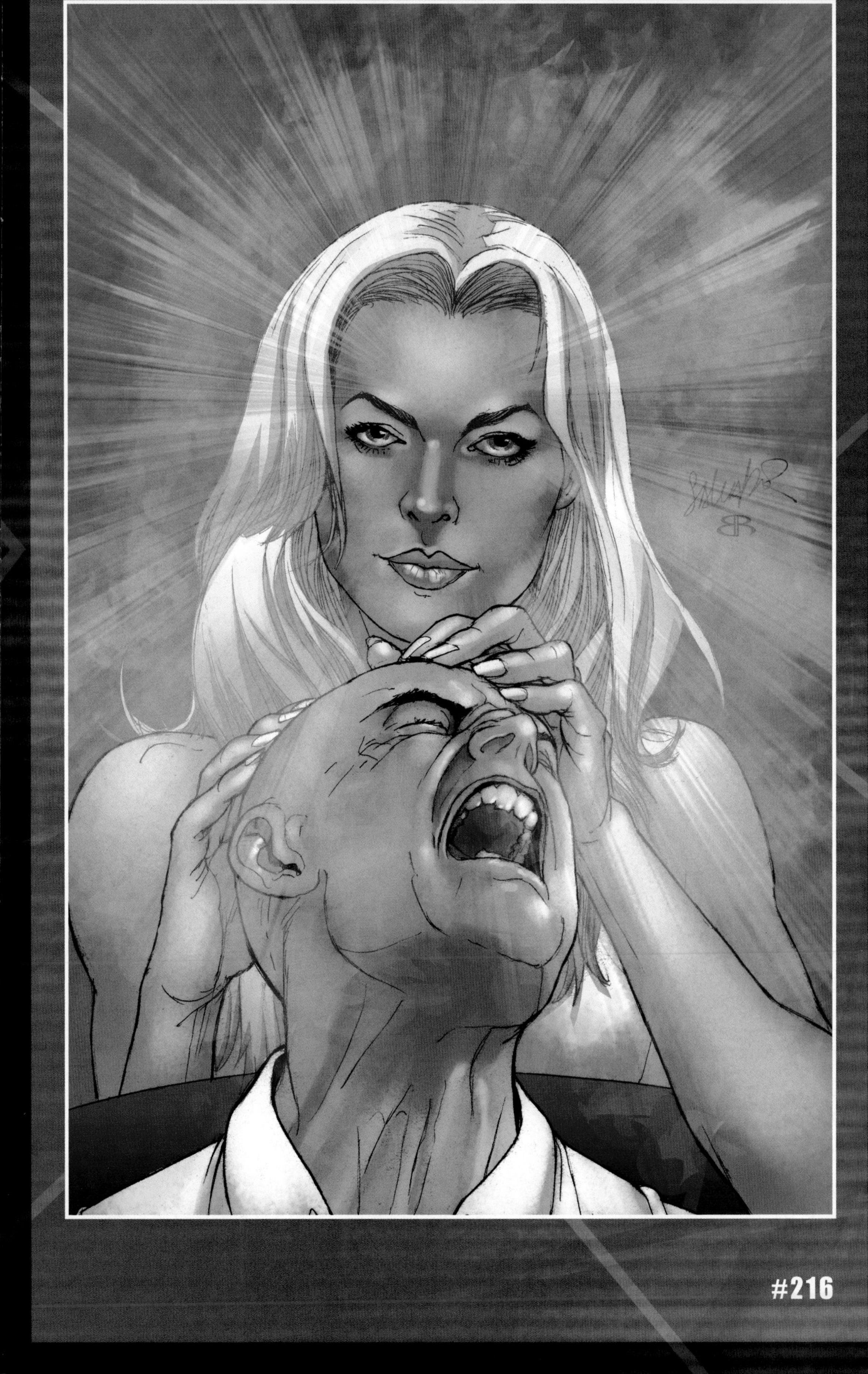

#216

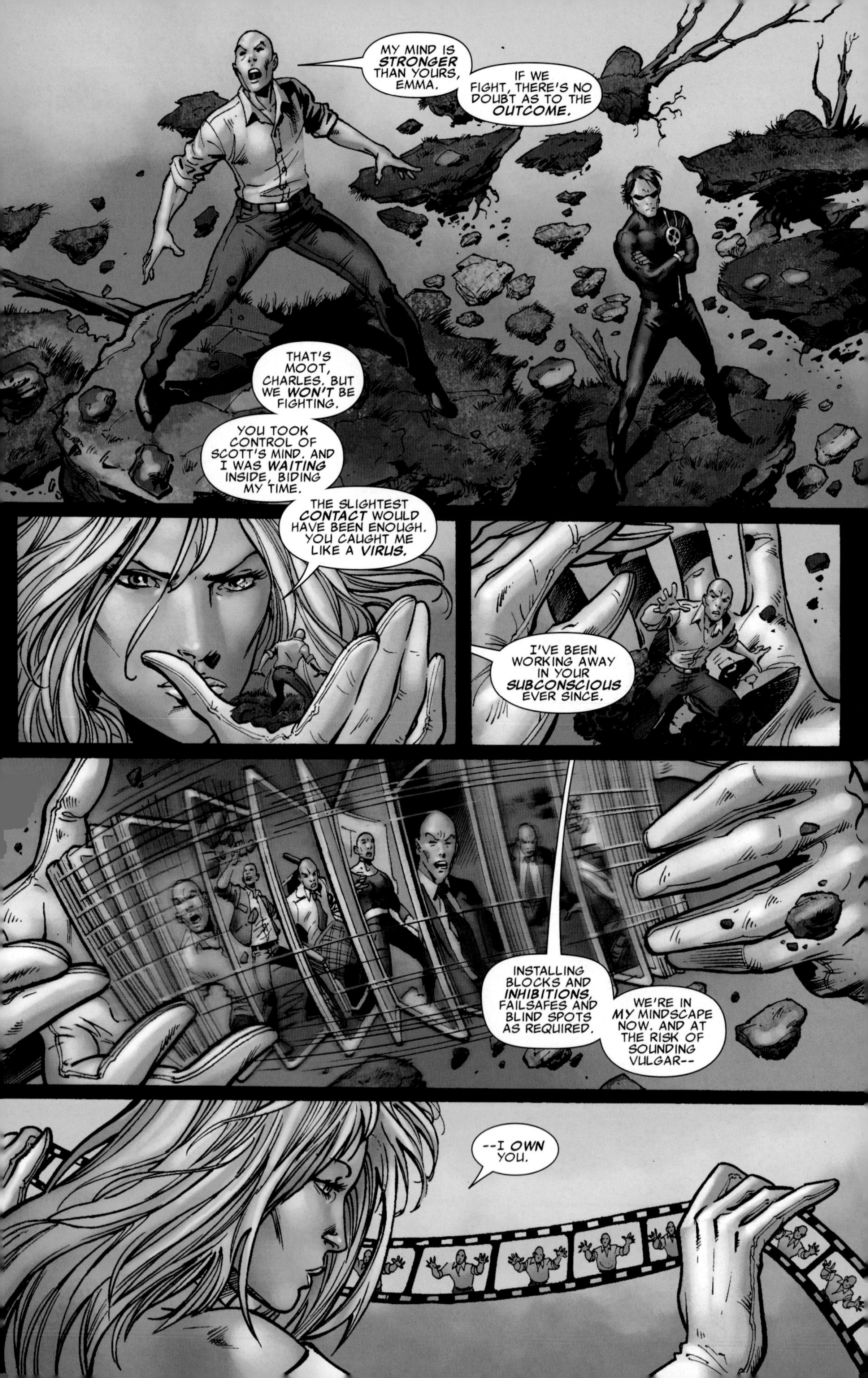
MY MIND IS STRONGER THAN YOURS, EMMA.
IF WE FIGHT, THERE'S NO DOUBT AS TO THE OUTCOME.
THAT'S MOOT, CHARLES. BUT WE WON'T BE FIGHTING.
YOU TOOK CONTROL OF SCOTT'S MIND. AND I WAS WAITING INSIDE, BIDING MY TIME.
THE SLIGHTEST CONTACT WOULD HAVE BEEN ENOUGH. YOU CAUGHT ME LIKE A VIRUS.
I'VE BEEN WORKING AWAY IN YOUR SUBCONSCIOUS EVER SINCE.
INSTALLING BLOCKS AND INHIBITIONS, FAILSAFES AND BLIND SPOTS AS REQUIRED.
WE'RE IN MY MINDSCAPE NOW. AND AT THE RISK OF SOUNDING VULGAR--
--I OWN YOU.

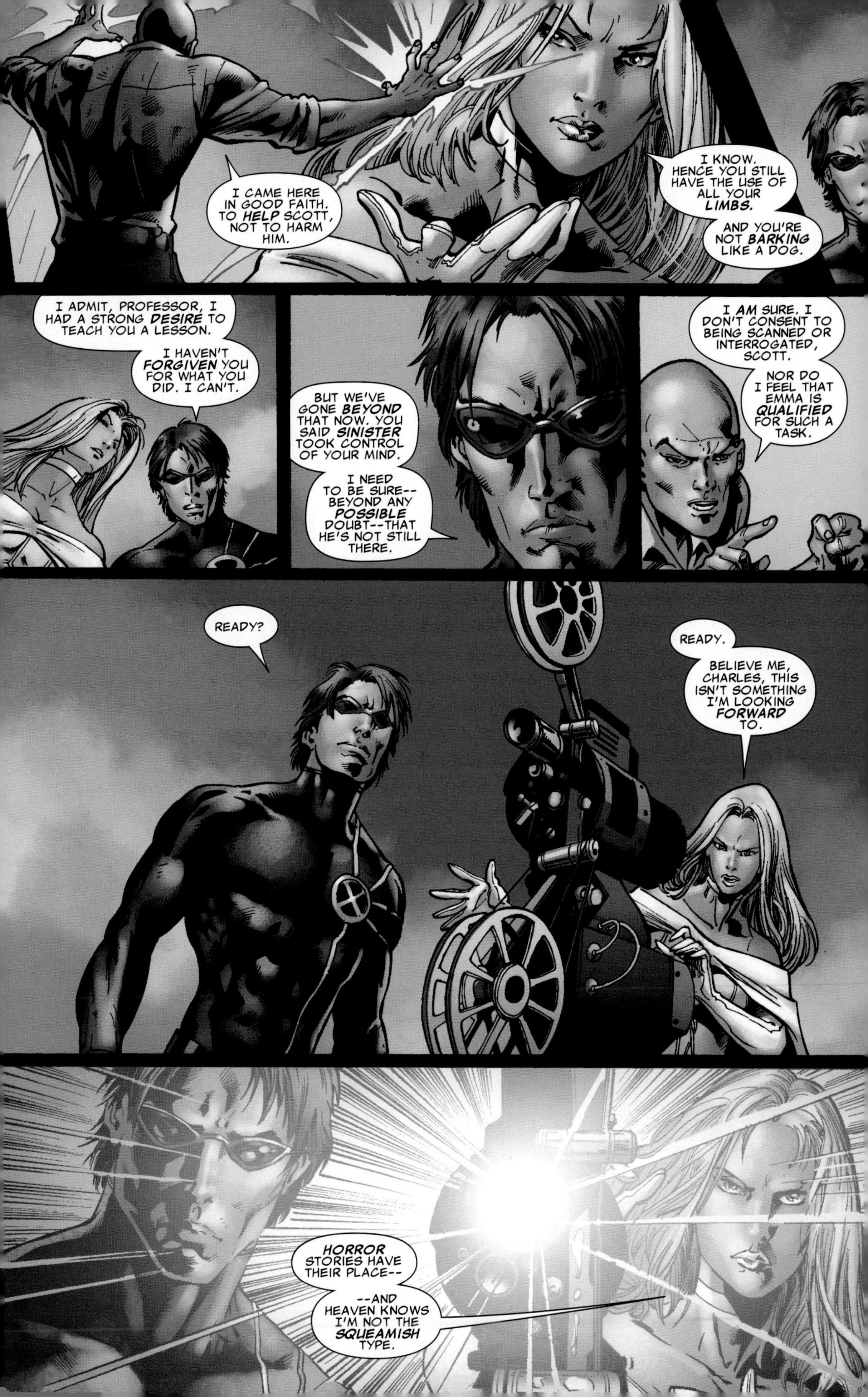
I CAME HERE IN GOOD FAITH. TO HELP SCOTT, NOT TO HARM HIM.
I KNOW. HENCE YOU STILL HAVE THE USE OF ALL YOUR LIMBS.
AND YOU'RE NOT BARKING LIKE A DOG.
I ADMIT, PROFESSOR, I HAD A STRONG DESIRE TO TEACH YOU A LESSON.
I HAVEN'T FORGIVEN YOU FOR WHAT YOU DID. I CAN'T.
BUT WE'VE GONE BEYOND THAT NOW. YOU SAID SINISTER TOOK CONTROL OF YOUR MIND.
I NEED TO BE SURE--BEYOND ANY POSSIBLE DOUBT--THAT HE'S NOT STILL THERE.
I AM SURE. I DON'T CONSENT TO BEING SCANNED OR INTERROGATED, SCOTT.
NOR DO I FEEL THAT EMMA IS QUALIFIED FOR SUCH A TASK.
READY?
READY.
BELIEVE ME, CHARLES, THIS ISN'T SOMETHING I'M LOOKING FORWARD TO.
HORROR STORIES HAVE THEIR PLACE--
--AND HEAVEN KNOWS I'M NOT THE SQUEAMISH TYPE.

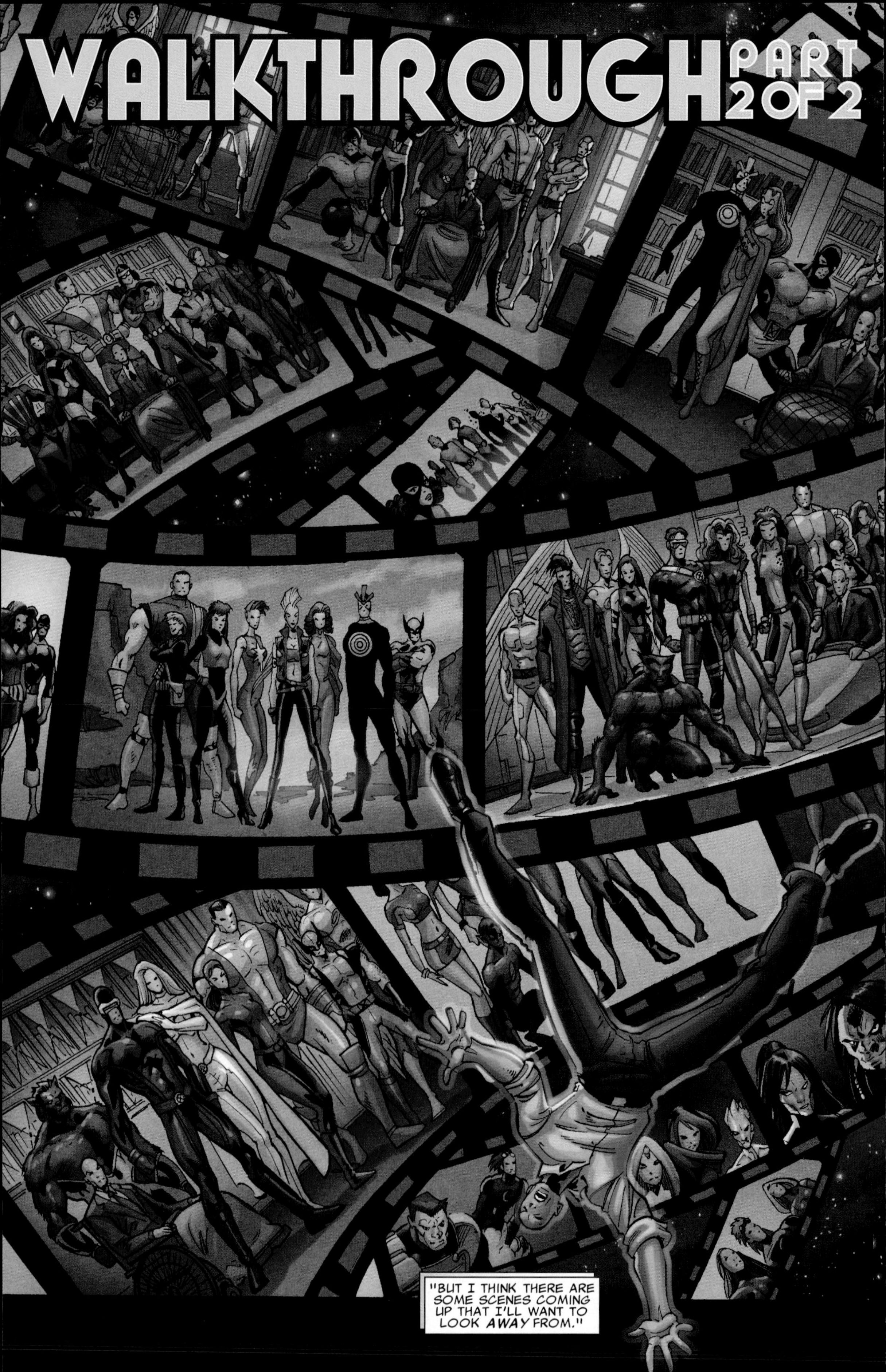
WALKTHROUGH PART 2 OF 2
"BUT I THINK THERE ARE SOME SCENES COMING UP THAT I'LL WANT TO LOOK AWAY FROM."

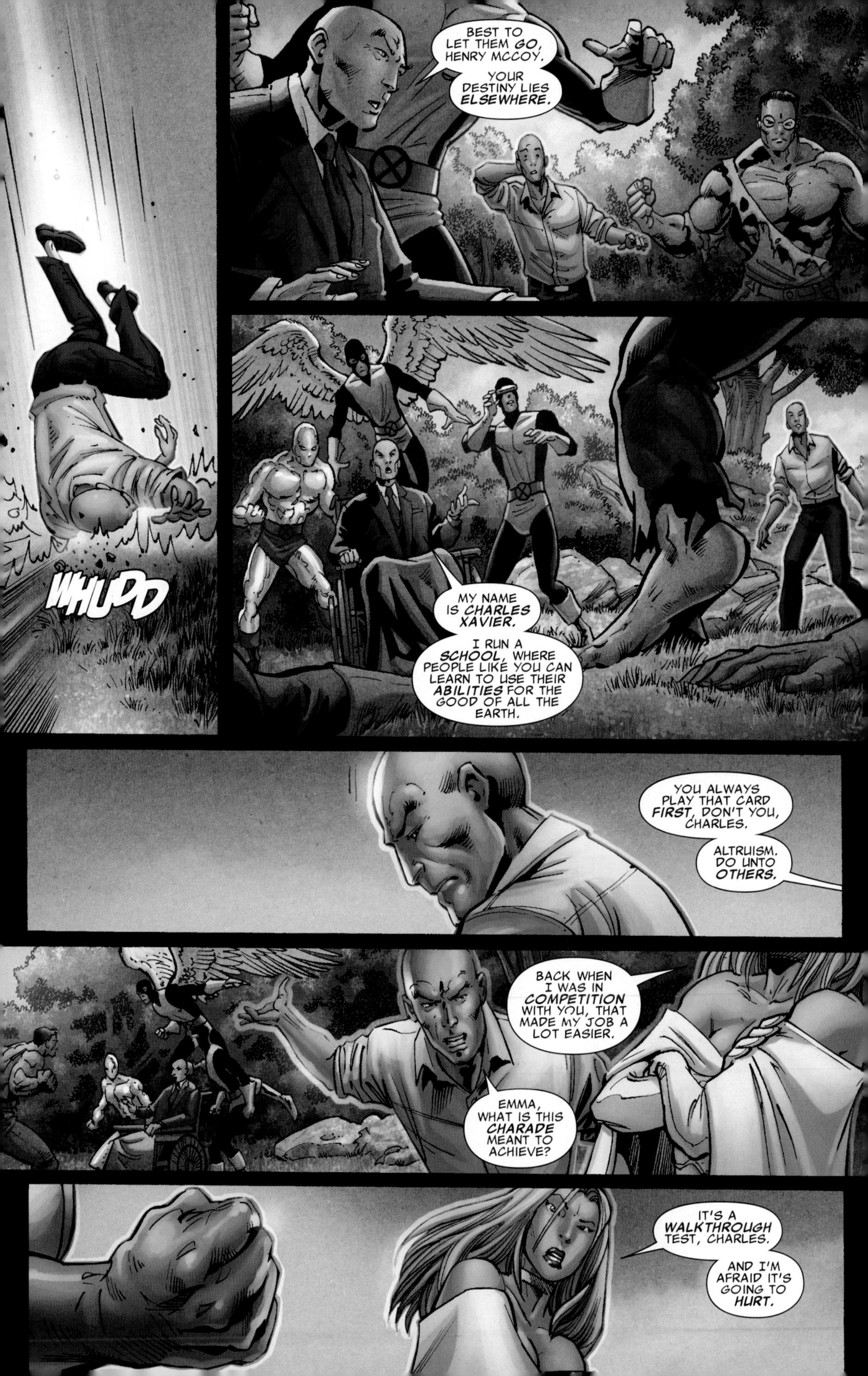
BEST TO LET THEM GO, HENRY McCOY.
YOUR DESTINY LIES ELSEWHERE.
WHUDD
MY NAME IS CHARLES XAVIER.
I RUN A SCHOOL, WHERE PEOPLE LIKE YOU CAN LEARN TO USE THEIR ABILITIES FOR THE GOOD OF ALL THE EARTH.
YOU ALWAYS PLAY THAT CARD FIRST, DON'T YOU, CHARLES.
ALTRUISM. DO UNTO OTHERS.
BACK WHEN I WAS IN COMPETITION WITH YOU, THAT MADE MY JOB A LOT EASIER.
EMMA, WHAT IS THIS CHARADE MEANT TO ACHIEVE?
IT'S A WALKTHROUGH TEST, CHARLES.
AND I'M AFRAID IT'S GOING TO HURT.

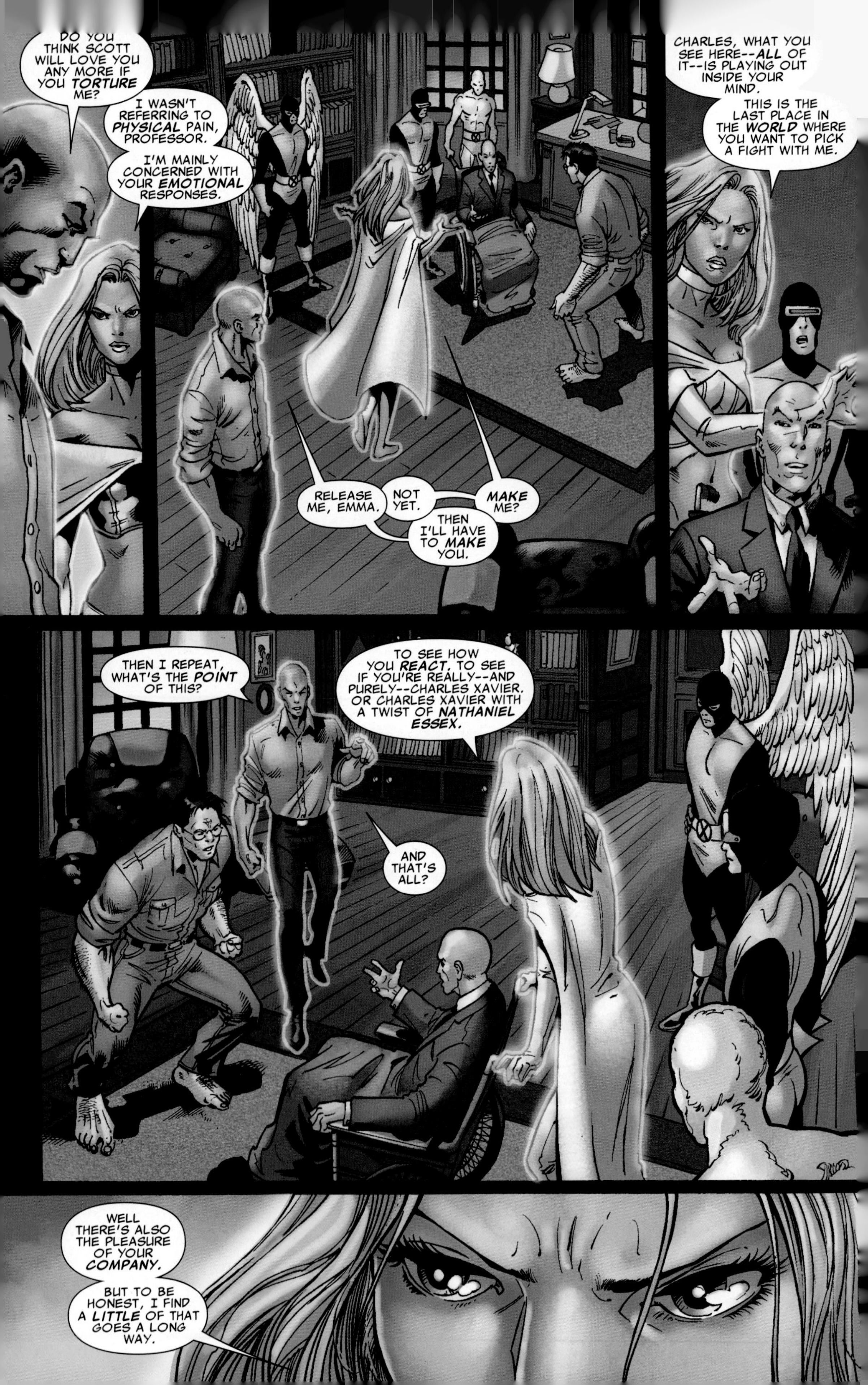

DO YOU THINK SCOTT WILL LOVE YOU ANY MORE IF YOU TORTURE ME?
I WASN'T REFERRING TO PHYSICAL PAIN, PROFESSOR.
I'M MAINLY CONCERNED WITH YOUR EMOTIONAL RESPONSES.
RELEASE ME, EMMA.
NOT YET.
MAKE ME?
THEN I'LL HAVE TO MAKE YOU.
CHARLES, WHAT YOU SEE HERE--ALL OF IT--IS PLAYING OUT INSIDE YOUR MIND.
THIS IS THE LAST PLACE IN THE WORLD WHERE YOU WANT TO PICK A FIGHT WITH ME.
THEN I REPEAT, WHAT'S THE POINT OF THIS?
TO SEE HOW YOU REACT. TO SEE IF YOU'RE REALLY--AND PURELY--CHARLES XAVIER. OR CHARLES XAVIER WITH A TWIST OF NATHANIEL ESSEX.
AND THAT'S ALL?
WELL THERE'S ALSO THE PLEASURE OF YOUR COMPANY.
BUT TO BE HONEST, I FIND A LITTLE OF THAT GOES A LONG WAY.

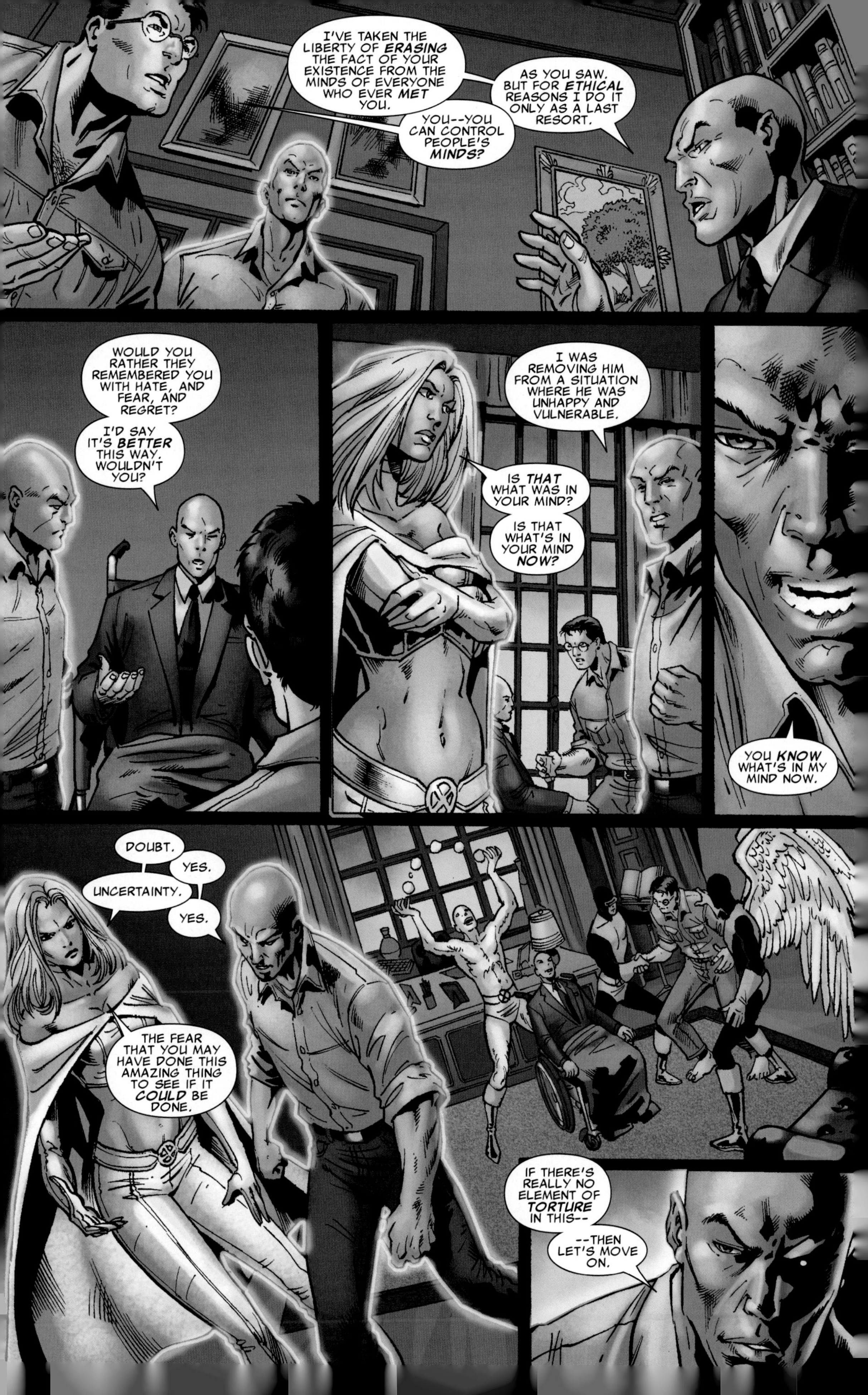
I'VE TAKEN THE LIBERTY OF ERASING THE FACT OF YOUR EXISTENCE FROM THE MINDS OF EVERYONE WHO EVER MET YOU.
YOU--YOU CAN CONTROL PEOPLE'S MINDS?
AS YOU SAW. BUT FOR ETHICAL REASONS I DO IT ONLY AS A LAST RESORT.
WOULD YOU RATHER THEY REMEMBERED YOU WITH HATE, AND FEAR, AND REGRET?
I'D SAY IT'S BETTER THIS WAY. WOULDN'T YOU?
I WAS REMOVING HIM FROM A SITUATION WHERE HE WAS UNHAPPY AND VULNERABLE.
IS THAT WHAT WAS IN YOUR MIND?
IS THAT WHAT'S IN YOUR MIND NOW?
YOU KNOW WHAT'S IN MY MIND NOW.
DOUBT.
YES.
UNCERTAINTY.
YES.
THE FEAR THAT YOU MAY HAVE DONE THIS AMAZING THING TO SEE IF IT COULD BE DONE.
IF THERE'S REALLY NO ELEMENT OF TORTURE IN THIS--
--THEN LET'S MOVE ON.

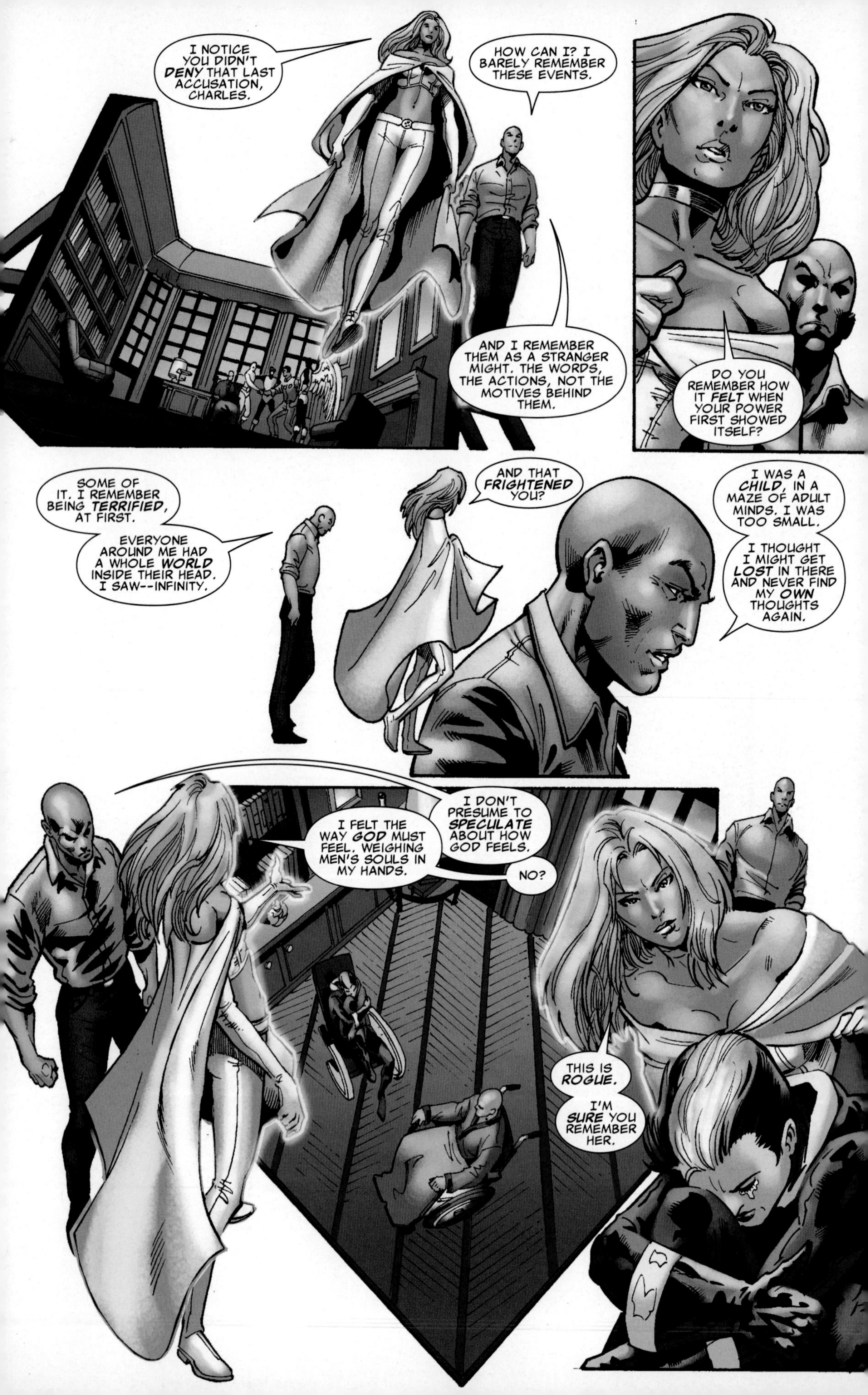

I NOTICE YOU DIDN'T **DENY** THAT LAST ACCUSATION, CHARLES.
HOW CAN I? I BARELY REMEMBER THESE EVENTS.
AND I REMEMBER THEM AS A STRANGER MIGHT. THE WORDS, THE ACTIONS, NOT THE MOTIVES BEHIND THEM.
DO YOU REMEMBER HOW IT **FELT** WHEN YOUR POWER FIRST SHOWED ITSELF?
SOME OF IT. I REMEMBER BEING **TERRIFIED**, AT FIRST.
EVERYONE AROUND ME HAD A WHOLE **WORLD** INSIDE THEIR HEAD. I SAW--INFINITY.
AND THAT **FRIGHTENED** YOU?
I WAS A **CHILD**, IN A MAZE OF ADULT MINDS. I WAS TOO SMALL.
I THOUGHT I MIGHT GET **LOST** IN THERE AND NEVER FIND MY **OWN** THOUGHTS AGAIN.
I FELT THE WAY **GOD** MUST FEEL. WEIGHING MEN'S SOULS IN MY HANDS.
I DON'T PRESUME TO **SPECULATE** ABOUT HOW GOD FEELS.
NO?
THIS IS **ROGUE.**
I'M **SURE** YOU REMEMBER HER.

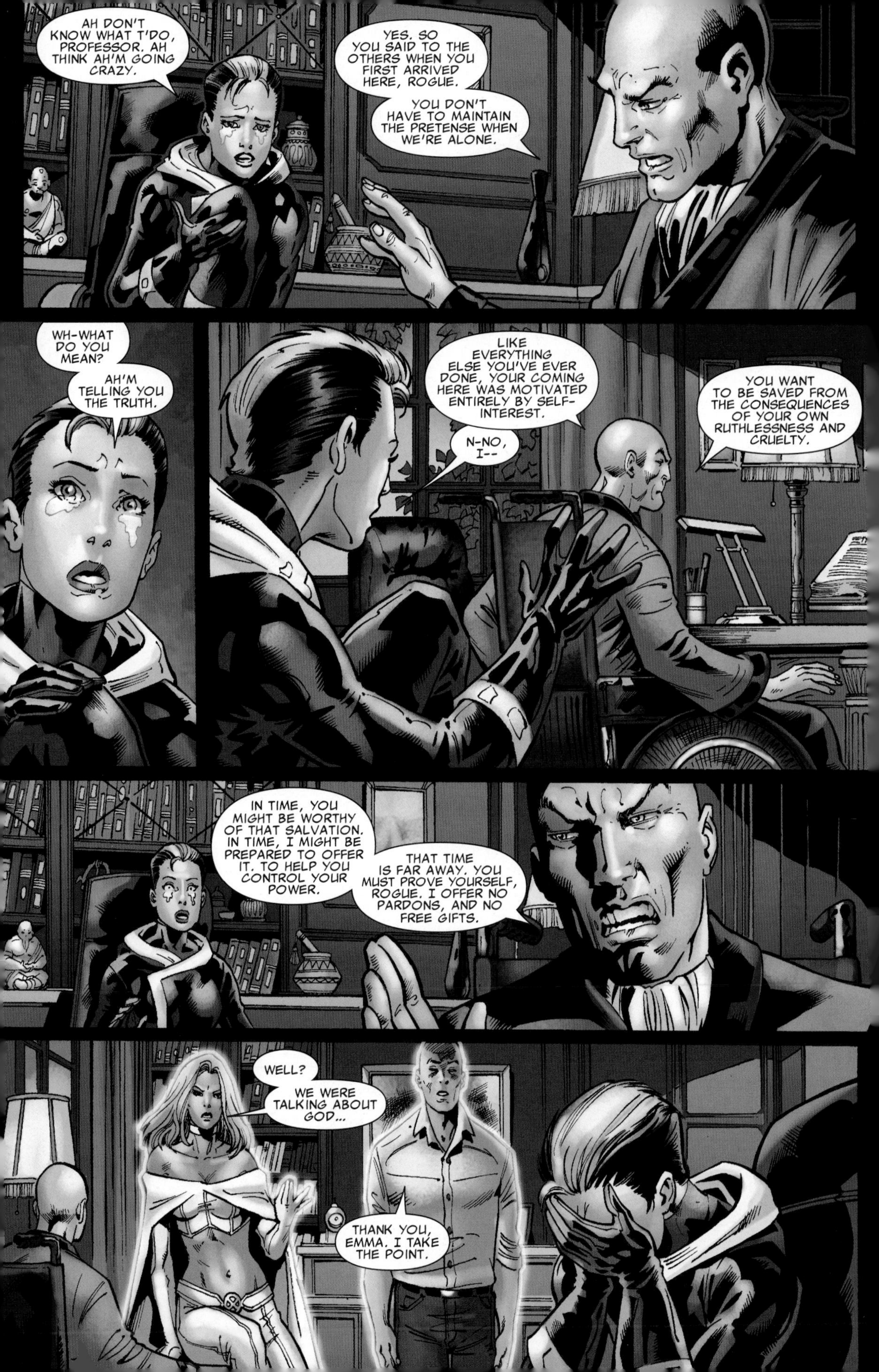
AH DON'T KNOW WHAT T'DO, PROFESSOR. AH THINK AH'M GOING CRAZY.
YES. SO YOU SAID TO THE OTHERS WHEN YOU FIRST ARRIVED HERE, ROGUE.
YOU DON'T HAVE TO MAINTAIN THE PRETENSE WHEN WE'RE ALONE.
WH-WHAT DO YOU MEAN?
AH'M TELLING YOU THE TRUTH.
LIKE EVERYTHING ELSE YOU'VE EVER DONE, YOUR COMING HERE WAS MOTIVATED ENTIRELY BY SELF-INTEREST.
N-NO, I--
YOU WANT TO BE SAVED FROM THE CONSEQUENCES OF YOUR OWN RUTHLESSNESS AND CRUELTY.
IN TIME, YOU MIGHT BE WORTHY OF THAT SALVATION. IN TIME, I MIGHT BE PREPARED TO OFFER IT. TO HELP YOU CONTROL YOUR POWER.
THAT TIME IS FAR AWAY. YOU MUST PROVE YOURSELF, ROGUE. I OFFER NO PARDONS, AND NO FREE GIFTS.
WELL?
WE WERE TALKING ABOUT GOD...
THANK YOU, EMMA. I TAKE THE POINT.

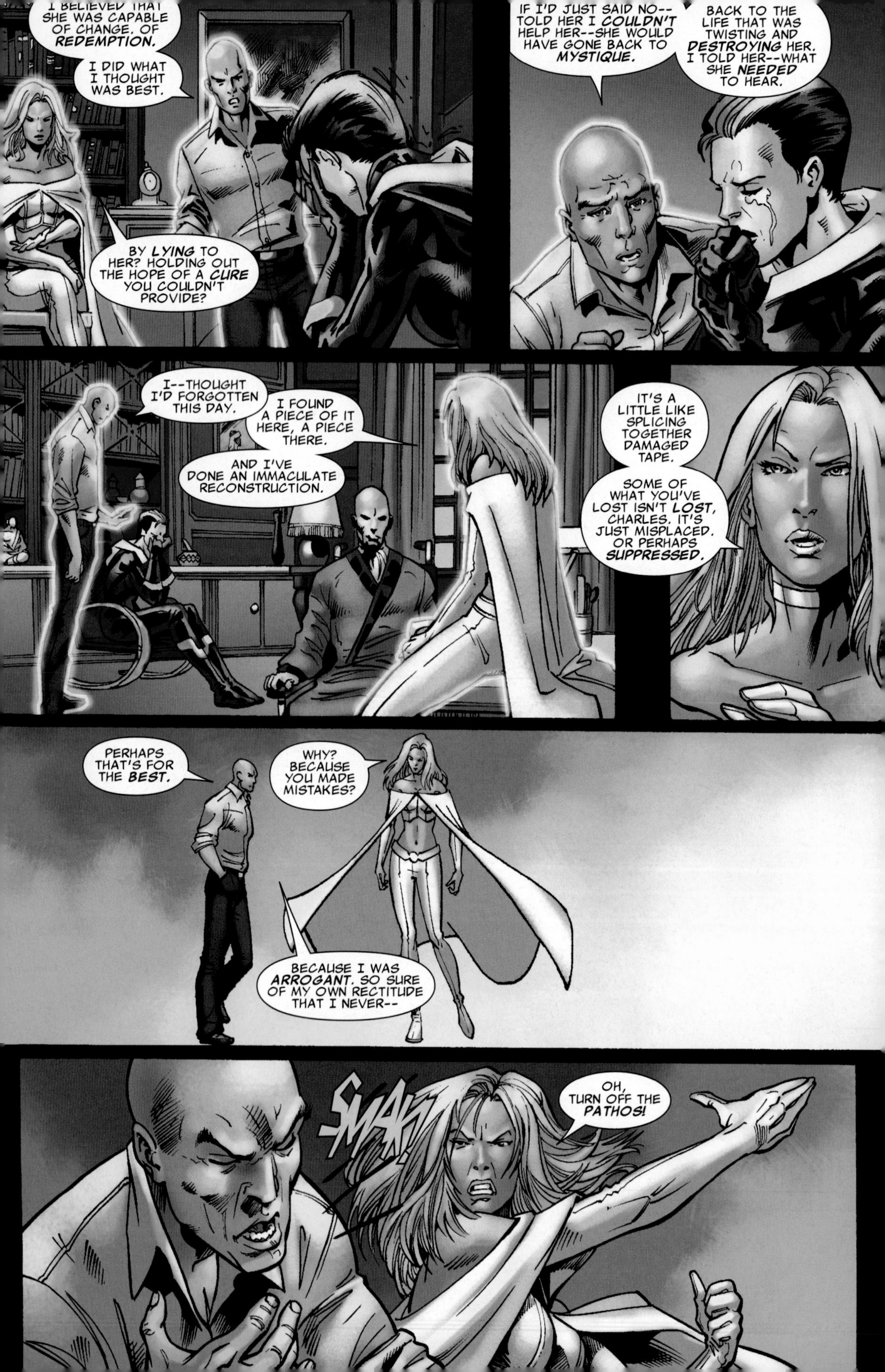

I BELIEVED THAT SHE WAS CAPABLE OF CHANGE. OF REDEMPTION.
I DID WHAT I THOUGHT WAS BEST.
BY LYING TO HER? HOLDING OUT THE HOPE OF A CURE YOU COULDN'T PROVIDE?
IF I'D JUST SAID NO--TOLD HER I COULDN'T HELP HER--SHE WOULD HAVE GONE BACK TO MYSTIQUE.
BACK TO THE LIFE THAT WAS TWISTING AND DESTROYING HER. I TOLD HER--WHAT SHE NEEDED TO HEAR.
I--THOUGHT I'D FORGOTTEN THIS DAY.
I FOUND A PIECE OF IT HERE, A PIECE THERE.
AND I'VE DONE AN IMMACULATE RECONSTRUCTION.
IT'S A LITTLE LIKE SPLICING TOGETHER DAMAGED TAPE.
SOME OF WHAT YOU'VE LOST ISN'T LOST, CHARLES. IT'S JUST MISPLACED. OR PERHAPS SUPPRESSED.
PERHAPS THAT'S FOR THE BEST.
WHY? BECAUSE YOU MADE MISTAKES?
BECAUSE I WAS ARROGANT. SO SURE OF MY OWN RECTITUDE THAT I NEVER--
SMAK!
OH, TURN OFF THE PATHOS!

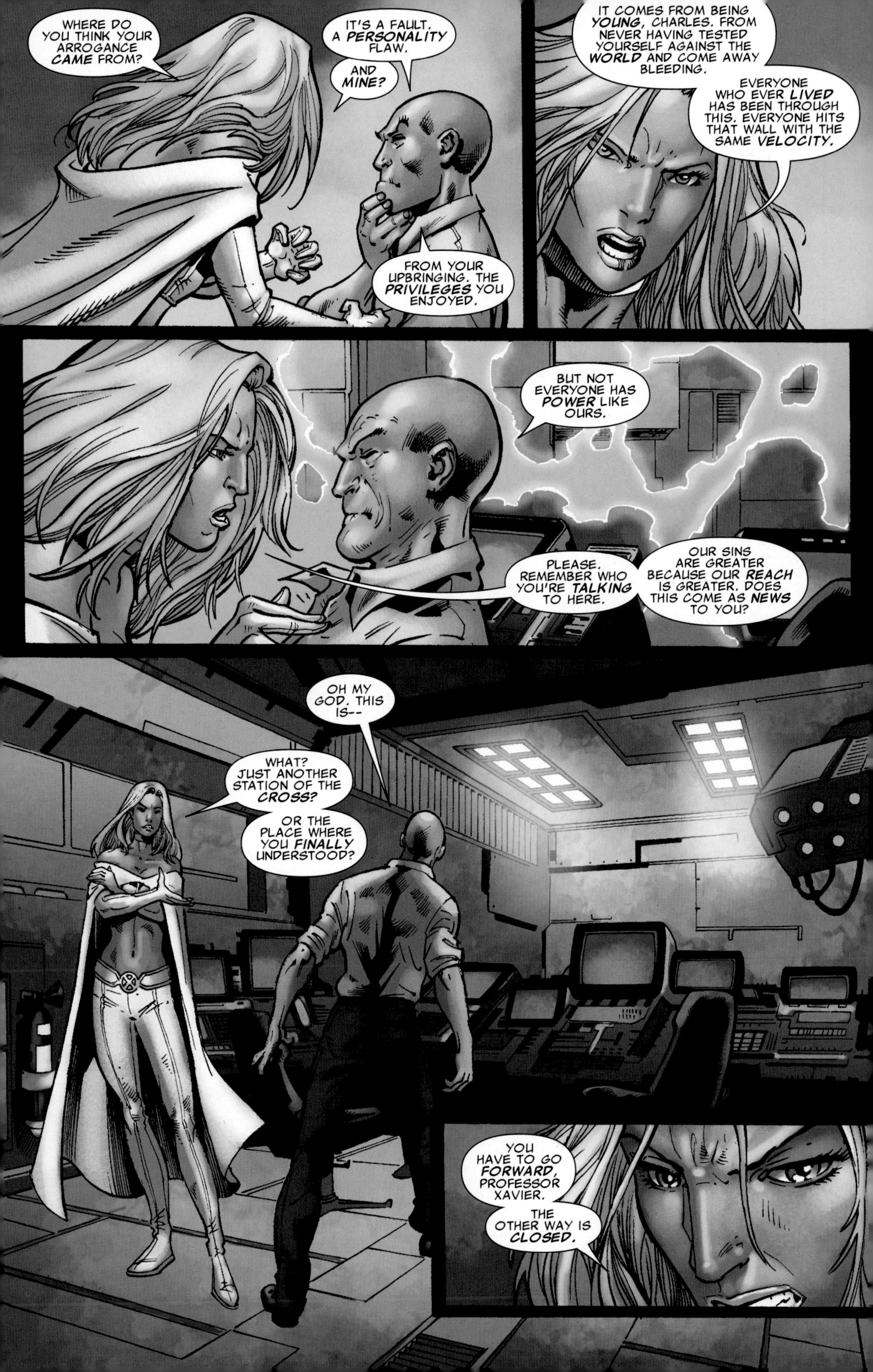
WHERE DO YOU THINK YOUR ARROGANCE CAME FROM?
IT'S A FAULT. A PERSONALITY FLAW.
AND MINE?
FROM YOUR UPBRINGING. THE PRIVILEGES YOU ENJOYED.
IT COMES FROM BEING YOUNG, CHARLES. FROM NEVER HAVING TESTED YOURSELF AGAINST THE WORLD AND COME AWAY BLEEDING.
EVERYONE WHO EVER LIVED HAS BEEN THROUGH THIS. EVERYONE HITS THAT WALL WITH THE SAME VELOCITY.
BUT NOT EVERYONE HAS POWER LIKE OURS.
PLEASE. REMEMBER WHO YOU'RE TALKING TO HERE.
OUR SINS ARE GREATER BECAUSE OUR REACH IS GREATER. DOES THIS COME AS NEWS TO YOU?
OH MY GOD. THIS IS--
WHAT? JUST ANOTHER STATION OF THE CROSS?
OR THE PLACE WHERE YOU FINALLY UNDERSTOOD?
YOU HAVE TO GO FORWARD, PROFESSOR XAVIER.
THE OTHER WAY IS CLOSED.

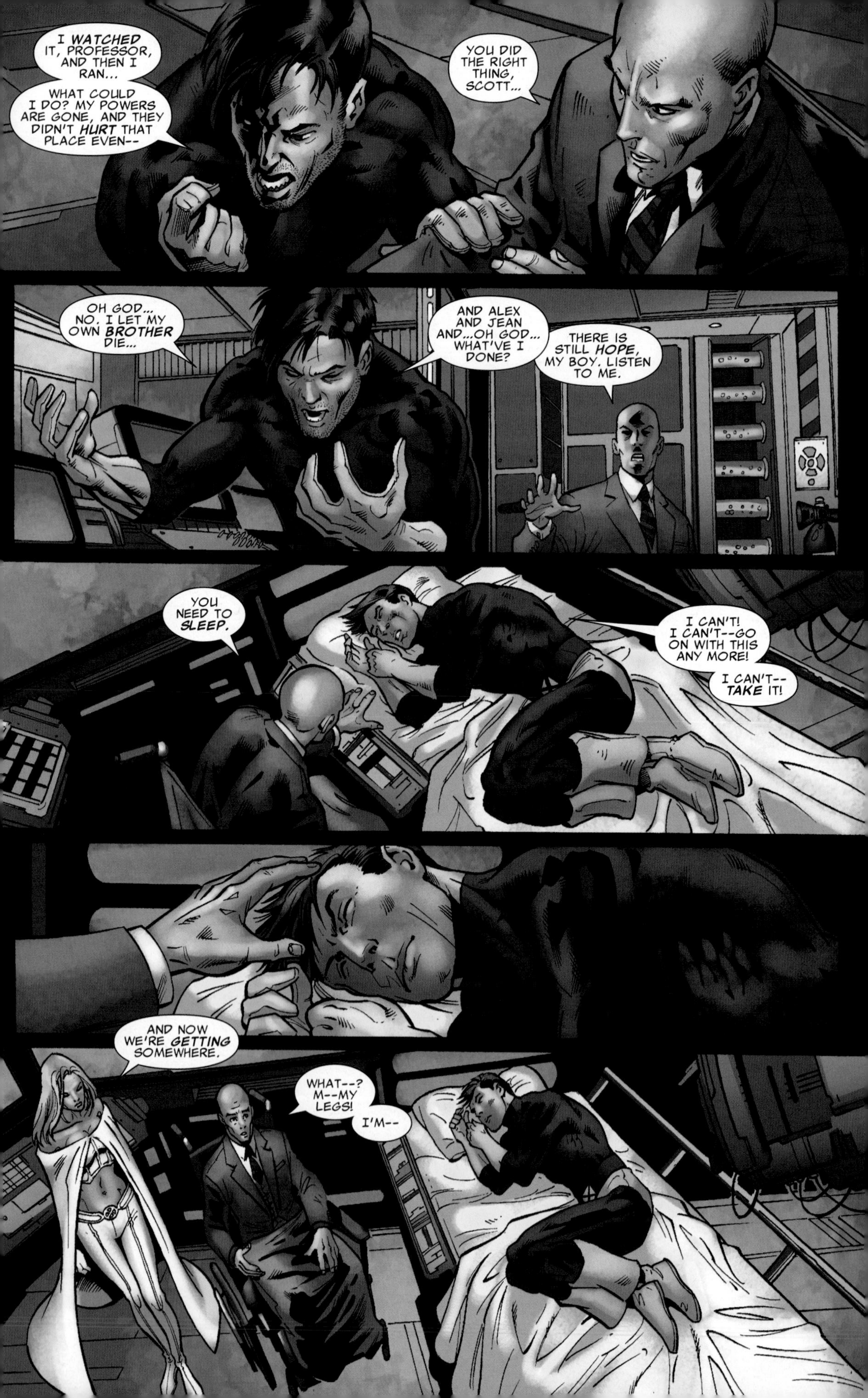
I WATCHED IT, PROFESSOR, AND THEN I RAN...
WHAT COULD I DO? MY POWERS ARE GONE, AND THEY DIDN'T HURT THAT PLACE EVEN--
YOU DID THE RIGHT THING, SCOTT...
OH GOD... NO. I LET MY OWN BROTHER DIE...
AND ALEX AND JEAN AND...OH GOD... WHAT'VE I DONE?
THERE IS STILL HOPE, MY BOY. LISTEN TO ME.
YOU NEED TO SLEEP.
I CAN'T! I CAN'T--GO ON WITH THIS ANY MORE!
I CAN'T--TAKE IT!
AND NOW WE'RE GETTING SOMEWHERE.
WHAT--? M--MY LEGS!
I'M--

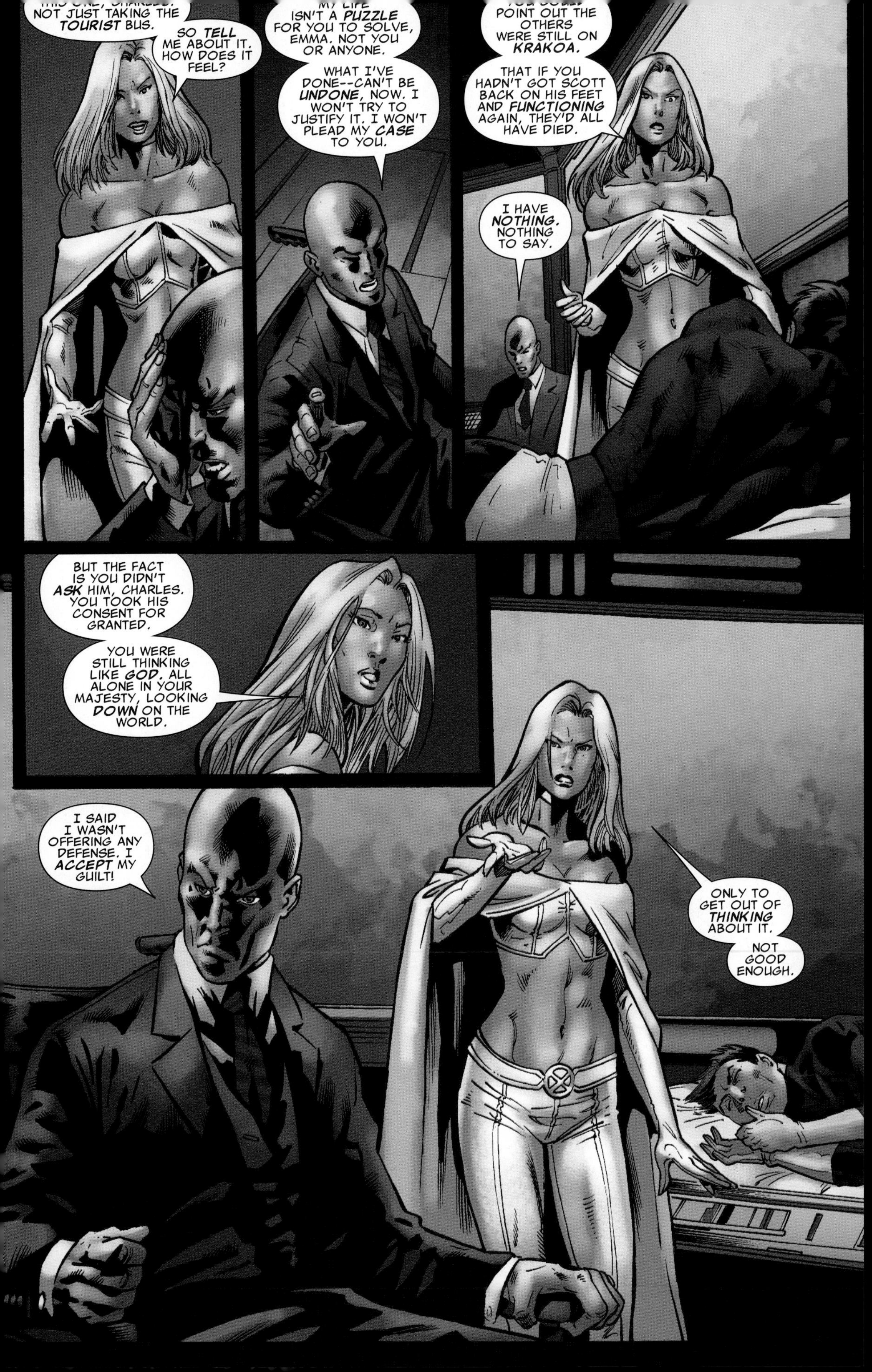
NOT JUST TAKING THE TOURIST BUS.
SO TELL ME ABOUT IT. HOW DOES IT FEEL?
MY LIFE ISN'T A PUZZLE FOR YOU TO SOLVE, EMMA. NOT YOU OR ANYONE.
WHAT I'VE DONE--CAN'T BE UNDONE, NOW. I WON'T TRY TO JUSTIFY IT. I WON'T PLEAD MY CASE TO YOU.
POINT OUT THE OTHERS WERE STILL ON KRAKOA.
THAT IF YOU HADN'T GOT SCOTT BACK ON HIS FEET AND FUNCTIONING AGAIN, THEY'D ALL HAVE DIED.
I HAVE NOTHING. NOTHING TO SAY.
BUT THE FACT IS YOU DIDN'T ASK HIM, CHARLES. YOU TOOK HIS CONSENT FOR GRANTED.
YOU WERE STILL THINKING LIKE GOD. ALL ALONE IN YOUR MAJESTY, LOOKING DOWN ON THE WORLD.
I SAID I WASN'T OFFERING ANY DEFENSE. I ACCEPT MY GUILT!
ONLY TO GET OUT OF THINKING ABOUT IT.
NOT GOOD ENOUGH.

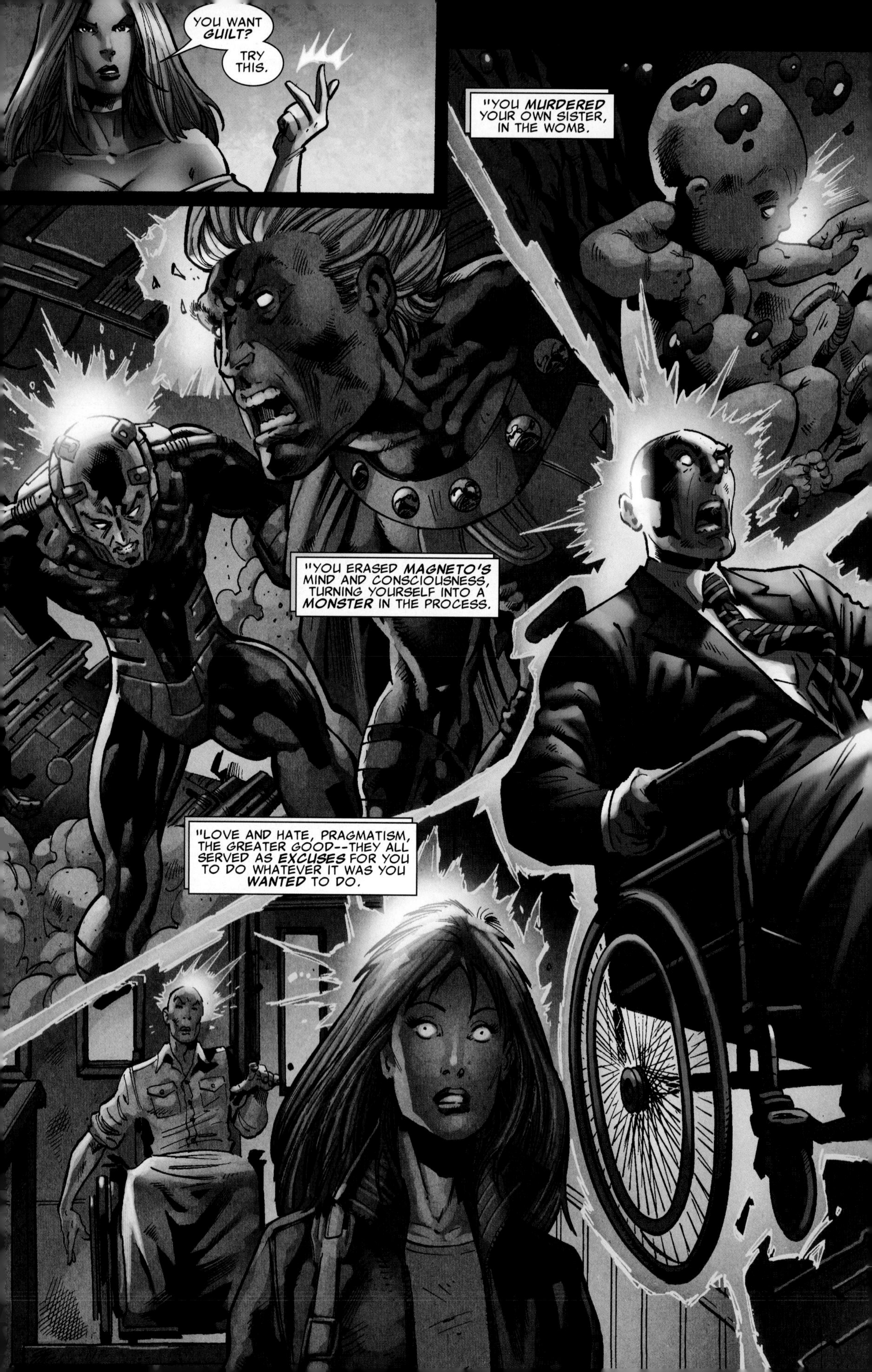

YOU WANT GUILT? TRY THIS.
"YOU MURDERED YOUR OWN SISTER, IN THE WOMB.
"YOU ERASED MAGNETO'S MIND AND CONSCIOUSNESS, TURNING YOURSELF INTO A MONSTER IN THE PROCESS.
"LOVE AND HATE, PRAGMATISM, THE GREATER GOOD--THEY ALL SERVED AS EXCUSES FOR YOU TO DO WHATEVER IT WAS YOU WANTED TO DO.

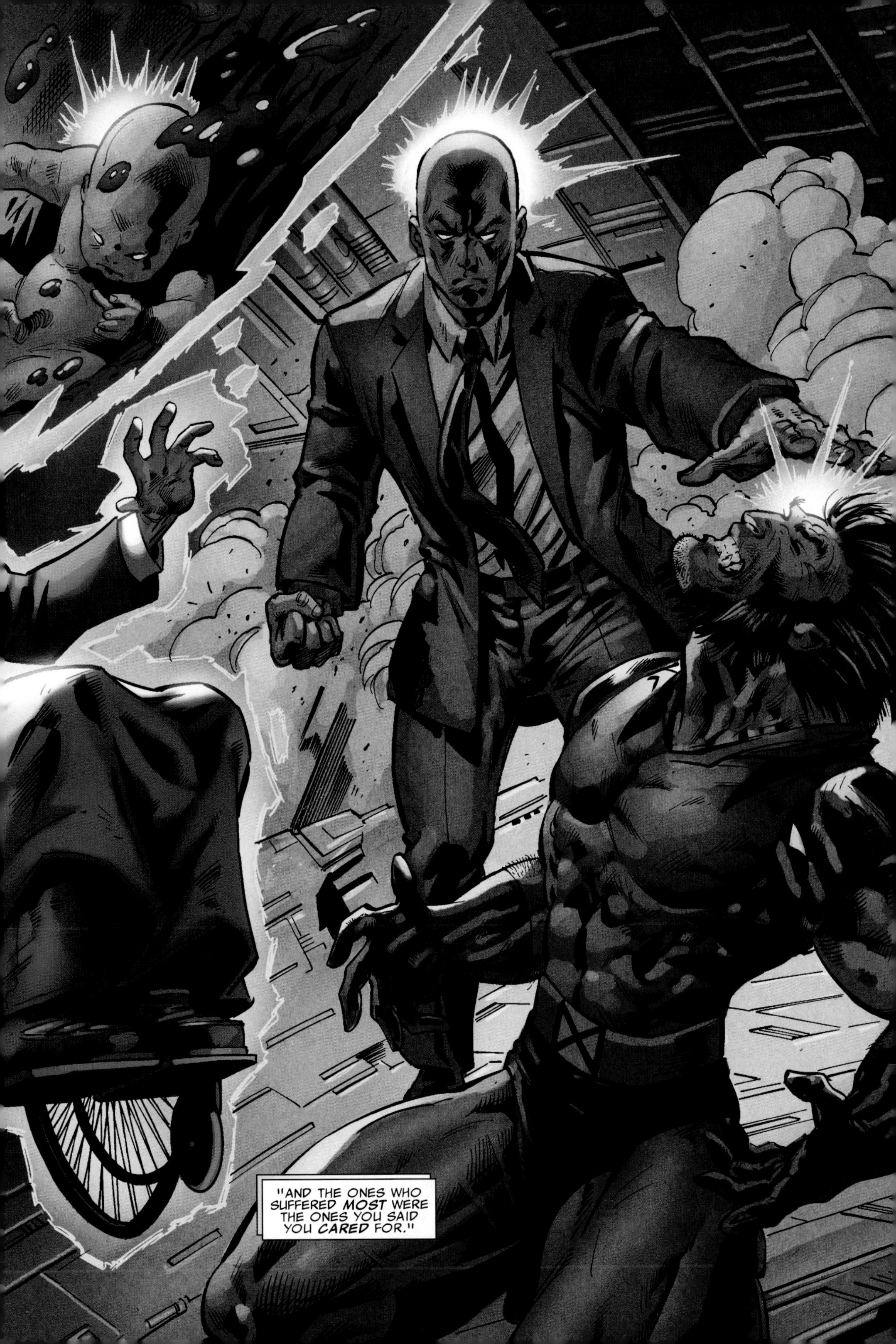
"AND THE ONES WHO SUFFERED MOST WERE THE ONES YOU SAID YOU CARED FOR."

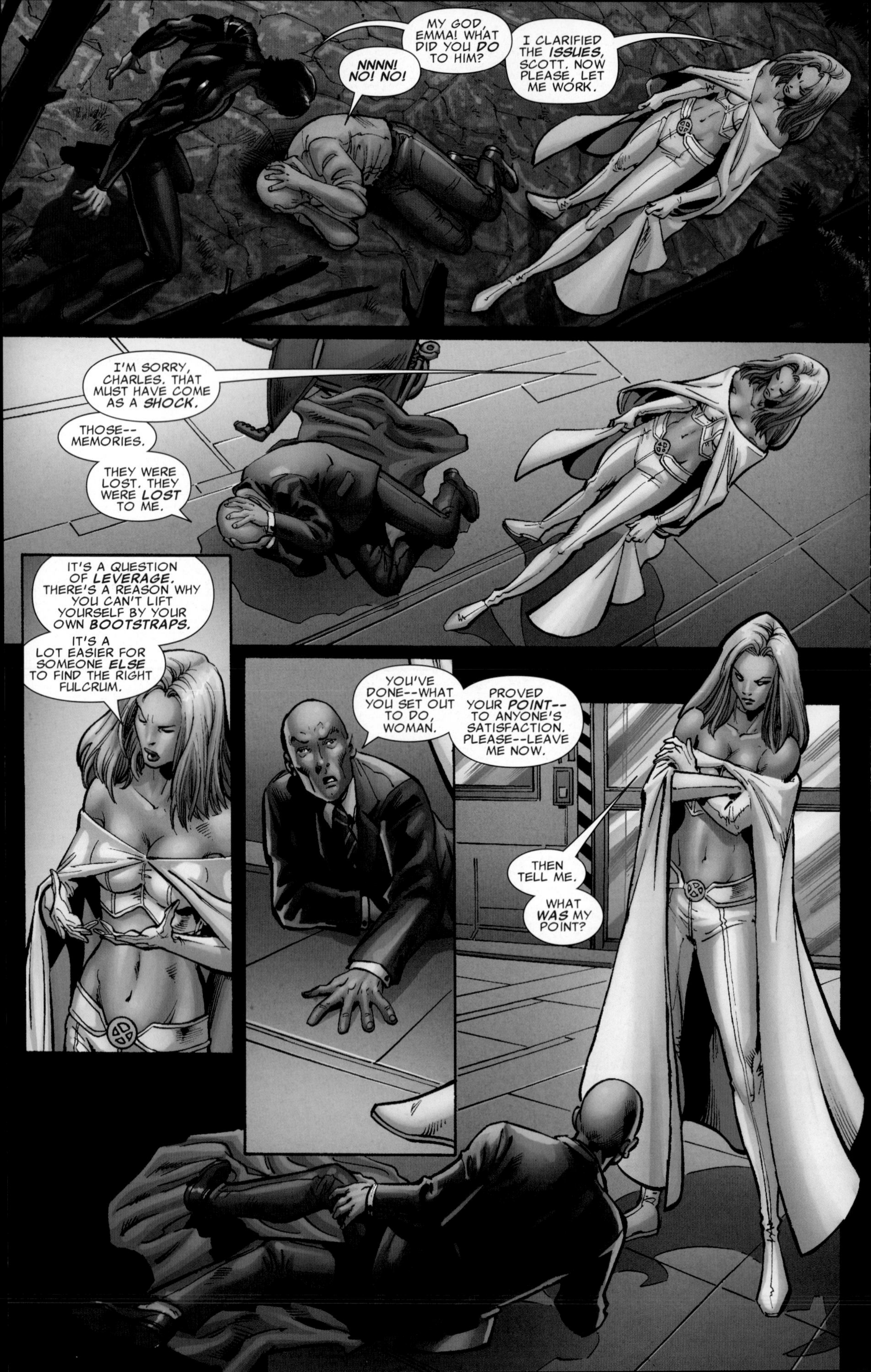
MY GOD, EMMA! WHAT DID YOU DO TO HIM?
NNNN! NO! NO!
I CLARIFIED THE ISSUES, SCOTT. NOW PLEASE, LET ME WORK.
I'M SORRY, CHARLES. THAT MUST HAVE COME AS A SHOCK.
THOSE-- MEMORIES.
THEY WERE LOST. THEY WERE LOST TO ME.
IT'S A QUESTION OF LEVERAGE. THERE'S A REASON WHY YOU CAN'T LIFT YOURSELF BY YOUR OWN BOOTSTRAPS.
IT'S A LOT EASIER FOR SOMEONE ELSE TO FIND THE RIGHT FULCRUM.
YOU'VE DONE--WHAT YOU SET OUT TO DO, WOMAN.
PROVED YOUR POINT-- TO ANYONE'S SATISFACTION. PLEASE--LEAVE ME NOW.
THEN TELL ME.
WHAT WAS MY POINT?

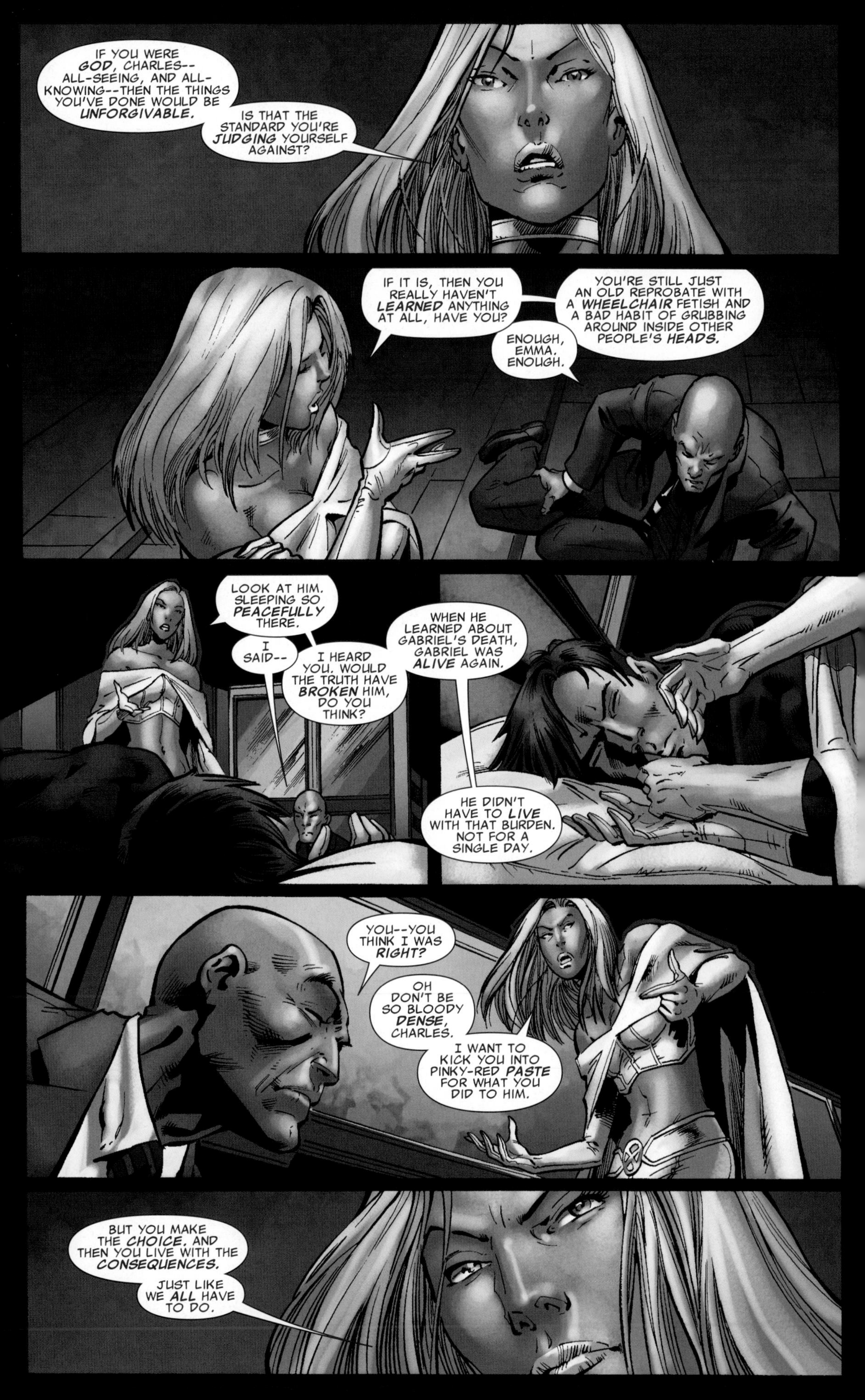

IF YOU WERE GOD, CHARLES-- ALL-SEEING, AND ALL-KNOWING--THEN THE THINGS YOU'VE DONE WOULD BE UNFORGIVABLE.
IS THAT THE STANDARD YOU'RE JUDGING YOURSELF AGAINST?
IF IT IS, THEN YOU REALLY HAVEN'T LEARNED ANYTHING AT ALL, HAVE YOU?
YOU'RE STILL JUST AN OLD REPROBATE WITH A WHEELCHAIR FETISH AND A BAD HABIT OF GRUBBING AROUND INSIDE OTHER PEOPLE'S HEADS.
ENOUGH, EMMA. ENOUGH.
LOOK AT HIM. SLEEPING SO PEACEFULLY THERE.
I SAID--
I HEARD YOU. WOULD THE TRUTH HAVE BROKEN HIM, DO YOU THINK?
WHEN HE LEARNED ABOUT GABRIEL'S DEATH, GABRIEL WAS ALIVE AGAIN.
HE DIDN'T HAVE TO LIVE WITH THAT BURDEN. NOT FOR A SINGLE DAY.
YOU--YOU THINK I WAS RIGHT?
OH DON'T BE SO BLOODY DENSE, CHARLES.
I WANT TO KICK YOU INTO PINKY-RED PASTE FOR WHAT YOU DID TO HIM.
BUT YOU MAKE THE CHOICE, AND THEN YOU LIVE WITH THE CONSEQUENCES.
JUST LIKE WE ALL HAVE TO DO.

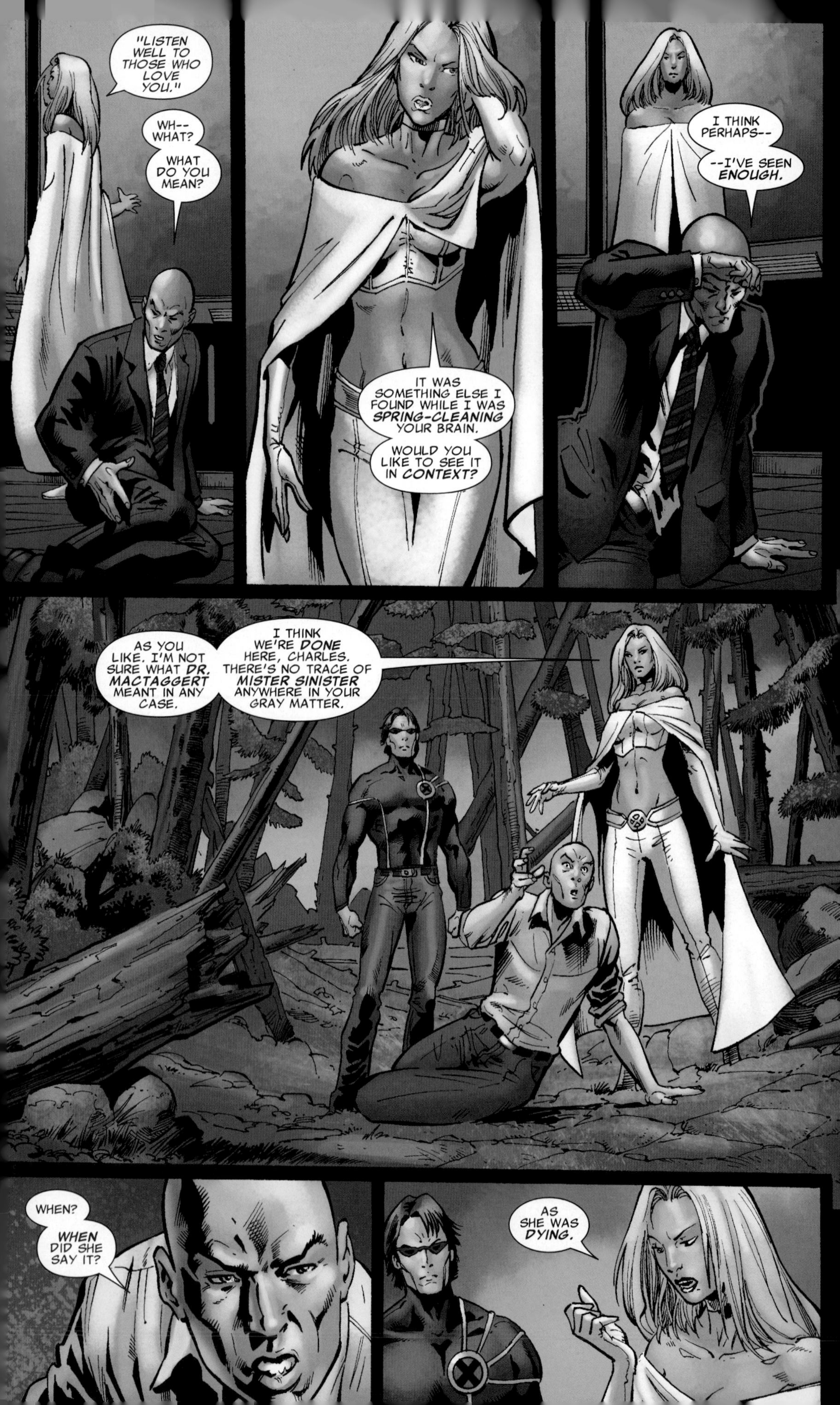
"LISTEN WELL TO THOSE WHO LOVE YOU."
WH-- WHAT?
WHAT DO YOU MEAN?
IT WAS SOMETHING ELSE I FOUND WHILE I WAS SPRING-CLEANING YOUR BRAIN.
WOULD YOU LIKE TO SEE IT IN CONTEXT?
I THINK PERHAPS--
--I'VE SEEN ENOUGH.
AS YOU LIKE. I'M NOT SURE WHAT DR. MACTAGGERT MEANT IN ANY CASE.
I THINK WE'RE DONE HERE, CHARLES. THERE'S NO TRACE OF MISTER SINISTER ANYWHERE IN YOUR GRAY MATTER.
WHEN?
WHEN DID SHE SAY IT?
AS SHE WAS DYING.

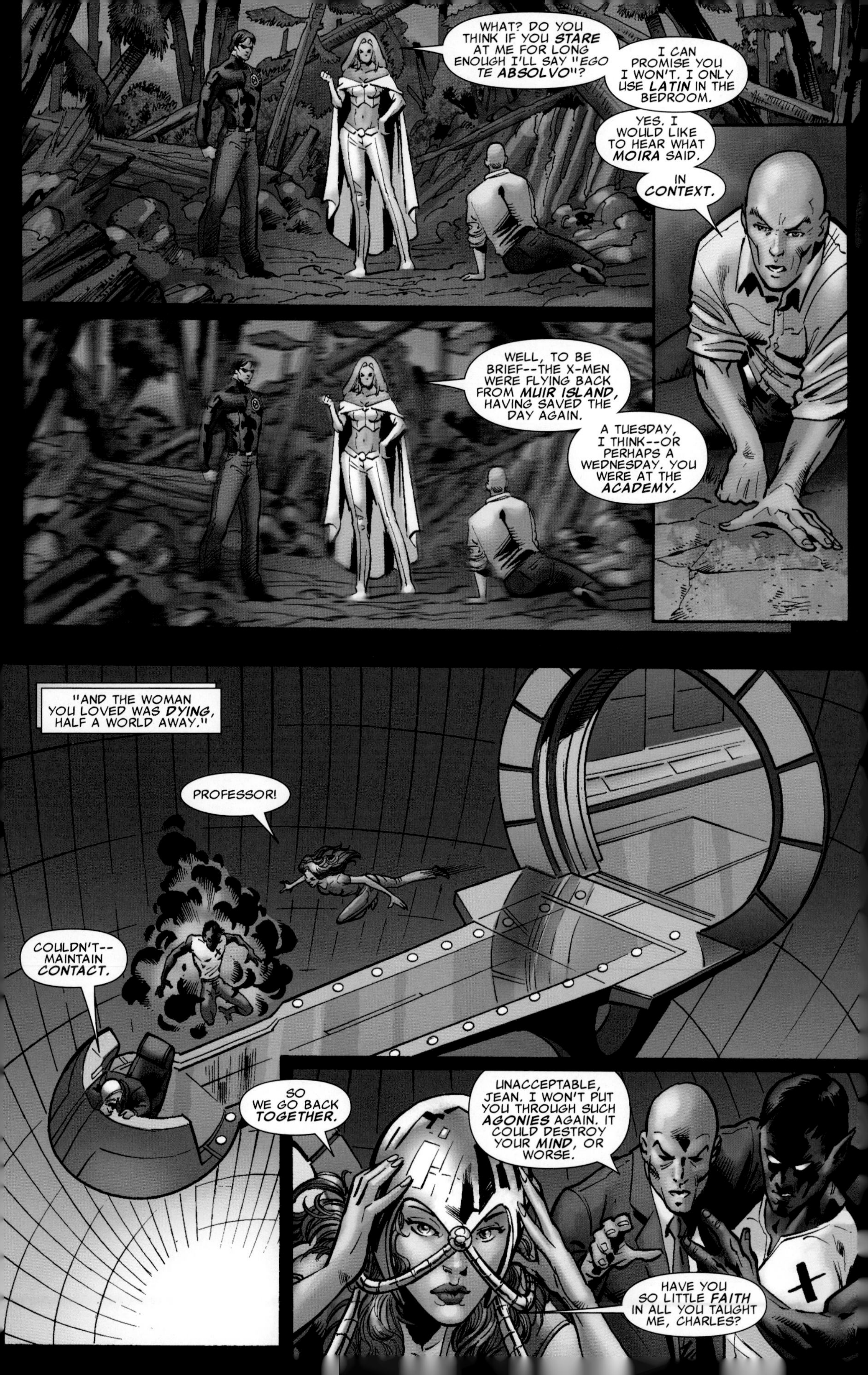
WHAT? DO YOU THINK IF YOU STARE AT ME FOR LONG ENOUGH I'LL SAY "EGO TE ABSOLVO"?
I CAN PROMISE YOU I WON'T. I ONLY USE LATIN IN THE BEDROOM.
YES. I WOULD LIKE TO HEAR WHAT MOIRA SAID.
IN CONTEXT.
WELL, TO BE BRIEF--THE X-MEN WERE FLYING BACK FROM MUIR ISLAND, HAVING SAVED THE DAY AGAIN.
A TUESDAY, I THINK--OR PERHAPS A WEDNESDAY. YOU WERE AT THE ACADEMY.
"AND THE WOMAN YOU LOVED WAS DYING, HALF A WORLD AWAY."
PROFESSOR!
COULDN'T-- MAINTAIN CONTACT.
SO WE GO BACK TOGETHER.
UNACCEPTABLE, JEAN. I WON'T PUT YOU THROUGH SUCH AGONIES AGAIN. IT COULD DESTROY YOUR MIND, OR WORSE.
HAVE YOU SO LITTLE FAITH IN ALL YOU TAUGHT ME, CHARLES?

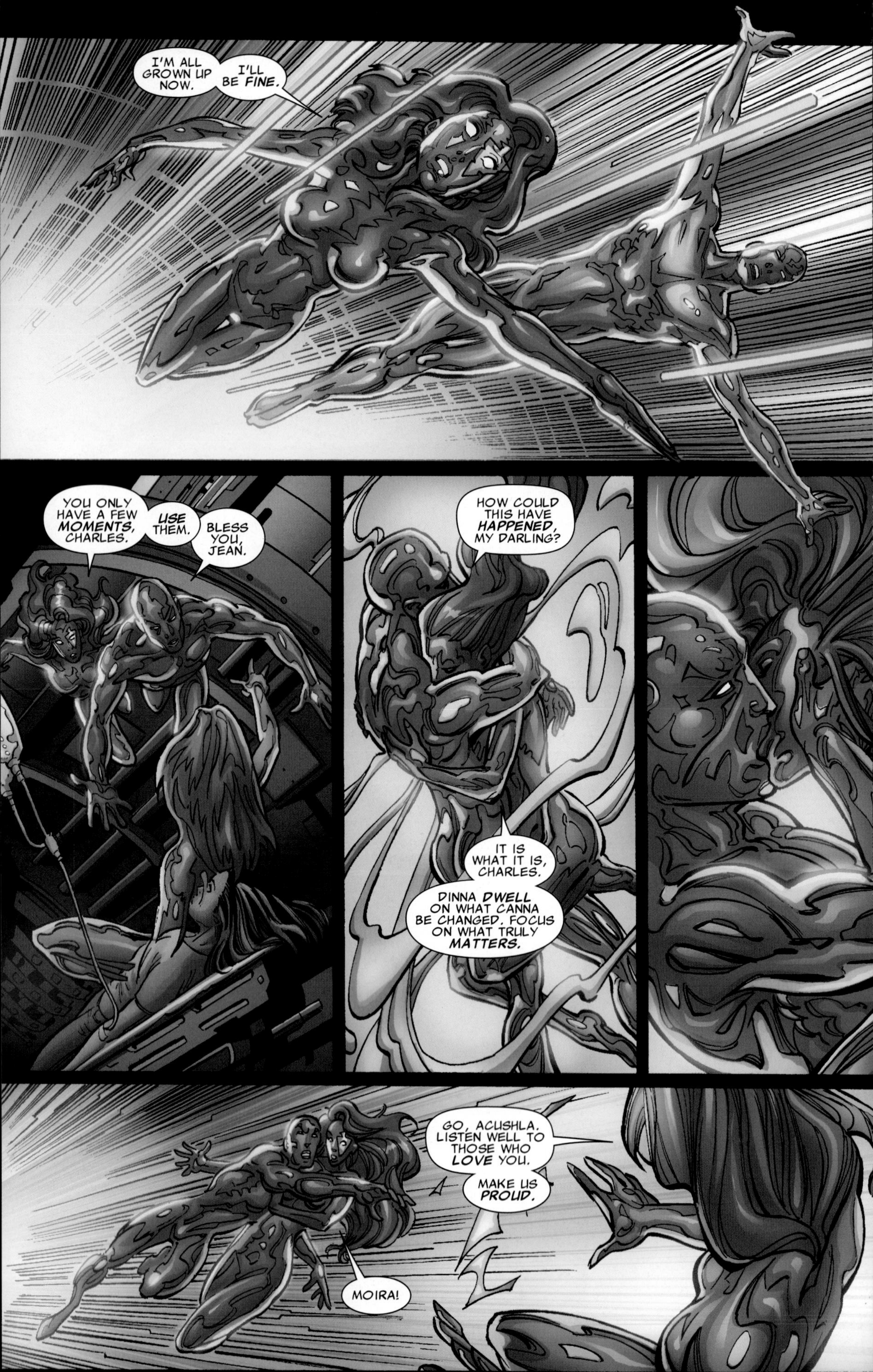
I'M ALL GROWN UP NOW.
I'LL BE FINE.
YOU ONLY HAVE A FEW MOMENTS, CHARLES.
USE THEM.
BLESS YOU, JEAN.
HOW COULD THIS HAVE HAPPENED, MY DARLING?
IT IS WHAT IT IS, CHARLES.
DINNA DWELL ON WHAT CANNA BE CHANGED. FOCUS ON WHAT TRULY MATTERS.
GO, ACUSHLA. LISTEN WELL TO THOSE WHO LOVE YOU.
MAKE US PROUD.
MOIRA!

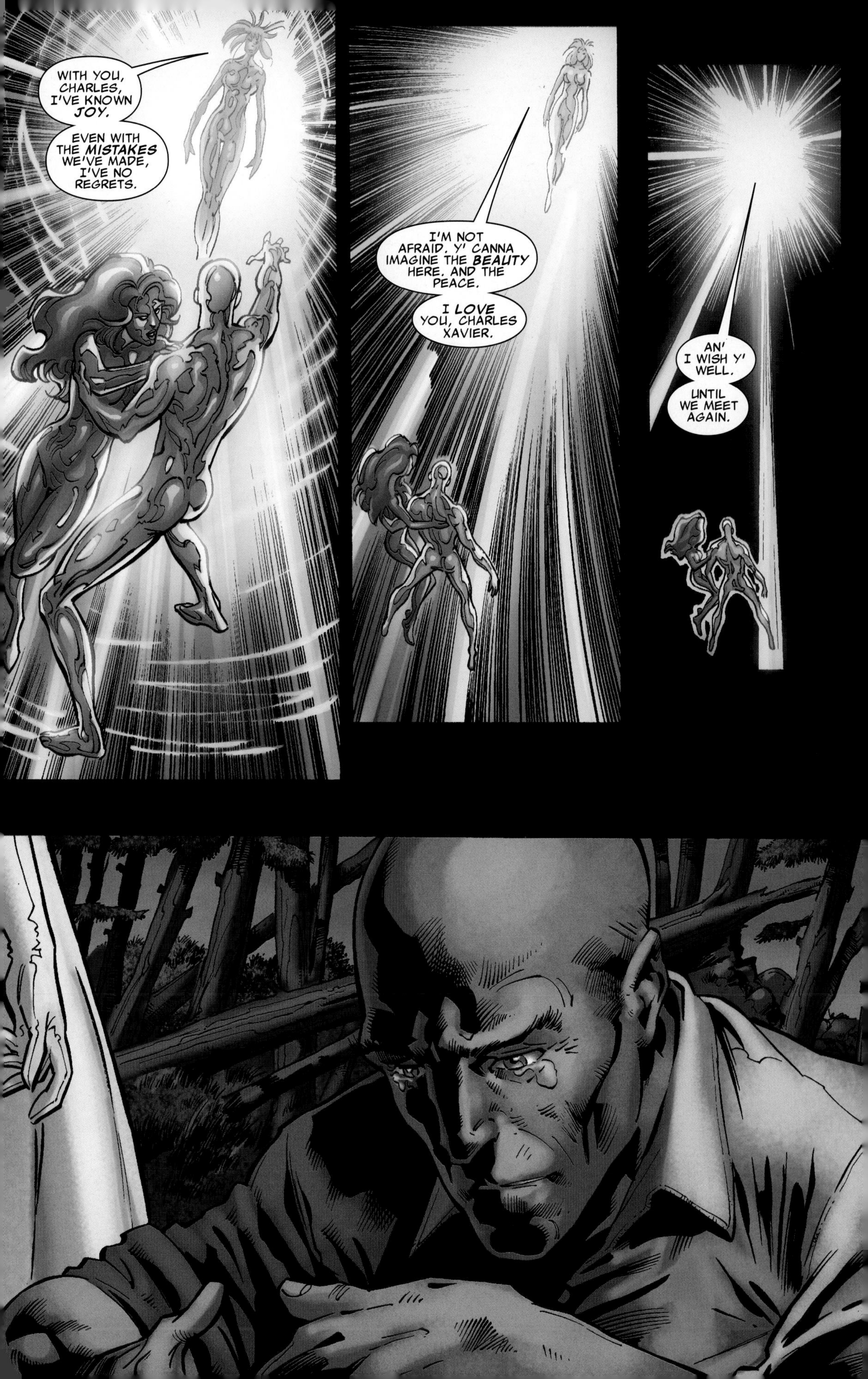
WITH YOU, CHARLES, I'VE KNOWN JOY.
EVEN WITH THE MISTAKES WE'VE MADE, I'VE NO REGRETS.
I'M NOT AFRAID. Y' CANNA IMAGINE THE BEAUTY HERE. AND THE PEACE.
I LOVE YOU, CHARLES XAVIER.
AN' I WISH Y' WELL.
UNTIL WE MEET AGAIN.

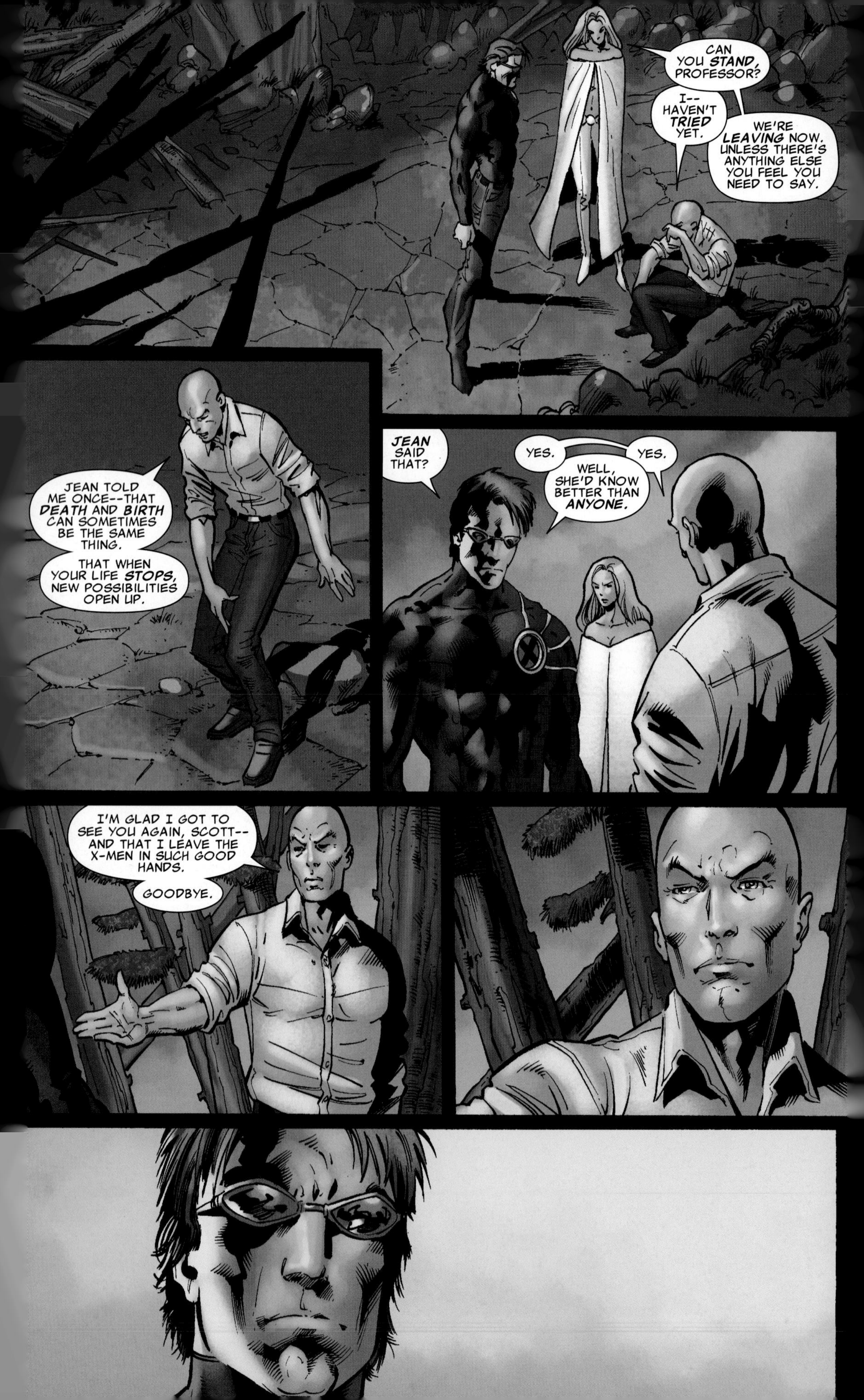
CAN YOU STAND, PROFESSOR?
I-- HAVEN'T TRIED YET.
WE'RE LEAVING NOW. UNLESS THERE'S ANYTHING ELSE YOU FEEL YOU NEED TO SAY.
JEAN TOLD ME ONCE--THAT DEATH AND BIRTH CAN SOMETIMES BE THE SAME THING.
THAT WHEN YOUR LIFE STOPS, NEW POSSIBILITIES OPEN UP.
JEAN SAID THAT?
YES.
YES.
WELL, SHE'D KNOW BETTER THAN ANYONE.
I'M GLAD I GOT TO SEE YOU AGAIN, SCOTT-- AND THAT I LEAVE THE X-MEN IN SUCH GOOD HANDS.
GOODBYE.

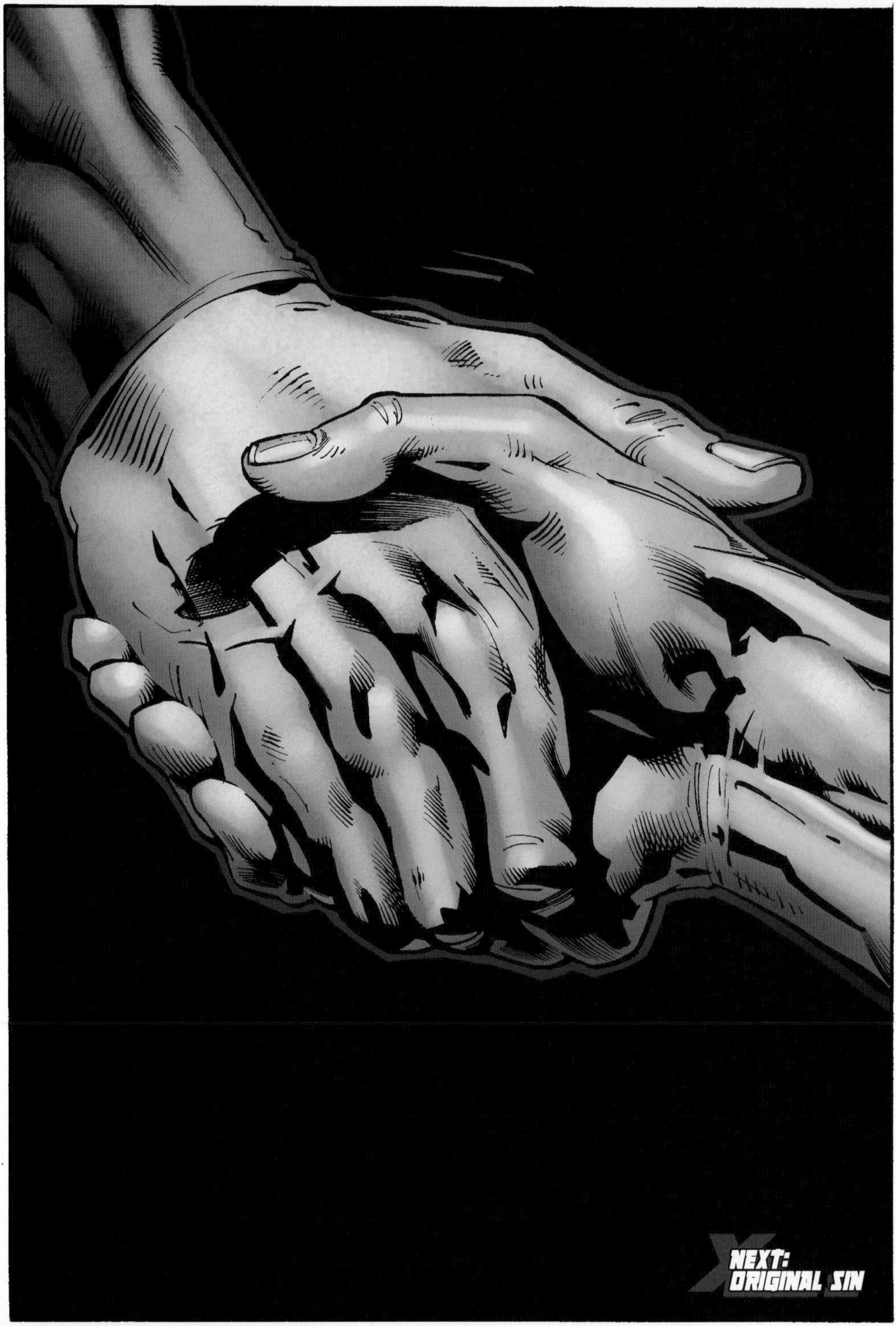
NEXT:
ORIGINAL SIN

THE MINDSCAPE PAPERS

The book you're reading covers the climax of the second Legacy storyline, "Sins of the Father", and the whole of the third, "Walkthrough". Both stories took to the limit the "mindscape" device that we'd been using to define Professor Xavier's quest on the page, to illustrate the way in which he was re-experiencing the memories of his past life as he recovered them. Each issue was basically a tapestry, weaving through a great deal of past X-Men continuity and tying it to the theme of Professor X's self-examination: his attempt to understand his own past actions and motivations.

When I was writing these issues, I had to layer in a lot of references to a lot of different X-Men stories, stretching back over four decades. Obviously this was a labour of love, in a lot of ways: I was choosing moments that had been significant in the life of Professor X, but I was also going for stories that had meant something to me as a reader. It's an armchair anthology of the stories that brought Charles Xavier to the fore as the creator and leader of the X-Men: his greatest hours, his blood and sweat and tears.

For completists, these notes comprise a list of the stories we referenced. If I've missed out something important, remember that I caught a ricochet from Bishop's bullet.

#213, SINS OF THE FATHER PART 3

P6&7: "I ordered Jean's silence…" This first scene is from *Uncanny #65*. Professor X was playing dead while he figured out a way to defeat the Z'Nox, and this was the issue where Marvel Girl and Havok spilled the beans to the rest of the team.

The second sequence ("Professor, can I talk to you?") is from the early heyday of the Claremont era — *Uncanny #129*. It's a fascinating example of how differently Professor Xavier and Cyclops approached the training and management of the new X-Men team. I can't read this page without thinking of Arthur Miller's *All My Sons*.

P10: "He took out part of your brain…" The origin of Gambit's association with Sinister, as portrayed in *Gambit* (3rd series) *#14*.

For Jacob Shaw's involvement with Mister Sinister, see the *X-Men: Hellfire Club* miniseries — especially *#3*. I don't think we ever learned until now what Sinister got out of that deal.

P13: Amanda Mueller's involvement in the Alamogordo project and her alliance with Sinister is documented in *X-Men Forever #4*. The visual of her sitting in the dark like a withered, ageless spider in a digital web, manipulating events from a distance, was one that stayed with me. Thank (or blame) Fabian Nicieza and penciler Kevin Maguire.

#214: SINS OF THE FATHER, PART 4

P1: Professor X originally gave this speech way, way, way back in *Uncanny #1*. He didn't repeat himself back then, though.

P7: This lovely splash brings together images from a whole lot of different places:

- Child Xavier being thrashed by Kurt Marko
- The hate-crime beating that almost killed Xavier in *UXM #192*
- Xavier's heart attack from *UXM #200*
- The shattering of Xavier's spine (second time around) in the Muir Island Saga
- Xavier on the cross from "Eve of Destruction"
- Xavier dying in Hank's arms in *XM #120* (I know, I know, it's actually Xavier's mind in Cassandra Nova's body.)
- Xavier being shot in the head by Bishop in the "Messiah Complex" Crossover

P10: Xavier took a bullet from Stryfe in *Uncanny #294*, the issue that launched The "X-Cutioner's Song". The bullet infected the Professor with the techno-organic virus, and there was all sorts of hell to pay.

P13: The reference here is to *Uncanny #167*, when the Brood queen that had been incubating in the Professor's body from the start of his relationship with the New Mutants finally hatched out. That was also the issue in which the X-Men came back to Earth after their own traumatic encounter with the Brood. Happy days.

P15: Xavier as Onslaught. Hmm. Not so happy days, for a reader of my era, but it had to be there.

#215: WALKTHROUGH, PART 1

P1: "I told my sister…" He did, but it was in another mindscape sequence, in *Legacy #211*, not in reality. The graduation photo is a reference to the events of *Uncanny #7*.

P2: "Maynards Plains". Okay, I just flat-out made that up. The X-Men took over the Reavers' ghost town HQ in *Uncanny #229*, but I couldn't find a single issue in which it was ever given a name.

The Rogue/Colossus scene takes place in *Uncanny #231*. I loved those playful moments when they came. It's amazing how seldom I write them, though.

P13: For young Scott Summers' exploits at the Nebraska orphanage, and for his relationship with Lefty, see *Classic X-Men #41*.

The image of Mister Sinister observing a ten-year-old Jean Grey isn't a specific flashback: it's just something I think we can assume to have happened, given his obsessive nature and what we know of his interest in her bloodline.

P16: This very poignant scene is in canon: I got it from *Uncanny #244*. I loved the tortured, twisted interplay between Rogue and Carol Danvers, and around about this time it was getting particularly fascinating.

#216: WALKTHROUGH, PART 2

P4: The first place where the story of Beast's joining the X-Men was told was as a back-up story in *Uncanny*, issues *#49-53*. I retold it recently in an *X-Men: Origins* book: this beat – Professor X erasing Hank McCoy from living memory – still amazes me. Okay, it was dreamed up in a more innocent age, but as an illustration of the sheer brute-force scale of Professor X's powers, this is the supreme example.

P7: The story I'm referencing here is in *Uncanny #171*. We see Rogue arriving at the mansion, and we see Professor X taking her away to his study for a one-to-one conversation. The content of that conversation was never revealed before this issue.

P11: Referencing the events of *Deadly Genesis #6*, although again we're seeing what happened between the moments that we saw there.

P13&14: The spread here is built around the theme of the most questionable and disturbing things that Professor X has done over the years. Xavier mind-wiping Magneto (from "Fatal Attractions" – *X-Men #25*) takes pride of place. Alongside this, we have:

- Xavier fighting Cassandra Nova in the womb.
- Xavier and the X-Men confronting Danger in the Savage Land, from the second Astonishing arc.
- Xavier stopping Amelia Voght from leaving him (only momentarily, but still…) from *UXM #309*.
- A non-canonical scene, teasing the events of "Original Sin" – Wolverine in classic yellow and black costume kneels at Xavier's feet, head thrown back, screaming to the skies, as Xavier stands over him, one hand raised, and works on his mind: brain surgery without a scalpel or anaesthetic.

P17: "Listen well to those who love you". To see this sequence, and the death of Moira MacTaggert, in its full narrative context, you should (you really should) obtain and read *X-Men #108*. It's part of the Muir Island Saga (well, "Dreams End") so it's got to have been reprinted somewhere.* Okay, you either get a lump in your throat at Moira's death or you don't, but I defy you not to be moved by the Xavier/Jean stuff.

P21: "Jean told me…" As with the Xavier-Cassandra dialogue, don't give yourself a nose-bleed looking for this one. I made it up, and put it into *Legacy #211*.

And that's it. In case I didn't say this already, writing this book draws a zig-zag line through so much of my own childhood that I almost feel it's my mind we're walking through. My big brother Chris gave me my first X-Men comic, and tore me off a strip because I creased the cover. I was seven years old, and kids still cleaned chimneys or went to work in mines.

My job is better.

—Mike Carey, *October 2008*

---

*It's reprinted in *X-Men: Dream's End!* On sale now! —Jen "Trade Monger" Grünwald

ALAN DAVIS COVER PROCESS

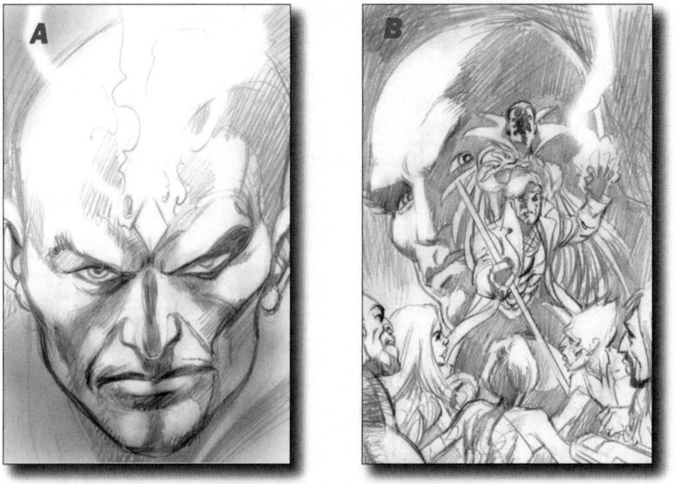
A
B

ISSUE #213 SKETCHES

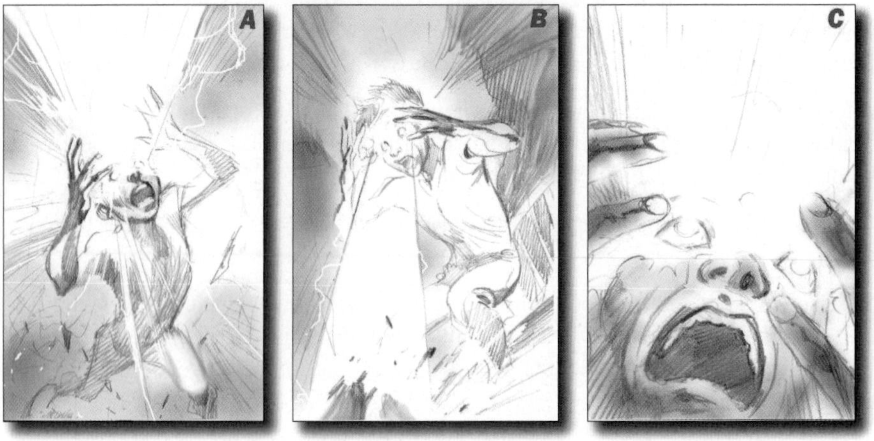
A
B
C

ISSUE #214 SKETCHES

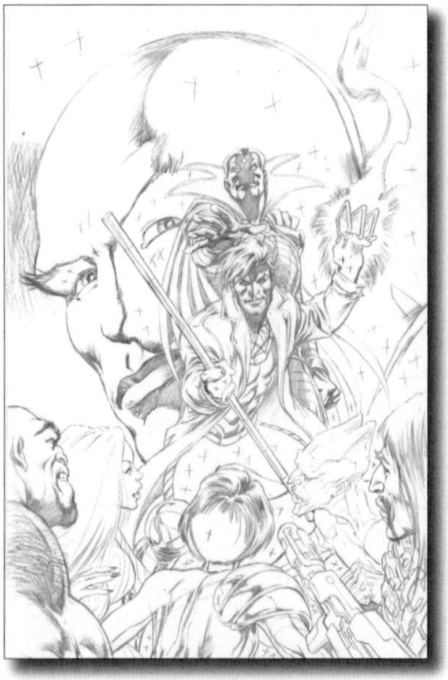

ISSUE #213 PENCILS

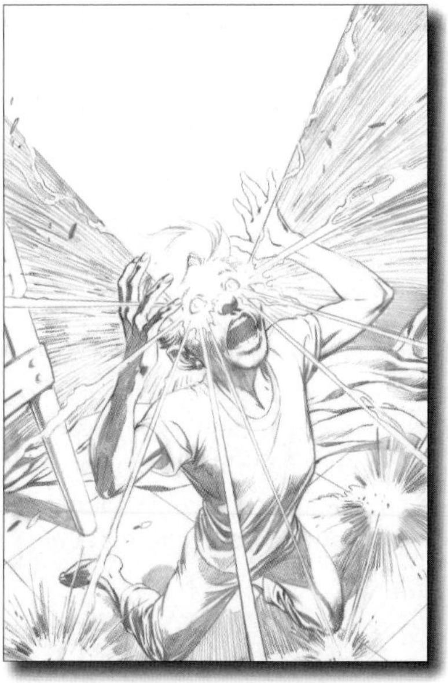

ISSUE #214 PENCILS

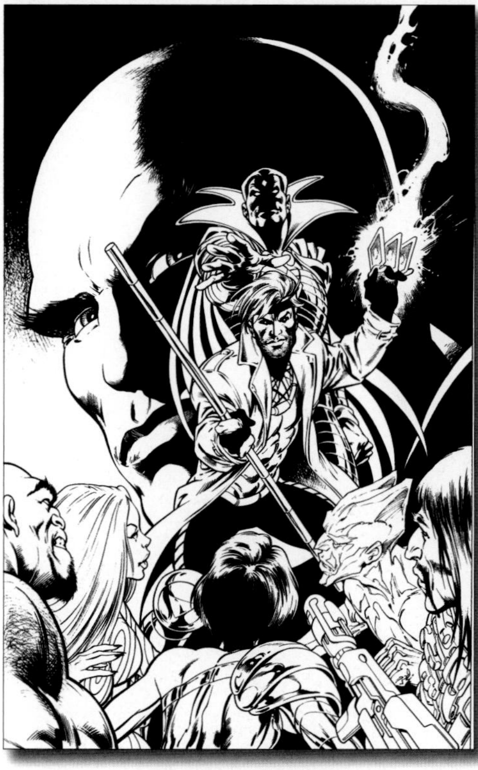

ISSUE #213 INKS

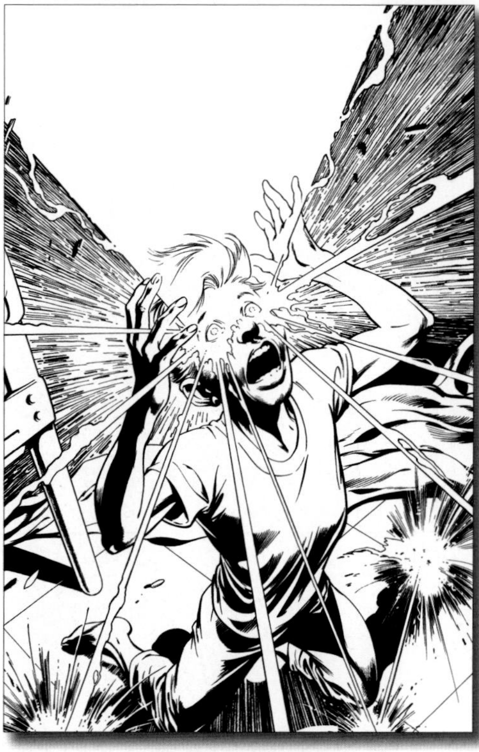

ISSUE #214 INKS

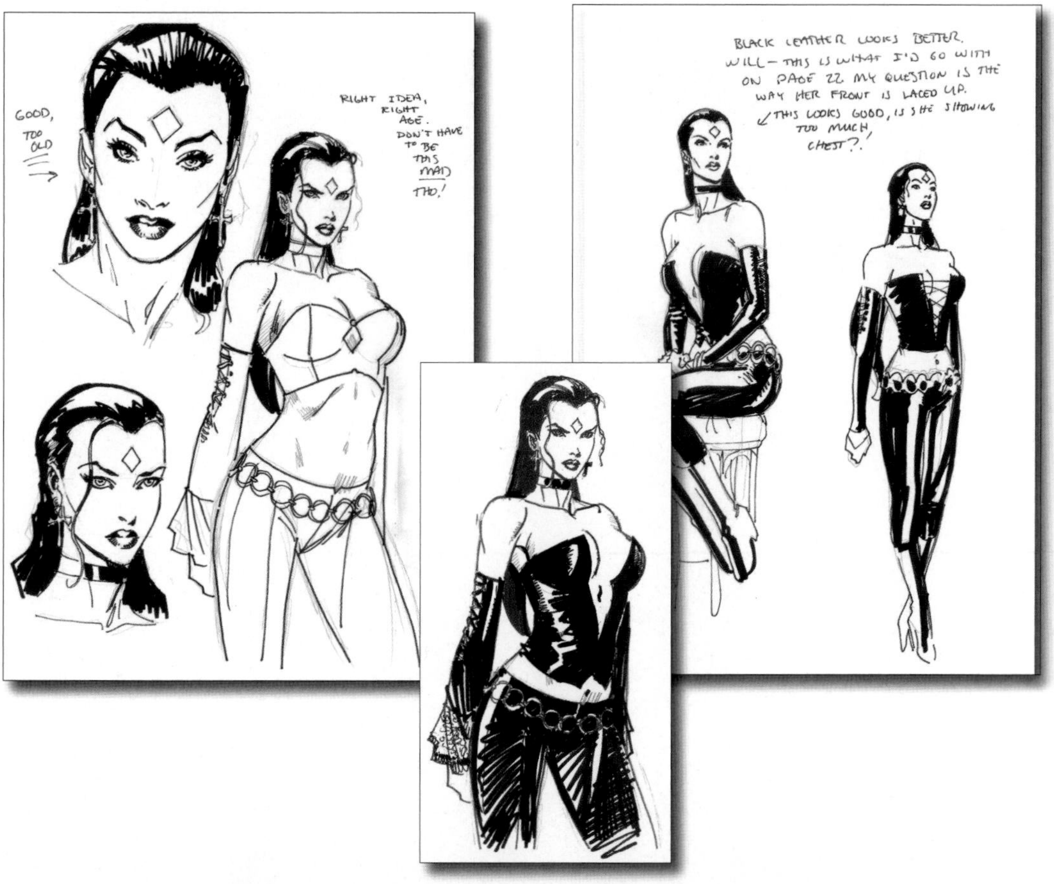
GOOD, TOO OLD
RIGHT IDEA, RIGHT AGE. DON'T HAVE TO BE THIS MAD THO,!
BLACK LEATHER LOOKS BETTER. WILL— THIS IS WHAT I'D GO WITH ON PAGE 22 MY QUESTION IS THE WAY HER FRONT IS LACED UP.
THIS LOOKS GOOD, IS SHE SHOWING TOO MUCH CHEST?!

MISS SINISTER CHARACTER SKETCHES BY SCOT EATON

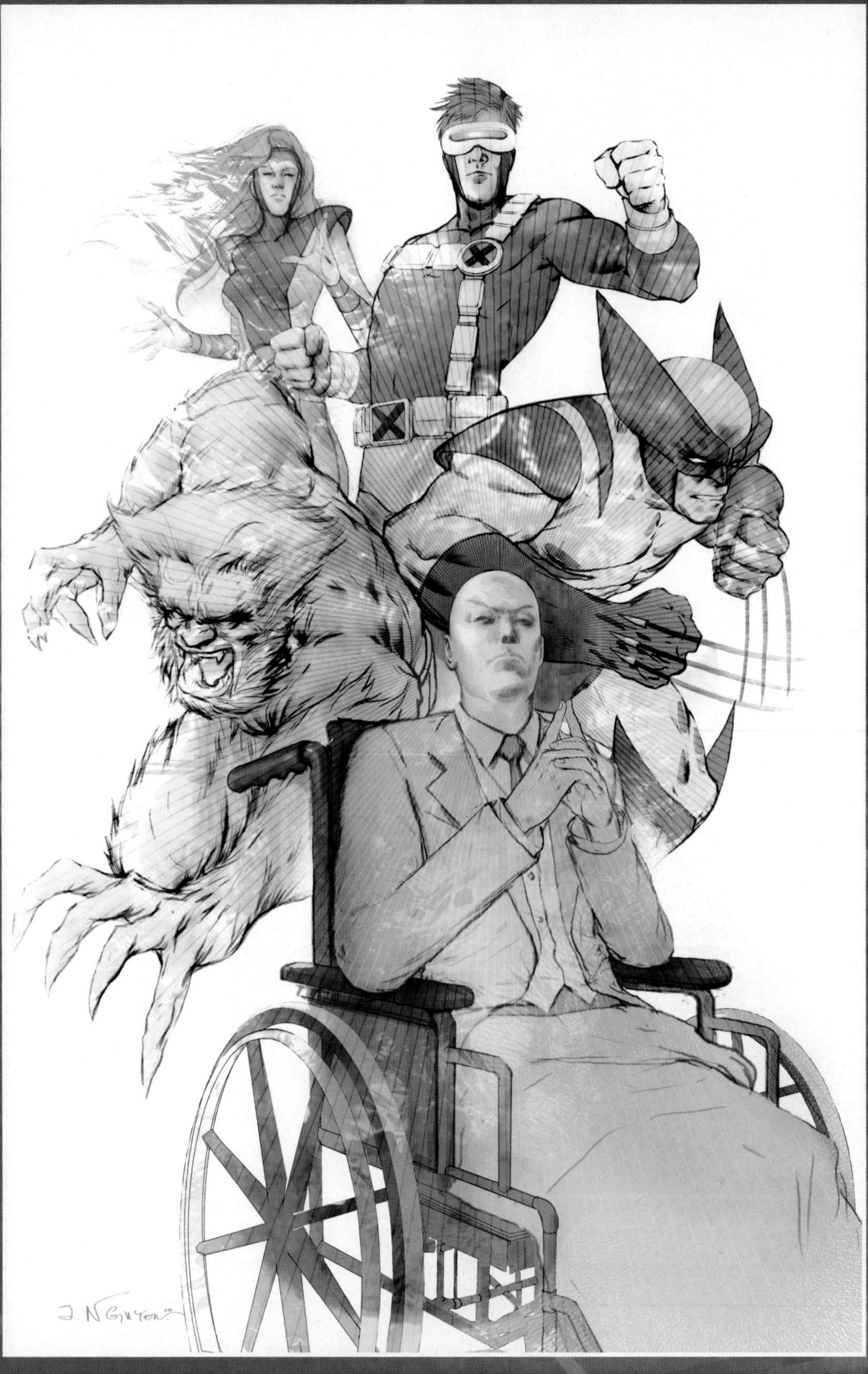

X-MEN: ODD MEN OUT

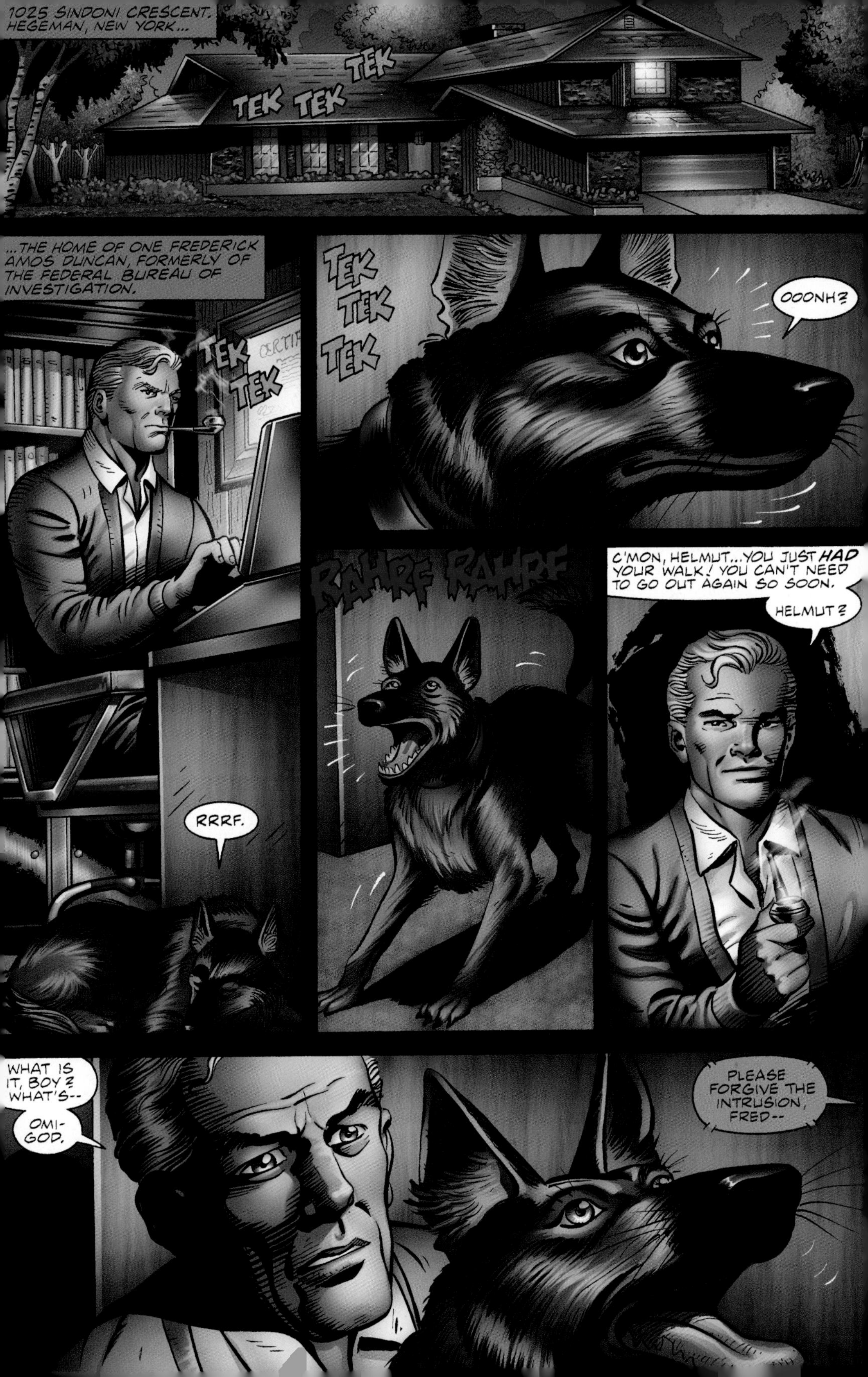
1025 SINDONI CRESCENT, HEGEMAN, NEW YORK...
TEK TEK TEK
...THE HOME OF ONE FREDERICK AMOS DUNCAN, FORMERLY OF THE FEDERAL BUREAU OF INVESTIGATION.
TEK TEK
RRRF.
TEK TEK TEK
OOONH?
RAHRF RAHRF
C'MON, HELMUT...YOU JUST HAD YOUR WALK! YOU CAN'T NEED TO GO OUT AGAIN SO SOON.
HELMUT?
WHAT IS IT, BOY? WHAT'S--
OMI-GOD.
PLEASE FORGIVE THE INTRUSION, FRED--

ODD MEN OUT

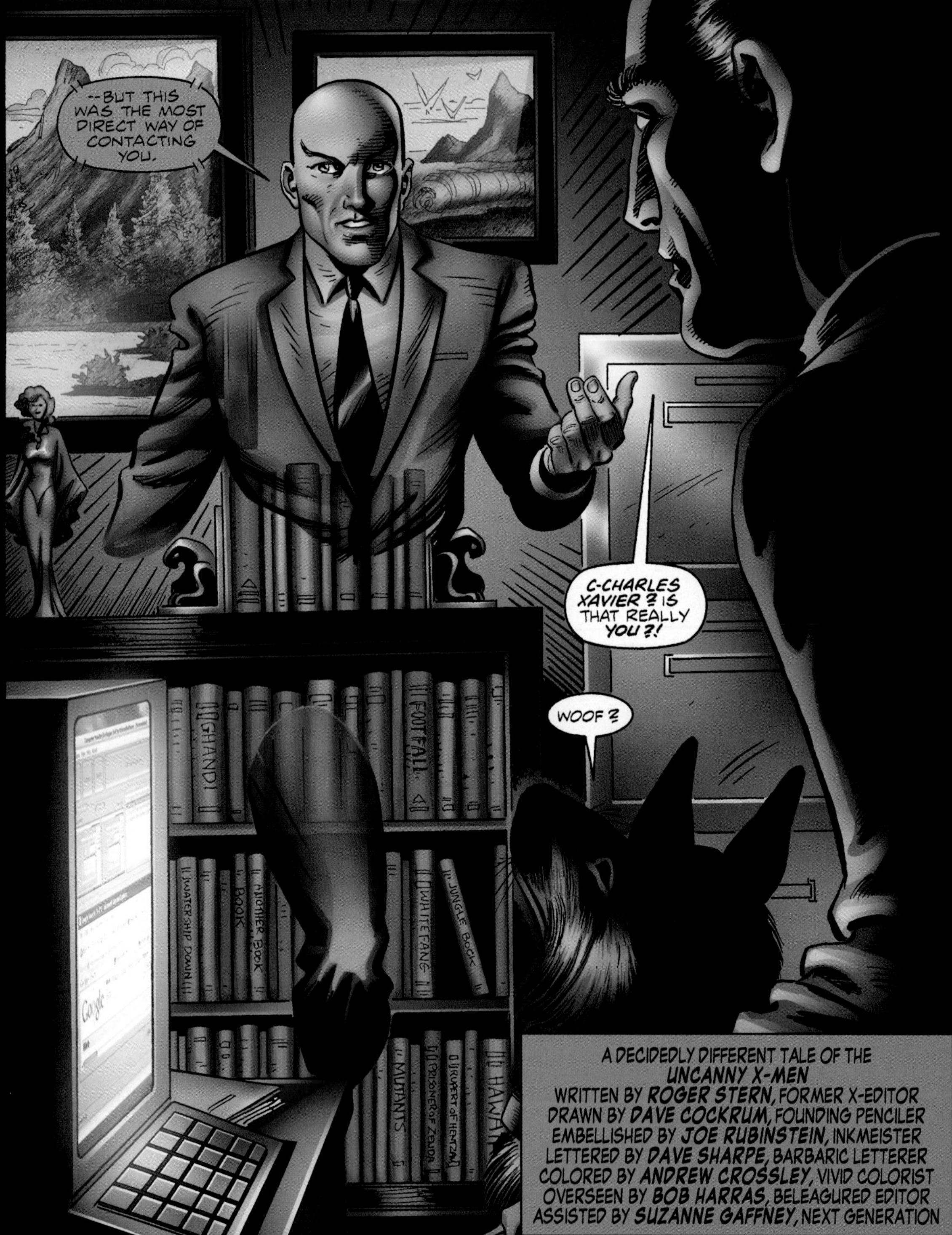

--BUT THIS WAS THE MOST DIRECT WAY OF CONTACTING YOU.
C-CHARLES XAVIER ?! IS THAT REALLY YOU ?!
WOOF ?
GHANDI
FOOTFALL
WATERSHIP DOWN
ANOTHER BOOK
BOOK
WHITE FANG
JUNGLE BOOK
MUTANTS
PRISONER OF ZENDA
RUPERT OF HENTZAU
HAWAII

A DECIDEDLY DIFFERENT TALE OF THE
UNCANNY X-MEN
WRITTEN BY ***ROGER STERN***, FORMER X-EDITOR
DRAWN BY ***DAVE COCKRUM***, FOUNDING PENCILER
EMBELLISHED BY ***JOE RUBINSTEIN***, INKMEISTER
LETTERED BY ***DAVE SHARPE***, BARBARIC LETTERER
COLORED BY ***ANDREW CROSSLEY***, VIVID COLORIST
OVERSEEN BY ***BOB HARRAS***, BELEAGURED EDITOR
ASSISTED BY ***SUZANNE GAFFNEY***, NEXT GENERATION

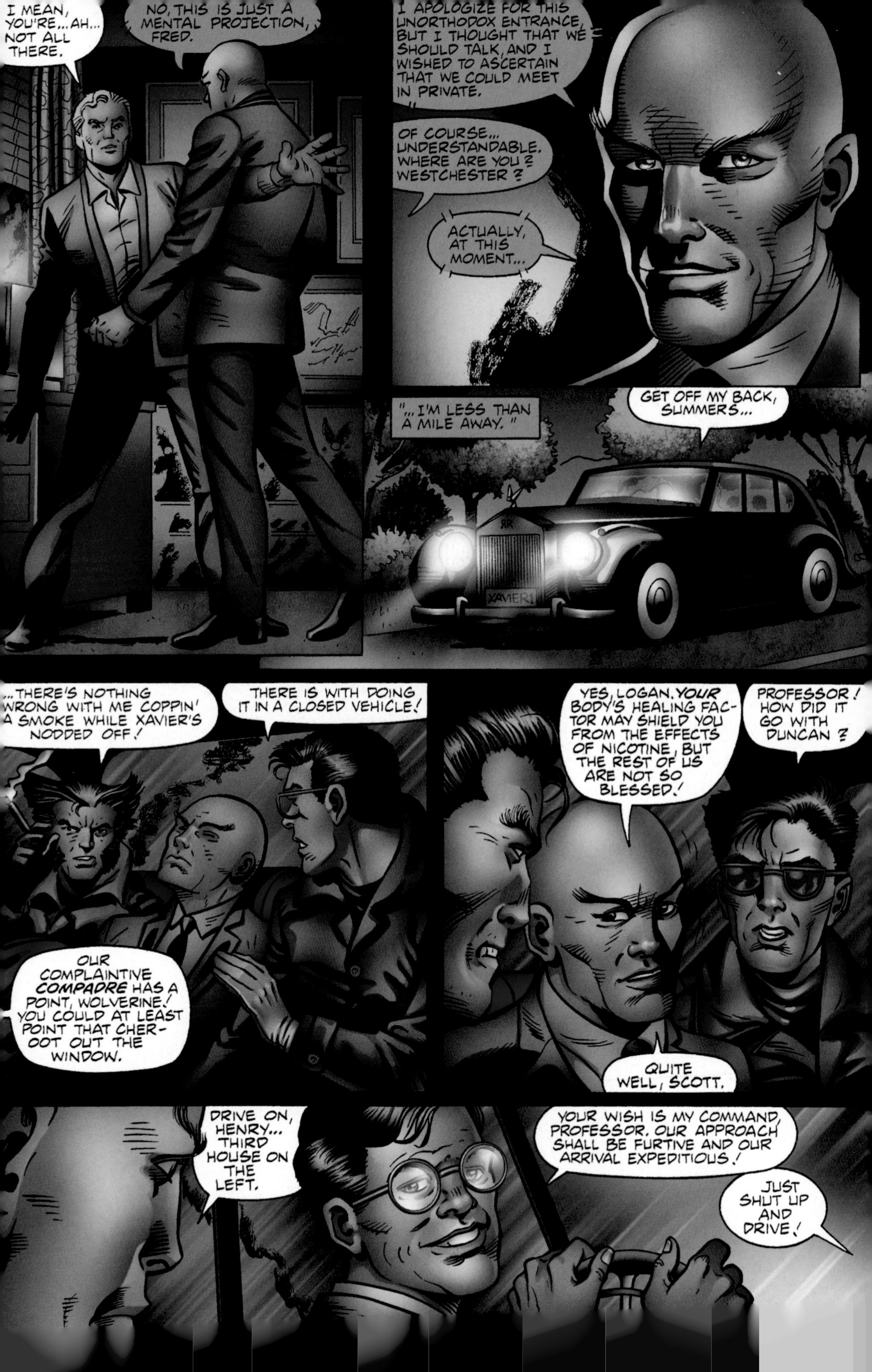
I MEAN, YOU'RE...AH... NOT ALL THERE.
NO, THIS IS JUST A MENTAL PROJECTION, FRED.
I APOLOGIZE FOR THIS UNORTHODOX ENTRANCE, BUT I THOUGHT THAT WE SHOULD TALK, AND I WISHED TO ASCERTAIN THAT WE COULD MEET IN PRIVATE.
OF COURSE... UNDERSTANDABLE. WHERE ARE YOU? WESTCHESTER?
ACTUALLY, AT THIS MOMENT...
"...I'M LESS THAN A MILE AWAY."
GET OFF MY BACK, SUMMERS...
XAVIER1
...THERE'S NOTHING WRONG WITH ME COPPIN' A SMOKE WHILE XAVIER'S NODDED OFF!
THERE IS WITH DOING IT IN A CLOSED VEHICLE!
OUR COMPLAINTIVE COMPADRE HAS A POINT, WOLVERINE! YOU COULD AT LEAST POINT THAT CHEROOT OUT THE WINDOW.
YES, LOGAN. YOUR BODY'S HEALING FACTOR MAY SHIELD YOU FROM THE EFFECTS OF NICOTINE, BUT THE REST OF US ARE NOT SO BLESSED!
PROFESSOR! HOW DID IT GO WITH DUNCAN?
QUITE WELL, SCOTT.
DRIVE ON, HENRY... THIRD HOUSE ON THE LEFT.
YOUR WISH IS MY COMMAND, PROFESSOR. OUR APPROACH SHALL BE FURTIVE AND OUR ARRIVAL EXPEDITIOUS!
JUST SHUT UP AND DRIVE!

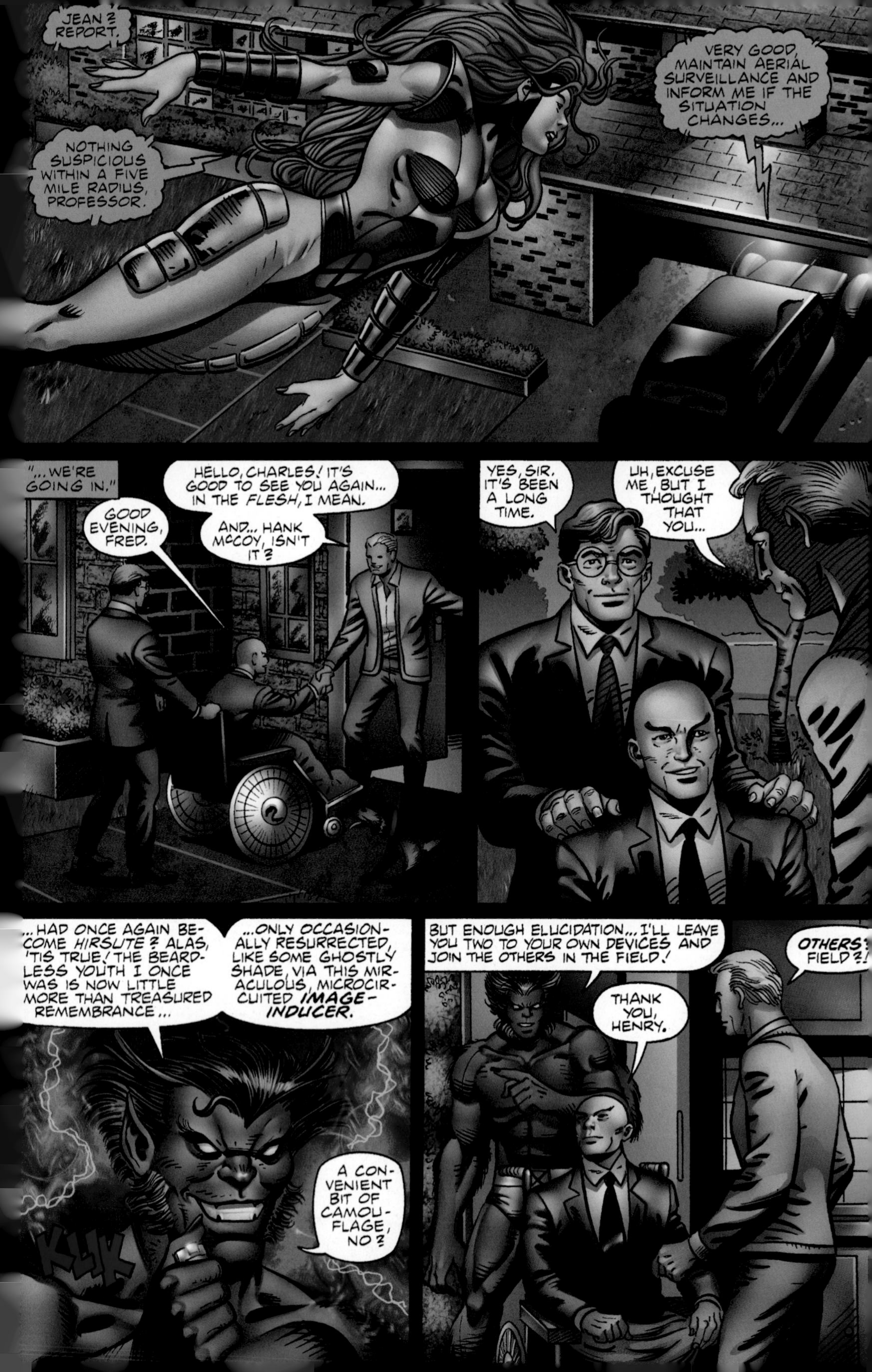
JEAN? REPORT.
NOTHING SUSPICIOUS WITHIN A FIVE MILE RADIUS, PROFESSOR.
VERY GOOD, MAINTAIN AERIAL SURVEILLANCE AND INFORM ME IF THE SITUATION CHANGES...
"...WE'RE GOING IN."
GOOD EVENING, FRED.
HELLO, CHARLES! IT'S GOOD TO SEE YOU AGAIN... IN THE *FLESH*, I MEAN.
AND... HANK McCOY, ISN'T IT?
YES, SIR. IT'S BEEN A LONG TIME.
UH, EXCUSE ME, BUT I THOUGHT THAT YOU...
...HAD ONCE AGAIN BECOME *HIRSUTE*? ALAS, 'TIS TRUE! THE BEARDLESS YOUTH I ONCE WAS IS NOW LITTLE MORE THAN TREASURED REMEMBRANCE...
...ONLY OCCASIONALLY RESURRECTED, LIKE SOME GHOSTLY SHADE, VIA THIS MIRACULOUS, MICROCIRCUITED *IMAGE-INDUCER*.
KLIK
A CONVENIENT BIT OF CAMOUFLAGE, NO?
BUT ENOUGH ELUCIDATION... I'LL LEAVE YOU TWO TO YOUR OWN DEVICES AND JOIN THE OTHERS IN THE FIELD!
THANK YOU, HENRY.
OTHERS? FIELD?!

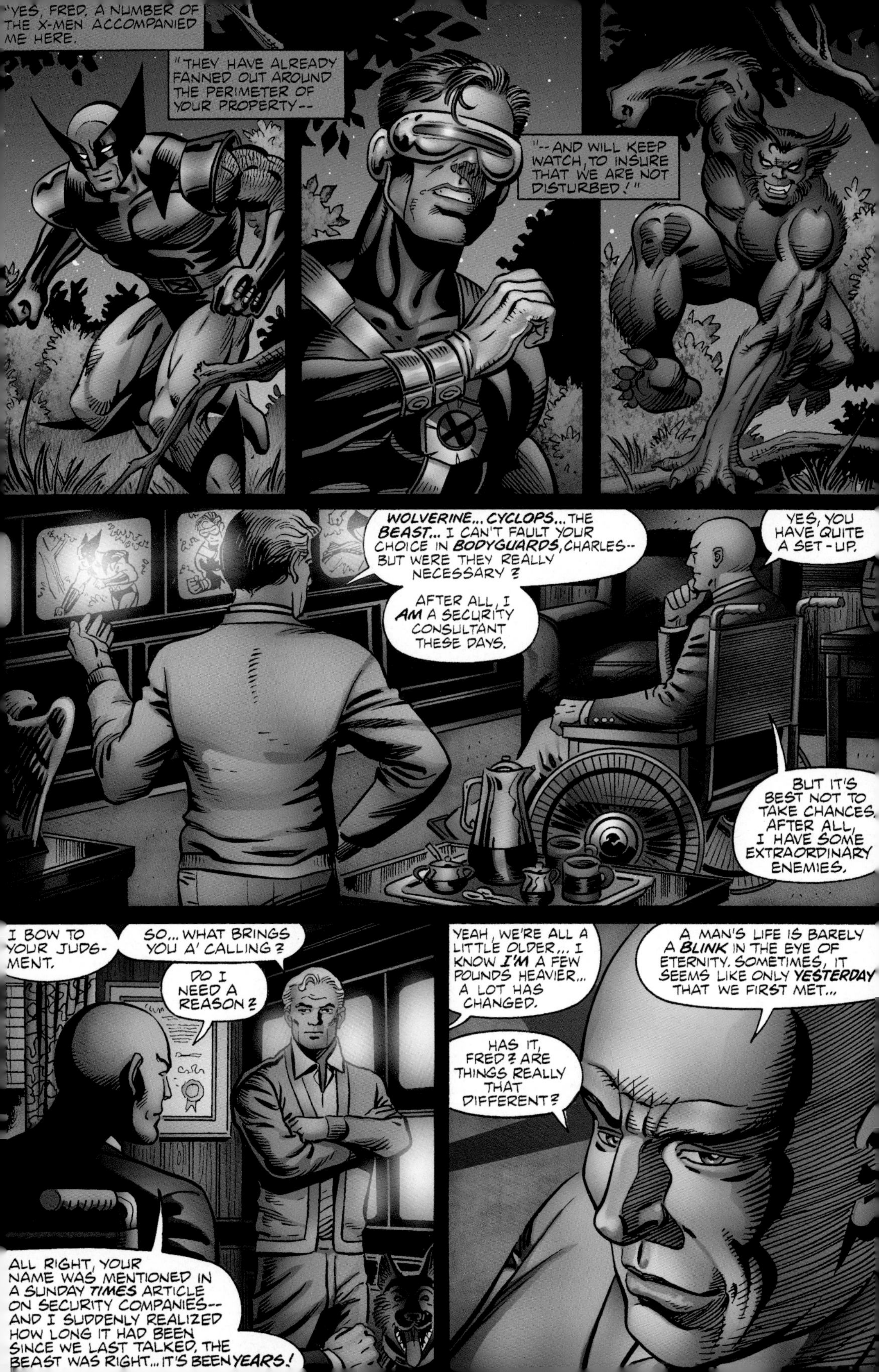
"YES, FRED. A NUMBER OF THE X-MEN ACCOMPANIED ME HERE.
"THEY HAVE ALREADY FANNED OUT AROUND THE PERIMETER OF YOUR PROPERTY--
"--AND WILL KEEP WATCH, TO INSURE THAT WE ARE NOT DISTURBED!"
WOLVERINE... CYCLOPS... THE BEAST... I CAN'T FAULT YOUR CHOICE IN BODYGUARDS, CHARLES-- BUT WERE THEY REALLY NECESSARY?
AFTER ALL, I AM A SECURITY CONSULTANT THESE DAYS.
YES, YOU HAVE QUITE A SET-UP.
BUT IT'S BEST NOT TO TAKE CHANCES. AFTER ALL, I HAVE SOME EXTRAORDINARY ENEMIES.
I BOW TO YOUR JUDGMENT.
SO... WHAT BRINGS YOU A' CALLING?
DO I NEED A REASON?
ALL RIGHT, YOUR NAME WAS MENTIONED IN A SUNDAY TIMES ARTICLE ON SECURITY COMPANIES-- AND I SUDDENLY REALIZED HOW LONG IT HAD BEEN SINCE WE LAST TALKED. THE BEAST WAS RIGHT... IT'S BEEN YEARS!
YEAH, WE'RE ALL A LITTLE OLDER... I KNOW I'M A FEW POUNDS HEAVIER... A LOT HAS CHANGED.
HAS IT, FRED? ARE THINGS REALLY THAT DIFFERENT?
A MAN'S LIFE IS BARELY A BLINK IN THE EYE OF ETERNITY. SOMETIMES, IT SEEMS LIKE ONLY YESTERDAY THAT WE FIRST MET...

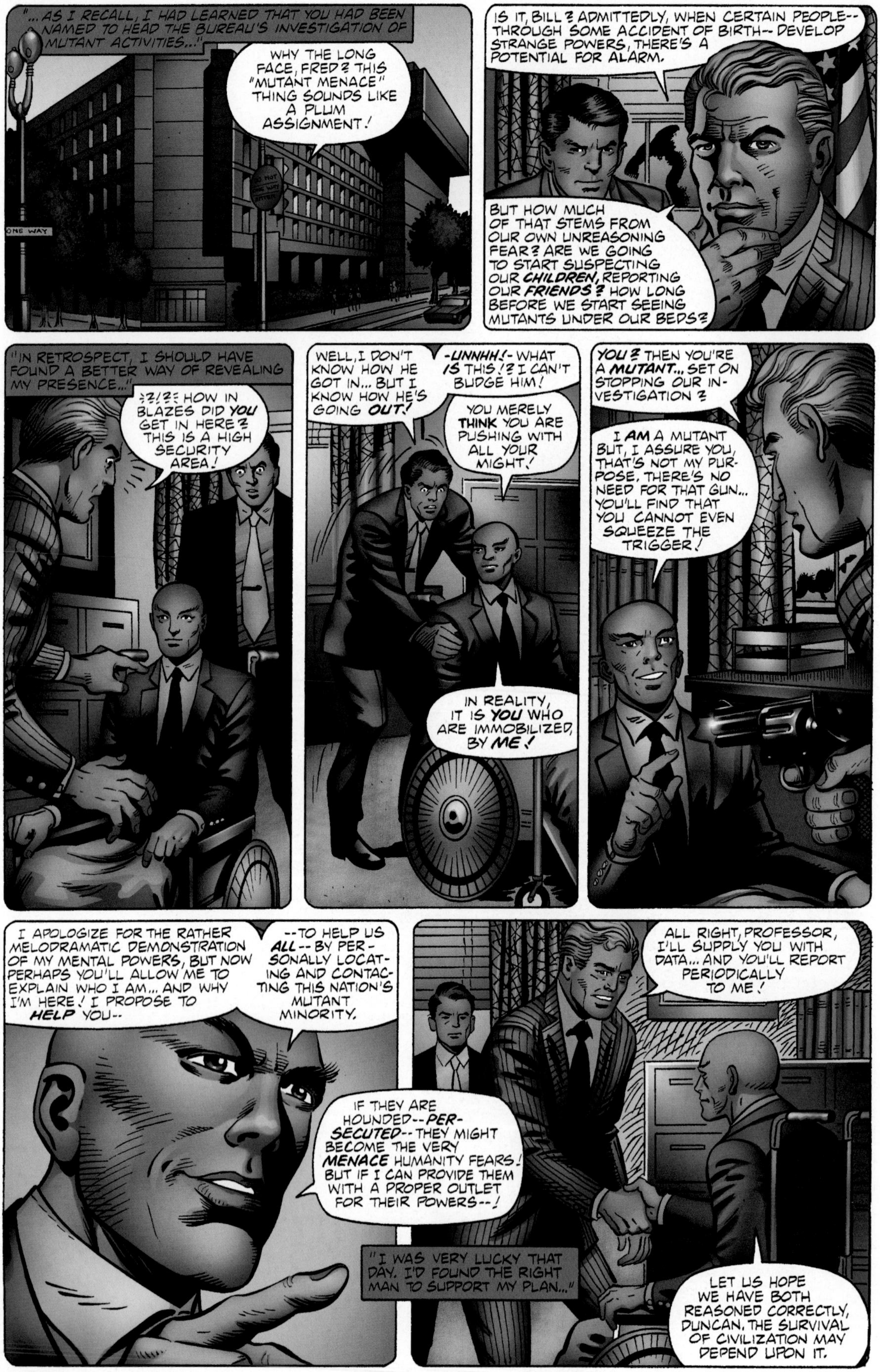
"...AS I RECALL, I HAD LEARNED THAT YOU HAD BEEN NAMED TO HEAD THE BUREAU'S INVESTIGATION OF MUTANT ACTIVITIES..."
WHY THE LONG FACE, FRED? THIS "MUTANT MENACE" THING SOUNDS LIKE A PLUM ASSIGNMENT!
ONE WAY
IS IT, BILL? ADMITTEDLY, WHEN CERTAIN PEOPLE--THROUGH SOME ACCIDENT OF BIRTH--DEVELOP STRANGE POWERS, THERE'S A POTENTIAL FOR ALARM.
BUT HOW MUCH OF THAT STEMS FROM OUR OWN UNREASONING FEAR? ARE WE GOING TO START SUSPECTING OUR CHILDREN, REPORTING OUR FRIENDS? HOW LONG BEFORE WE START SEEING MUTANTS UNDER OUR BEDS?
"IN RETROSPECT, I SHOULD HAVE FOUND A BETTER WAY OF REVEALING MY PRESENCE..."
?!?! HOW IN BLAZES DID YOU GET IN HERE? THIS IS A HIGH SECURITY AREA!
WELL, I DON'T KNOW HOW HE GOT IN... BUT I KNOW HOW HE'S GOING OUT!
-UNNHH!- WHAT IS THIS!? I CAN'T BUDGE HIM!
YOU MERELY THINK YOU ARE PUSHING WITH ALL YOUR MIGHT!
IN REALITY, IT IS YOU WHO ARE IMMOBILIZED, BY ME!
YOU? THEN YOU'RE A MUTANT... SET ON STOPPING OUR INVESTIGATION?
I AM A MUTANT BUT, I ASSURE YOU, THAT'S NOT MY PURPOSE. THERE'S NO NEED FOR THAT GUN... YOU'LL FIND THAT YOU CANNOT EVEN SQUEEZE THE TRIGGER!
I APOLOGIZE FOR THE RATHER MELODRAMATIC DEMONSTRATION OF MY MENTAL POWERS, BUT NOW PERHAPS YOU'LL ALLOW ME TO EXPLAIN WHO I AM... AND WHY I'M HERE! I PROPOSE TO HELP YOU--
--TO HELP US ALL--BY PERSONALLY LOCATING AND CONTACTING THIS NATION'S MUTANT MINORITY.
IF THEY ARE HOUNDED--PERSECUTED--THEY MIGHT BECOME THE VERY MENACE HUMANITY FEARS! BUT IF I CAN PROVIDE THEM WITH A PROPER OUTLET FOR THEIR POWERS--!
ALL RIGHT, PROFESSOR, I'LL SUPPLY YOU WITH DATA... AND YOU'LL REPORT PERIODICALLY TO ME!
"I WAS VERY LUCKY THAT DAY. I'D FOUND THE RIGHT MAN TO SUPPORT MY PLAN..."
LET US HOPE WE HAVE BOTH REASONED CORRECTLY, DUNCAN. THE SURVIVAL OF CIVILIZATION MAY DEPEND UPON IT.

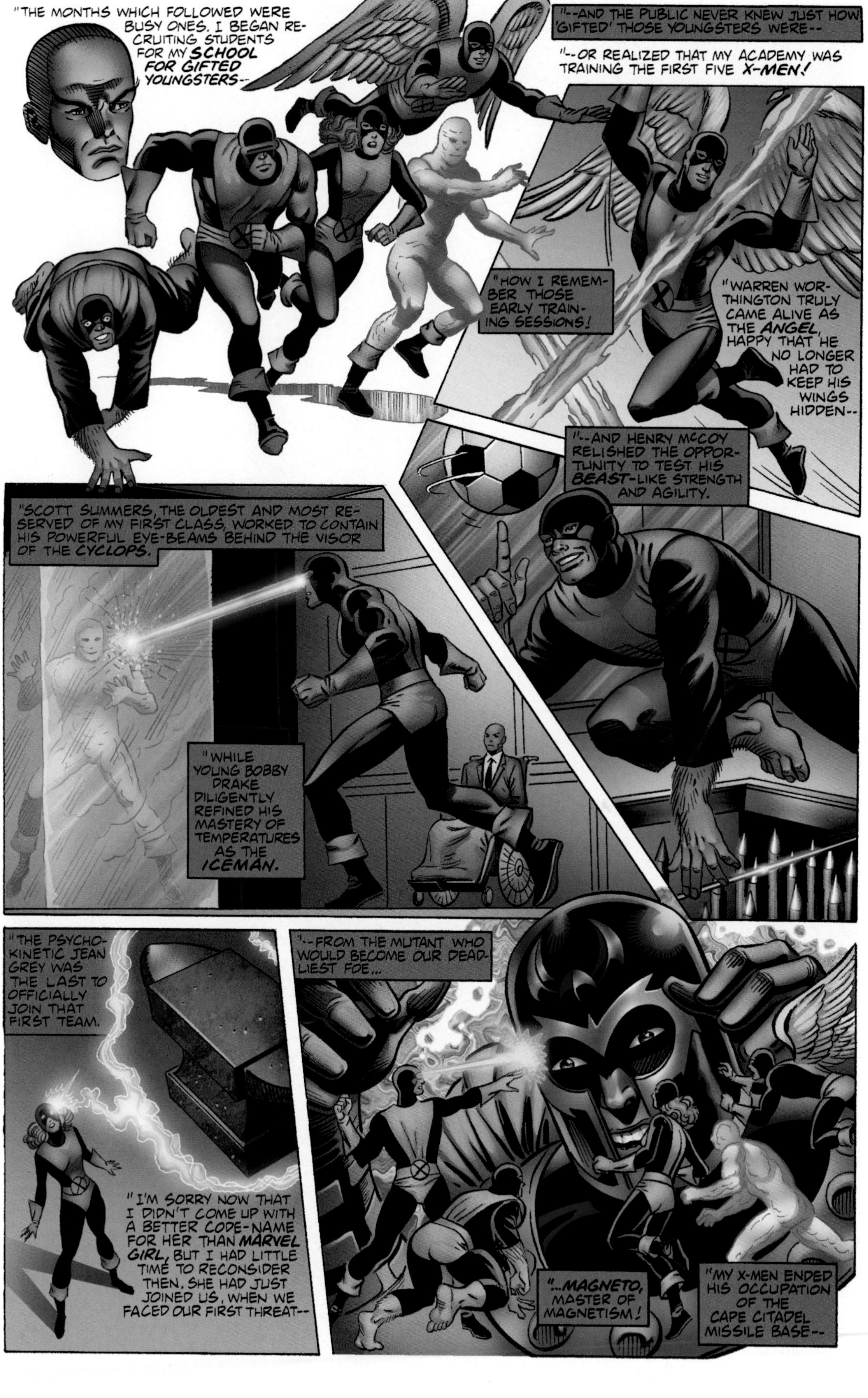
"THE MONTHS WHICH FOLLOWED WERE BUSY ONES. I BEGAN RECRUITING STUDENTS FOR MY SCHOOL FOR GIFTED YOUNGSTERS--
"--AND THE PUBLIC NEVER KNEW JUST HOW 'GIFTED' THOSE YOUNGSTERS WERE--
"--OR REALIZED THAT MY ACADEMY WAS TRAINING THE FIRST FIVE X-MEN!
"HOW I REMEMBER THOSE EARLY TRAINING SESSIONS!
"WARREN WORTHINGTON TRULY CAME ALIVE AS THE ANGEL, HAPPY THAT HE NO LONGER HAD TO KEEP HIS WINGS HIDDEN--
"--AND HENRY McCOY RELISHED THE OPPORTUNITY TO TEST HIS BEAST-LIKE STRENGTH AND AGILITY.
"SCOTT SUMMERS, THE OLDEST AND MOST RESERVED OF MY FIRST CLASS, WORKED TO CONTAIN HIS POWERFUL EYE-BEAMS BEHIND THE VISOR OF THE CYCLOPS.
"WHILE YOUNG BOBBY DRAKE DILIGENTLY REFINED HIS MASTERY OF TEMPERATURES AS THE ICEMAN.
"THE PSYCHOKINETIC JEAN GREY WAS THE LAST TO OFFICIALLY JOIN THAT FIRST TEAM.
"I'M SORRY NOW THAT I DIDN'T COME UP WITH A BETTER CODE-NAME FOR HER THAN MARVEL GIRL, BUT I HAD LITTLE TIME TO RECONSIDER THEN. SHE HAD JUST JOINED US, WHEN WE FACED OUR FIRST THREAT--
"--FROM THE MUTANT WHO WOULD BECOME OUR DEADLIEST FOE...
"...MAGNETO, MASTER OF MAGNETISM!
"MY X-MEN ENDED HIS OCCUPATION OF THE CAPE CITADEL MISSILE BASE--

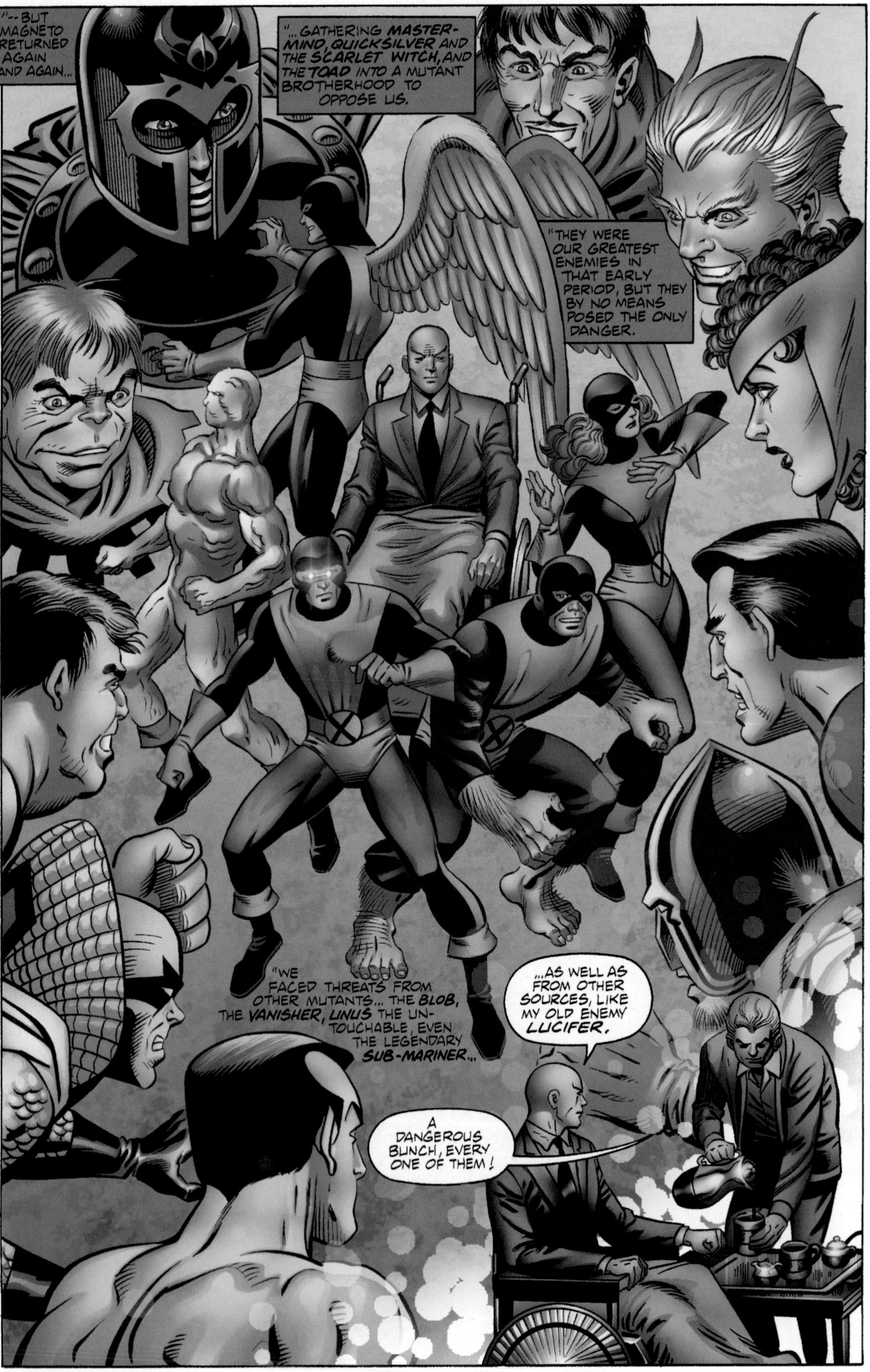
"--BUT MAGNETO RETURNED AGAIN AND AGAIN...
"...GATHERING MASTERMIND, QUICKSILVER AND THE SCARLET WITCH, AND THE TOAD INTO A MUTANT BROTHERHOOD TO OPPOSE US.
"THEY WERE OUR GREATEST ENEMIES IN THAT EARLY PERIOD, BUT THEY BY NO MEANS POSED THE ONLY DANGER.
"WE FACED THREATS FROM OTHER MUTANTS... THE BLOB, THE VANISHER, LINUS THE UNTOUCHABLE, EVEN THE LEGENDARY SUB-MARINER...
...AS WELL AS FROM OTHER SOURCES, LIKE MY OLD ENEMY LUCIFER.
A DANGEROUS BUNCH, EVERY ONE OF THEM!

YOU CAN BE PROUD, CHARLES. YOUR KIDS FACED SOME OF THE TOUGHEST OPPONENTS THAT EVER WALKED THE EARTH--AND *WON* EVERY TIME!

NOT *EVERY* TIME, FRED. THEY NEVER TOTALLY OVERCAME MAGNETO.

MAYBE NOT, BUT THEY ALWAYS MANAGED TO SAVE THE DAY.

YOU TRAINED THEM SO WELL THAT THEY WERE EVEN ABLE TO GET ALONG WITHOUT YOU. I'LL NEVER FORGET THAT TIME...

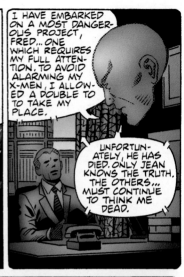

I HAVE EMBARKED ON A MOST DANGEROUS PROJECT, FRED... ONE WHICH REQUIRES MY FULL ATTENTION. TO AVOID ALARMING MY X-MEN, I ALLOWED A DOUBLE TO TAKE MY PLACE.

UNFORTUNATELY, HE HAS DIED. ONLY JEAN KNOWS THE TRUTH. THE OTHERS... MUST CONTINUE TO THINK ME DEAD.

"I FOLLOWED YOUR WISHES, AND PAID THEM A VISIT AT YOUR 'GRAVE-SITE'..."

PARDON MY INTRUSION... BUT IT'S URGENT THAT I TALK WITH YOU.

"WE WENT BACK TO YOUR MANSION, BUT BEFORE WE COULD GET DOWN TO TERMS, THERE WAS A MAJOR INTERRUPTION CALLED... *JUGGERNAUT!*"

"HE LOOKED LIKE HALF-A-TON OF PURE RAGE. I THOUGHT IT WAS ALL OVER, BUT SOMEHOW YOUR KIDS' DEALT WITH HIM.

"ONCE THAT WAS OVER, I GAVE THEM MY SONG AND DANCE, ORDERING THEM TO SPLIT UP INTO SMALLER UNITS AND SPREAD OUT ACROSS THE COUNTRY.

"AS THEY STOOD THERE, IN THEIR NEW OUTFITS, I TRIED NOT TO LOOK MS. GREY IN THE EYE. I KNEW THAT SHE WAS KEEPING YOUR SECRET--

"--AND HAD SUSPECTED THE REAL REASON FOR MY ORDER...

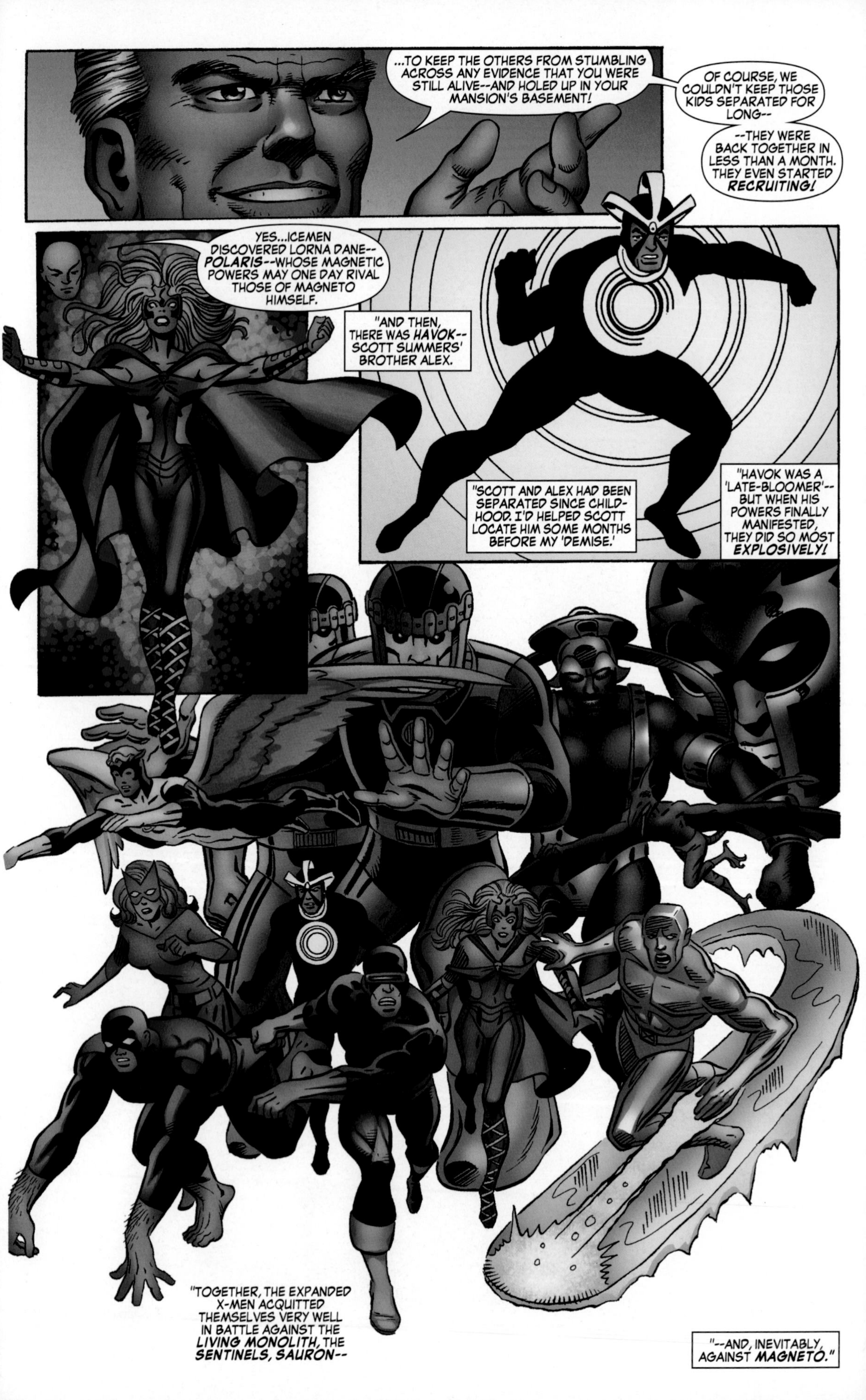
...TO KEEP THE OTHERS FROM STUMBLING ACROSS ANY EVIDENCE THAT YOU WERE STILL ALIVE--AND HOLED UP IN YOUR MANSION'S BASEMENT!
OF COURSE, WE COULDN'T KEEP THOSE KIDS SEPARATED FOR LONG--
--THEY WERE BACK TOGETHER IN LESS THAN A MONTH. THEY EVEN STARTED RECRUITING!
YES...ICEMEN DISCOVERED LORNA DANE--POLARIS--WHOSE MAGNETIC POWERS MAY ONE DAY RIVAL THOSE OF MAGNETO HIMSELF.
"AND THEN, THERE WAS HAVOK--SCOTT SUMMERS' BROTHER ALEX.
"SCOTT AND ALEX HAD BEEN SEPARATED SINCE CHILD-HOOD. I'D HELPED SCOTT LOCATE HIM SOME MONTHS BEFORE MY 'DEMISE.'
"HAVOK WAS A 'LATE-BLOOMER'--BUT WHEN HIS POWERS FINALLY MANIFESTED, THEY DID SO MOST EXPLOSIVELY!
"TOGETHER, THE EXPANDED X-MEN ACQUITTED THEMSELVES VERY WELL IN BATTLE AGAINST THE LIVING MONOLITH, THE SENTINELS, SAURON--
"--AND, INEVITABLY, AGAINST MAGNETO."

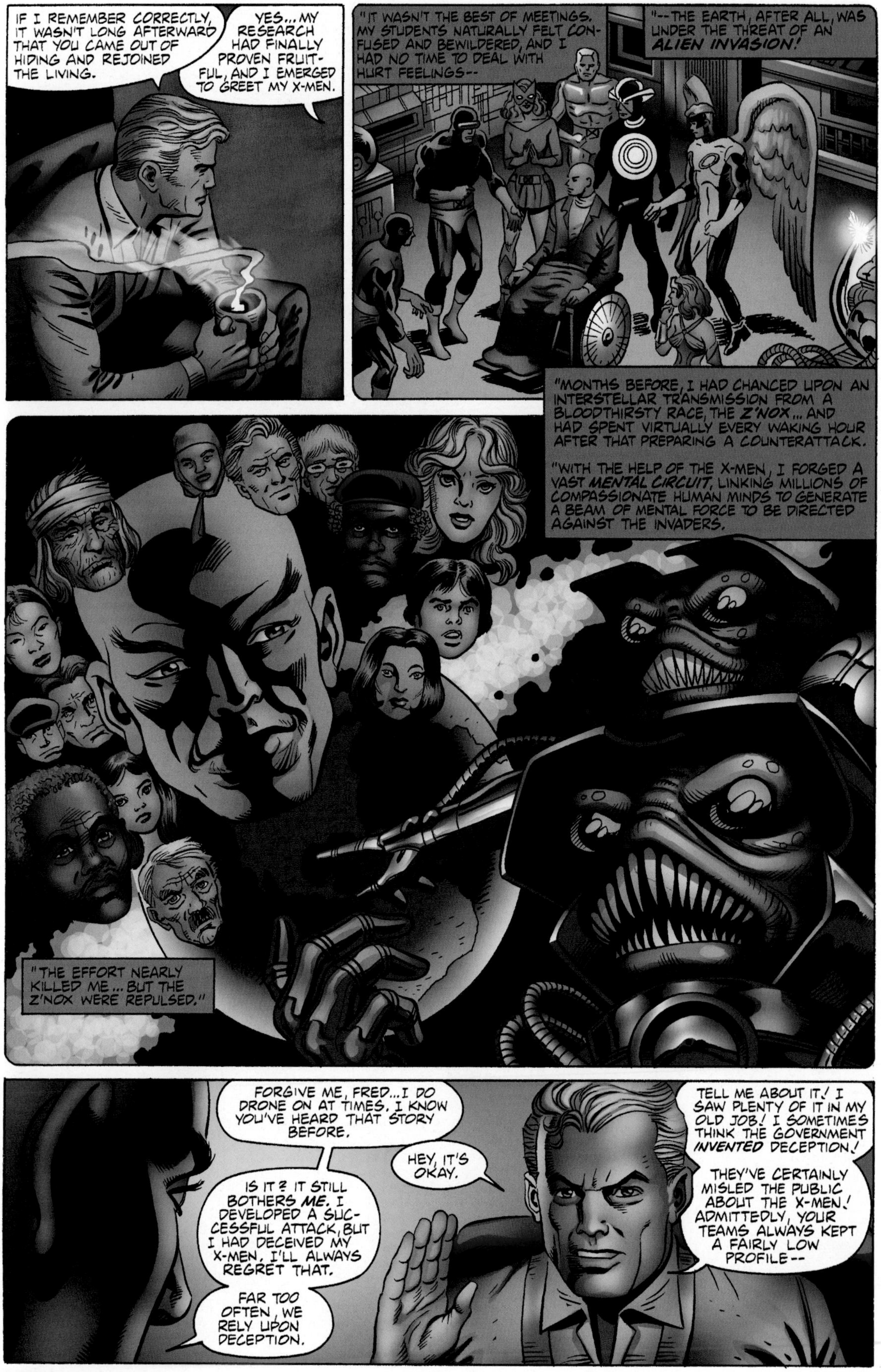
IF I REMEMBER CORRECTLY, IT WASN'T LONG AFTERWARD THAT YOU CAME OUT OF HIDING AND REJOINED THE LIVING.
YES... MY RESEARCH HAD FINALLY PROVEN FRUIT-FUL, AND I EMERGED TO GREET MY X-MEN.
"IT WASN'T THE BEST OF MEETINGS. MY STUDENTS NATURALLY FELT CON-FUSED AND BEWILDERED, AND I HAD NO TIME TO DEAL WITH HURT FEELINGS--
"--THE EARTH, AFTER ALL, WAS UNDER THE THREAT OF AN ALIEN INVASION!
"MONTHS BEFORE, I HAD CHANCED UPON AN INTERSTELLAR TRANSMISSION FROM A BLOODTHIRSTY RACE, THE Z'NOX... AND HAD SPENT VIRTUALLY EVERY WAKING HOUR AFTER THAT PREPARING A COUNTERATTACK.
"WITH THE HELP OF THE X-MEN, I FORGED A VAST MENTAL CIRCUIT, LINKING MILLIONS OF COMPASSIONATE HUMAN MINDS TO GENERATE A BEAM OF MENTAL FORCE TO BE DIRECTED AGAINST THE INVADERS.
"THE EFFORT NEARLY KILLED ME... BUT THE Z'NOX WERE REPULSED."
FORGIVE ME, FRED... I DO DRONE ON AT TIMES. I KNOW YOU'VE HEARD THAT STORY BEFORE.
HEY, IT'S OKAY.
IS IT? IT STILL BOTHERS ME. I DEVELOPED A SUC-CESSFUL ATTACK, BUT I HAD DECEIVED MY X-MEN. I'LL ALWAYS REGRET THAT.
FAR TOO OFTEN, WE RELY UPON DECEPTION.
TELL ME ABOUT IT! I SAW PLENTY OF IT IN MY OLD JOB! I SOMETIMES THINK THE GOVERNMENT INVENTED DECEPTION!
THEY'VE CERTAINLY MISLED THE PUBLIC ABOUT THE X-MEN! ADMITTEDLY, YOUR TEAMS ALWAYS KEPT A FAIRLY LOW PROFILE--

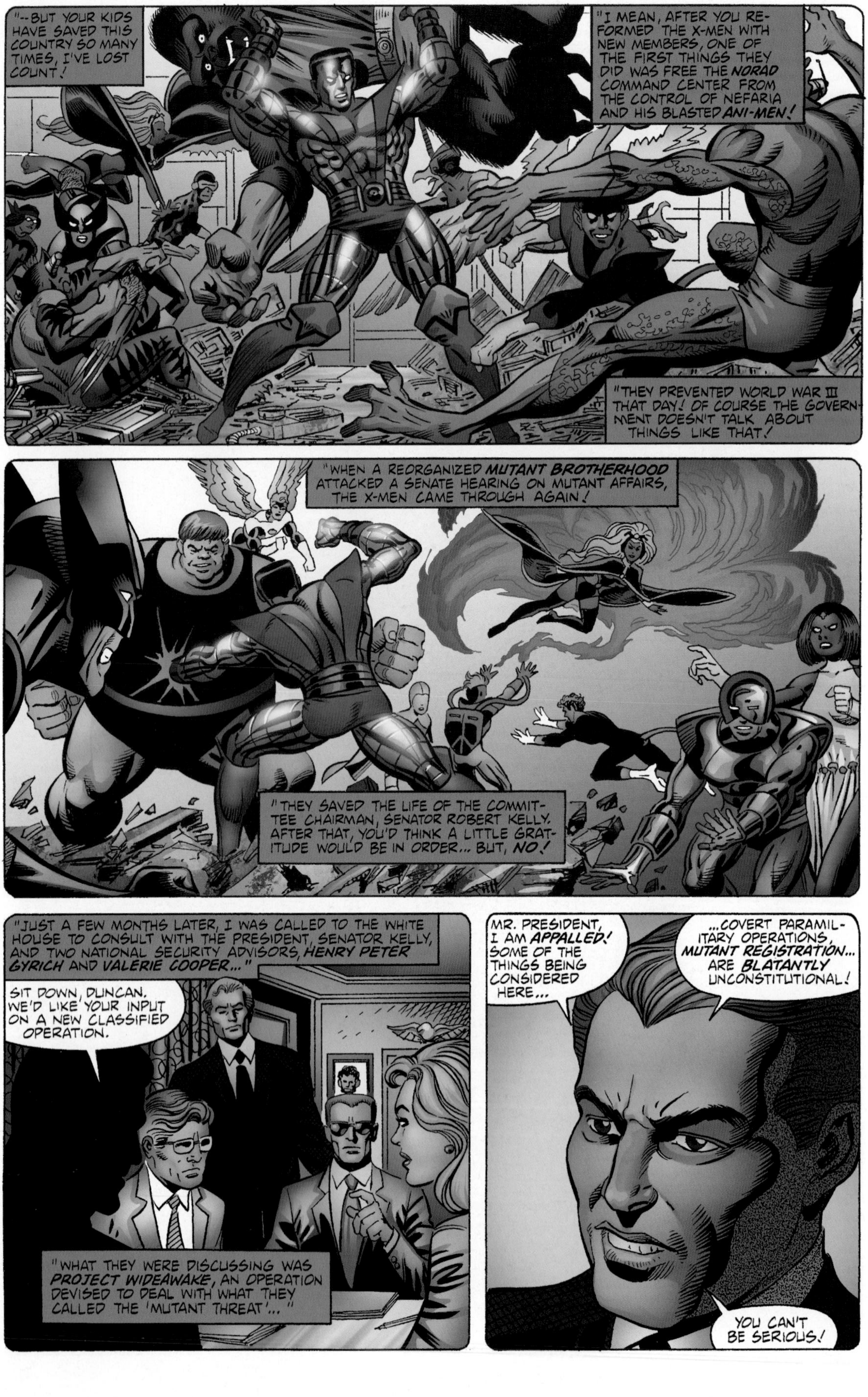
"--BUT YOUR KIDS HAVE SAVED THIS COUNTRY SO MANY TIMES, I'VE LOST COUNT!
"I MEAN, AFTER YOU RE-FORMED THE X-MEN WITH NEW MEMBERS, ONE OF THE FIRST THINGS THEY DID WAS FREE THE NORAD COMMAND CENTER FROM THE CONTROL OF NEFARIA AND HIS BLASTED ANI-MEN!
"THEY PREVENTED WORLD WAR III THAT DAY! OF COURSE THE GOVERNMENT DOESN'T TALK ABOUT THINGS LIKE THAT!
"WHEN A REORGANIZED MUTANT BROTHERHOOD ATTACKED A SENATE HEARING ON MUTANT AFFAIRS, THE X-MEN CAME THROUGH AGAIN!
"THEY SAVED THE LIFE OF THE COMMITTEE CHAIRMAN, SENATOR ROBERT KELLY. AFTER THAT, YOU'D THINK A LITTLE GRATITUDE WOULD BE IN ORDER... BUT, NO!
"JUST A FEW MONTHS LATER, I WAS CALLED TO THE WHITE HOUSE TO CONSULT WITH THE PRESIDENT, SENATOR KELLY, AND TWO NATIONAL SECURITY ADVISORS, HENRY PETER GYRICH AND VALERIE COOPER..."
SIT DOWN, DUNCAN. WE'D LIKE YOUR INPUT ON A NEW CLASSIFIED OPERATION.
"WHAT THEY WERE DISCUSSING WAS PROJECT WIDEAWAKE, AN OPERATION DEVISED TO DEAL WITH WHAT THEY CALLED THE 'MUTANT THREAT'..."
MR. PRESIDENT, I AM APPALLED! SOME OF THE THINGS BEING CONSIDERED HERE...
...COVERT PARAMILITARY OPERATIONS, MUTANT REGISTRATION... ARE BLATANTLY UNCONSTITUTIONAL!
YOU CAN'T BE SERIOUS!

WELL, NOW HOLD ON THERE, FRED... WE'RE NOT ABOUT TO GO VIOLATING THE RIGHTS OF ANY GOOD CITIZEN!

WE'RE JUST TRYING TO MAKE CONTINGENCIES FOR DEALING WITH THREATS TO NATIONAL SECURITY. AMERICA HARDLY HAS A MONOPOLY ON MUTANTS, NOW DO WE?

NO, SIR, BUT--!

"I PUT UP THE BEST ARGUMENT I COULD...

"...BUT INEVITABLY, I WAS DISMISSED. I GOT THE PICTURE THAT, WHATEVER PLANS THE ADMINISTRATION HAD IN REGARD TO MUTANTS--

"--I WAS GOING TO BE OUT OF THE LOOP. GYRICH AND COOPER CLEARLY HAD THE PRESIDENT'S EAR...

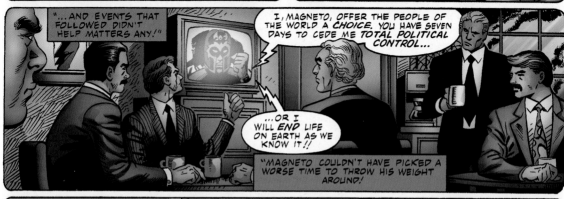

"...AND EVENTS THAT FOLLOWED DIDN'T HELP MATTERS ANY!"

I, MAGNETO, OFFER THE PEOPLE OF THE WORLD A *CHOICE*. YOU HAVE SEVEN DAYS TO CEDE ME *TOTAL POLITICAL CONTROL*...

...OR I WILL *END* LIFE ON EARTH AS WE KNOW IT!!

"MAGNETO COULDN'T HAVE PICKED A WORSE TIME TO THROW HIS WEIGHT AROUND!"

"I HEARD FROM YOU LATER HOW THE X-MEN WRECKED THAT LITTLE PLAN OF HIS. AND THEN, I DIDN'T HEAR ANY MORE UNTIL, ONE DAY..."

WHAT IN BLAZES IS GOING ON, DUNCAN?!

--?!?!

SPECIAL AGENT FRED DUNCAN

NICE TO SEE YOU TOO, GYRICH! TO WHAT DO I OWE THE PLEASURE?

ARE YOU TELLING ME THAT YOU *DON'T* KNOW?!

KNOW *WHAT*?

TRY ACCESSING YOUR FILES ON THE X-MEN... *JUST TRY!*

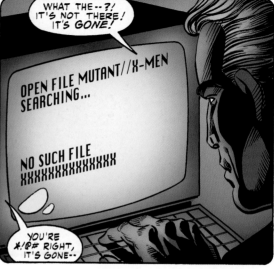

WHAT THE--?! IT'S NOT THERE! IT'S GONE!

OPEN FILE MUTANT//X-MEN
SEARCHING...

NO SUCH FILE
XXXXXXXXXXXXXX

YOU'RE *!@# RIGHT, IT'S GONE--

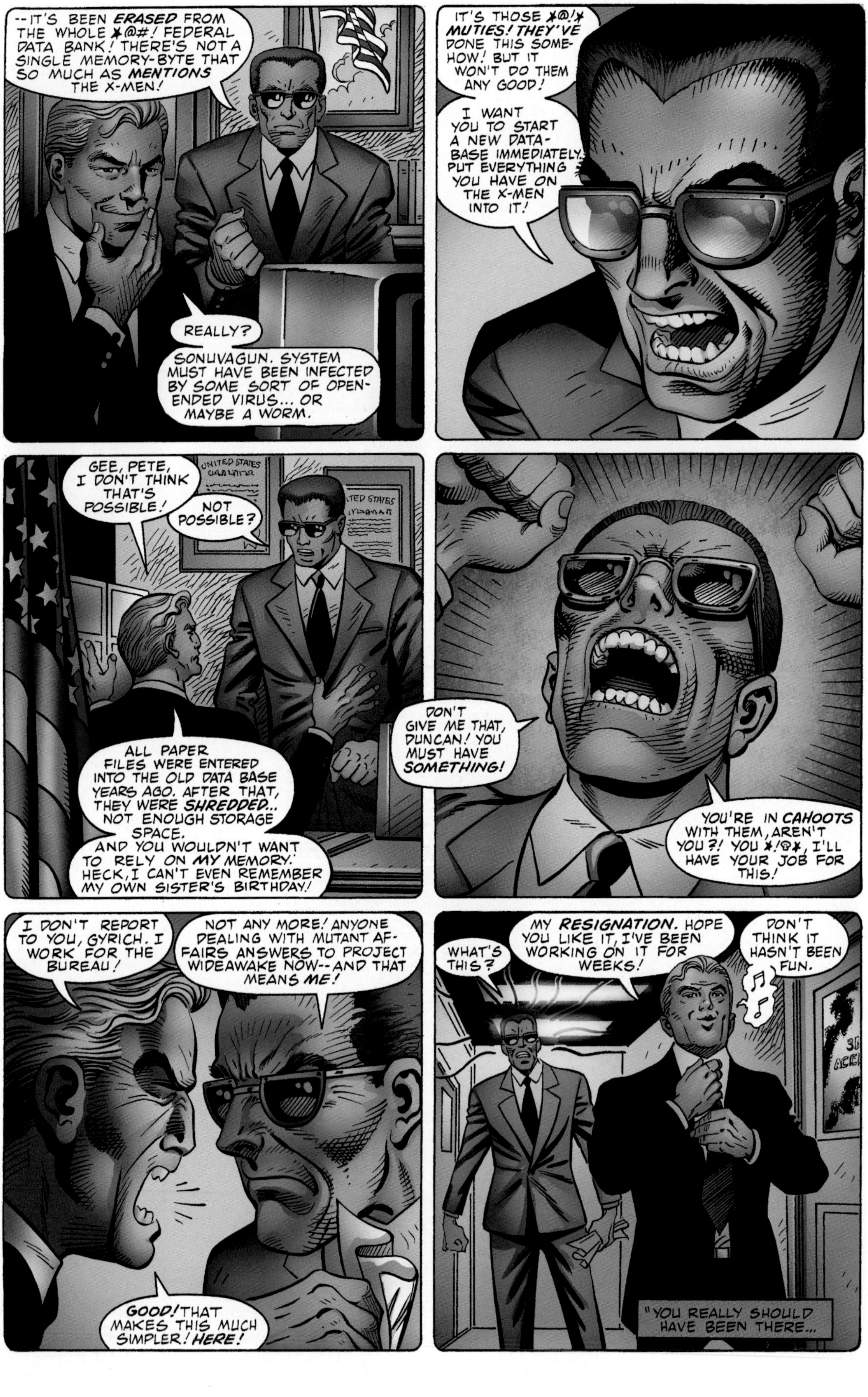
--IT'S BEEN ERASED FROM THE WHOLE ✱@#! FEDERAL DATA BANK! THERE'S NOT A SINGLE MEMORY-BYTE THAT SO MUCH AS MENTIONS THE X-MEN!
REALLY?
SONUVAGUN. SYSTEM MUST HAVE BEEN INFECTED BY SOME SORT OF OPEN-ENDED VIRUS... OR MAYBE A WORM.
IT'S THOSE ✱@!✱ MUTIES! THEY'VE DONE THIS SOMEHOW! BUT IT WON'T DO THEM ANY GOOD!
I WANT YOU TO START A NEW DATA-BASE IMMEDIATELY. PUT EVERYTHING YOU HAVE ON THE X-MEN INTO IT!
GEE, PETE, I DON'T THINK THAT'S POSSIBLE!
NOT POSSIBLE?
ALL PAPER FILES WERE ENTERED INTO THE OLD DATA BASE YEARS AGO. AFTER THAT, THEY WERE SHREDDED... NOT ENOUGH STORAGE SPACE.
AND YOU WOULDN'T WANT TO RELY ON MY MEMORY. HECK, I CAN'T EVEN REMEMBER MY OWN SISTER'S BIRTHDAY!
DON'T GIVE ME THAT, DUNCAN! YOU MUST HAVE SOMETHING!
YOU'RE IN CAHOOTS WITH THEM, AREN'T YOU?! YOU ✱!@✱, I'LL HAVE YOUR JOB FOR THIS!
I DON'T REPORT TO YOU, GYRICH. I WORK FOR THE BUREAU!
NOT ANY MORE! ANYONE DEALING WITH MUTANT AFFAIRS ANSWERS TO PROJECT WIDEAWAKE NOW--AND THAT MEANS ME!
GOOD! THAT MAKES THIS MUCH SIMPLER! HERE!
WHAT'S THIS?
MY RESIGNATION. HOPE YOU LIKE IT, I'VE BEEN WORKING ON IT FOR WEEKS!
DON'T THINK IT HASN'T BEEN FUN.
"YOU REALLY SHOULD HAVE BEEN THERE...

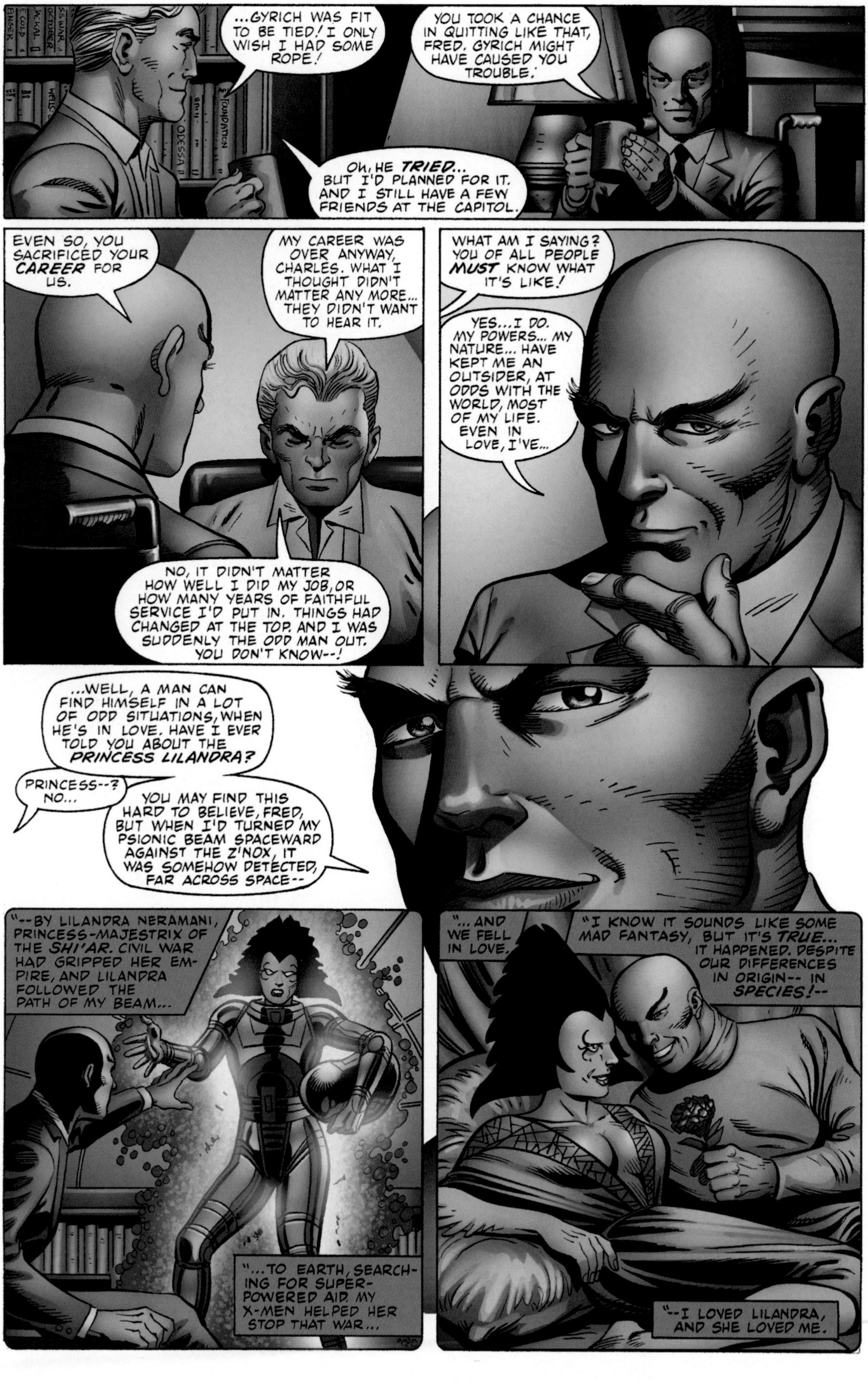
...GYRICH WAS FIT TO BE TIED! I ONLY WISH I HAD SOME ROPE!
YOU TOOK A CHANCE IN QUITTING LIKE THAT, FRED. GYRICH MIGHT HAVE CAUSED YOU TROUBLE.
OH, HE TRIED... BUT I'D PLANNED FOR IT. AND I STILL HAVE A FEW FRIENDS AT THE CAPITOL.
EVEN SO, YOU SACRIFICED YOUR CAREER FOR US.
MY CAREER WAS OVER ANYWAY, CHARLES. WHAT I THOUGHT DIDN'T MATTER ANY MORE... THEY DIDN'T WANT TO HEAR IT.
NO, IT DIDN'T MATTER HOW WELL I DID MY JOB, OR HOW MANY YEARS OF FAITHFUL SERVICE I'D PUT IN. THINGS HAD CHANGED AT THE TOP. AND I WAS SUDDENLY THE ODD MAN OUT. YOU DON'T KNOW--!
WHAT AM I SAYING? YOU OF ALL PEOPLE MUST KNOW WHAT IT'S LIKE!
YES... I DO. MY POWERS... MY NATURE... HAVE KEPT ME AN OUTSIDER, AT ODDS WITH THE WORLD, MOST OF MY LIFE. EVEN IN LOVE, I'VE...
...WELL, A MAN CAN FIND HIMSELF IN A LOT OF ODD SITUATIONS, WHEN HE'S IN LOVE. HAVE I EVER TOLD YOU ABOUT THE PRINCESS LILANDRA?
PRINCESS--? NO...
YOU MAY FIND THIS HARD TO BELIEVE, FRED, BUT WHEN I'D TURNED MY PSIONIC BEAM SPACEWARD AGAINST THE Z'NOX, IT WAS SOMEHOW DETECTED, FAR ACROSS SPACE--
"--BY LILANDRA NERAMANI, PRINCESS-MAJESTRIX OF THE SHI'AR. CIVIL WAR HAD GRIPPED HER EMPIRE, AND LILANDRA FOLLOWED THE PATH OF MY BEAM...
"...TO EARTH, SEARCHING FOR SUPER-POWERED AID. MY X-MEN HELPED HER STOP THAT WAR...
"...AND WE FELL IN LOVE.
"I KNOW IT SOUNDS LIKE SOME MAD FANTASY, BUT IT'S TRUE... IT HAPPENED. DESPITE OUR DIFFERENCES IN ORIGIN-- IN SPECIES!--
"--I LOVED LILANDRA, AND SHE LOVED ME.

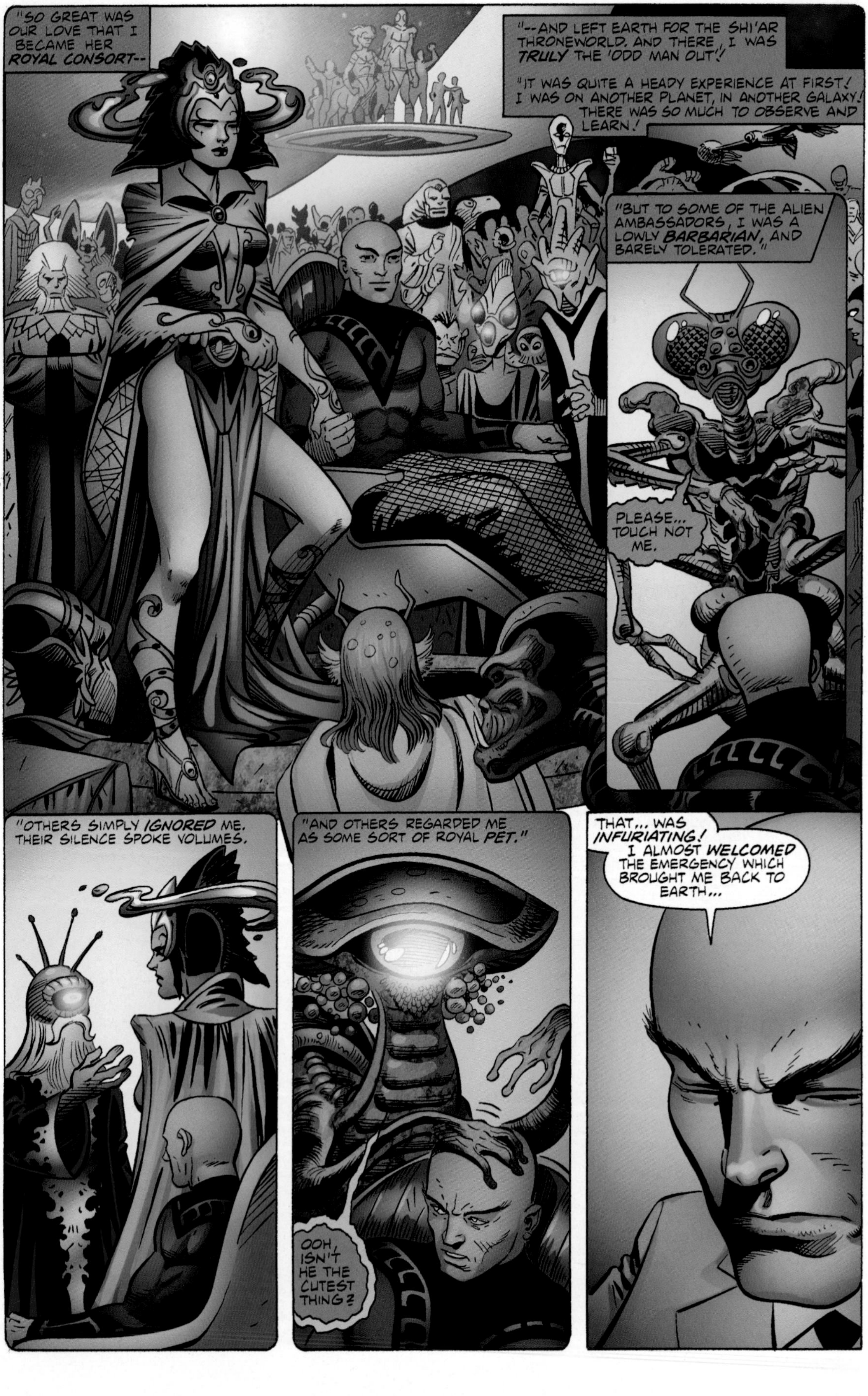
"SO GREAT WAS OUR LOVE THAT I BECAME HER ROYAL CONSORT--
"--AND LEFT EARTH FOR THE SHI'AR THRONEWORLD. AND THERE, I WAS TRULY THE 'ODD MAN OUT'!
"IT WAS QUITE A HEADY EXPERIENCE AT FIRST! I WAS ON ANOTHER PLANET, IN ANOTHER GALAXY! THERE WAS SO MUCH TO OBSERVE AND LEARN!
"BUT TO SOME OF THE ALIEN AMBASSADORS, I WAS A LOWLY BARBARIAN, AND BARELY TOLERATED."
PLEASE... TOUCH NOT ME.
"OTHERS SIMPLY IGNORED ME. THEIR SILENCE SPOKE VOLUMES.
"AND OTHERS REGARDED ME AS SOME SORT OF ROYAL PET."
OOH, ISN'T HE THE CUTEST THING?
THAT... WAS INFURIATING! I ALMOST WELCOMED THE EMERGENCY WHICH BROUGHT ME BACK TO EARTH...

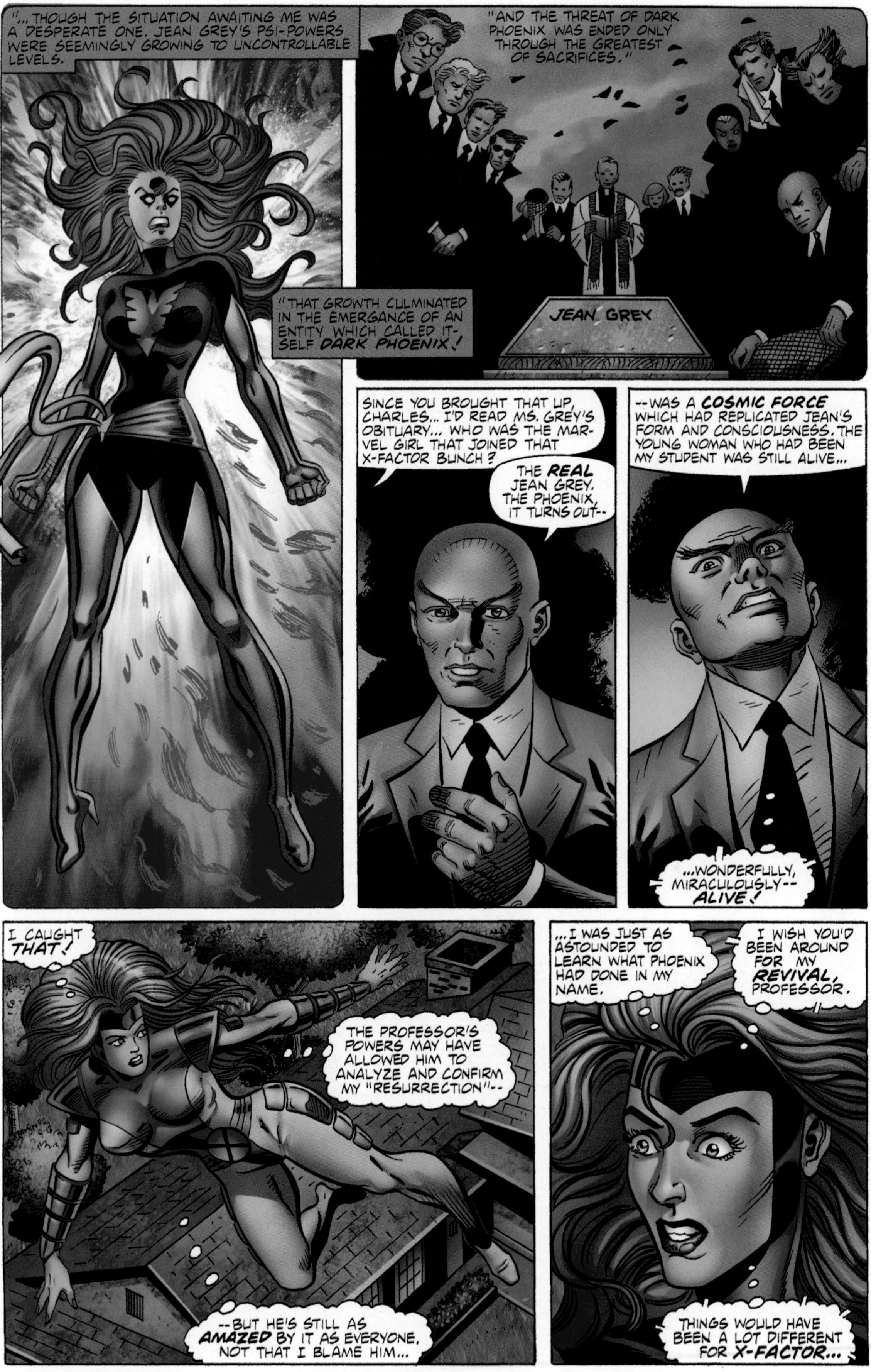
"...THOUGH THE SITUATION AWAITING ME WAS A DESPERATE ONE. JEAN GREY'S PSI-POWERS WERE SEEMINGLY GROWING TO UNCONTROLLABLE LEVELS.
"THAT GROWTH CULMINATED IN THE EMERGANCE OF AN ENTITY WHICH CALLED IT-SELF DARK PHOENIX!
"AND THE THREAT OF DARK PHOENIX WAS ENDED ONLY THROUGH THE GREATEST OF SACRIFICES."
JEAN GREY
SINCE YOU BROUGHT THAT UP, CHARLES... I'D READ MS. GREY'S OBITUARY... WHO WAS THE MAR-VEL GIRL THAT JOINED THAT X-FACTOR BUNCH?
THE REAL JEAN GREY. THE PHOENIX, IT TURNS OUT--
--WAS A COSMIC FORCE WHICH HAD REPLICATED JEAN'S FORM AND CONSCIOUSNESS. THE YOUNG WOMAN WHO HAD BEEN MY STUDENT WAS STILL ALIVE...
...WONDERFULLY, MIRACULOUSLY--ALIVE!
I CAUGHT THAT!
THE PROFESSOR'S POWERS MAY HAVE ALLOWED HIM TO ANALYZE AND CONFIRM MY "RESURRECTION"--
--BUT HE'S STILL AS AMAZED BY IT AS EVERYONE. NOT THAT I BLAME HIM...
...I WAS JUST AS ASTOUNDED TO LEARN WHAT PHOENIX HAD DONE IN MY NAME.
I WISH YOU'D BEEN AROUND FOR MY REVIVAL, PROFESSOR.
THINGS WOULD HAVE BEEN A LOT DIFFERENT FOR X-FACTOR...

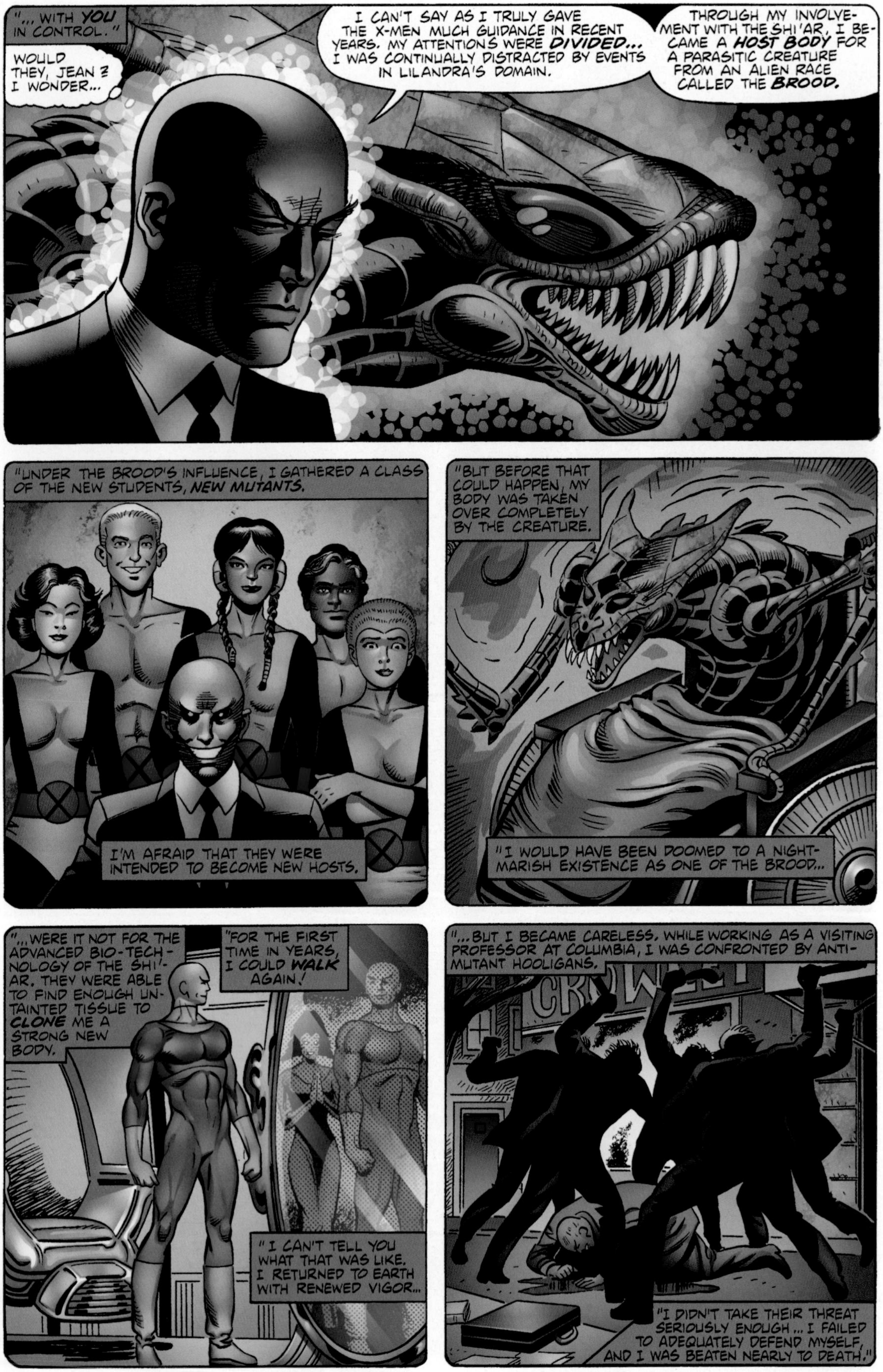
"...WITH YOU IN CONTROL."
WOULD THEY, JEAN? I WONDER...
I CAN'T SAY AS I TRULY GAVE THE X-MEN MUCH GUIDANCE IN RECENT YEARS. MY ATTENTIONS WERE DIVIDED... I WAS CONTINUALLY DISTRACTED BY EVENTS IN LILANDRA'S DOMAIN.
THROUGH MY INVOLVEMENT WITH THE SHI'AR, I BECAME A HOST BODY FOR A PARASITIC CREATURE FROM AN ALIEN RACE CALLED THE BROOD.
"UNDER THE BROOD'S INFLUENCE, I GATHERED A CLASS OF THE NEW STUDENTS, NEW MUTANTS.
I'M AFRAID THAT THEY WERE INTENDED TO BECOME NEW HOSTS.
"BUT BEFORE THAT COULD HAPPEN, MY BODY WAS TAKEN OVER COMPLETELY BY THE CREATURE.
"I WOULD HAVE BEEN DOOMED TO A NIGHTMARISH EXISTENCE AS ONE OF THE BROOD...
"...WERE IT NOT FOR THE ADVANCED BIO-TECHNOLOGY OF THE SHI'AR. THEY WERE ABLE TO FIND ENOUGH UNTAINTED TISSUE TO CLONE ME A STRONG NEW BODY.
"FOR THE FIRST TIME IN YEARS, I COULD WALK AGAIN!
"I CAN'T TELL YOU WHAT THAT WAS LIKE. I RETURNED TO EARTH WITH RENEWED VIGOR...
"...BUT I BECAME CARELESS. WHILE WORKING AS A VISITING PROFESSOR AT COLUMBIA, I WAS CONFRONTED BY ANTI-MUTANT HOOLIGANS.
"I DIDN'T TAKE THEIR THREAT SERIOUSLY ENOUGH... I FAILED TO ADEQUATELY DEFEND MYSELF, AND I WAS BEATEN NEARLY TO DEATH."

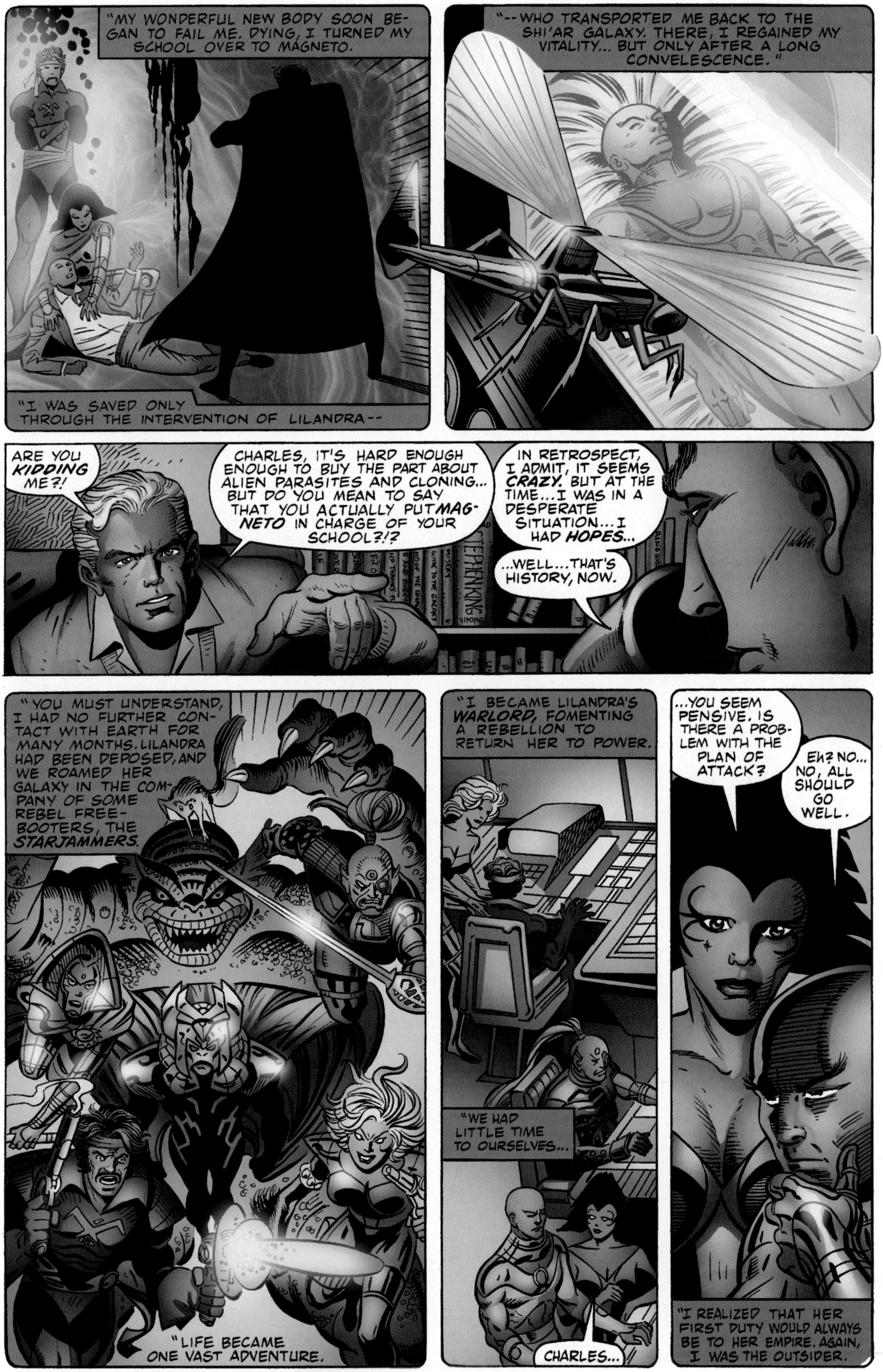
"MY WONDERFUL NEW BODY SOON BEGAN TO FAIL ME. DYING, I TURNED MY SCHOOL OVER TO MAGNETO.
"I WAS SAVED ONLY THROUGH THE INTERVENTION OF LILANDRA--
"--WHO TRANSPORTED ME BACK TO THE SHI'AR GALAXY. THERE, I REGAINED MY VITALITY... BUT ONLY AFTER A LONG CONVELESCENCE."
ARE YOU KIDDING ME?!
CHARLES, IT'S HARD ENOUGH TO BUY THE PART ABOUT ALIEN PARASITES AND CLONING... BUT DO YOU MEAN TO SAY THAT YOU ACTUALLY PUT MAGNETO IN CHARGE OF YOUR SCHOOL?!?
IN RETROSPECT, I ADMIT, IT SEEMS CRAZY. BUT AT THE TIME... I WAS IN A DESPERATE SITUATION... I HAD HOPES...
...WELL... THAT'S HISTORY, NOW.
"YOU MUST UNDERSTAND, I HAD NO FURTHER CONTACT WITH EARTH FOR MANY MONTHS. LILANDRA HAD BEEN DEPOSED, AND WE ROAMED HER GALAXY IN THE COMPANY OF SOME REBEL FREE-BOOTERS, THE STARJAMMERS.
"LIFE BECAME ONE VAST ADVENTURE.
"I BECAME LILANDRA'S WARLORD, FOMENTING A REBELLION TO RETURN HER TO POWER.
"WE HAD LITTLE TIME TO OURSELVES...
CHARLES...
...YOU SEEM PENSIVE. IS THERE A PROBLEM WITH THE PLAN OF ATTACK?
EH? NO... NO, ALL SHOULD GO WELL.
"I REALIZED THAT HER FIRST DUTY WOULD ALWAYS BE TO HER EMPIRE. AGAIN, I WAS THE OUTSIDER.

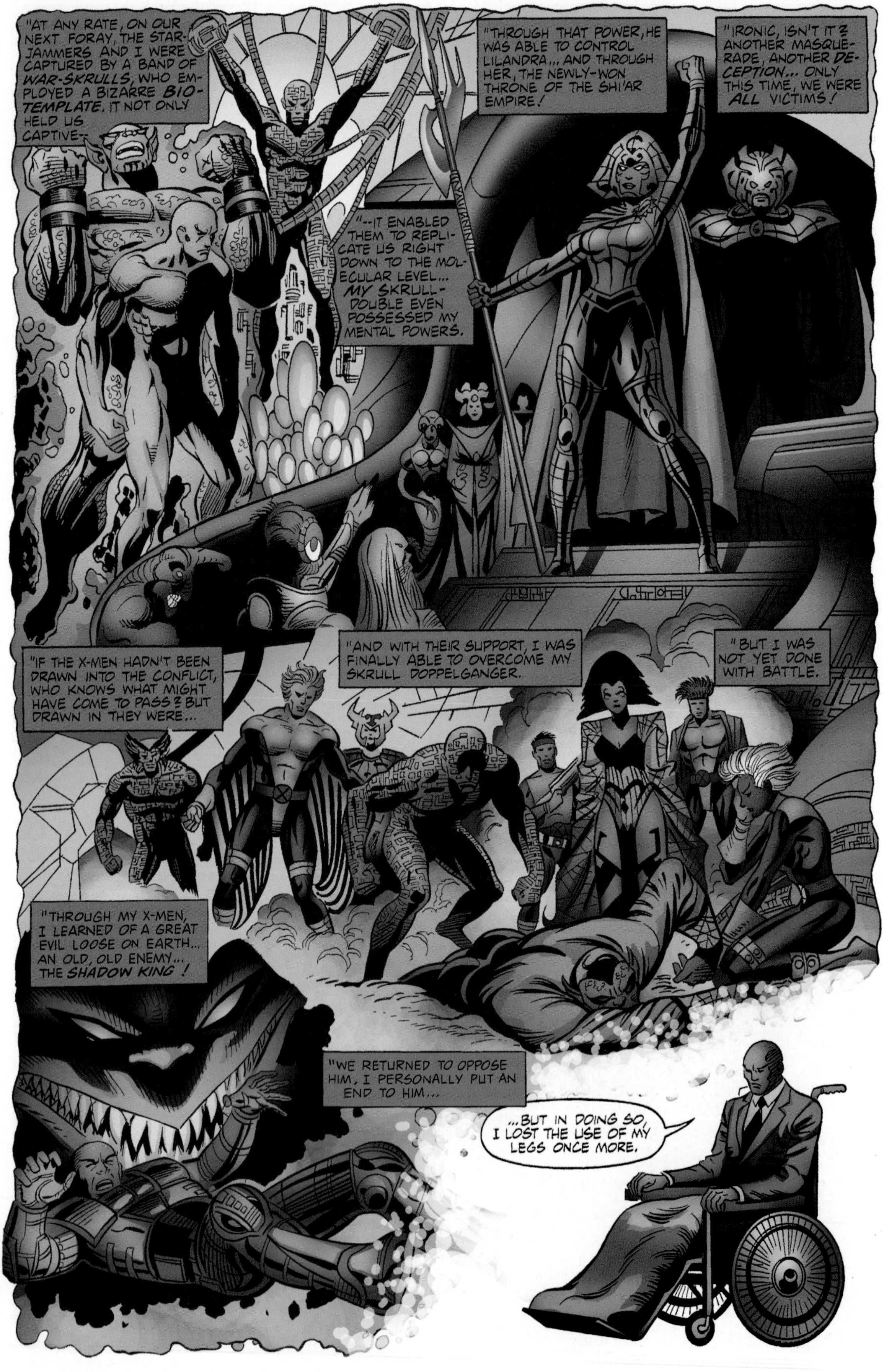
"AT ANY RATE, ON OUR NEXT FORAY, THE STAR-JAMMERS AND I WERE CAPTURED BY A BAND OF WAR-SKRULLS, WHO EMPLOYED A BIZARRE BIO-TEMPLATE. IT NOT ONLY HELD US CAPTIVE--
"--IT ENABLED THEM TO REPLICATE US RIGHT DOWN TO THE MOLECULAR LEVEL... MY SKRULL-DOUBLE EVEN POSSESSED MY MENTAL POWERS.
"THROUGH THAT POWER, HE WAS ABLE TO CONTROL LILANDRA... AND THROUGH HER, THE NEWLY-WON THRONE OF THE SHI'AR EMPIRE!
"IRONIC, ISN'T IT? ANOTHER MASQUERADE, ANOTHER DECEPTION... ONLY THIS TIME, WE WERE ALL VICTIMS!
"IF THE X-MEN HADN'T BEEN DRAWN INTO THE CONFLICT, WHO KNOWS WHAT MIGHT HAVE COME TO PASS? BUT DRAWN IN THEY WERE...
"AND WITH THEIR SUPPORT, I WAS FINALLY ABLE TO OVERCOME MY SKRULL DOPPELGANGER.
"BUT I WAS NOT YET DONE WITH BATTLE.
"THROUGH MY X-MEN, I LEARNED OF A GREAT EVIL LOOSE ON EARTH... AN OLD, OLD ENEMY... THE SHADOW KING!
"WE RETURNED TO OPPOSE HIM. I PERSONALLY PUT AN END TO HIM...
...BUT IN DOING SO, I LOST THE USE OF MY LEGS ONCE MORE.

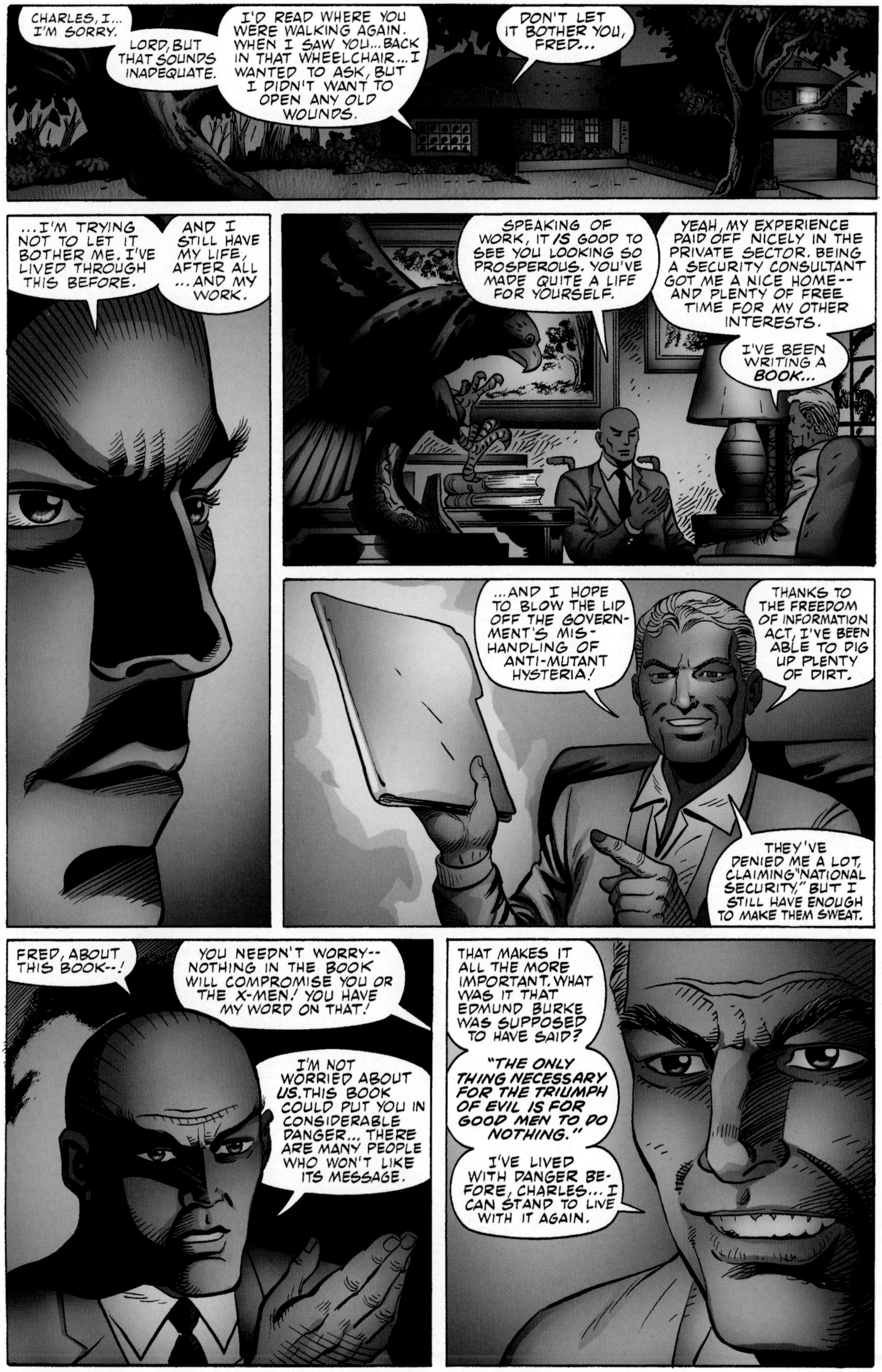
CHARLES, I... I'M SORRY.
LORD, BUT THAT SOUNDS INADEQUATE.
I'D READ WHERE YOU WERE WALKING AGAIN. WHEN I SAW YOU... BACK IN THAT WHEELCHAIR... I WANTED TO ASK, BUT I DIDN'T WANT TO OPEN ANY OLD WOUNDS.
DON'T LET IT BOTHER YOU, FRED...
...I'M TRYING NOT TO LET IT BOTHER ME. I'VE LIVED THROUGH THIS BEFORE.
AND I STILL HAVE MY LIFE, AFTER ALL ...AND MY WORK.
SPEAKING OF WORK, IT IS GOOD TO SEE YOU LOOKING SO PROSPEROUS. YOU'VE MADE QUITE A LIFE FOR YOURSELF.
YEAH, MY EXPERIENCE PAID OFF NICELY IN THE PRIVATE SECTOR. BEING A SECURITY CONSULTANT GOT ME A NICE HOME-- AND PLENTY OF FREE TIME FOR MY OTHER INTERESTS.
I'VE BEEN WRITING A BOOK...
...AND I HOPE TO BLOW THE LID OFF THE GOVERNMENT'S MISHANDLING OF ANTI-MUTANT HYSTERIA!
THANKS TO THE FREEDOM OF INFORMATION ACT, I'VE BEEN ABLE TO DIG UP PLENTY OF DIRT.
THEY'VE DENIED ME A LOT, CLAIMING "NATIONAL SECURITY," BUT I STILL HAVE ENOUGH TO MAKE THEM SWEAT.
FRED, ABOUT THIS BOOK--!
YOU NEEDN'T WORRY-- NOTHING IN THE BOOK WILL COMPROMISE YOU OR THE X-MEN! YOU HAVE MY WORD ON THAT!
I'M NOT WORRIED ABOUT US. THIS BOOK COULD PUT YOU IN CONSIDERABLE DANGER... THERE ARE MANY PEOPLE WHO WON'T LIKE ITS MESSAGE.
THAT MAKES IT ALL THE MORE IMPORTANT. WHAT WAS IT THAT EDMUND BURKE WAS SUPPOSED TO HAVE SAID?
"THE ONLY THING NECESSARY FOR THE TRIUMPH OF EVIL IS FOR GOOD MEN TO DO NOTHING."
I'VE LIVED WITH DANGER BEFORE, CHARLES... I CAN STAND TO LIVE WITH IT AGAIN.

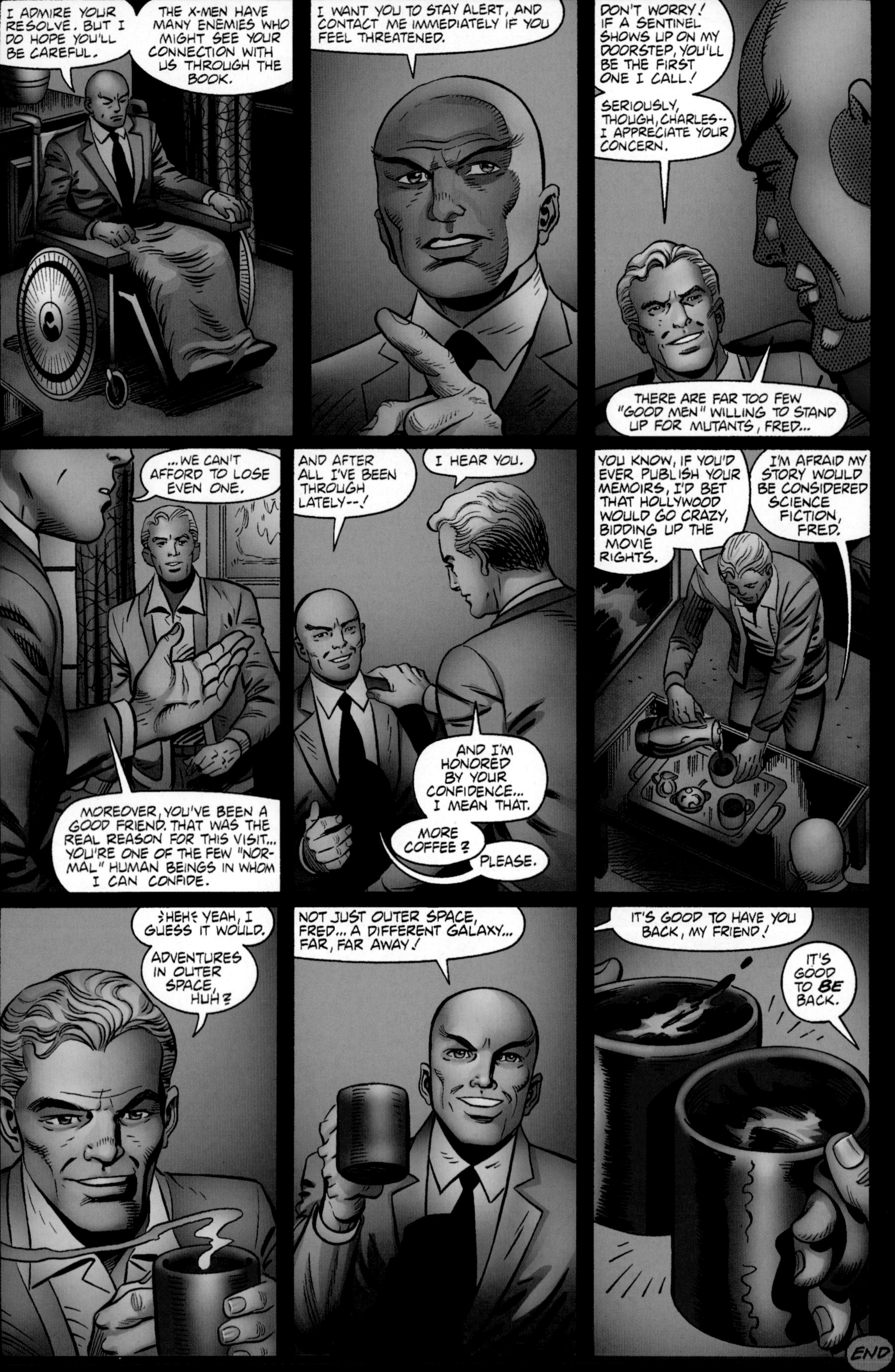
I ADMIRE YOUR RESOLVE. BUT I DO HOPE YOU'LL BE CAREFUL.
THE X-MEN HAVE MANY ENEMIES WHO MIGHT SEE YOUR CONNECTION WITH US THROUGH THE BOOK.
I WANT YOU TO STAY ALERT, AND CONTACT ME IMMEDIATELY IF YOU FEEL THREATENED.
DON'T WORRY! IF A SENTINEL SHOWS UP ON MY DOORSTEP, YOU'LL BE THE FIRST ONE I CALL!
SERIOUSLY, THOUGH, CHARLES-- I APPRECIATE YOUR CONCERN.
THERE ARE FAR TOO FEW "GOOD MEN" WILLING TO STAND UP FOR MUTANTS, FRED...
...WE CAN'T AFFORD TO LOSE EVEN ONE.
MOREOVER, YOU'VE BEEN A GOOD FRIEND. THAT WAS THE REAL REASON FOR THIS VISIT... YOU'RE ONE OF THE FEW "NOR-MAL" HUMAN BEINGS IN WHOM I CAN CONFIDE.
AND AFTER ALL I'VE BEEN THROUGH LATELY--!
I HEAR YOU.
AND I'M HONORED BY YOUR CONFIDENCE... I MEAN THAT.
MORE COFFEE?
PLEASE.
YOU KNOW, IF YOU'D EVER PUBLISH YOUR MEMOIRS, I'D BET THAT HOLLYWOOD WOULD GO CRAZY, BIDDING UP THE MOVIE RIGHTS.
I'M AFRAID MY STORY WOULD BE CONSIDERED SCIENCE FICTION, FRED.
HEH YEAH, I GUESS IT WOULD.
ADVENTURES IN OUTER SPACE, HUH?
NOT JUST OUTER SPACE, FRED... A DIFFERENT GALAXY... FAR, FAR AWAY!
IT'S GOOD TO HAVE YOU BACK, MY FRIEND!
IT'S GOOD TO BE BACK.
END

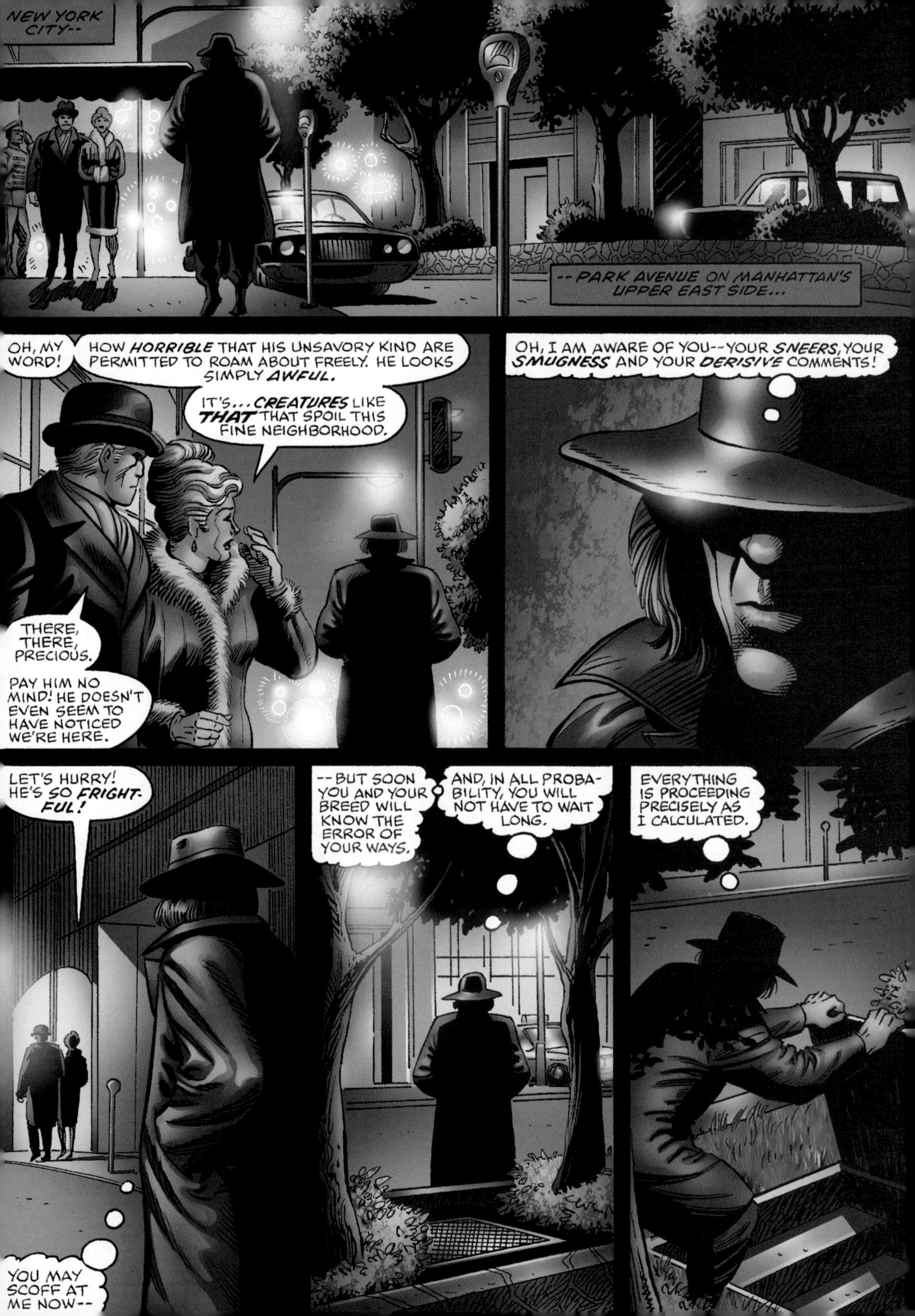

NEW YORK CITY--
--PARK AVENUE ON MANHATTAN'S UPPER EAST SIDE...
OH, MY WORD!
HOW HORRIBLE THAT HIS UNSAVORY KIND ARE PERMITTED TO ROAM ABOUT FREELY. HE LOOKS SIMPLY AWFUL.
IT'S...CREATURES LIKE THAT THAT SPOIL THIS FINE NEIGHBORHOOD.
THERE, THERE, PRECIOUS.
PAY HIM NO MIND! HE DOESN'T EVEN SEEM TO HAVE NOTICED WE'RE HERE.
OH, I AM AWARE OF YOU--YOUR SNEERS, YOUR SMUGNESS AND YOUR DERISIVE COMMENTS!
LET'S HURRY! HE'S SO FRIGHT-FUL!
YOU MAY SCOFF AT ME NOW--
--BUT SOON YOU AND YOUR BREED WILL KNOW THE ERROR OF YOUR WAYS.
AND, IN ALL PROBA-BILITY, YOU WILL NOT HAVE TO WAIT LONG.
EVERYTHING IS PROCEEDING PRECISELY AS I CALCULATED.

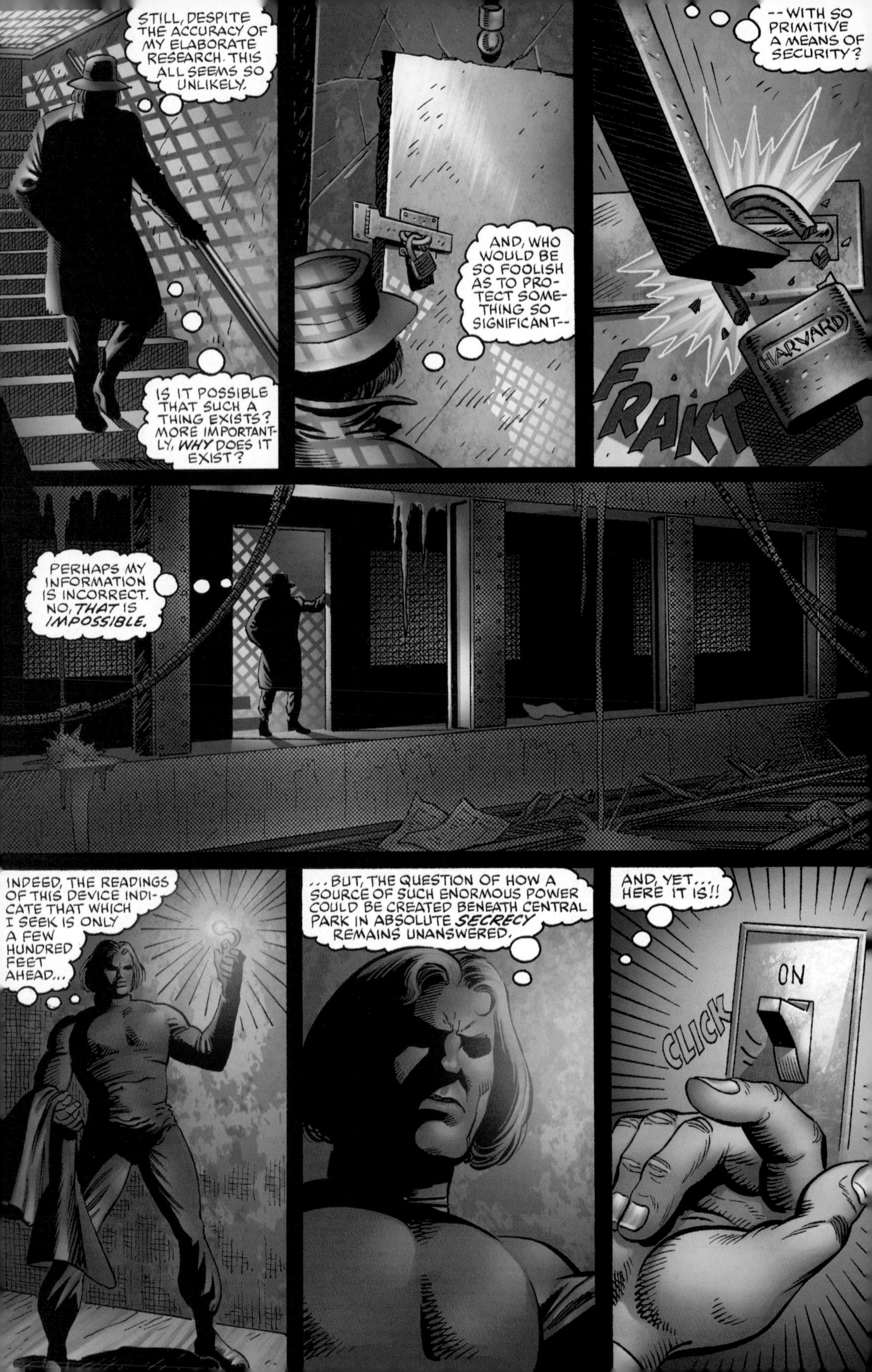
STILL, DESPITE THE ACCURACY OF MY ELABORATE RESEARCH. THIS ALL SEEMS SO UNLIKELY.
IS IT POSSIBLE THAT SUCH A THING EXISTS? MORE IMPORTANTLY, WHY DOES IT EXIST?
AND, WHO WOULD BE SO FOOLISH AS TO PROTECT SOMETHING SO SIGNIFICANT--
--WITH SO PRIMITIVE A MEANS OF SECURITY?
FRAKT
HARVARD
PERHAPS MY INFORMATION IS INCORRECT. NO, THAT IS IMPOSSIBLE.
INDEED, THE READINGS OF THIS DEVICE INDICATE THAT WHICH I SEEK IS ONLY A FEW HUNDRED FEET AHEAD...
...BUT, THE QUESTION OF HOW A SOURCE OF SUCH ENORMOUS POWER COULD BE CREATED BENEATH CENTRAL PARK IN ABSOLUTE SECRECY REMAINS UNANSWERED.
AND, YET... HERE IT IS!!
ON
CLICK

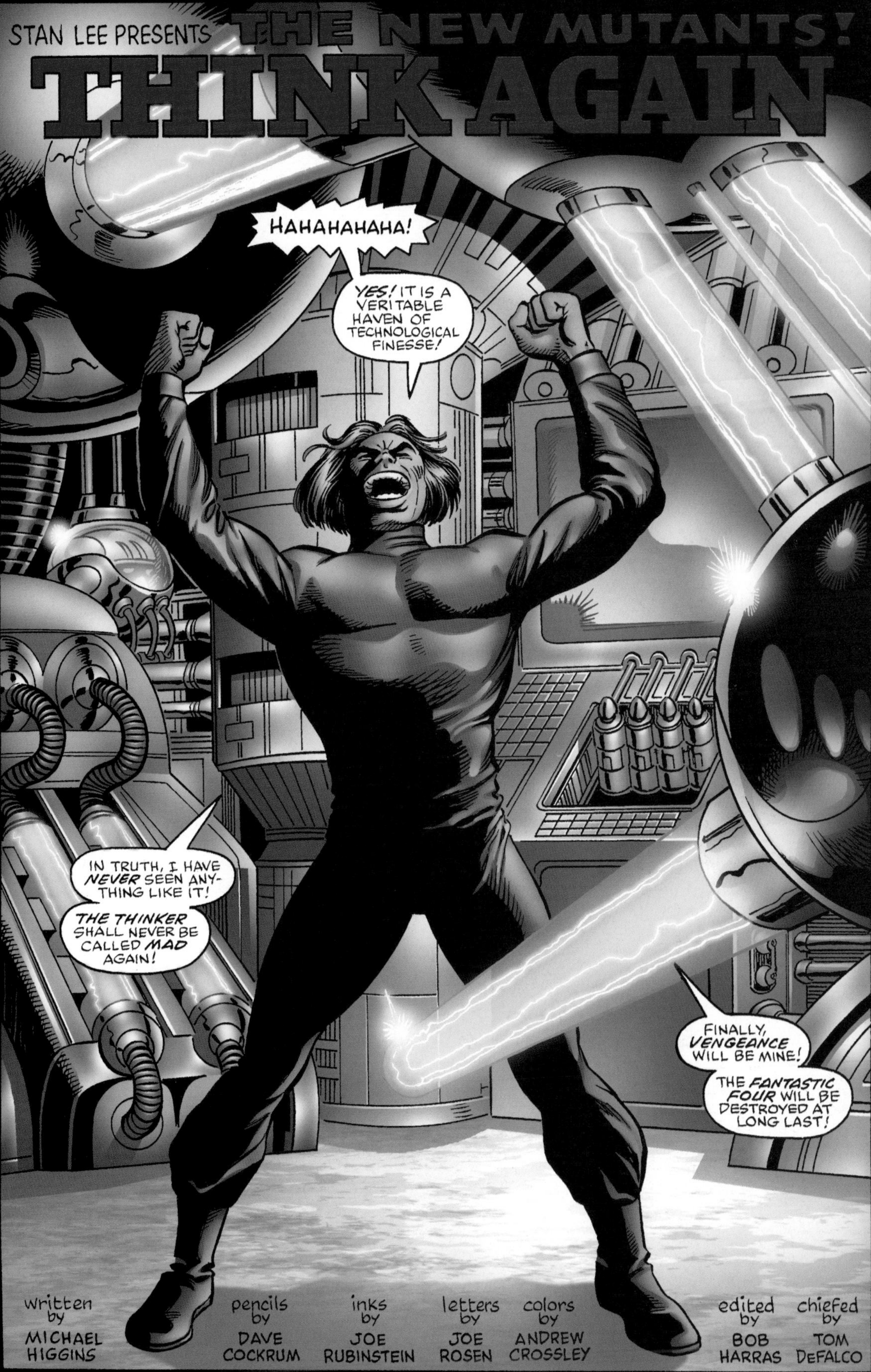
STAN LEE PRESENTS THE NEW MUTANTS!
THINK AGAIN
HAHAHAHAHA!
YES! IT IS A VERITABLE HAVEN OF TECHNOLOGICAL FINESSE!
IN TRUTH, I HAVE NEVER SEEN ANYTHING LIKE IT!
THE THINKER SHALL NEVER BE CALLED MAD AGAIN!
FINALLY, VENGEANCE WILL BE MINE!
THE FANTASTIC FOUR WILL BE DESTROYED AT LONG LAST!
written by MICHAEL HIGGINS
pencils by DAVE COCKRUM
inks by JOE RUBINSTEIN
letters by JOE ROSEN
colors by ANDREW CROSSLEY
edited by BOB HARRAS
chiefed by TOM DeFALCO

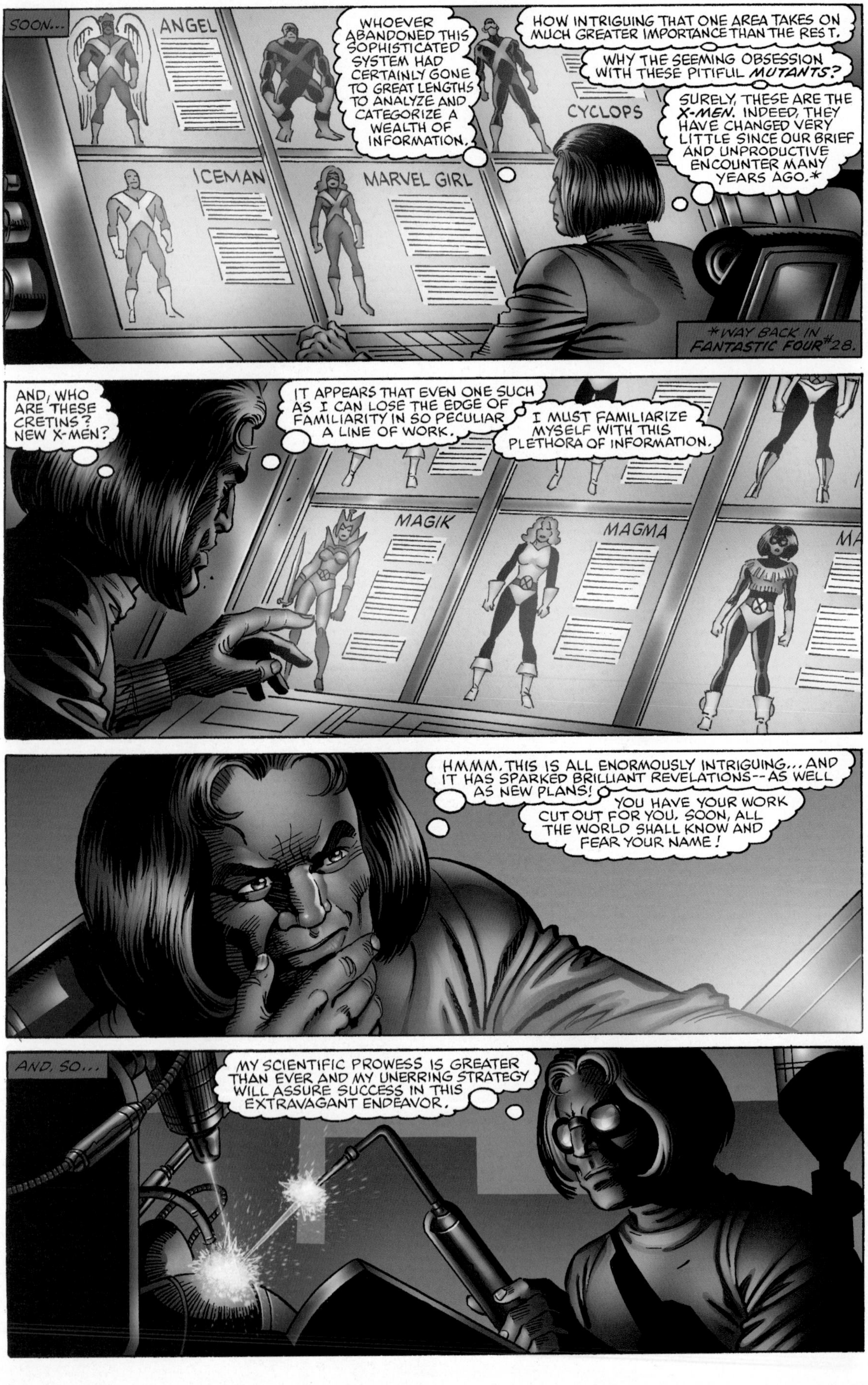
SOON...
ANGEL
CYCLOPS
ICEMAN
MARVEL GIRL
WHOEVER ABANDONED THIS SOPHISTICATED SYSTEM HAD CERTAINLY GONE TO GREAT LENGTHS TO ANALYZE AND CATEGORIZE A WEALTH OF INFORMATION.
HOW INTRIGUING THAT ONE AREA TAKES ON MUCH GREATER IMPORTANCE THAN THE REST.
WHY THE SEEMING OBSESSION WITH THESE PITIFUL MUTANTS?
SURELY, THESE ARE THE X-MEN. INDEED, THEY HAVE CHANGED VERY LITTLE SINCE OUR BRIEF AND UNPRODUCTIVE ENCOUNTER MANY YEARS AGO.*
*WAY BACK IN FANTASTIC FOUR #28.
AND, WHO ARE THESE CRETINS? NEW X-MEN?
IT APPEARS THAT EVEN ONE SUCH AS I CAN LOSE THE EDGE OF FAMILIARITY IN SO PECULIAR A LINE OF WORK.
I MUST FAMILIARIZE MYSELF WITH THIS PLETHORA OF INFORMATION.
MAGIK
MAGMA
HMMM. THIS IS ALL ENORMOUSLY INTRIGUING... AND IT HAS SPARKED BRILLIANT REVELATIONS--AS WELL AS NEW PLANS!
YOU HAVE YOUR WORK CUT OUT FOR YOU. SOON, ALL THE WORLD SHALL KNOW AND FEAR YOUR NAME!
AND, SO...
MY SCIENTIFIC PROWESS IS GREATER THAN EVER AND MY UNERRING STRATEGY WILL ASSURE SUCCESS IN THIS EXTRAVAGANT ENDEAVOR.

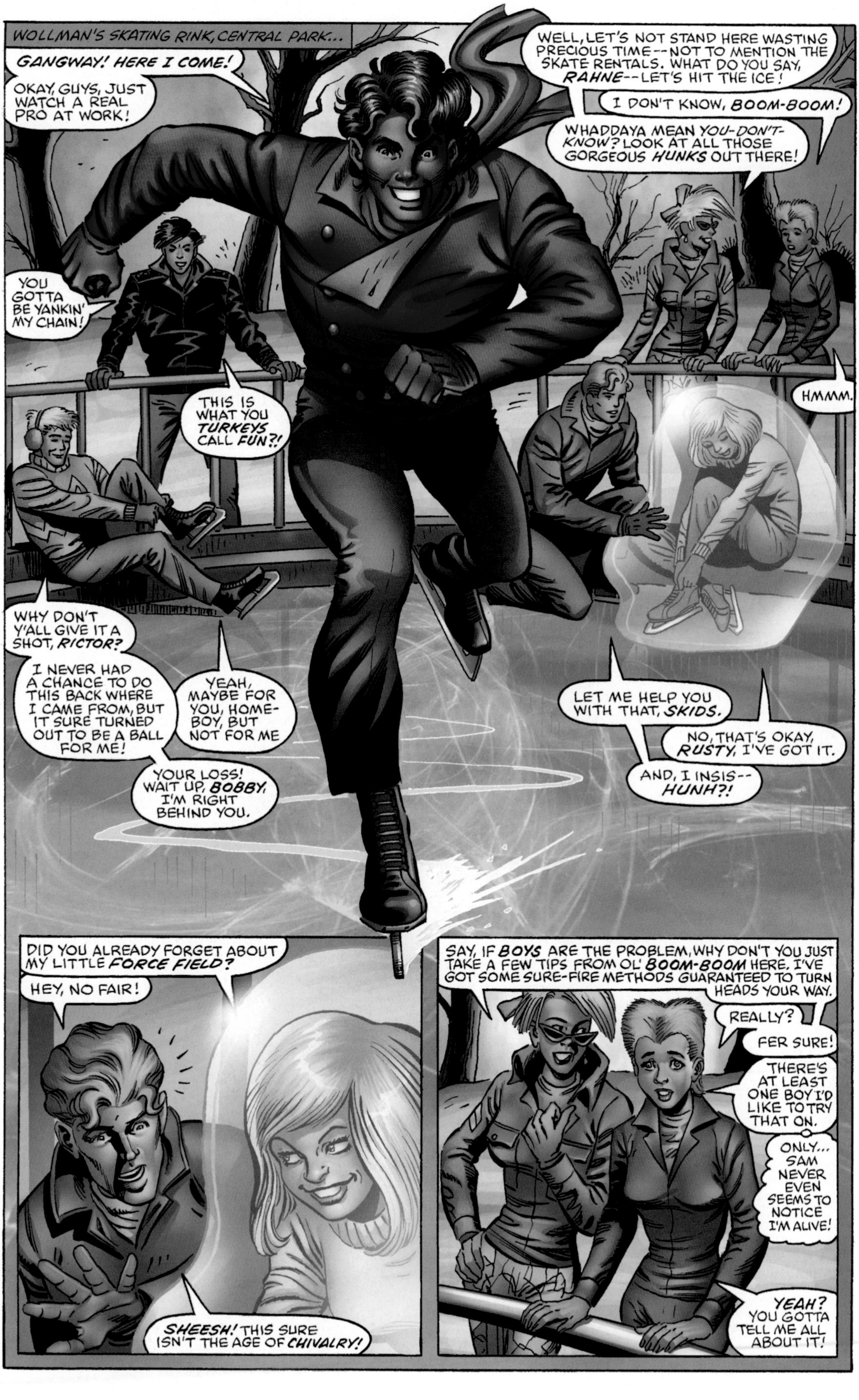

WOLLMAN'S SKATING RINK, CENTRAL PARK...
GANGWAY! HERE I COME!
OKAY, GUYS, JUST WATCH A REAL PRO AT WORK!
WELL, LET'S NOT STAND HERE WASTING PRECIOUS TIME--NOT TO MENTION THE SKATE RENTALS. WHAT DO YOU SAY, RAHNE--LET'S HIT THE ICE!
I DON'T KNOW, BOOM-BOOM!
WHADDAYA MEAN YOU-DON'T-KNOW? LOOK AT ALL THOSE GORGEOUS HUNKS OUT THERE!
YOU GOTTA BE YANKIN' MY CHAIN!
THIS IS WHAT YOU TURKEYS CALL FUN?!
HMMM.
WHY DON'T Y'ALL GIVE IT A SHOT, RICTOR?
I NEVER HAD A CHANCE TO DO THIS BACK WHERE I CAME FROM, BUT IT SURE TURNED OUT TO BE A BALL FOR ME!
YEAH, MAYBE FOR YOU, HOME-BOY, BUT NOT FOR ME
YOUR LOSS! WAIT UP, BOBBY, I'M RIGHT BEHIND YOU.
LET ME HELP YOU WITH THAT, SKIDS.
NO, THAT'S OKAY, RUSTY, I'VE GOT IT.
AND, I INSIS-- HUNH?!
DID YOU ALREADY FORGET ABOUT MY LITTLE FORCE FIELD?
HEY, NO FAIR!
SHEESH! THIS SURE ISN'T THE AGE OF CHIVALRY!
SAY, IF BOYS ARE THE PROBLEM, WHY DON'T YOU JUST TAKE A FEW TIPS FROM OL' BOOM-BOOM HERE. I'VE GOT SOME SURE-FIRE METHODS GUARANTEED TO TURN HEADS YOUR WAY.
REALLY?
FER SURE!
THERE'S AT LEAST ONE BOY I'D LIKE TO TRY THAT ON.
ONLY... SAM NEVER EVEN SEEMS TO NOTICE I'M ALIVE!
YEAH? YOU GOTTA TELL ME ALL ABOUT IT!

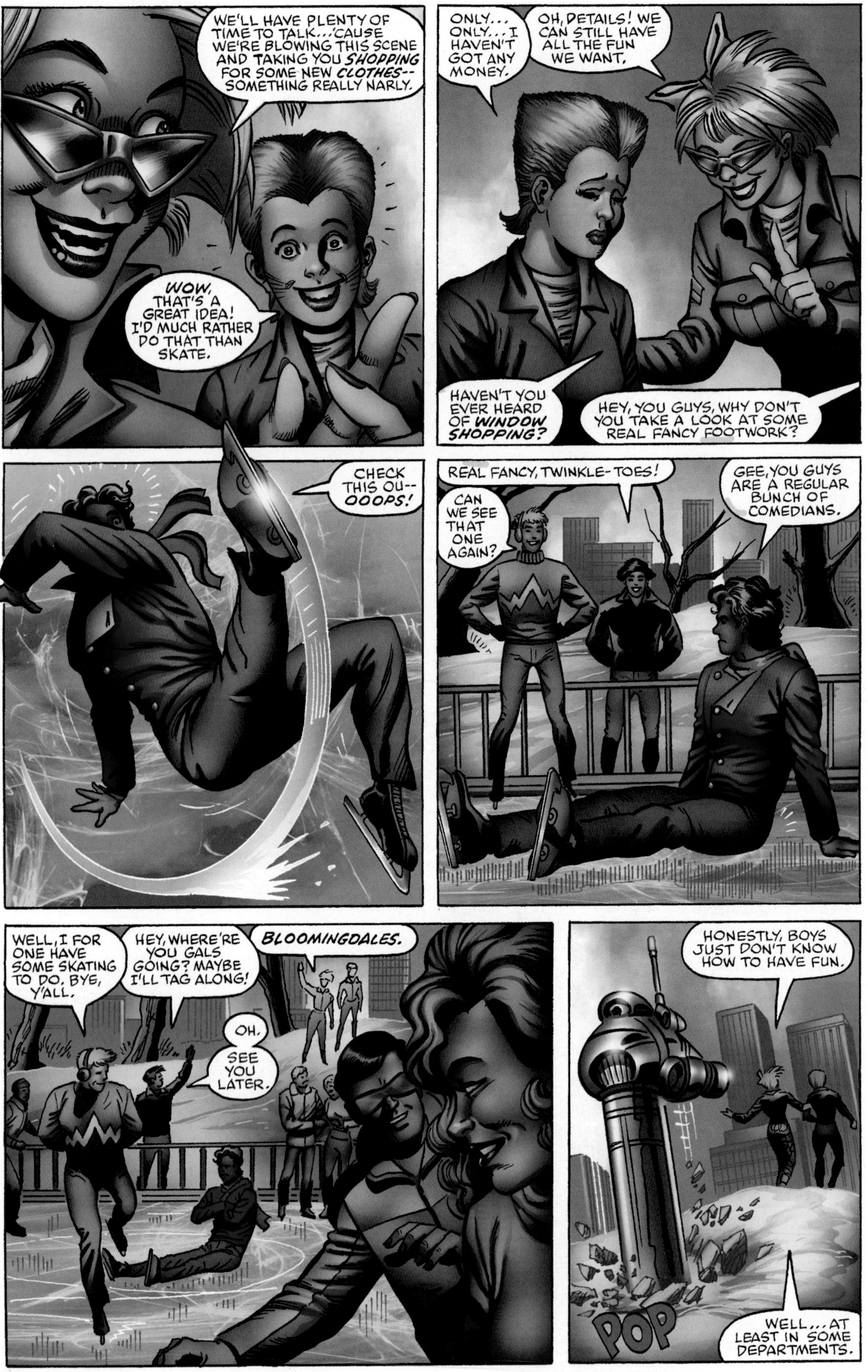

WE'LL HAVE PLENTY OF TIME TO TALK...'CAUSE WE'RE BLOWING THIS SCENE AND TAKING YOU SHOPPING FOR SOME NEW CLOTHES--SOMETHING REALLY NARLY.
WOW, THAT'S A GREAT IDEA! I'D MUCH RATHER DO THAT THAN SKATE.
ONLY... ONLY... I HAVEN'T GOT ANY MONEY.
OH, DETAILS! WE CAN STILL HAVE ALL THE FUN WE WANT.
HAVEN'T YOU EVER HEARD OF WINDOW SHOPPING?
HEY, YOU GUYS, WHY DON'T YOU TAKE A LOOK AT SOME REAL FANCY FOOTWORK?
CHECK THIS OU--OOOPS!
REAL FANCY, TWINKLE-TOES!
CAN WE SEE THAT ONE AGAIN?
GEE, YOU GUYS ARE A REGULAR BUNCH OF COMEDIANS.
WELL, I FOR ONE HAVE SOME SKATING TO DO. BYE, Y'ALL.
HEY, WHERE'RE YOU GALS GOING? MAYBE I'LL TAG ALONG!
BLOOMINGDALES.
OH. SEE YOU LATER.
HONESTLY, BOYS JUST DON'T KNOW HOW TO HAVE FUN.
POP
WELL,... AT LEAST IN SOME DEPARTMENTS.

HAVING DEDUCED ALL PROBABILITIES, THIS DUO APPEARED EXACTLY AS I ANTICIPATED. WHILE OTHERS MIGHT RELY UPON CHANCE, I RELY SOLELY UPON KNOWLEDGE AND PLANNING.

THE MOMENT HAS COME.

EVERYTHING IS IN READINESS. MY GREATEST CREATION AWAITS ONLY THE *SPARK OF LIFE*--

--SOMETHING I WILL NOW PROVIDE!

SURELY, THIS ANDROID WILL NOT BE FLAWED LIKE HIS PRIMITIVE PREDECESSOR, CONSTRUCTED UPON ERRONEOUS, SHALLOW RESEARCH GATHERED BY THE SIMPLE-MINDED *REED RICHARDS*.

THE INFORMATION PROVIDED BY THESE AMAZINGLY ADVANCED CIRCUITS CAN BE SYNTHESIZED IN A MANNER FAR BEYOND THE COMPREHENSION OF THE SO-CALLED *MISTER FANTASTIC*.

FEEL THE *POWER* THAT SURGES THROUGH YOU--

--AND RISE FROM YOUR LIFELESS STATE TO GREET THE FACE OF YOUR *MASTER!*

CLICK

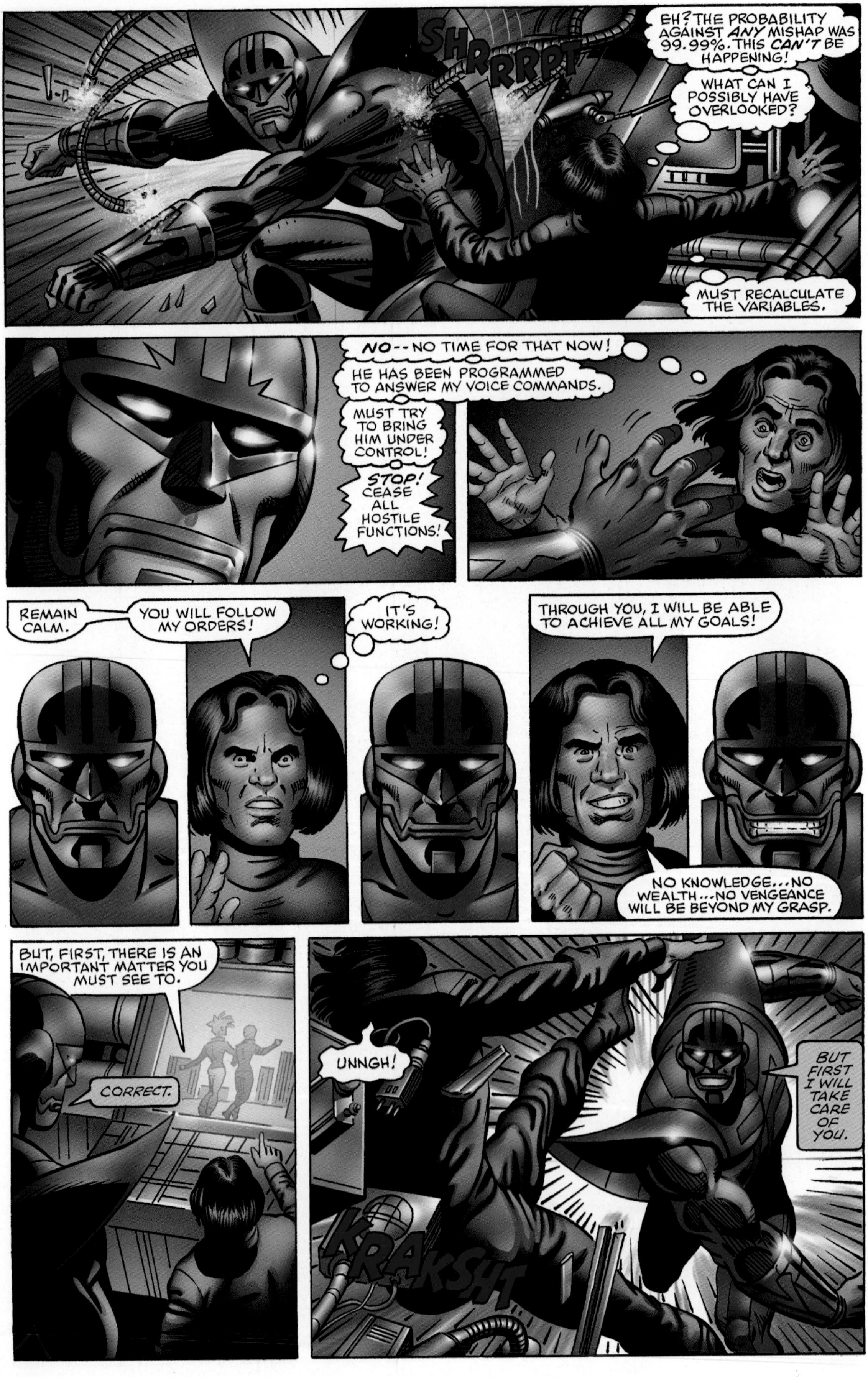

!
SHRRRRPT
EH? THE PROBABILITY AGAINST ANY MISHAP WAS 99.99%. THIS CAN'T BE HAPPENING!
WHAT CAN I POSSIBLY HAVE OVERLOOKED?
MUST RECALCULATE THE VARIABLES.
NO--NO TIME FOR THAT NOW!
HE HAS BEEN PROGRAMMED TO ANSWER MY VOICE COMMANDS.
MUST TRY TO BRING HIM UNDER CONTROL!
STOP! CEASE ALL HOSTILE FUNCTIONS!
REMAIN CALM.
YOU WILL FOLLOW MY ORDERS!
IT'S WORKING!
THROUGH YOU, I WILL BE ABLE TO ACHIEVE ALL MY GOALS!
NO KNOWLEDGE...NO WEALTH...NO VENGEANCE WILL BE BEYOND MY GRASP.
BUT, FIRST, THERE IS AN IMPORTANT MATTER YOU MUST SEE TO.
CORRECT.
UNNGH!
BUT FIRST I WILL TAKE CARE OF YOU.
KRAKSHT

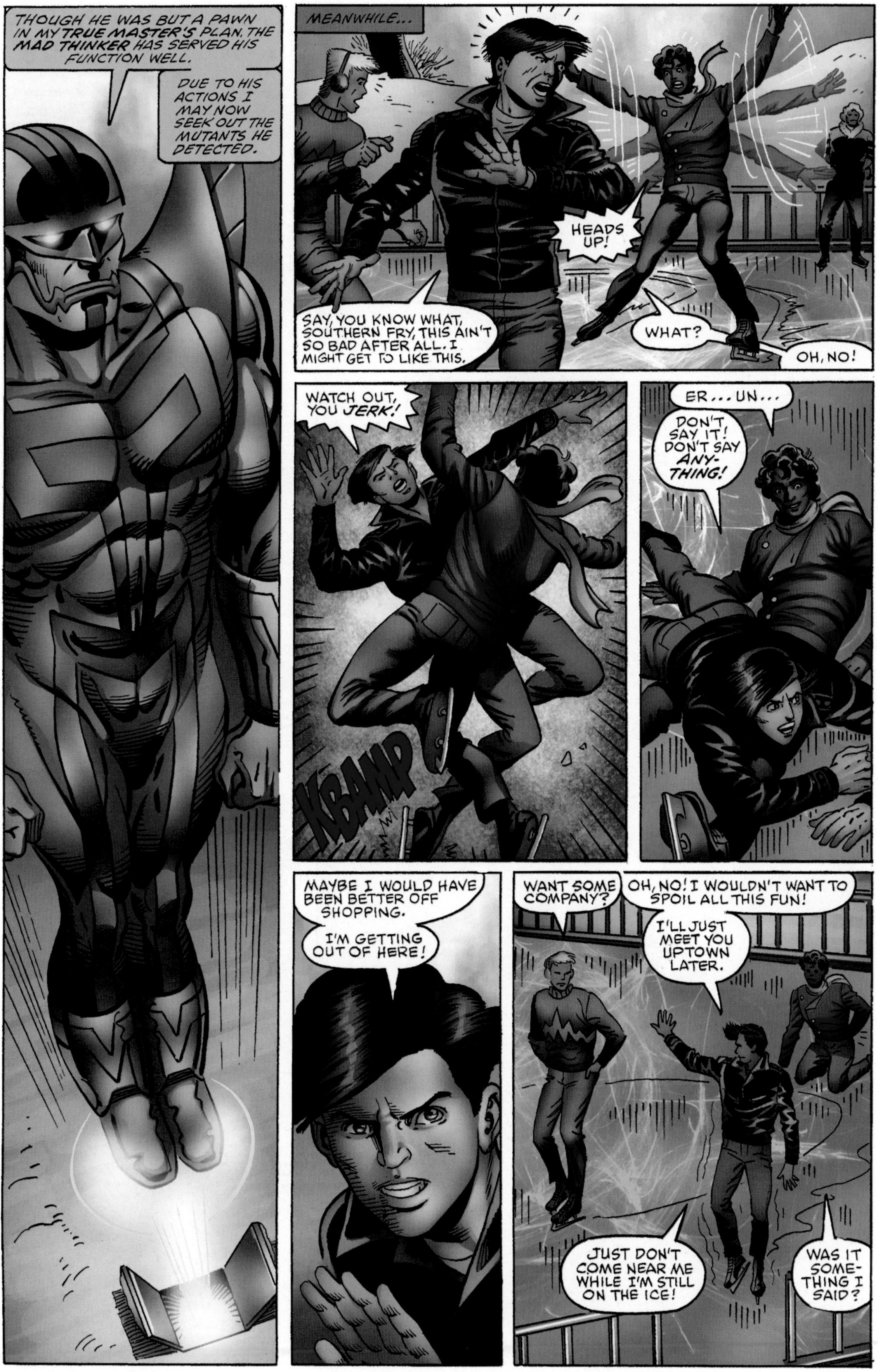
THOUGH HE WAS BUT A PAWN IN MY TRUE MASTER'S PLAN, THE MAD THINKER HAS SERVED HIS FUNCTION WELL.
DUE TO HIS ACTIONS I MAY NOW SEEK OUT THE MUTANTS HE DETECTED.
MEANWHILE...
HEADS UP!
SAY, YOU KNOW WHAT, SOUTHERN FRY, THIS AIN'T SO BAD AFTER ALL. I MIGHT GET TO LIKE THIS.
WHAT?
OH, NO!
WATCH OUT, YOU JERK!
KBAMP
ER... UN...
DON'T SAY IT! DON'T SAY ANY-THING!
MAYBE I WOULD HAVE BEEN BETTER OFF SHOPPING.
I'M GETTING OUT OF HERE!
WANT SOME COMPANY?
OH, NO! I WOULDN'T WANT TO SPOIL ALL THIS FUN!
I'LL JUST MEET YOU UPTOWN LATER.
JUST DON'T COME NEAR ME WHILE I'M STILL ON THE ICE!
WAS IT SOME-THING I SAID?

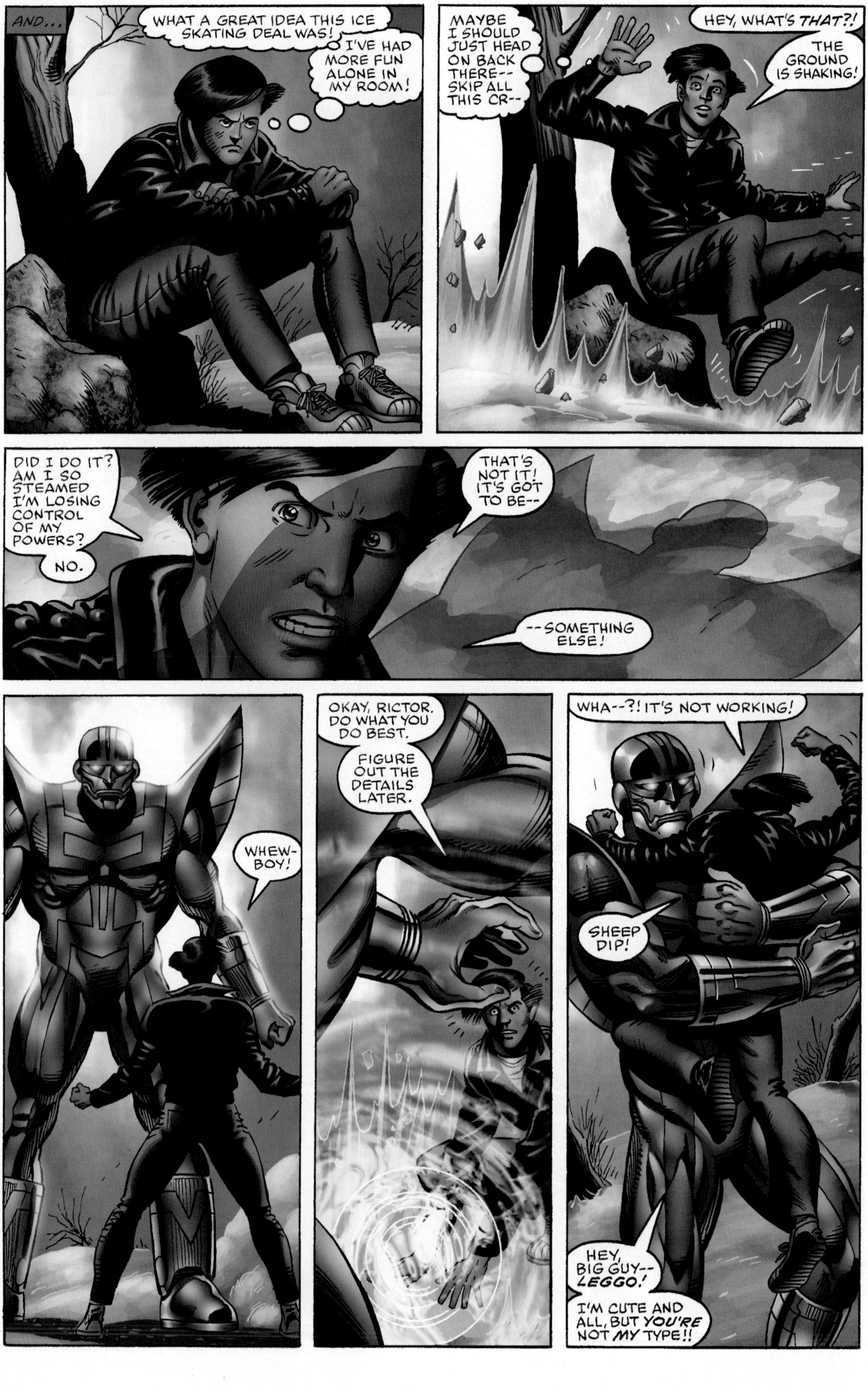

AND...
WHAT A GREAT IDEA THIS ICE SKATING DEAL WAS!
I'VE HAD MORE FUN ALONE IN MY ROOM!
MAYBE I SHOULD JUST HEAD ON BACK THERE-- SKIP ALL THIS CR--
HEY, WHAT'S *THAT?!*
THE GROUND IS SHAKING!
DID I DO IT? AM I SO STEAMED I'M LOSING CONTROL OF MY POWERS?
NO.
THAT'S NOT IT! IT'S GOT TO BE--
--SOMETHING ELSE!
WHEW-BOY!
OKAY, RICTOR. DO WHAT YOU DO BEST.
FIGURE OUT THE DETAILS LATER.
WHA--?! IT'S NOT WORKING!
SHEEP DIP!
HEY, BIG GUY-- *LEGGO!*
I'M CUTE AND ALL, BUT *YOU'RE* NOT *MY* TYPE!!

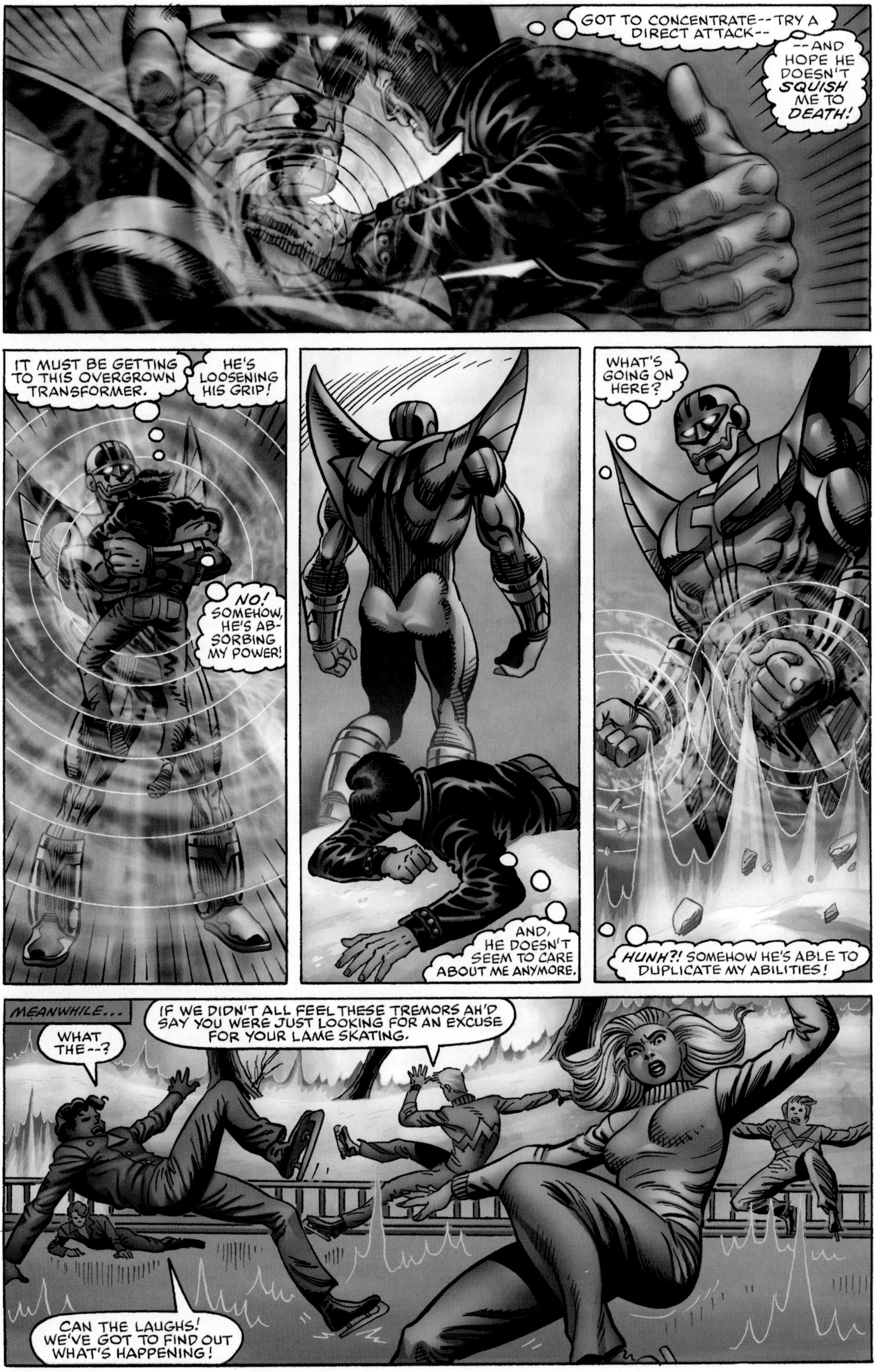
GOT TO CONCENTRATE--TRY A DIRECT ATTACK--
--AND HOPE HE DOESN'T SQUISH ME TO DEATH!
IT MUST BE GETTING TO THIS OVERGROWN TRANSFORMER.
HE'S LOOSENING HIS GRIP!
NO! SOMEHOW, HE'S ABSORBING MY POWER!
AND, HE DOESN'T SEEM TO CARE ABOUT ME ANYMORE.
WHAT'S GOING ON HERE?
HUNH?! SOMEHOW HE'S ABLE TO DUPLICATE MY ABILITIES!
MEANWHILE...
WHAT THE--?
IF WE DIDN'T ALL FEEL THESE TREMORS AH'D SAY YOU WERE JUST LOOKING FOR AN EXCUSE FOR YOUR LAME SKATING.
CAN THE LAUGHS! WE'VE GOT TO FIND OUT WHAT'S HAPPENING!

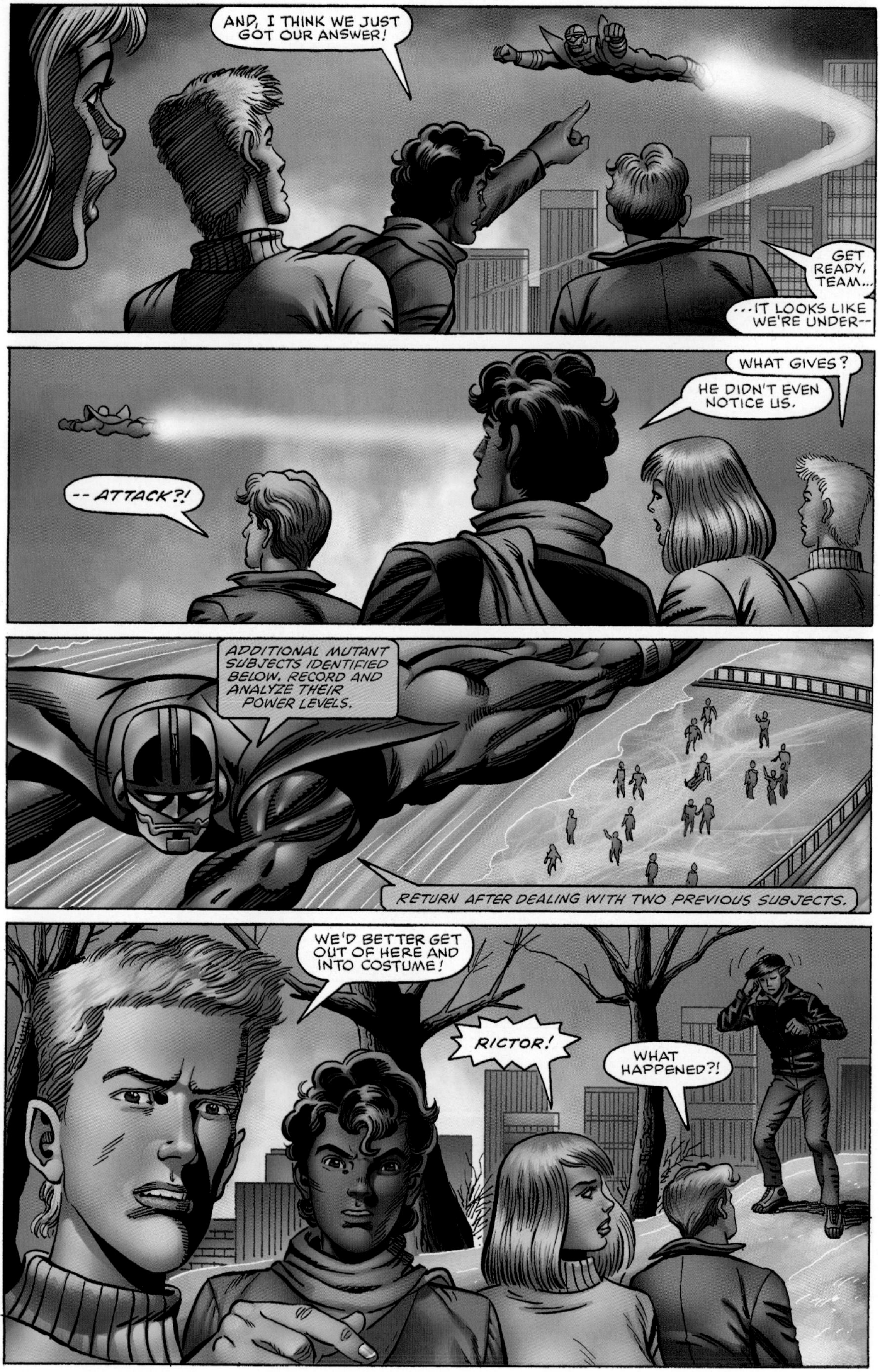
AND, I THINK WE JUST GOT OUR ANSWER!
GET READY, TEAM...
...IT LOOKS LIKE WE'RE UNDER--
WHAT GIVES?
HE DIDN'T EVEN NOTICE US.
-- ATTACK?!
ADDITIONAL MUTANT SUBJECTS IDENTIFIED BELOW. RECORD AND ANALYZE THEIR POWER LEVELS.
RETURN AFTER DEALING WITH TWO PREVIOUS SUBJECTS.
WE'D BETTER GET OUT OF HERE AND INTO COSTUME!
RICTOR!
WHAT HAPPENED?!

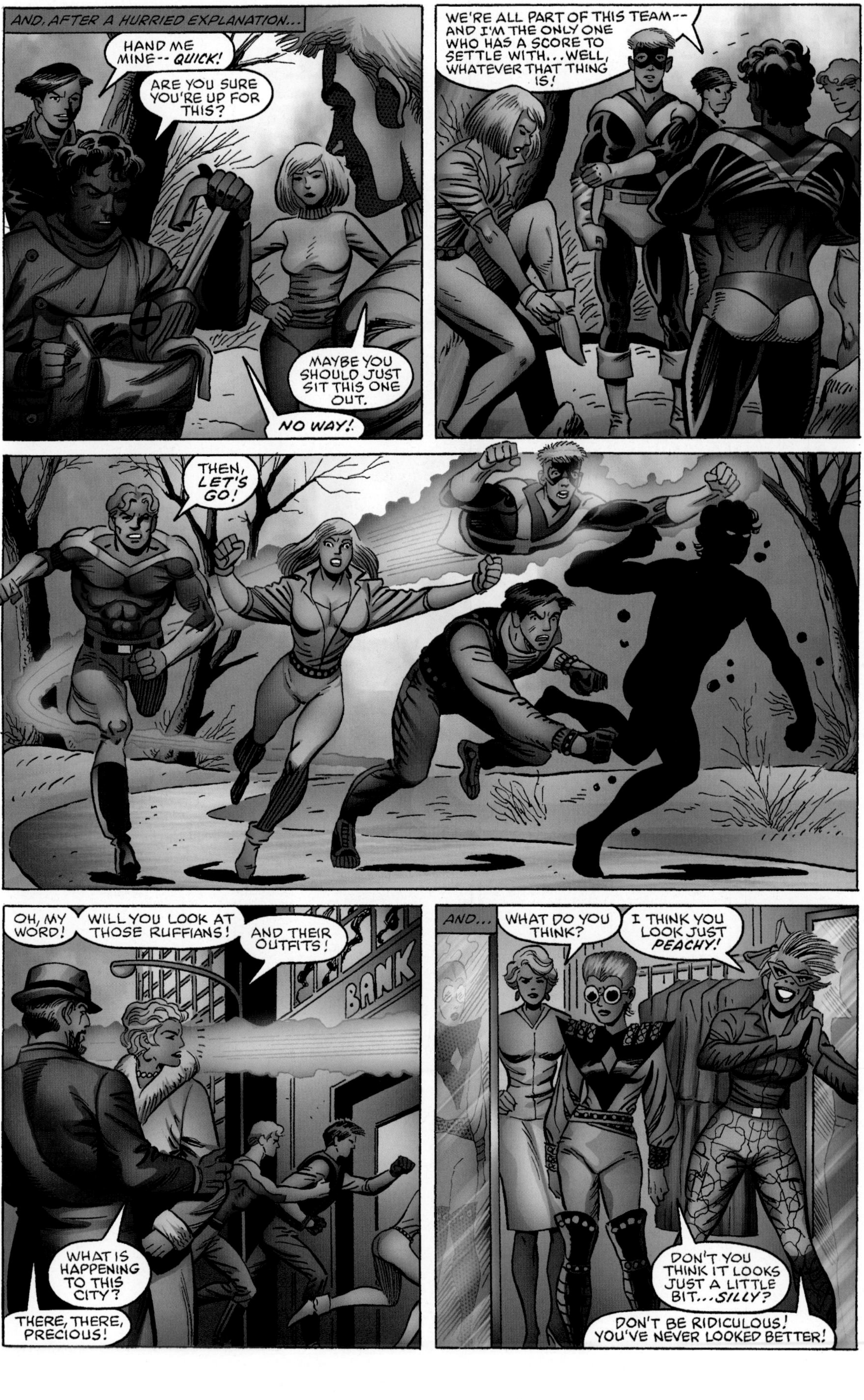
AND, AFTER A HURRIED EXPLANATION...
HAND ME MINE-- QUICK!
ARE YOU SURE YOU'RE UP FOR THIS?
MAYBE YOU SHOULD JUST SIT THIS ONE OUT.
NO WAY!
WE'RE ALL PART OF THIS TEAM-- AND I'M THE ONLY ONE WHO HAS A SCORE TO SETTLE WITH...WELL, WHATEVER THAT THING IS!
THEN, LET'S GO!
OH, MY WORD!
WILL YOU LOOK AT THOSE RUFFIANS!
AND THEIR OUTFITS!
BANK
WHAT IS HAPPENING TO THIS CITY?
THERE, THERE, PRECIOUS!
AND...
WHAT DO YOU THINK?
I THINK YOU LOOK JUST PEACHY!
DON'T YOU THINK IT LOOKS JUST A LITTLE BIT...SILLY?
DON'T BE RIDICULOUS! YOU'VE NEVER LOOKED BETTER!

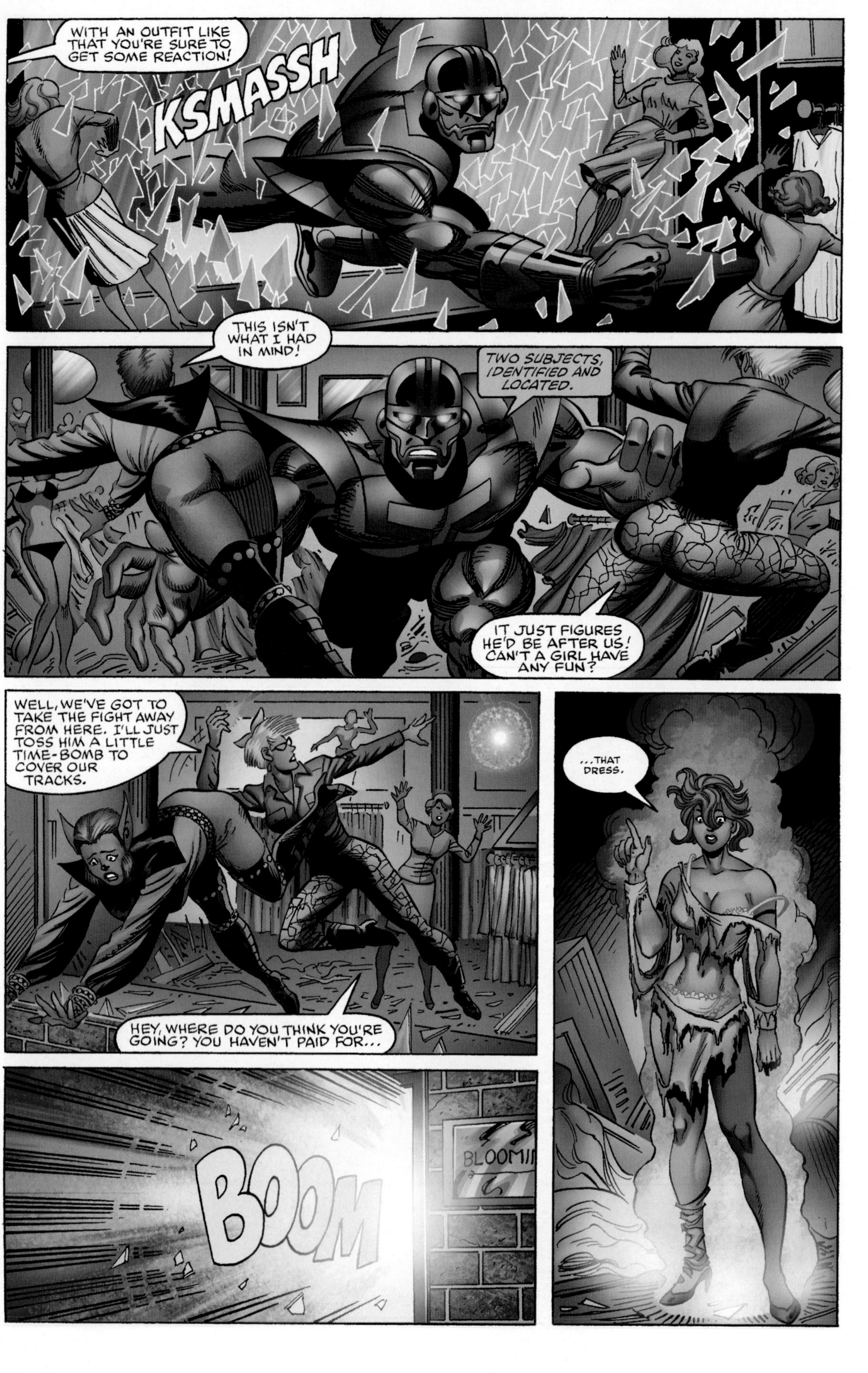
WITH AN OUTFIT LIKE THAT YOU'RE SURE TO GET SOME REACTION!
KSMASSH
THIS ISN'T WHAT I HAD IN MIND!
TWO SUBJECTS, IDENTIFIED AND LOCATED.
IT JUST FIGURES HE'D BE AFTER US! CAN'T A GIRL HAVE ANY FUN?
WELL, WE'VE GOT TO TAKE THE FIGHT AWAY FROM HERE. I'LL JUST TOSS HIM A LITTLE TIME-BOMB TO COVER OUR TRACKS.
HEY, WHERE DO YOU THINK YOU'RE GOING? YOU HAVEN'T PAID FOR...
BOOM
BLOOMI
...THAT DRESS.

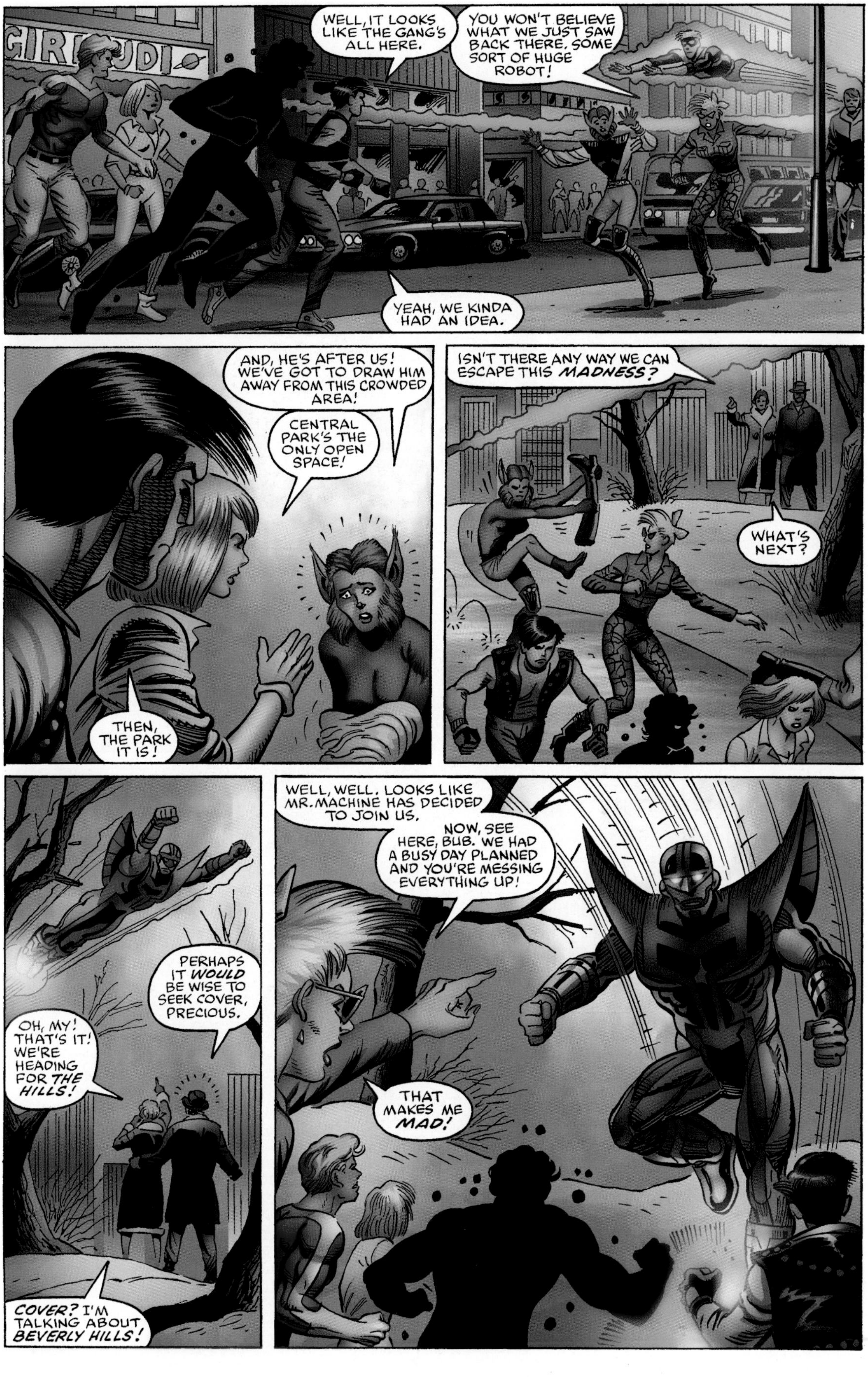

WELL, IT LOOKS LIKE THE GANG'S ALL HERE.
YOU WON'T BELIEVE WHAT WE JUST SAW BACK THERE. SOME SORT OF HUGE ROBOT!
YEAH, WE KINDA HAD AN IDEA.
AND, HE'S AFTER US! WE'VE GOT TO DRAW HIM AWAY FROM THIS CROWDED AREA!
CENTRAL PARK'S THE ONLY OPEN SPACE!
THEN, THE PARK IT IS!
ISN'T THERE ANY WAY WE CAN ESCAPE THIS MADNESS?
WHAT'S NEXT?
PERHAPS IT WOULD BE WISE TO SEEK COVER, PRECIOUS.
OH, MY! THAT'S IT! WE'RE HEADING FOR THE HILLS!
COVER? I'M TALKING ABOUT BEVERLY HILLS!
WELL, WELL. LOOKS LIKE MR. MACHINE HAS DECIDED TO JOIN US.
NOW, SEE HERE, BUB. WE HAD A BUSY DAY PLANNED AND YOU'RE MESSING EVERYTHING UP!
THAT MAKES ME MAD!

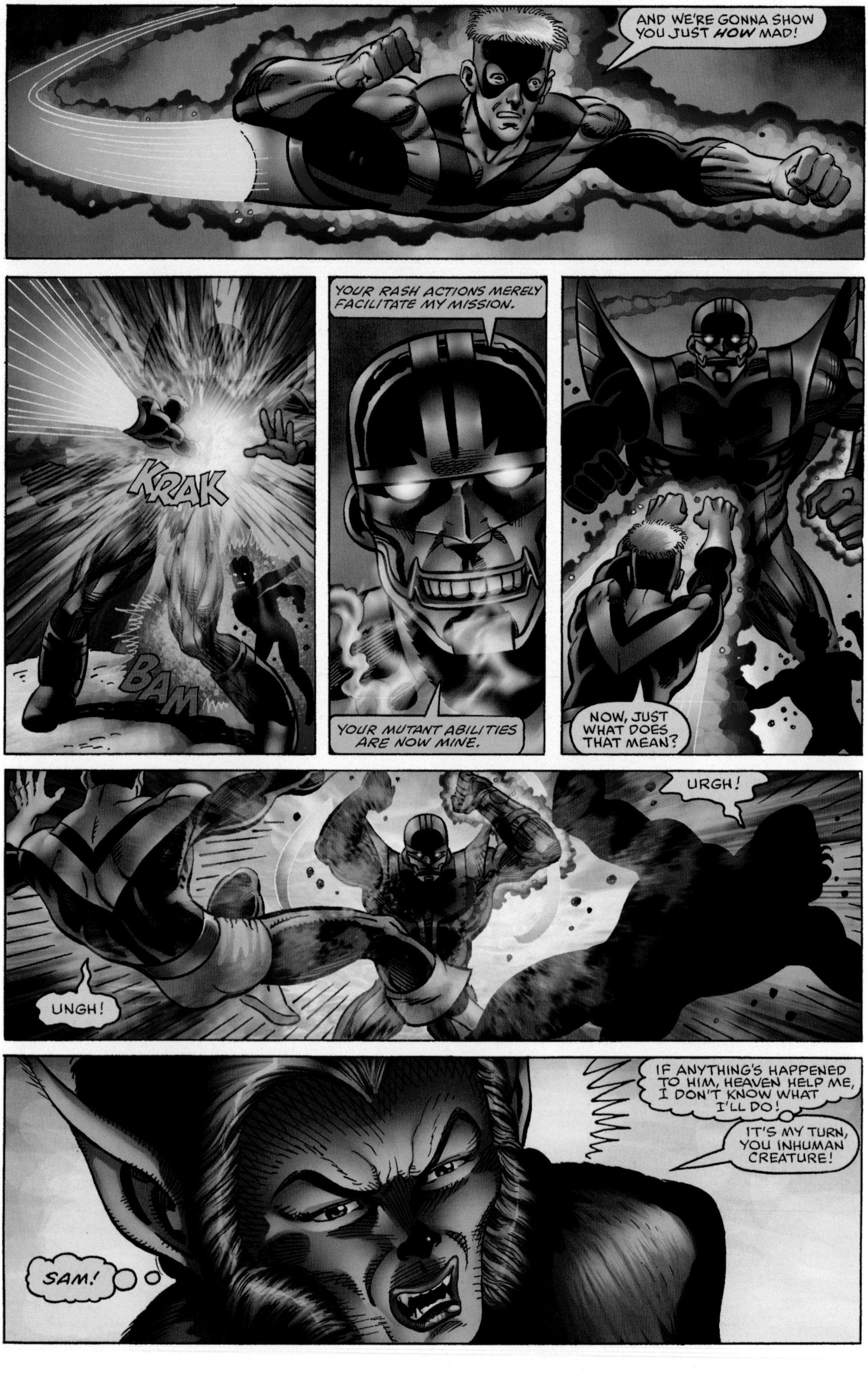
AND WE'RE GONNA SHOW YOU JUST HOW MAD!
KRAK
BAM
YOUR RASH ACTIONS MERELY FACILITATE MY MISSION.
YOUR MUTANT ABILITIES ARE NOW MINE.
NOW, JUST WHAT DOES THAT MEAN?
URGH!
UNGH!
IF ANYTHING'S HAPPENED TO HIM, HEAVEN HELP ME, I DON'T KNOW WHAT I'LL DO!
IT'S MY TURN, YOU INHUMAN CREATURE!
SAM!

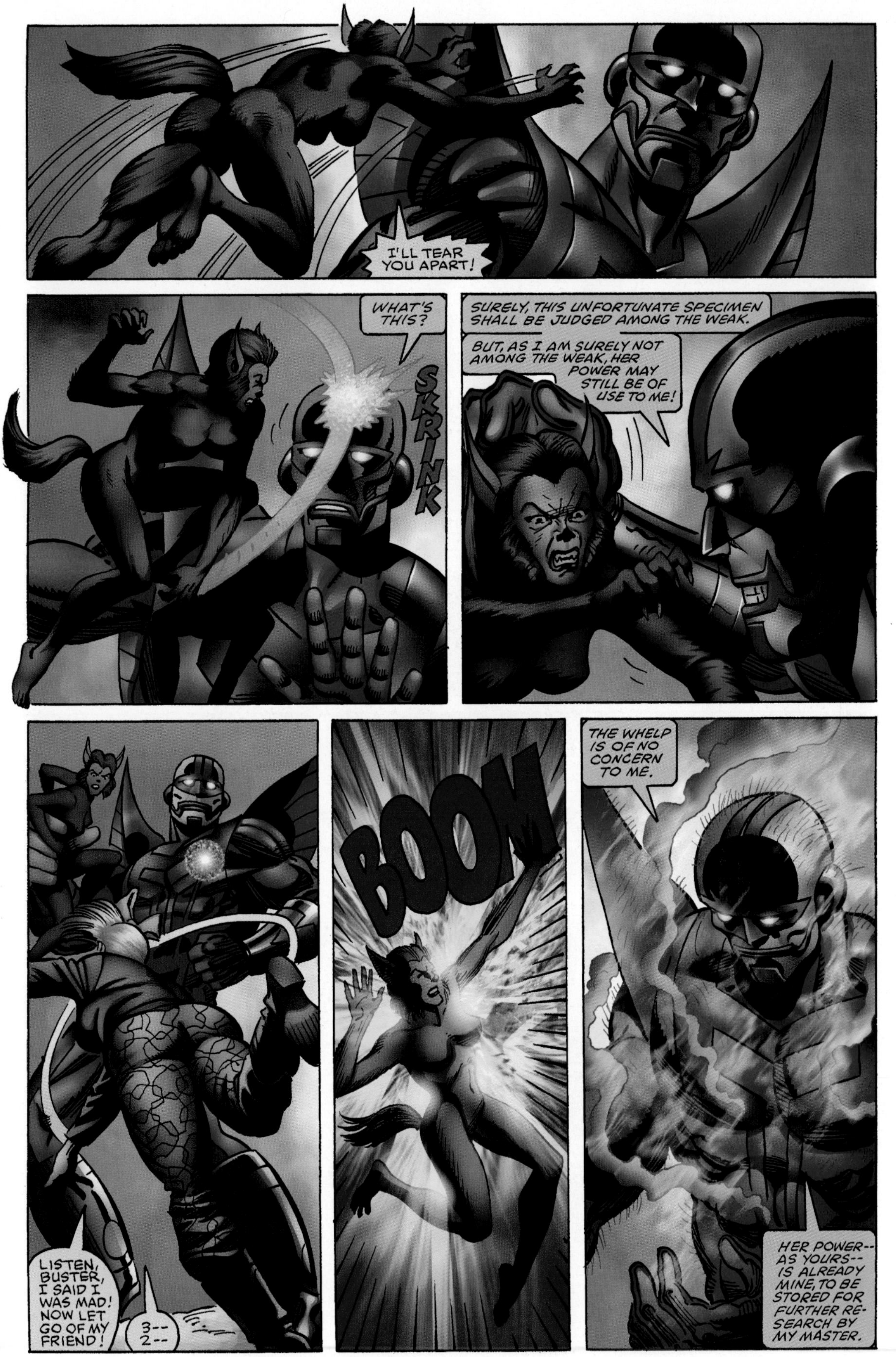
I'LL TEAR YOU APART!
WHAT'S THIS?
SKRINK
SURELY, THIS UNFORTUNATE SPECIMEN SHALL BE JUDGED AMONG THE WEAK.
BUT, AS I AM SURELY NOT AMONG THE WEAK, HER POWER MAY STILL BE OF USE TO ME!
LISTEN, BUSTER, I SAID I WAS MAD! NOW LET GO OF MY FRIEND!
3-- 2--
BOOM
THE WHELP IS OF NO CONCERN TO ME.
HER POWER-- AS YOURS-- IS ALREADY MINE, TO BE STORED FOR FURTHER RE-SEARCH BY MY MASTER.

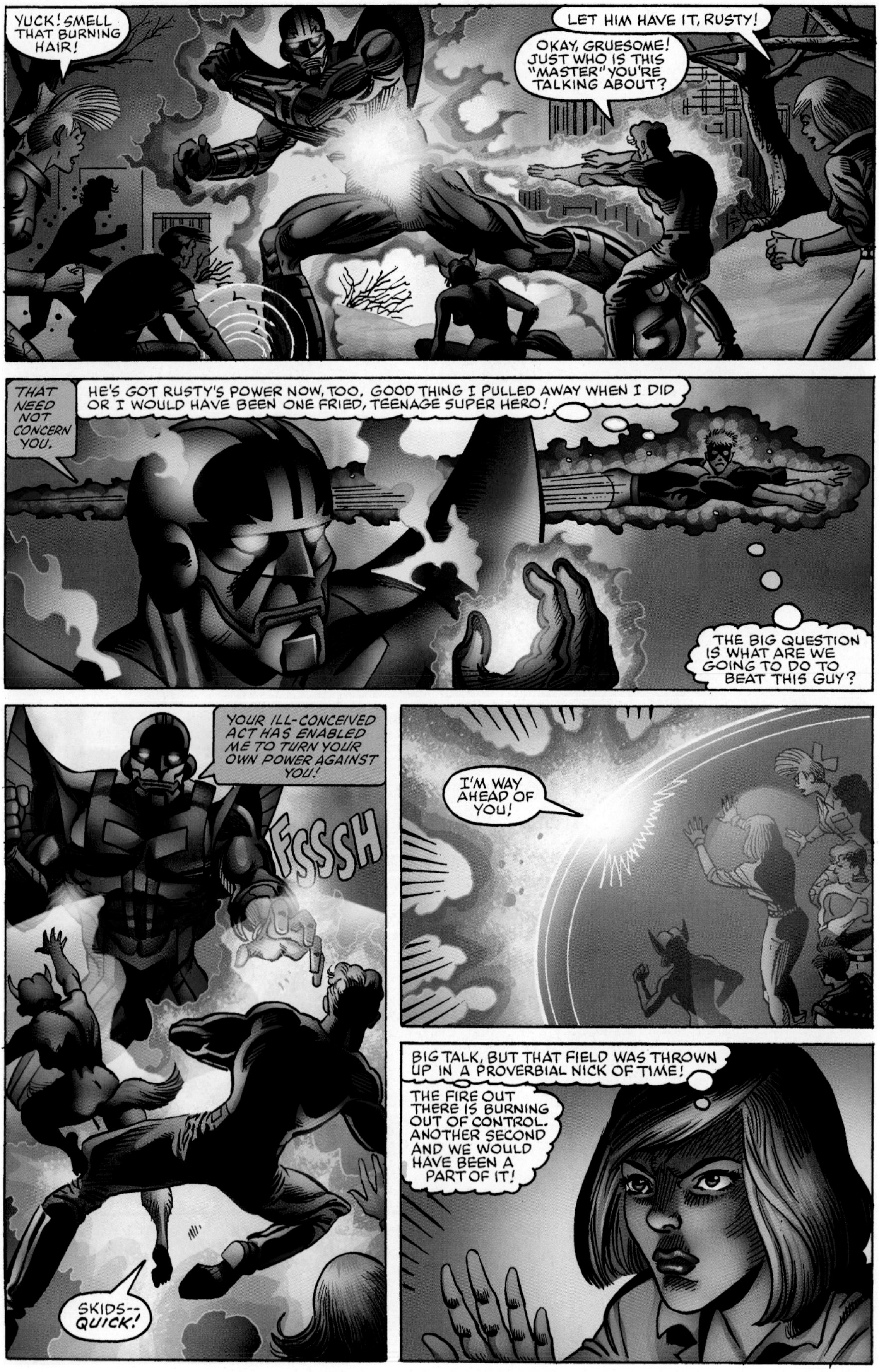
YUCK! SMELL THAT BURNING HAIR!
LET HIM HAVE IT, RUSTY!
OKAY, GRUESOME! JUST WHO IS THIS "MASTER" YOU'RE TALKING ABOUT?
THAT NEED NOT CONCERN YOU.
HE'S GOT RUSTY'S POWER NOW, TOO. GOOD THING I PULLED AWAY WHEN I DID OR I WOULD HAVE BEEN ONE FRIED, TEENAGE SUPER HERO!
THE BIG QUESTION IS WHAT ARE WE GOING TO DO TO BEAT THIS GUY?
YOUR ILL-CONCEIVED ACT HAS ENABLED ME TO TURN YOUR OWN POWER AGAINST YOU!
FSSSH
SKIDS-- QUICK!
I'M WAY AHEAD OF YOU!
BIG TALK, BUT THAT FIELD WAS THROWN UP IN A PROVERBIAL NICK OF TIME!
THE FIRE OUT THERE IS BURNING OUT OF CONTROL. ANOTHER SECOND AND WE WOULD HAVE BEEN A PART OF IT!

SKIDS, YOU'VE GOT TO LOWER YOUR FIELD, JUST ENOUGH TO RELEASE ME. I'VE GOT TO GET THAT FIRE UNDER CONTROL. WHO KNOWS WHAT COULD HAPPEN IF THE BLAZE WERE TO RAGE UNCHECKED?

NEVER AGAIN WILL I LET SOMEONE WHO'S INNOCENT BE HURT BECAUSE OF MY CARELESSNESS!

GOT TO ABSORB THIS *INFERNO*!

HURRY, RUSTY, GET BACK IN HERE!

I CAN'T! YOU'D ALL BE BURNED TO CRISPS!

TAKE CARE OF YOUR-SELVES!

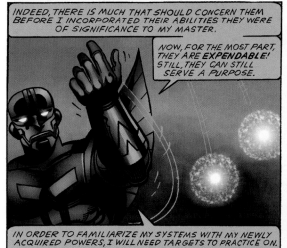

INDEED, THERE IS MUCH THAT SHOULD CONCERN THEM BEFORE I INCORPORATED THEIR ABILITIES THEY WERE OF SIGNIFICANCE TO MY MASTER.

NOW, FOR THE MOST PART, THEY ARE *EXPENDABLE!* STILL, THEY CAN STILL SERVE A PURPOSE.

IN ORDER TO FAMILIARIZE MY SYSTEMS WITH MY NEWLY ACQUIRED POWERS, I WILL NEED TARGETS TO PRACTICE ON.

THANK GOODNESS I'VE STILL GOT MOST OF THE TEAM PROTECTED!

BUT WHAT ABOUT--

RUSTY!!!

ARRGH!

IT WASN'T A DIRECT HIT!

LISTEN, TALL-DARK-GRUESOME, THERE'S NO WAY YOU'LL BE ABLE TO PENETRATE MY FIELD!

THERE WILL BE NO NEED FOR THAT!

BY SIMPLY MAKING CONTACT WITH IT...

...I HAVE DONE ALL THAT IS NECESSARY.

YOUR POWER HAS BEEN ADDED TO MY EXPANDING ARRAY OF RESOURCES --

--AND YOUR FIELD IS NOW SUBJECT TO MY WILL AS READILY AS YOUR OWN.

UH-OH!

I'VE GOT TO TRY SOMETHING. MAYBE, INSTEAD OF RELEASING MY ENERGY IN SINGLE BLASTS, I CAN STORE IT UP--CONCENTRATE IT--AND RELEASE IT ALL AT ONCE!

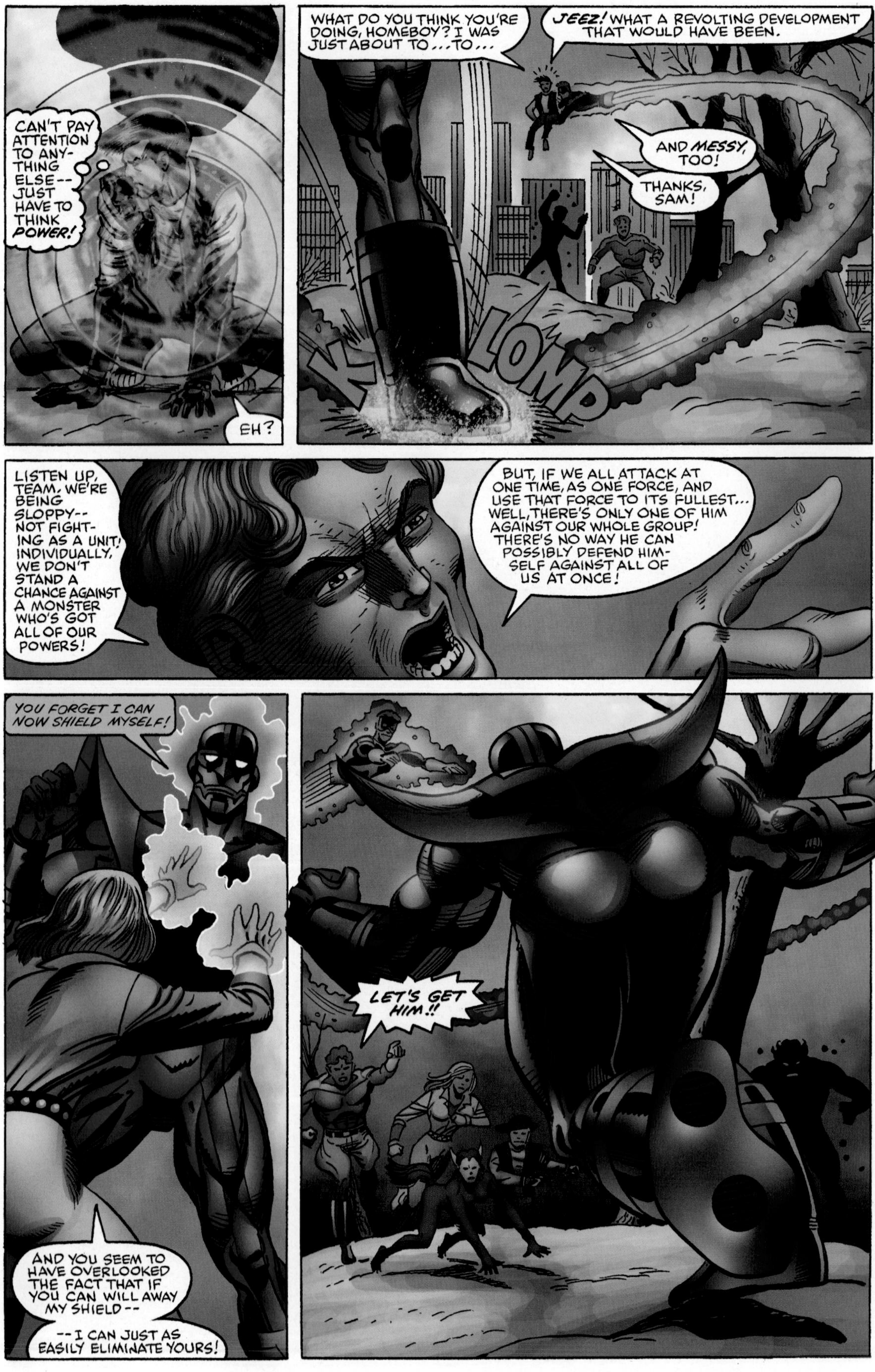
CAN'T PAY ATTENTION TO ANYTHING ELSE-- JUST HAVE TO THINK POWER!
EH?
WHAT DO YOU THINK YOU'RE DOING, HOMEBOY? I WAS JUST ABOUT TO...TO...
JEEZ! WHAT A REVOLTING DEVELOPMENT THAT WOULD HAVE BEEN.
AND MESSY, TOO!
THANKS, SAM!
KLOMP
LISTEN UP, TEAM. WE'RE BEING SLOPPY-- NOT FIGHTING AS A UNIT! INDIVIDUALLY, WE DON'T STAND A CHANCE AGAINST A MONSTER WHO'S GOT ALL OF OUR POWERS!
BUT, IF WE ALL ATTACK AT ONE TIME, AS ONE FORCE, AND USE THAT FORCE TO ITS FULLEST... WELL, THERE'S ONLY ONE OF HIM AGAINST OUR WHOLE GROUP! THERE'S NO WAY HE CAN POSSIBLY DEFEND HIMSELF AGAINST ALL OF US AT ONCE!
YOU FORGET I CAN NOW SHIELD MYSELF!
AND YOU SEEM TO HAVE OVERLOOKED THE FACT THAT IF YOU CAN WILL AWAY MY SHIELD--
--I CAN JUST AS EASILY ELIMINATE YOURS!
LET'S GET HIM!!

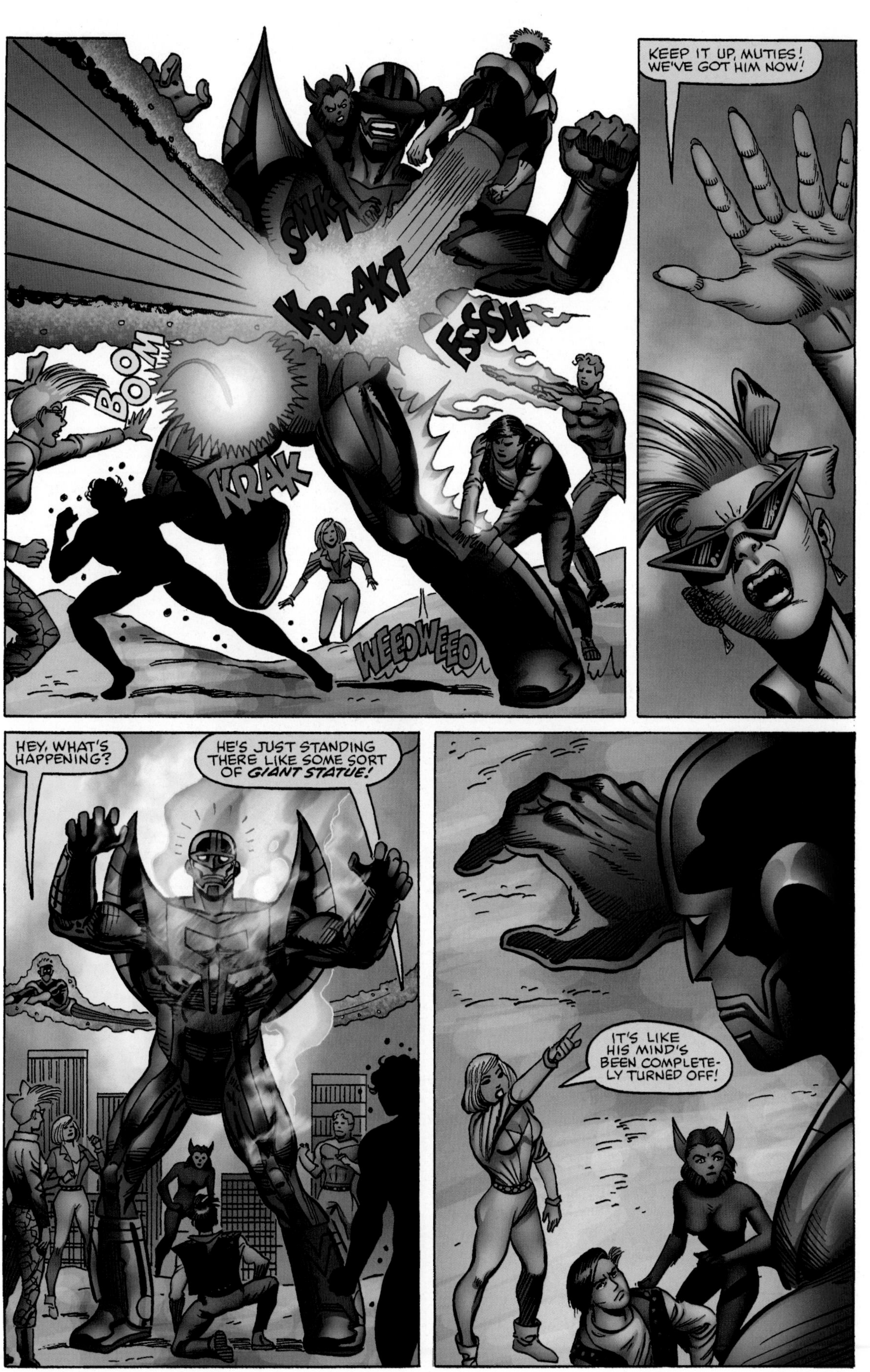
SNIKT
KBRAKT
FSSSH
BOOM
KRAK
WEEOWEEO
KEEP IT UP, MUTIES! WE'VE GOT HIM NOW!
HEY, WHAT'S HAPPENING?
HE'S JUST STANDING THERE LIKE SOME SORT OF *GIANT STATUE!*
IT'S LIKE HIS MIND'S BEEN COMPLETELY TURNED OFF!

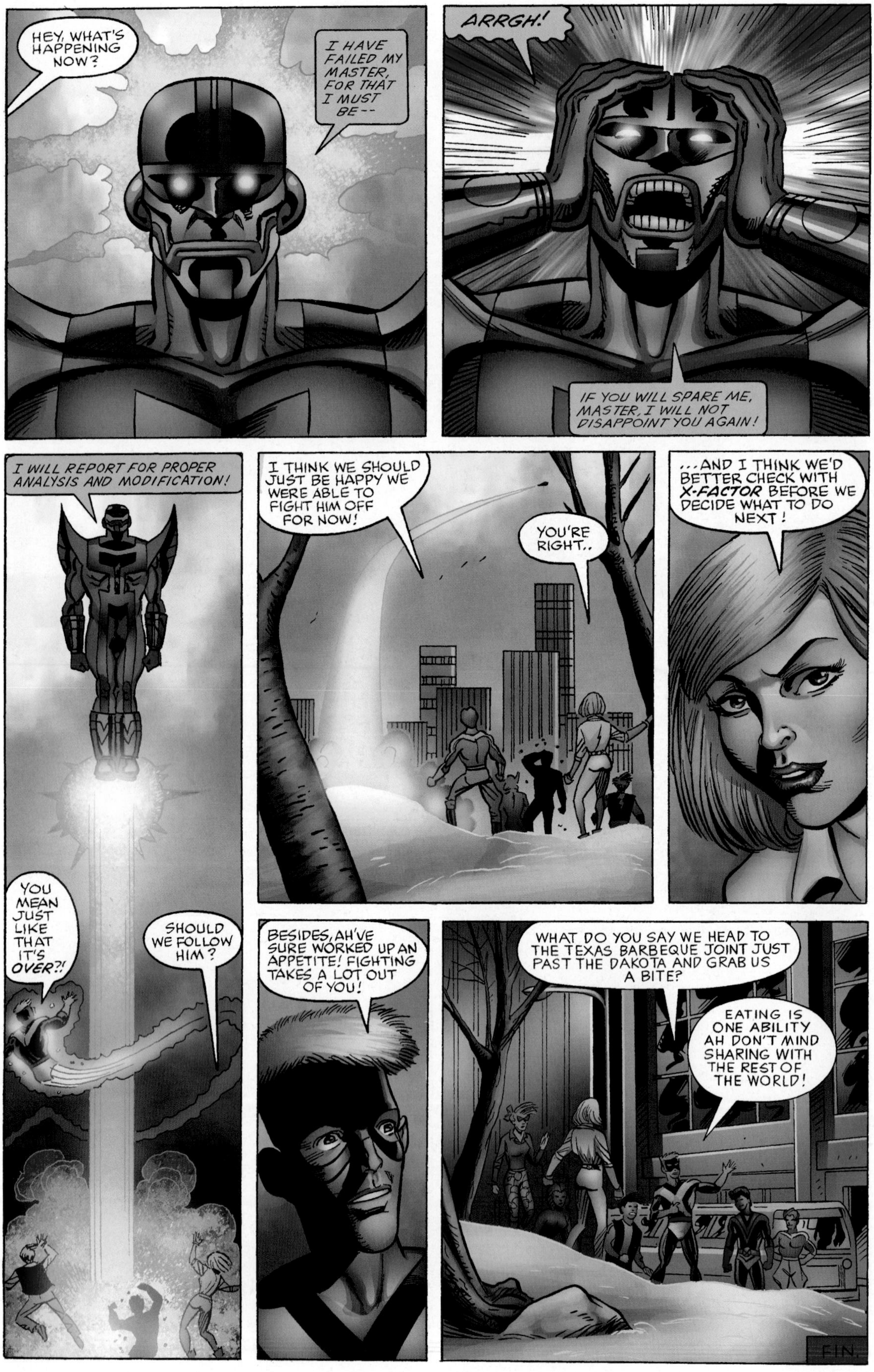
HEY, WHAT'S HAPPENING NOW?
I HAVE FAILED MY MASTER, FOR THAT I MUST BE--
ARRGH!
IF YOU WILL SPARE ME, MASTER, I WILL NOT DISAPPOINT YOU AGAIN!
I WILL REPORT FOR PROPER ANALYSIS AND MODIFICATION!
YOU MEAN JUST LIKE THAT IT'S OVER?!
SHOULD WE FOLLOW HIM?
I THINK WE SHOULD JUST BE HAPPY WE WERE ABLE TO FIGHT HIM OFF FOR NOW!
YOU'RE RIGHT..
...AND I THINK WE'D BETTER CHECK WITH X-FACTOR BEFORE WE DECIDE WHAT TO DO NEXT!
BESIDES, AH'VE SURE WORKED UP AN APPETITE! FIGHTING TAKES A LOT OUT OF YOU!
WHAT DO YOU SAY WE HEAD TO THE TEXAS BARBEQUE JOINT JUST PAST THE DAKOTA AND GRAB US A BITE?
EATING IS ONE ABILITY AH DON'T MIND SHARING WITH THE REST OF THE WORLD!
FIN.

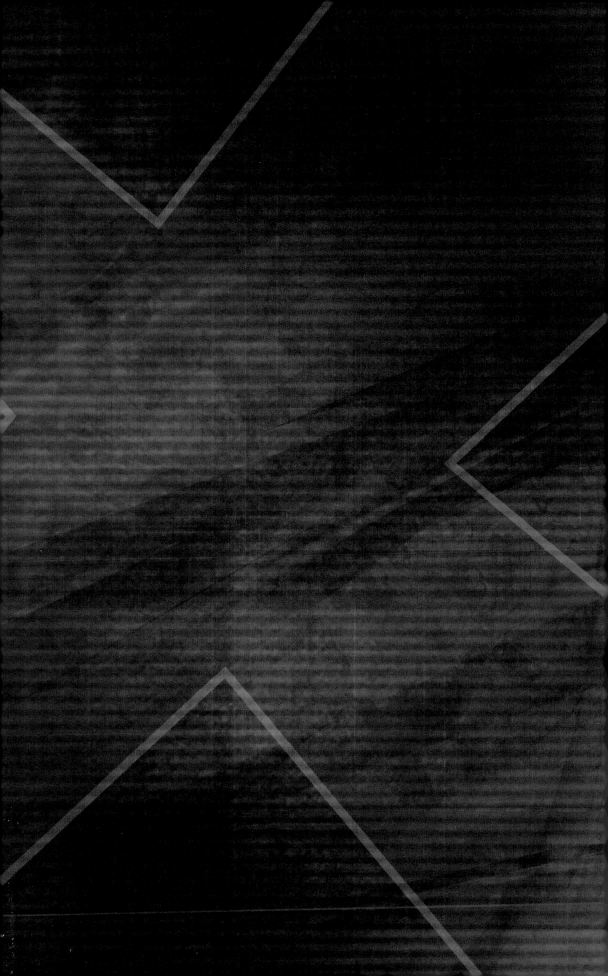

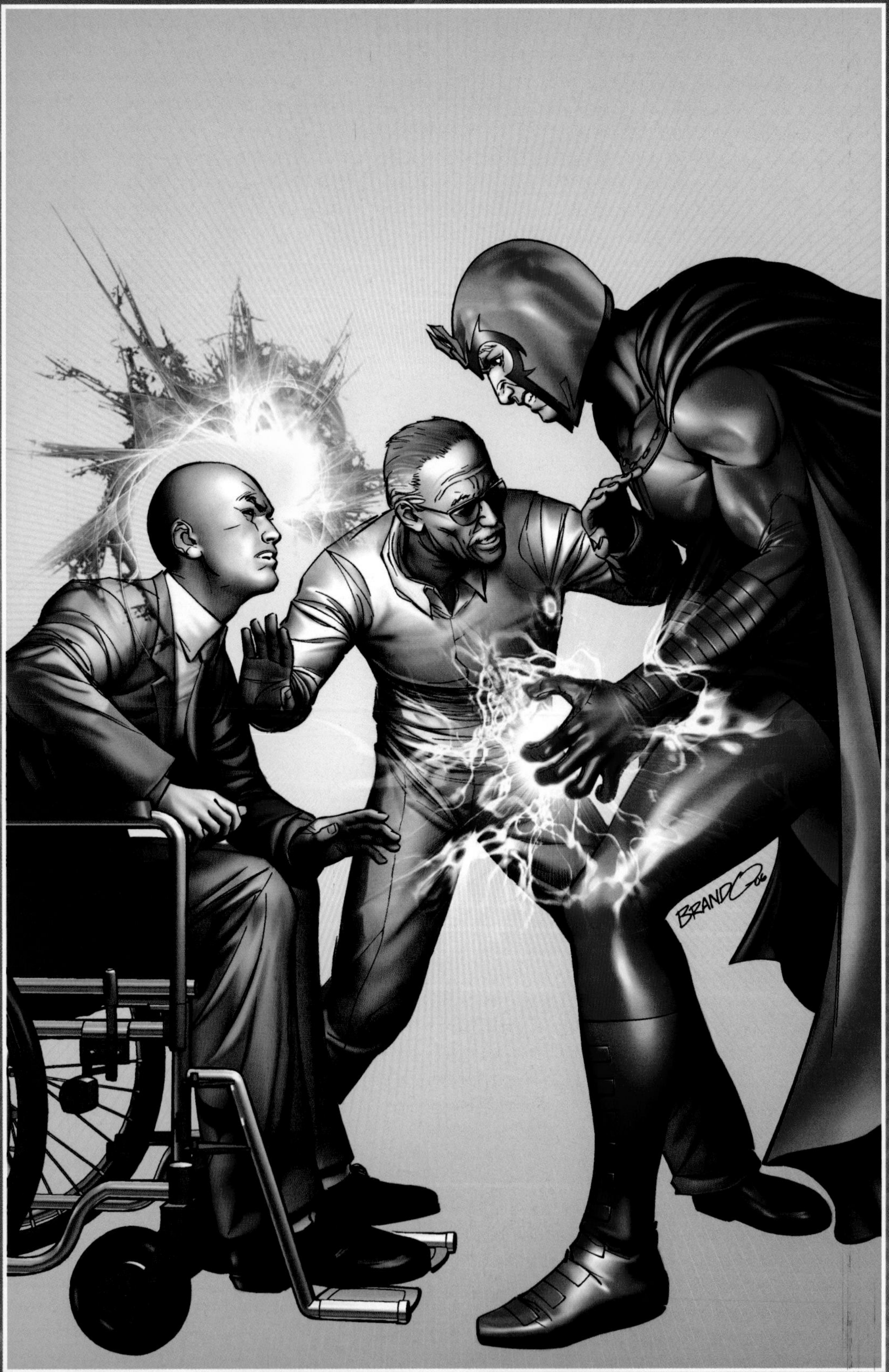
BRANDO '06

X-MEN: THE UNLIKEY SAGA OF XAVIER, MAGNETO AND STAN

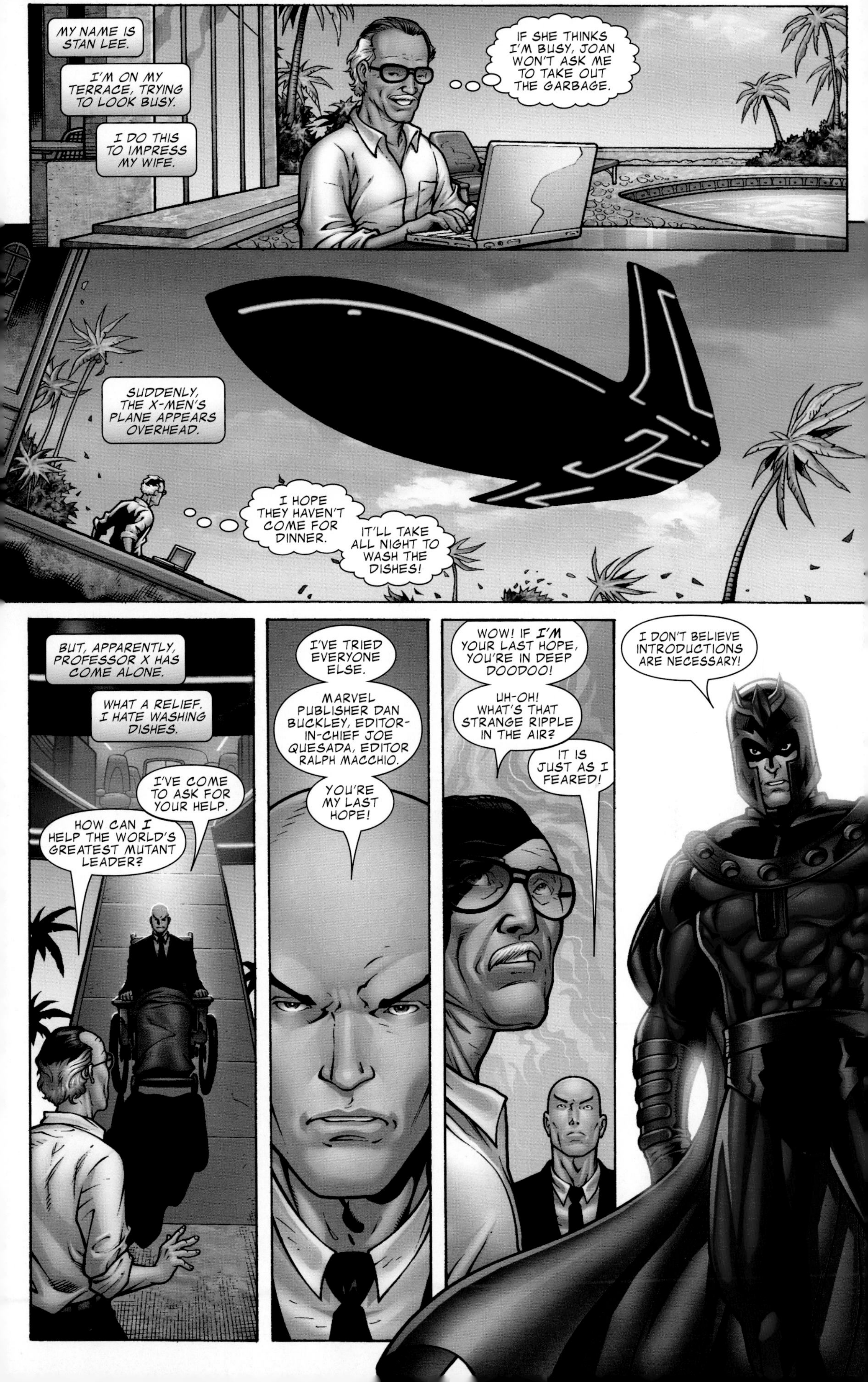
MY NAME IS STAN LEE.
I'M ON MY TERRACE, TRYING TO LOOK BUSY.
I DO THIS TO IMPRESS MY WIFE.
IF SHE THINKS I'M BUSY, JOAN WON'T ASK ME TO TAKE OUT THE GARBAGE.
SUDDENLY, THE X-MEN'S PLANE APPEARS OVERHEAD.
I HOPE THEY HAVEN'T COME FOR DINNER.
IT'LL TAKE ALL NIGHT TO WASH THE DISHES!
BUT, APPARENTLY, PROFESSOR X HAS COME ALONE.
WHAT A RELIEF. I HATE WASHING DISHES.
HOW CAN I HELP THE WORLD'S GREATEST MUTANT LEADER?
I'VE COME TO ASK FOR YOUR HELP.
I'VE TRIED EVERYONE ELSE.
MARVEL PUBLISHER DAN BUCKLEY, EDITOR-IN-CHIEF JOE QUESADA, EDITOR RALPH MACCHIO.
YOU'RE MY LAST HOPE!
WOW! IF I'M YOUR LAST HOPE, YOU'RE IN DEEP DOODOO!
UH-OH! WHAT'S THAT STRANGE RIPPLE IN THE AIR?
IT IS JUST AS I FEARED!
I DON'T BELIEVE INTRODUCTIONS ARE NECESSARY!

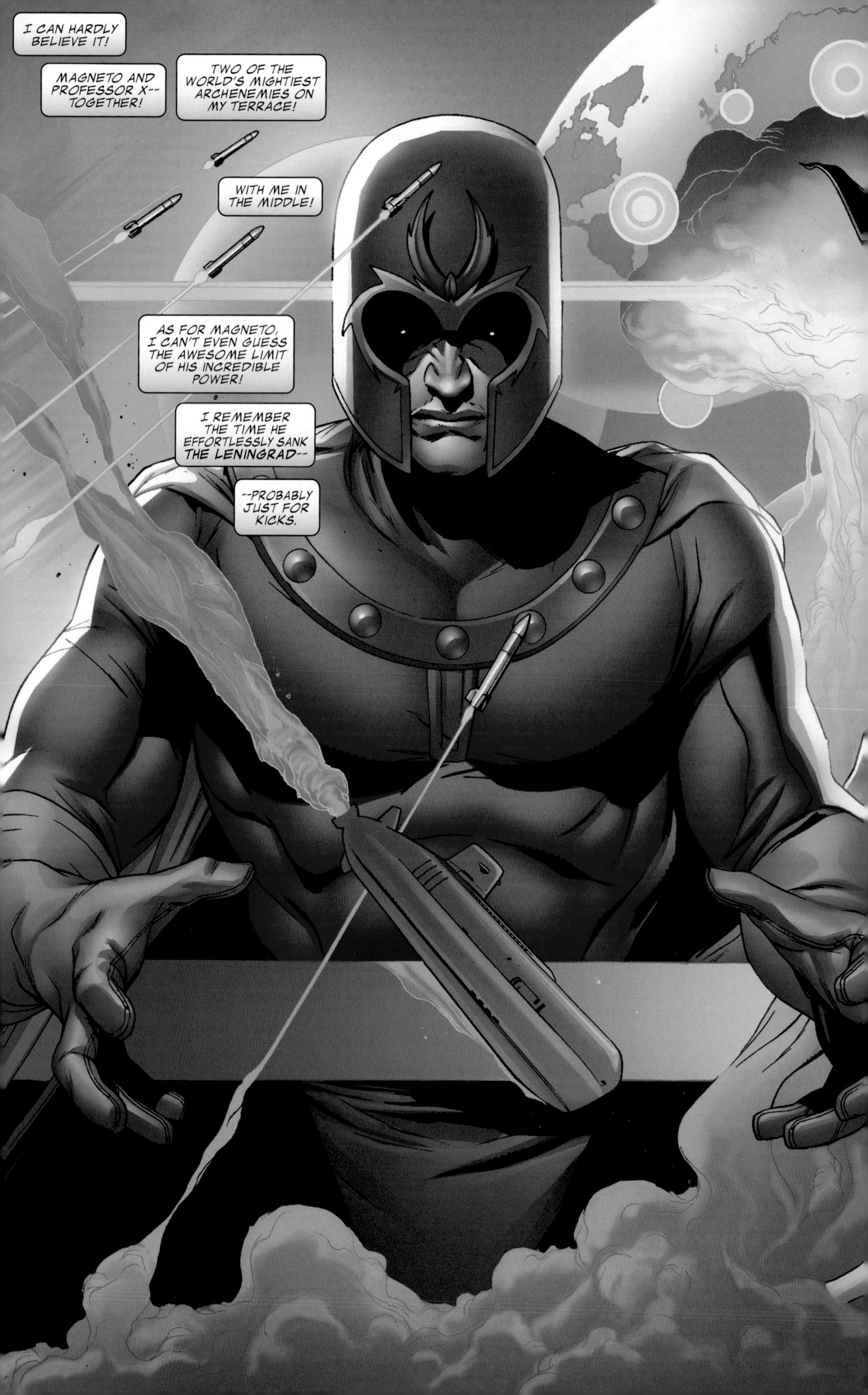
I CAN HARDLY BELIEVE IT!
MAGNETO AND PROFESSOR X--TOGETHER!
TWO OF THE WORLD'S MIGHTIEST ARCHENEMIES ON MY TERRACE!
WITH ME IN THE MIDDLE!
AS FOR MAGNETO, I CAN'T EVEN GUESS THE AWESOME LIMIT OF HIS INCREDIBLE POWER!
I REMEMBER THE TIME HE EFFORTLESSLY SANK THE LENINGRAD--
--PROBABLY JUST FOR KICKS.

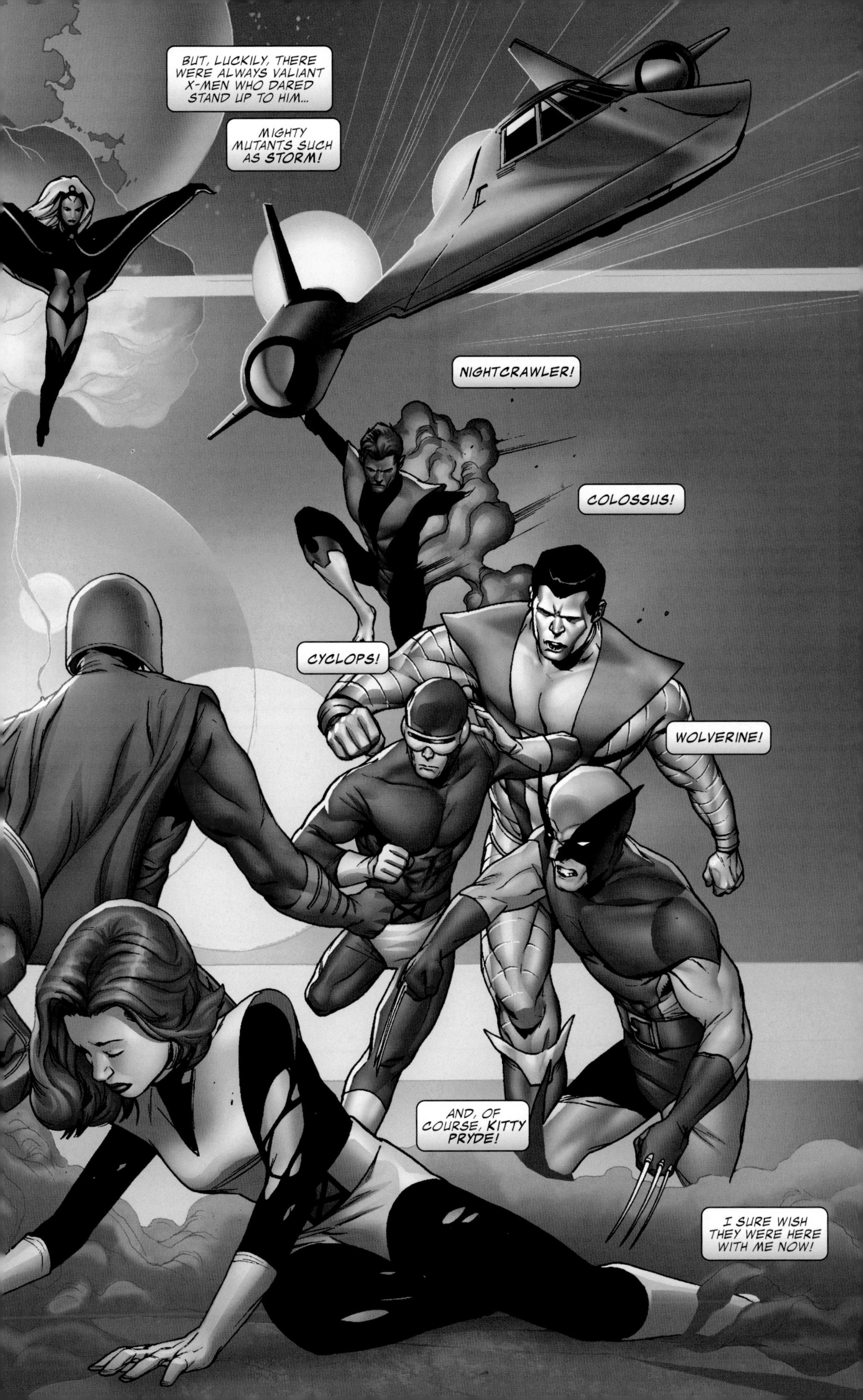
BUT, LUCKILY, THERE WERE ALWAYS VALIANT X-MEN WHO DARED STAND UP TO HIM...
MIGHTY MUTANTS SUCH AS STORM!
NIGHTCRAWLER!
COLOSSUS!
CYCLOPS!
WOLVERINE!
AND, OF COURSE, KITTY PRYDE!
I SURE WISH THEY WERE HERE WITH ME NOW!

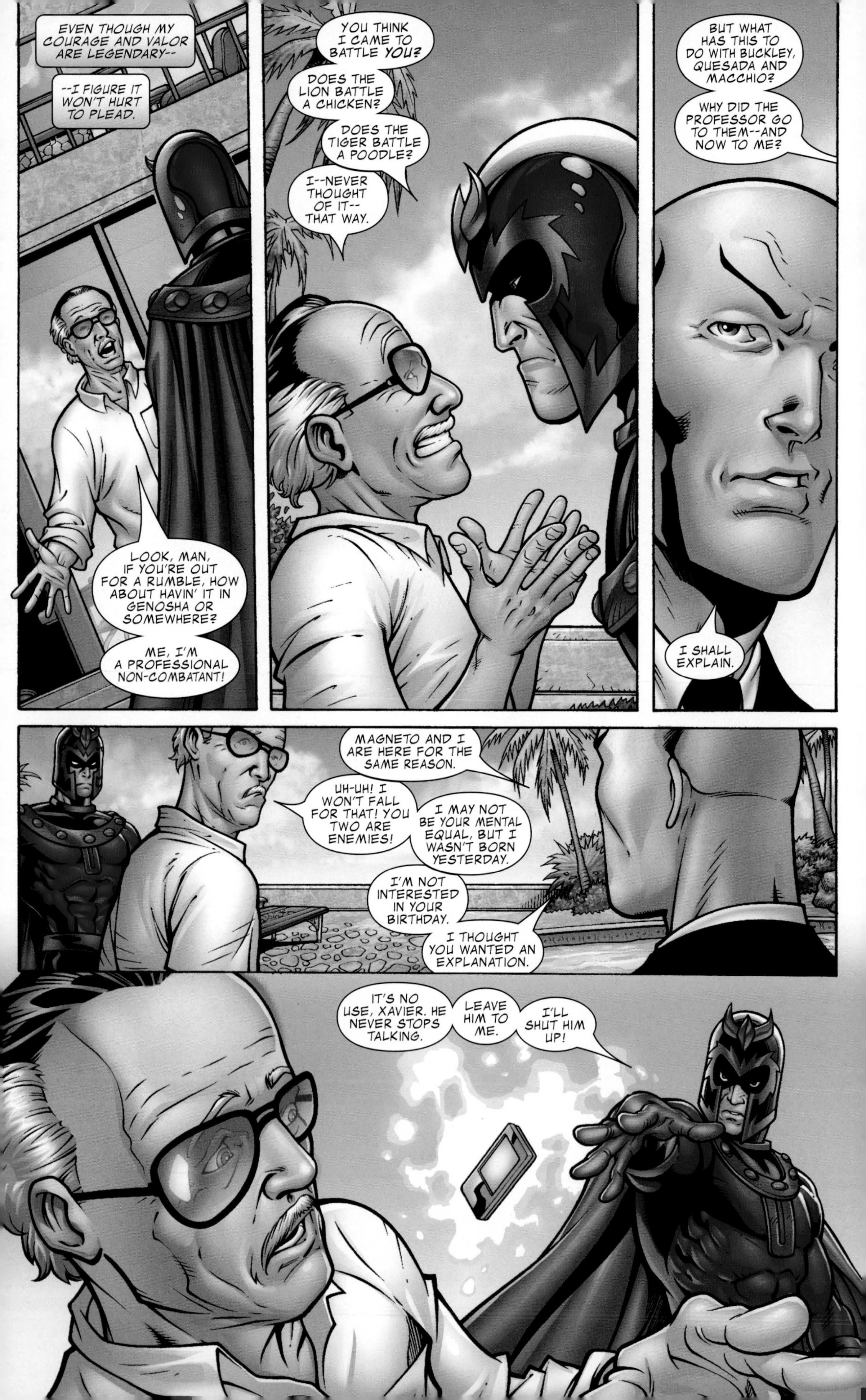
EVEN THOUGH MY COURAGE AND VALOR ARE LEGENDARY--
--I FIGURE IT WON'T HURT TO PLEAD.
LOOK, MAN, IF YOU'RE OUT FOR A RUMBLE, HOW ABOUT HAVIN' IT IN GENOSHA OR SOMEWHERE?
ME, I'M A PROFESSIONAL NON-COMBATANT!
YOU THINK I CAME TO BATTLE YOU?
DOES THE LION BATTLE A CHICKEN?
DOES THE TIGER BATTLE A POODLE?
I--NEVER THOUGHT OF IT--THAT WAY.
BUT WHAT HAS THIS TO DO WITH BUCKLEY, QUESADA AND MACCHIO?
WHY DID THE PROFESSOR GO TO THEM--AND NOW TO ME?
I SHALL EXPLAIN.
MAGNETO AND I ARE HERE FOR THE SAME REASON.
UH-UH! I WON'T FALL FOR THAT! YOU TWO ARE ENEMIES!
I MAY NOT BE YOUR MENTAL EQUAL, BUT I WASN'T BORN YESTERDAY.
I'M NOT INTERESTED IN YOUR BIRTHDAY.
I THOUGHT YOU WANTED AN EXPLANATION.
IT'S NO USE, XAVIER. HE NEVER STOPS TALKING.
LEAVE HIM TO ME.
I'LL SHUT HIM UP!

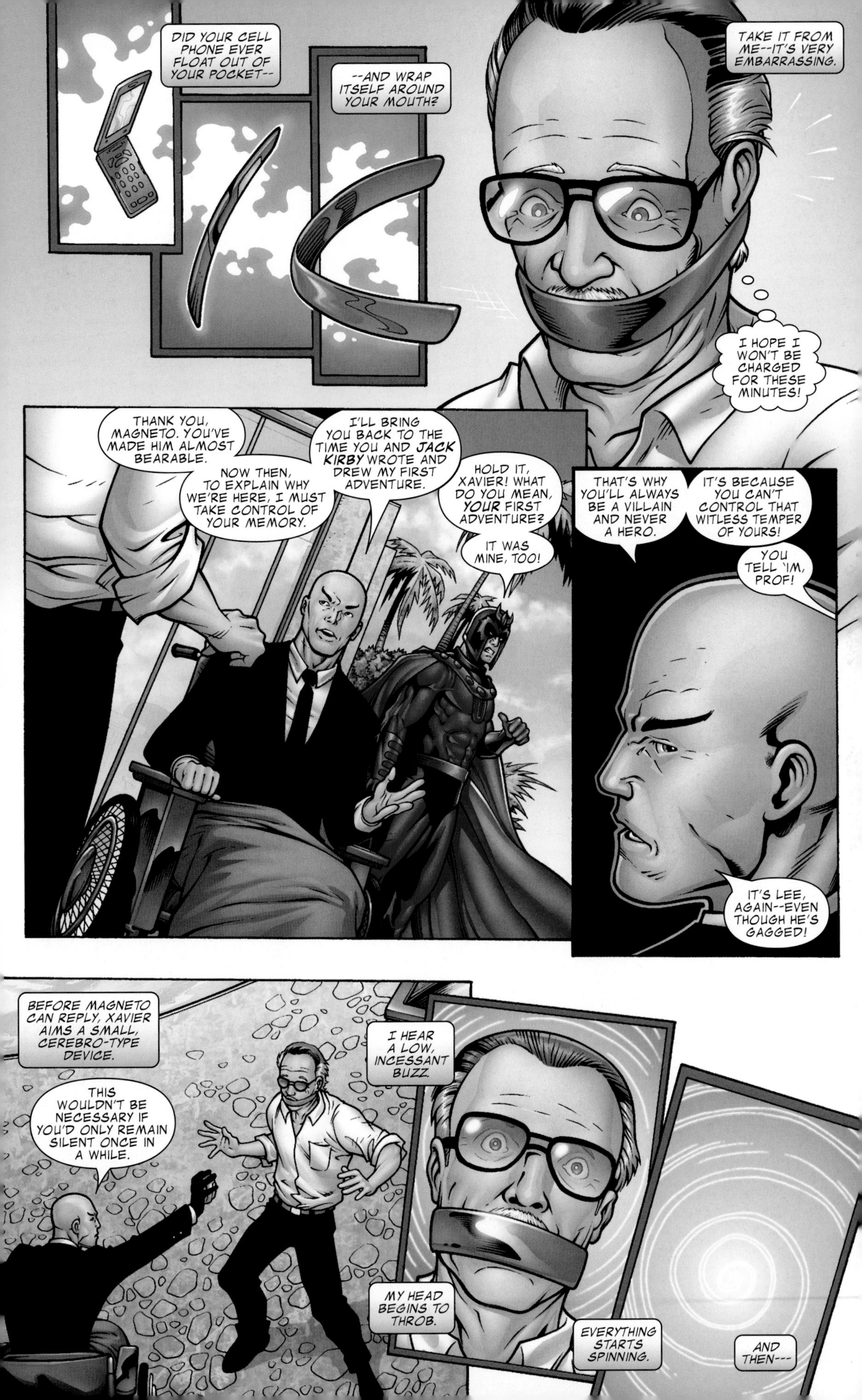

DID YOUR CELL PHONE EVER FLOAT OUT OF YOUR POCKET--
--AND WRAP ITSELF AROUND YOUR MOUTH?
TAKE IT FROM ME--IT'S VERY EMBARRASSING.
I HOPE I WON'T BE CHARGED FOR THESE MINUTES!
THANK YOU, MAGNETO. YOU'VE MADE HIM ALMOST BEARABLE.
NOW THEN, TO EXPLAIN WHY WE'RE HERE, I MUST TAKE CONTROL OF YOUR MEMORY.
I'LL BRING YOU BACK TO THE TIME YOU AND JACK KIRBY WROTE AND DREW MY FIRST ADVENTURE.
HOLD IT, XAVIER! WHAT DO YOU MEAN, YOUR FIRST ADVENTURE?
IT WAS MINE, TOO!
THAT'S WHY YOU'LL ALWAYS BE A VILLAIN AND NEVER A HERO.
IT'S BECAUSE YOU CAN'T CONTROL THAT WITLESS TEMPER OF YOURS!
YOU TELL 'IM, PROF!
IT'S LEE, AGAIN--EVEN THOUGH HE'S GAGGED!
BEFORE MAGNETO CAN REPLY, XAVIER AIMS A SMALL, CEREBRO-TYPE DEVICE.
THIS WOULDN'T BE NECESSARY IF YOU'D ONLY REMAIN SILENT ONCE IN A WHILE.
I HEAR A LOW, INCESSANT BUZZ.
MY HEAD BEGINS TO THROB.
EVERYTHING STARTS SPINNING.
AND THEN---

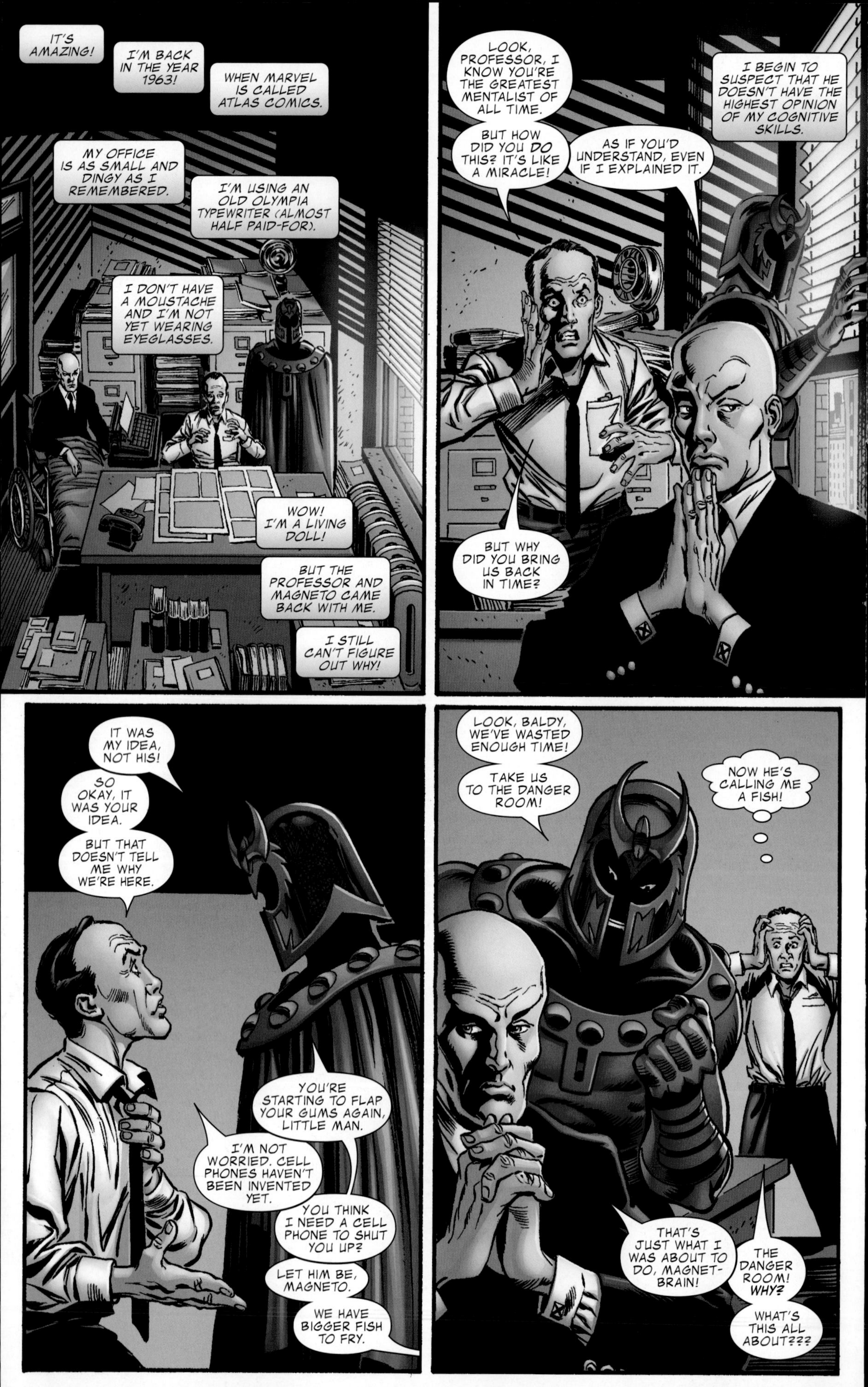
IT'S AMAZING!
I'M BACK IN THE YEAR 1963!
WHEN MARVEL IS CALLED ATLAS COMICS.
MY OFFICE IS AS SMALL AND DINGY AS I REMEMBERED.
I'M USING AN OLD OLYMPIA TYPEWRITER (ALMOST HALF PAID-FOR).
I DON'T HAVE A MOUSTACHE AND I'M NOT YET WEARING EYEGLASSES.
WOW! I'M A LIVING DOLL!
BUT THE PROFESSOR AND MAGNETO CAME BACK WITH ME.
I STILL CAN'T FIGURE OUT WHY!
LOOK, PROFESSOR, I KNOW YOU'RE THE GREATEST MENTALIST OF ALL TIME.
BUT HOW DID YOU DO THIS? IT'S LIKE A MIRACLE!
AS IF YOU'D UNDERSTAND, EVEN IF I EXPLAINED IT.
I BEGIN TO SUSPECT THAT HE DOESN'T HAVE THE HIGHEST OPINION OF MY COGNITIVE SKILLS.
BUT WHY DID YOU BRING US BACK IN TIME?
IT WAS MY IDEA, NOT HIS!
SO OKAY, IT WAS YOUR IDEA.
BUT THAT DOESN'T TELL ME WHY WE'RE HERE.
YOU'RE STARTING TO FLAP YOUR GUMS AGAIN, LITTLE MAN.
I'M NOT WORRIED. CELL PHONES HAVEN'T BEEN INVENTED YET.
YOU THINK I NEED A CELL PHONE TO SHUT YOU UP?
LET HIM BE, MAGNETO.
WE HAVE BIGGER FISH TO FRY.
LOOK, BALDY, WE'VE WASTED ENOUGH TIME!
TAKE US TO THE DANGER ROOM!
NOW HE'S CALLING ME A FISH!
THAT'S JUST WHAT I WAS ABOUT TO DO, MAGNET-BRAIN!
THE DANGER ROOM! WHY?
WHAT'S THIS ALL ABOUT???

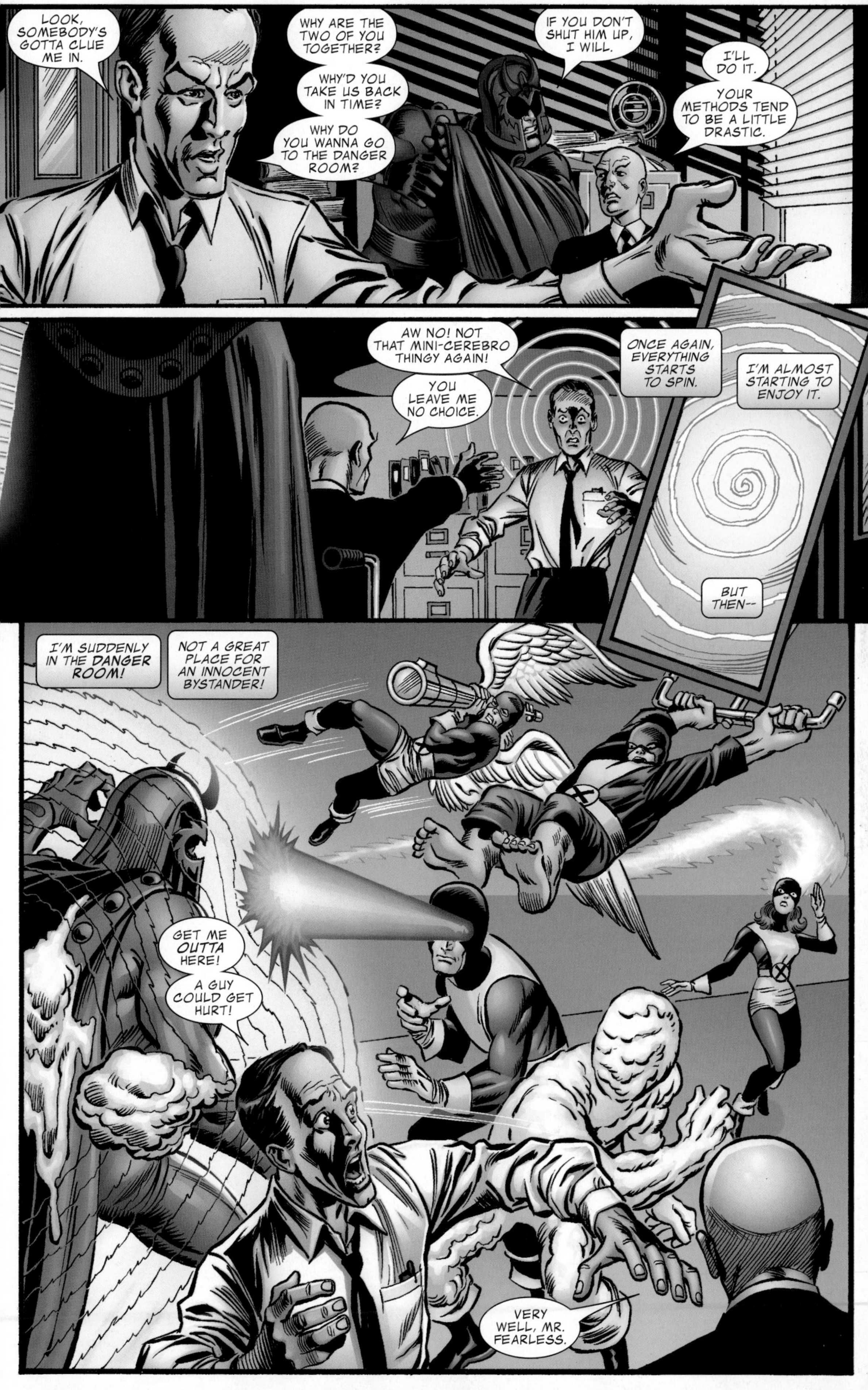
LOOK, SOMEBODY'S GOTTA CLUE ME IN.
WHY ARE THE TWO OF YOU TOGETHER?
WHY'D YOU TAKE US BACK IN TIME?
WHY DO YOU WANNA GO TO THE DANGER ROOM?
IF YOU DON'T SHUT HIM UP, I WILL.
I'LL DO IT.
YOUR METHODS TEND TO BE A LITTLE DRASTIC.
AW NO! NOT THAT MINI-CEREBRO THINGY AGAIN!
YOU LEAVE ME NO CHOICE.
ONCE AGAIN, EVERYTHING STARTS TO SPIN.
I'M ALMOST STARTING TO ENJOY IT.
BUT THEN--
I'M SUDDENLY IN THE DANGER ROOM!
NOT A GREAT PLACE FOR AN INNOCENT BYSTANDER!
GET ME OUTTA HERE!
A GUY COULD GET HURT!
VERY WELL, MR. FEARLESS.

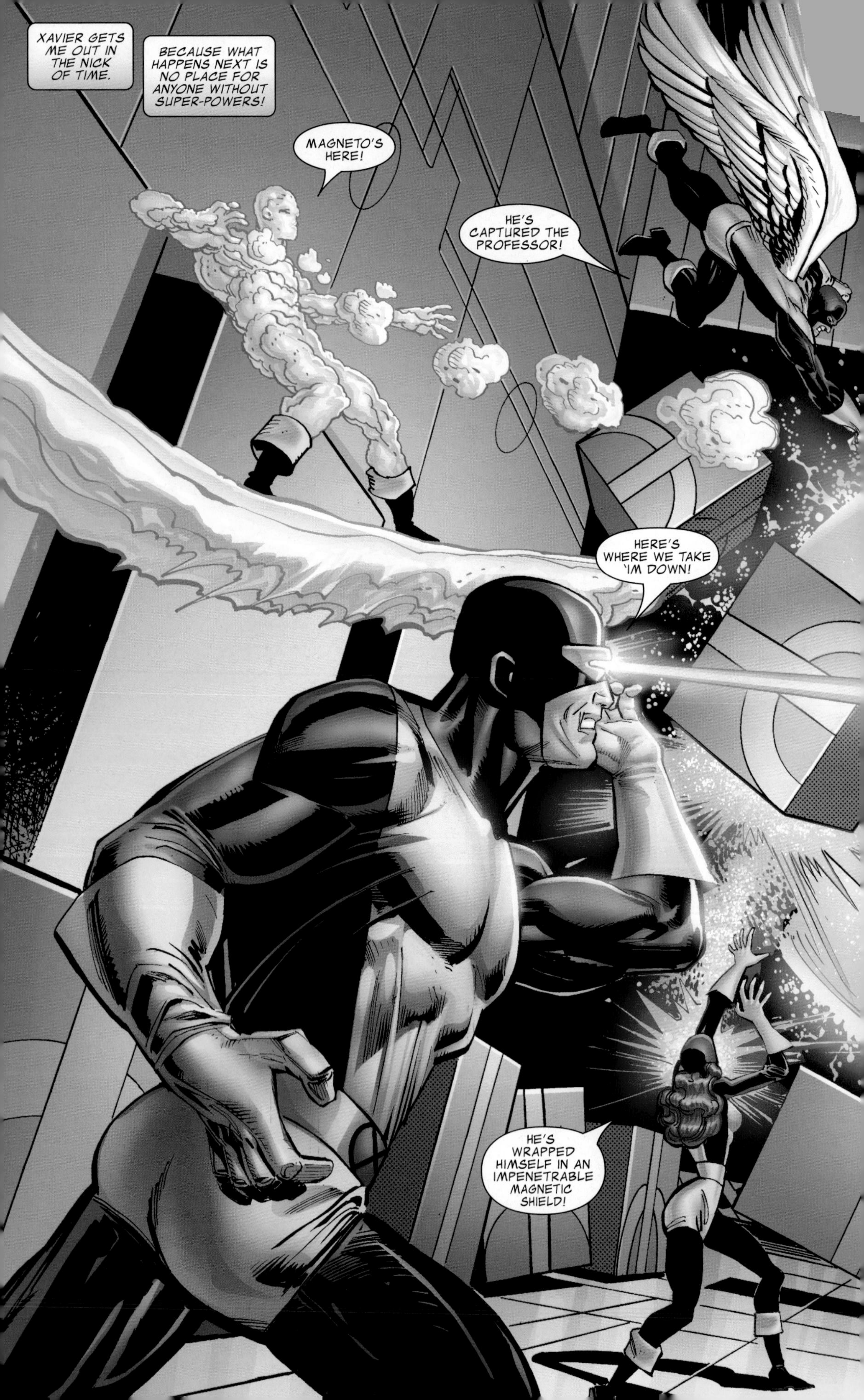
XAVIER GETS ME OUT IN THE NICK OF TIME.
BECAUSE WHAT HAPPENS NEXT IS NO PLACE FOR ANYONE WITHOUT SUPER-POWERS!
MAGNETO'S HERE!
HE'S CAPTURED THE PROFESSOR!
HERE'S WHERE WE TAKE 'IM DOWN!
HE'S WRAPPED HIMSELF IN AN IMPENETRABLE MAGNETIC SHIELD!

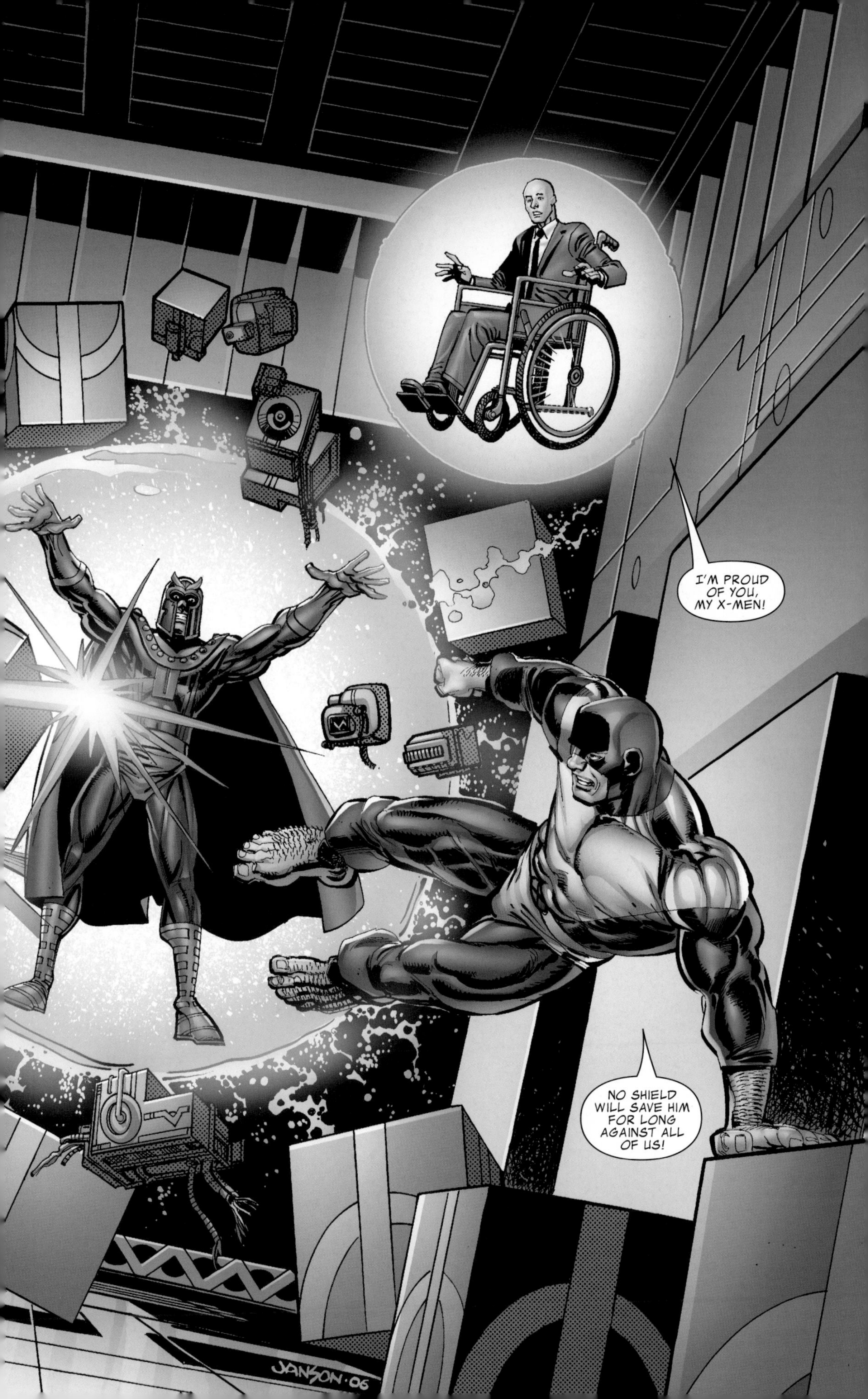
I'M PROUD OF YOU, MY X-MEN!
NO SHIELD WILL SAVE HIM FOR LONG AGAINST ALL OF US!
JANSON·06

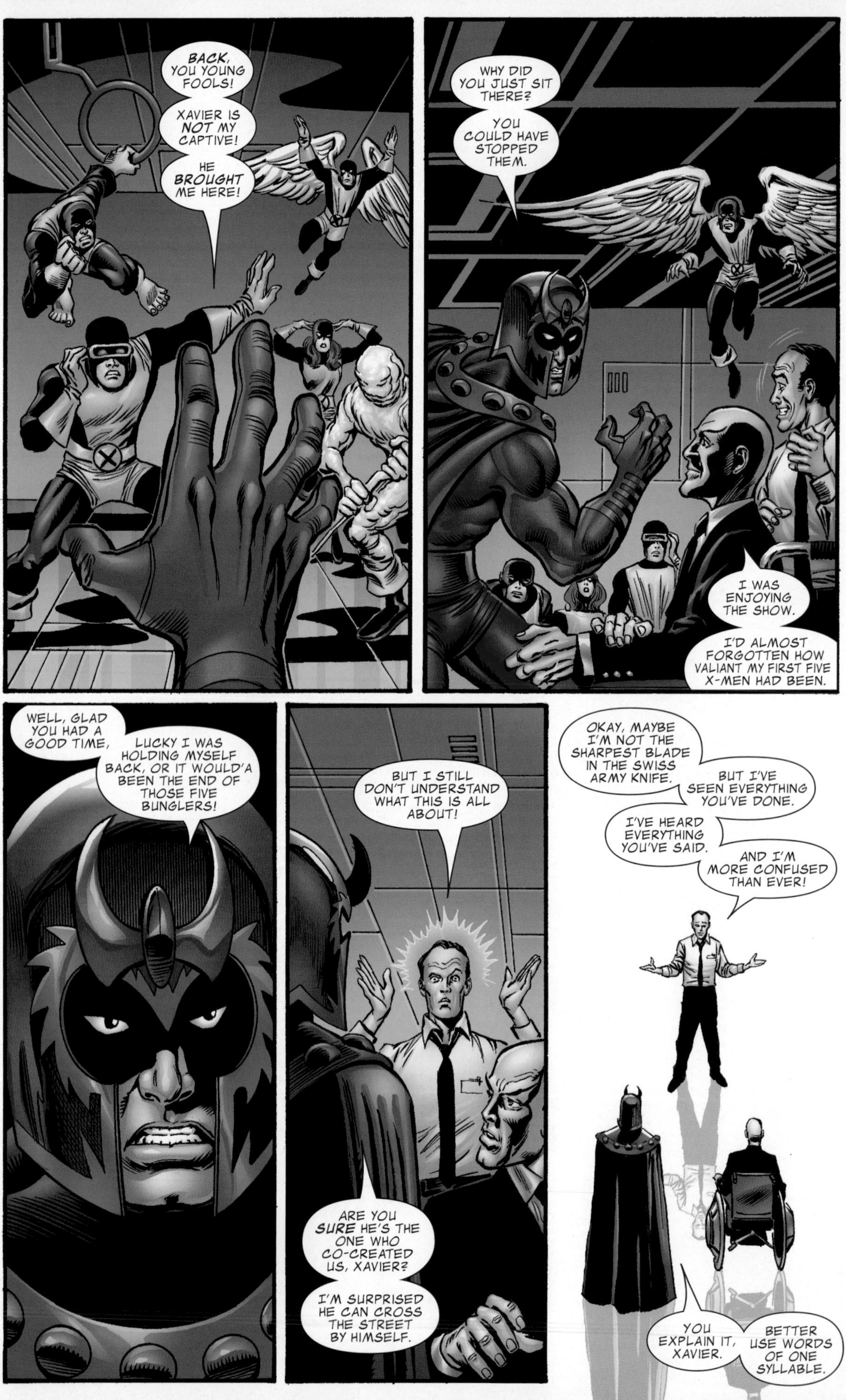
BACK, YOU YOUNG FOOLS!
XAVIER IS NOT MY CAPTIVE!
HE BROUGHT ME HERE!
WHY DID YOU JUST SIT THERE?
YOU COULD HAVE STOPPED THEM.
I WAS ENJOYING THE SHOW.
I'D ALMOST FORGOTTEN HOW VALIANT MY FIRST FIVE X-MEN HAD BEEN.
WELL, GLAD YOU HAD A GOOD TIME.
LUCKY I WAS HOLDING MYSELF BACK, OR IT WOULD'A BEEN THE END OF THOSE FIVE BUNGLERS!
BUT I STILL DON'T UNDERSTAND WHAT THIS IS ALL ABOUT!
ARE YOU SURE HE'S THE ONE WHO CO-CREATED US, XAVIER?
I'M SURPRISED HE CAN CROSS THE STREET BY HIMSELF.
OKAY, MAYBE I'M NOT THE SHARPEST BLADE IN THE SWISS ARMY KNIFE.
BUT I'VE SEEN EVERYTHING YOU'VE DONE.
I'VE HEARD EVERYTHING YOU'VE SAID.
AND I'M MORE CONFUSED THAN EVER!
YOU EXPLAIN IT, XAVIER.
BETTER USE WORDS OF ONE SYLLABLE.

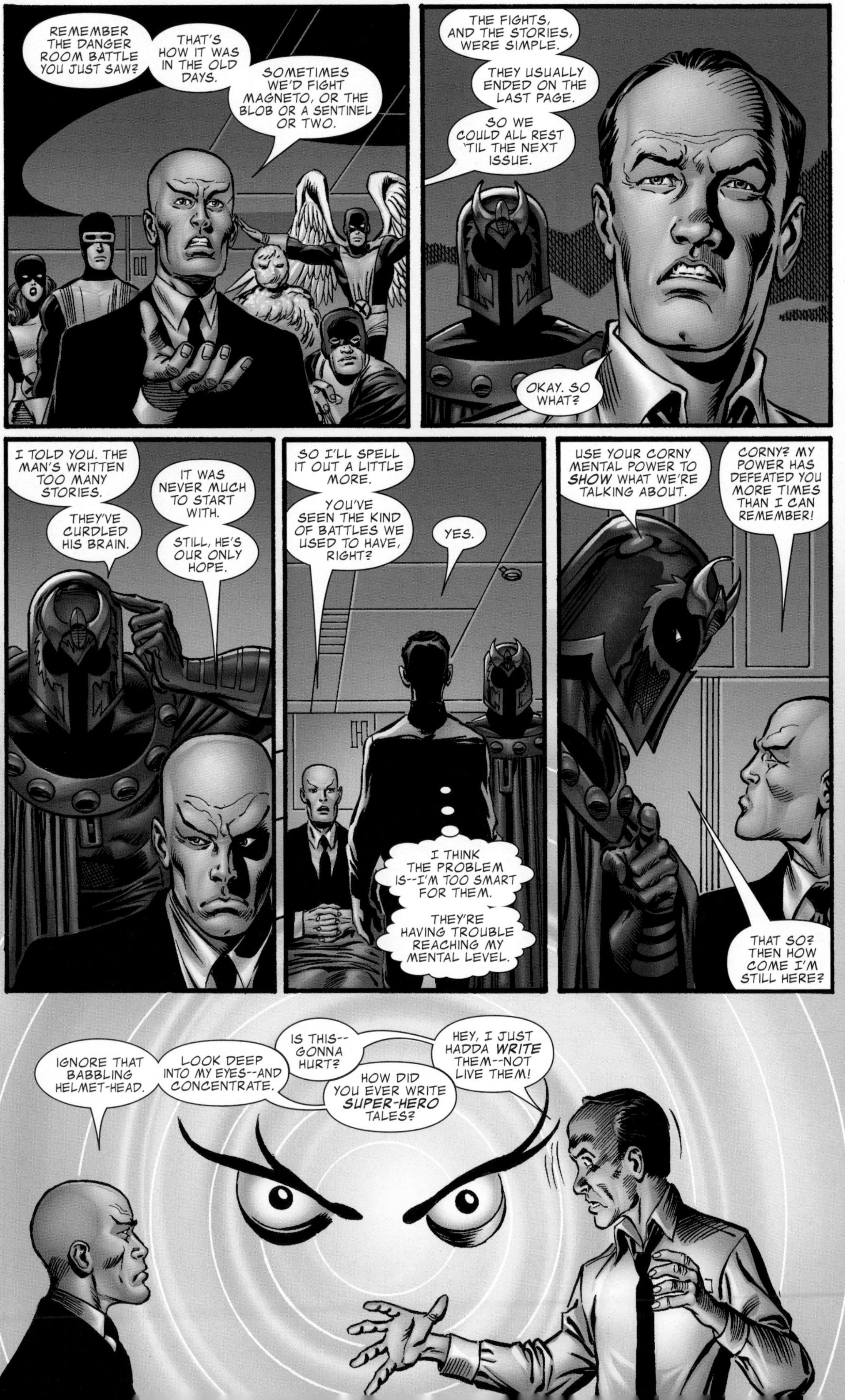
REMEMBER THE DANGER ROOM BATTLE YOU JUST SAW?
THAT'S HOW IT WAS IN THE OLD DAYS.
SOMETIMES WE'D FIGHT MAGNETO, OR THE BLOB OR A SENTINEL OR TWO.
THE FIGHTS, AND THE STORIES, WERE SIMPLE.
THEY USUALLY ENDED ON THE LAST PAGE.
SO WE COULD ALL REST 'TIL THE NEXT ISSUE.
OKAY. SO WHAT?
I TOLD YOU. THE MAN'S WRITTEN TOO MANY STORIES.
THEY'VE CURDLED HIS BRAIN.
IT WAS NEVER MUCH TO START WITH.
STILL, HE'S OUR ONLY HOPE.
SO I'LL SPELL IT OUT A LITTLE MORE.
YOU'VE SEEN THE KIND OF BATTLES WE USED TO HAVE, RIGHT?
YES.
I THINK THE PROBLEM IS--I'M TOO SMART FOR THEM.
THEY'RE HAVING TROUBLE REACHING MY MENTAL LEVEL.
USE YOUR CORNY MENTAL POWER TO SHOW WHAT WE'RE TALKING ABOUT.
CORNY? MY POWER HAS DEFEATED YOU MORE TIMES THAN I CAN REMEMBER!
THAT SO? THEN HOW COME I'M STILL HERE?
IGNORE THAT BABBLING HELMET-HEAD.
LOOK DEEP INTO MY EYES--AND CONCENTRATE.
IS THIS--GONNA HURT?
HOW DID YOU EVER WRITE SUPER-HERO TALES?
HEY, I JUST HADDA WRITE THEM--NOT LIVE THEM!

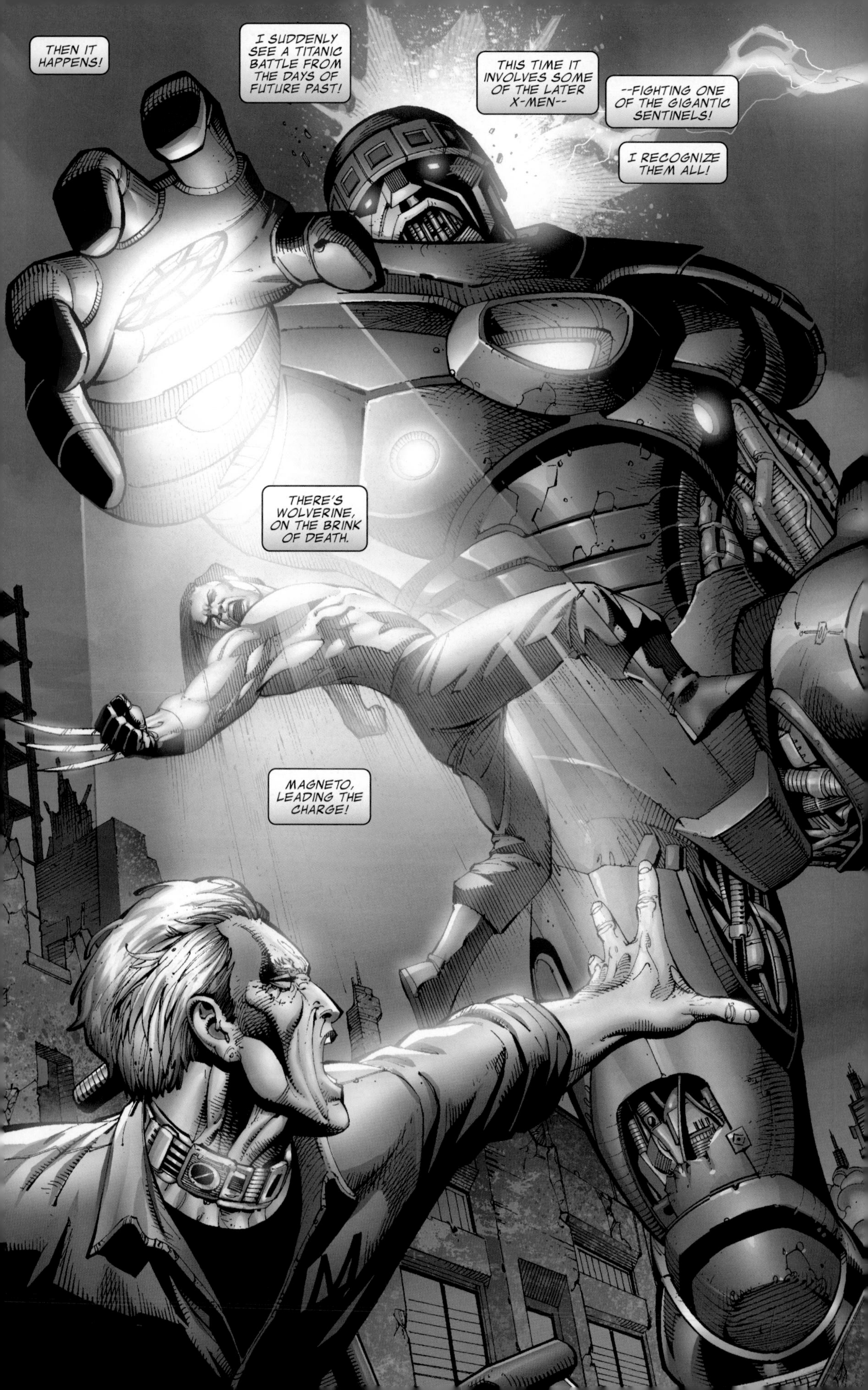
THEN IT HAPPENS!
I SUDDENLY SEE A TITANIC BATTLE FROM THE DAYS OF FUTURE PAST!
THIS TIME IT INVOLVES SOME OF THE LATER X-MEN--
--FIGHTING ONE OF THE GIGANTIC SENTINELS!
I RECOGNIZE THEM ALL!
THERE'S WOLVERINE, ON THE BRINK OF DEATH.
MAGNETO, LEADING THE CHARGE!

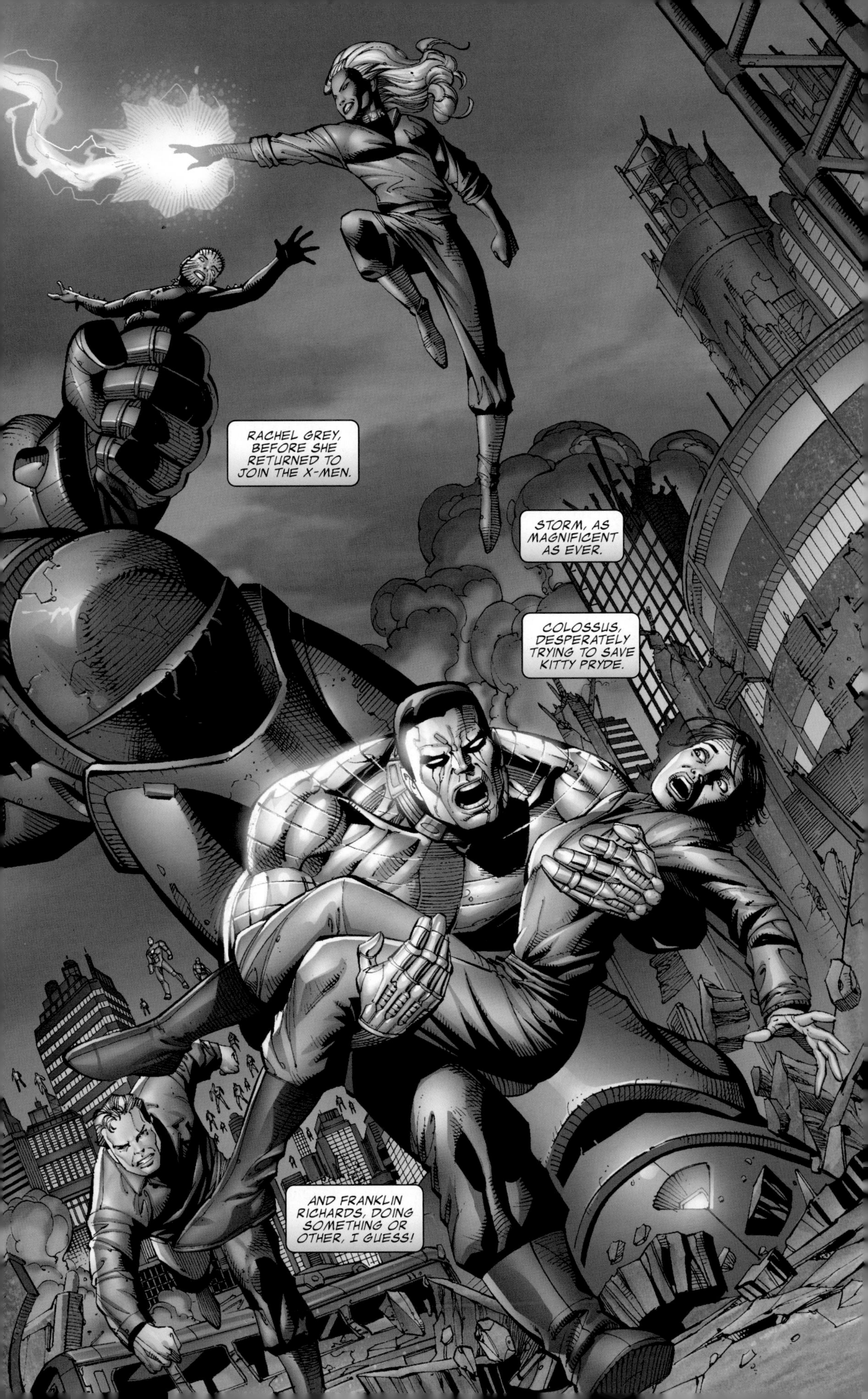
RACHEL GREY, BEFORE SHE RETURNED TO JOIN THE X-MEN.
STORM, AS MAGNIFICENT AS EVER.
COLOSSUS, DESPERATELY TRYING TO SAVE KITTY PRYDE.
AND FRANKLIN RICHARDS, DOING SOMETHING OR OTHER, I GUESS!

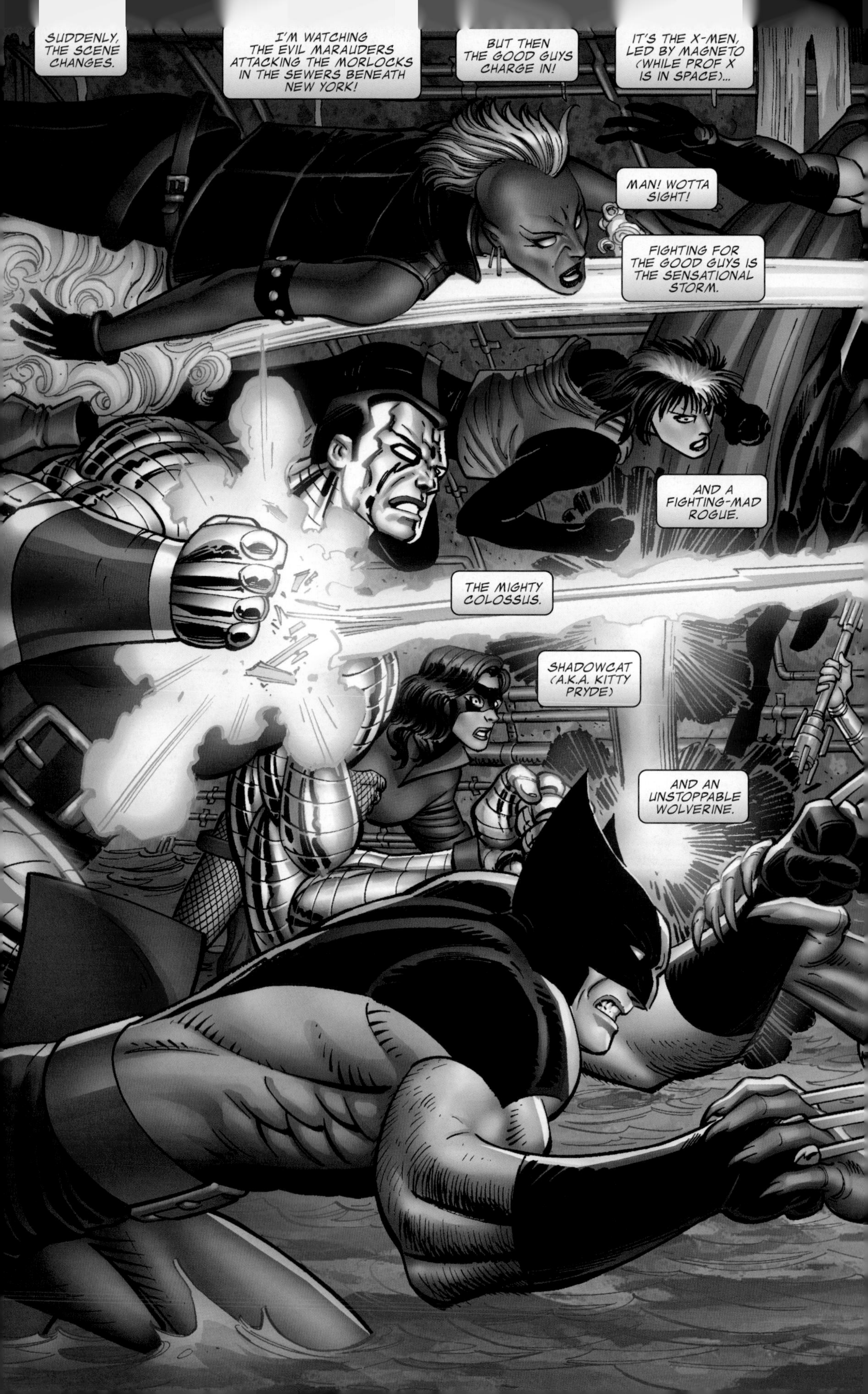
SUDDENLY, THE SCENE CHANGES.
I'M WATCHING THE EVIL MARAUDERS ATTACKING THE MORLOCKS IN THE SEWERS BENEATH NEW YORK!
BUT THEN THE GOOD GUYS CHARGE IN!
IT'S THE X-MEN, LED BY MAGNETO (WHILE PROF X IS IN SPACE)...
MAN! WOTTA SIGHT!
FIGHTING FOR THE GOOD GUYS IS THE SENSATIONAL STORM.
AND A FIGHTING-MAD ROGUE.
THE MIGHTY COLOSSUS.
SHADOWCAT (A.K.A. KITTY PRYDE)
AND AN UNSTOPPABLE WOLVERINE.

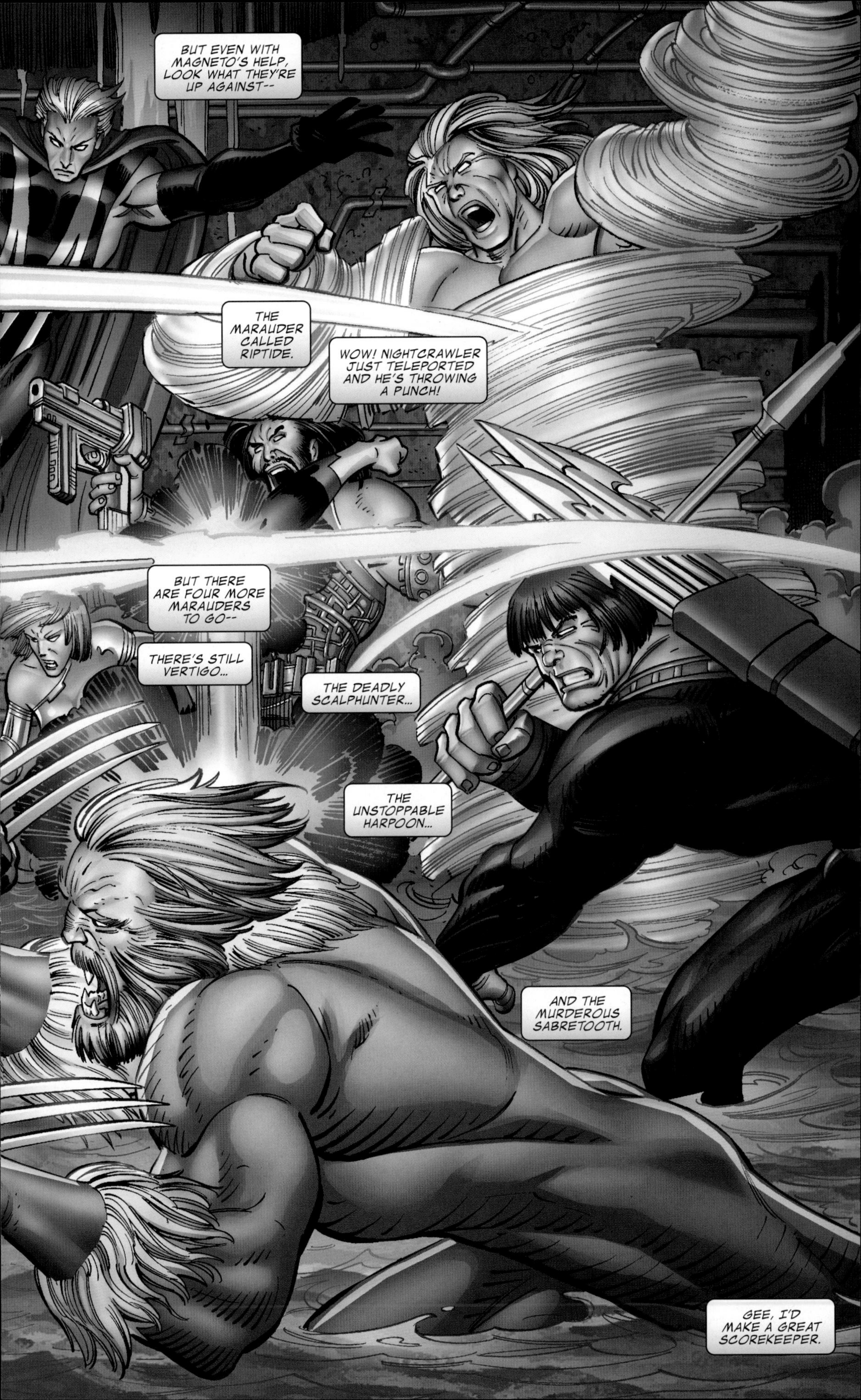
BUT EVEN WITH MAGNETO'S HELP, LOOK WHAT THEY'RE UP AGAINST--
THE MARAUDER CALLED RIPTIDE.
WOW! NIGHTCRAWLER JUST TELEPORTED AND HE'S THROWING A PUNCH!
BUT THERE ARE FOUR MORE MARAUDERS TO GO--
THERE'S STILL VERTIGO...
THE DEADLY SCALPHUNTER...
THE UNSTOPPABLE HARPOON...
AND THE MURDEROUS SABRETOOTH.
GEE, I'D MAKE A GREAT SCOREKEEPER.

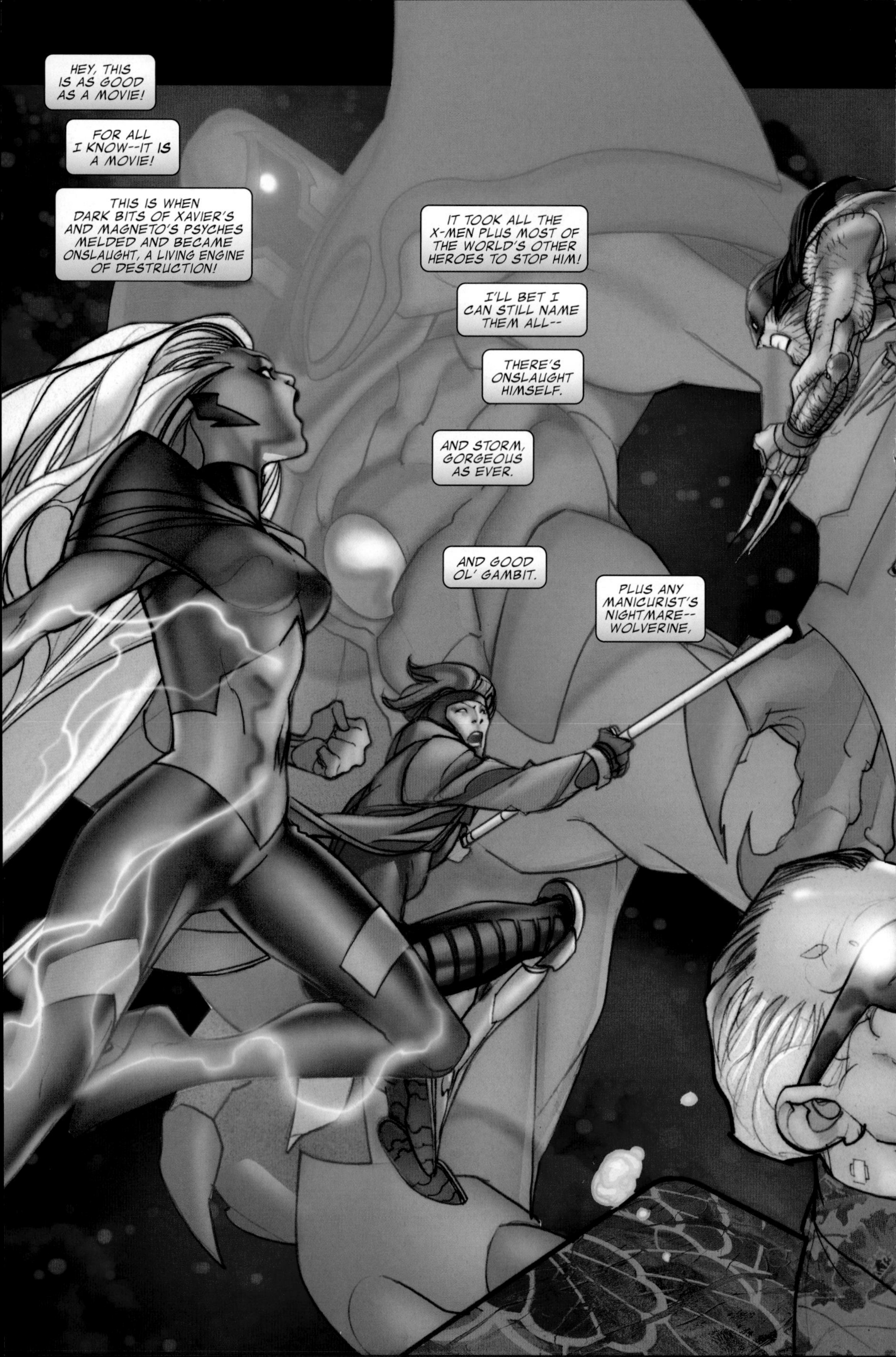
HEY, THIS IS AS GOOD AS A MOVIE!
FOR ALL I KNOW--IT IS A MOVIE!
THIS IS WHEN DARK BITS OF XAVIER'S AND MAGNETO'S PSYCHES MELDED AND BECAME ONSLAUGHT, A LIVING ENGINE OF DESTRUCTION!
IT TOOK ALL THE X-MEN PLUS MOST OF THE WORLD'S OTHER HEROES TO STOP HIM!
I'LL BET I CAN STILL NAME THEM ALL--
THERE'S ONSLAUGHT HIMSELF.
AND STORM, GORGEOUS AS EVER.
AND GOOD OL' GAMBIT.
PLUS ANY MANICURIST'S NIGHTMARE--WOLVERINE,

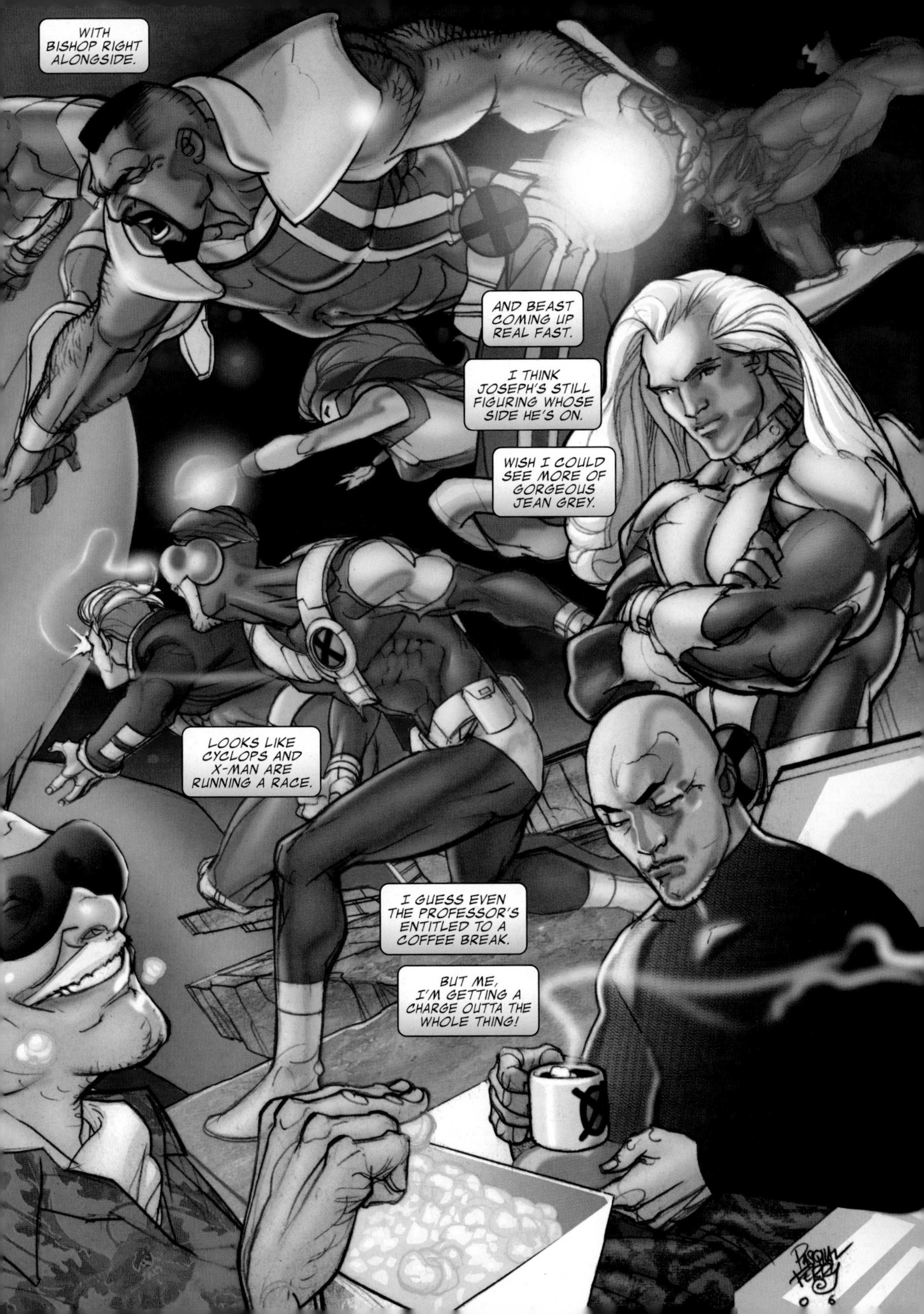
WITH BISHOP RIGHT ALONGSIDE.
AND BEAST COMING UP REAL FAST.
I THINK JOSEPH'S STILL FIGURING WHOSE SIDE HE'S ON.
WISH I COULD SEE MORE OF GORGEOUS JEAN GREY.
LOOKS LIKE CYCLOPS AND X-MAN ARE RUNNING A RACE.
I GUESS EVEN THE PROFESSOR'S ENTITLED TO A COFFEE BREAK.
BUT ME, I'M GETTING A CHARGE OUTTA THE WHOLE THING!

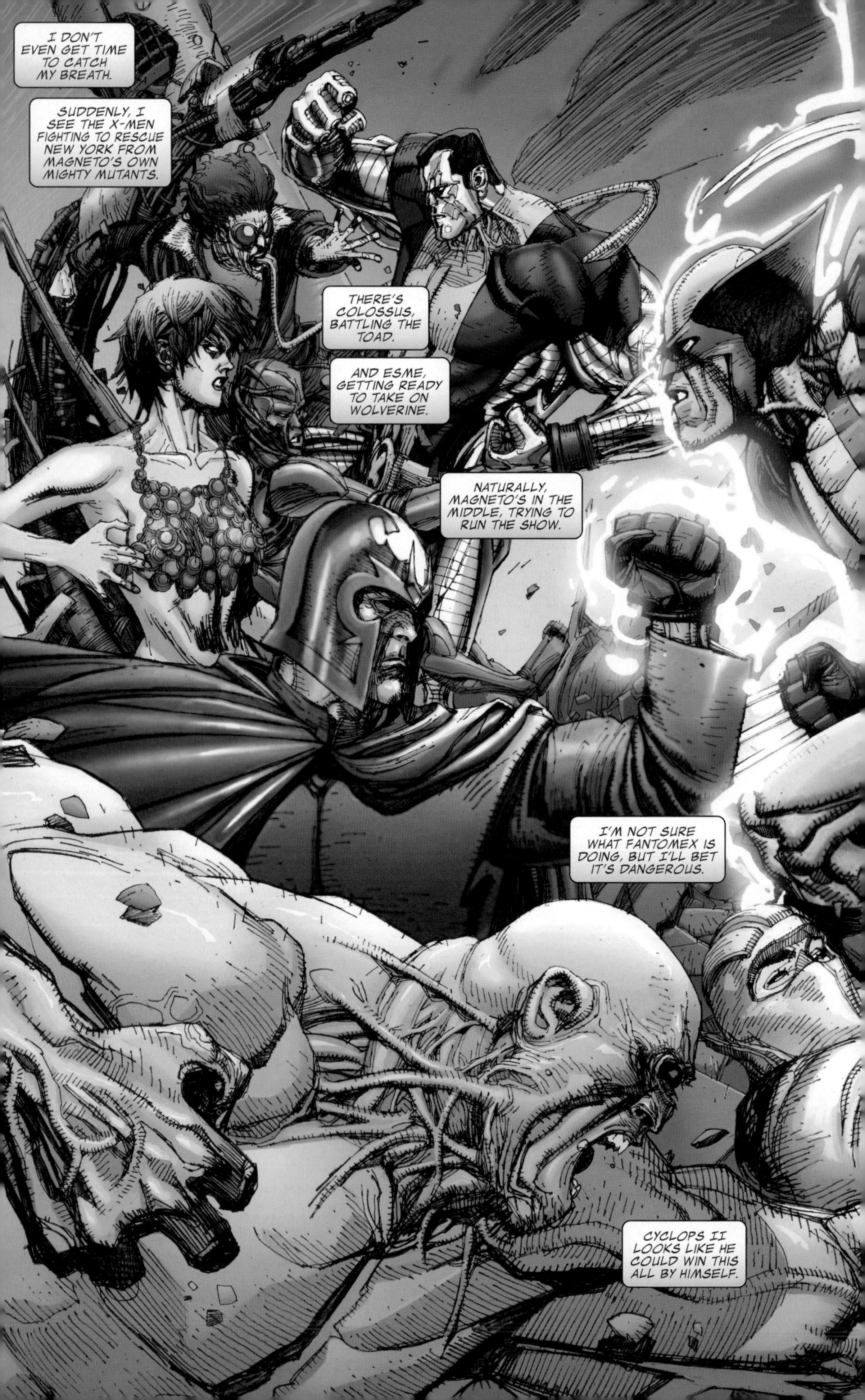
I DON'T EVEN GET TIME TO CATCH MY BREATH.
SUDDENLY, I SEE THE X-MEN FIGHTING TO RESCUE NEW YORK FROM MAGNETO'S OWN MIGHTY MUTANTS.
THERE'S COLOSSUS, BATTLING THE TOAD.
AND ESME, GETTING READY TO TAKE ON WOLVERINE.
NATURALLY, MAGNETO'S IN THE MIDDLE, TRYING TO RUN THE SHOW.
I'M NOT SURE WHAT FANTOMEX IS DOING, BUT I'LL BET IT'S DANGEROUS.
CYCLOPS II LOOKS LIKE HE COULD WIN THIS ALL BY HIMSELF.

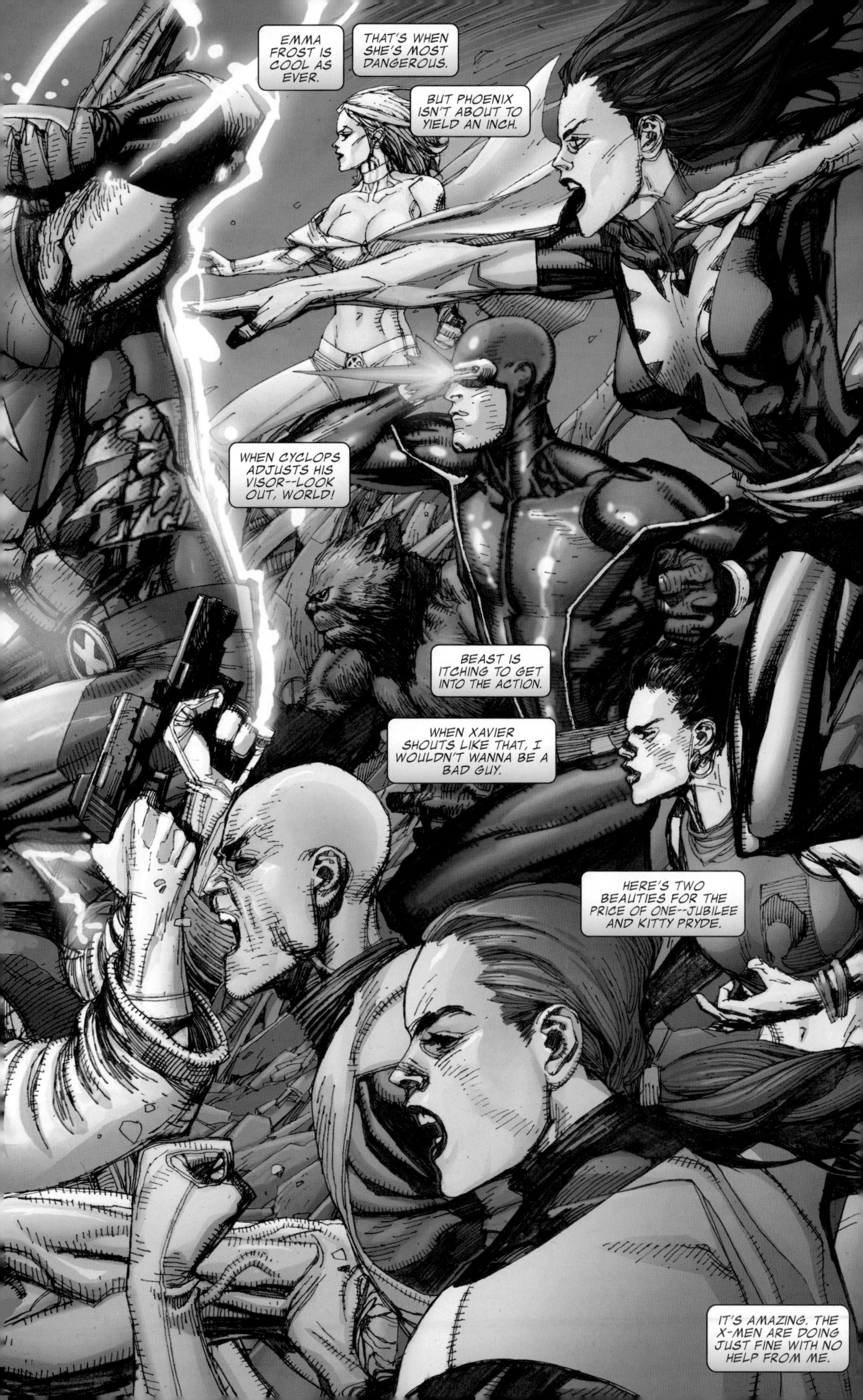
EMMA FROST IS COOL AS EVER.
THAT'S WHEN SHE'S MOST DANGEROUS.
BUT PHOENIX ISN'T ABOUT TO YIELD AN INCH.
WHEN CYCLOPS ADJUSTS HIS VISOR--LOOK OUT, WORLD!
BEAST IS ITCHING TO GET INTO THE ACTION.
WHEN XAVIER SHOUTS LIKE THAT, I WOULDN'T WANNA BE A BAD GUY.
HERE'S TWO BEAUTIES FOR THE PRICE OF ONE--JUBILEE AND KITTY PRYDE.
IT'S AMAZING. THE X-MEN ARE DOING JUST FINE WITH NO HELP FROM ME.

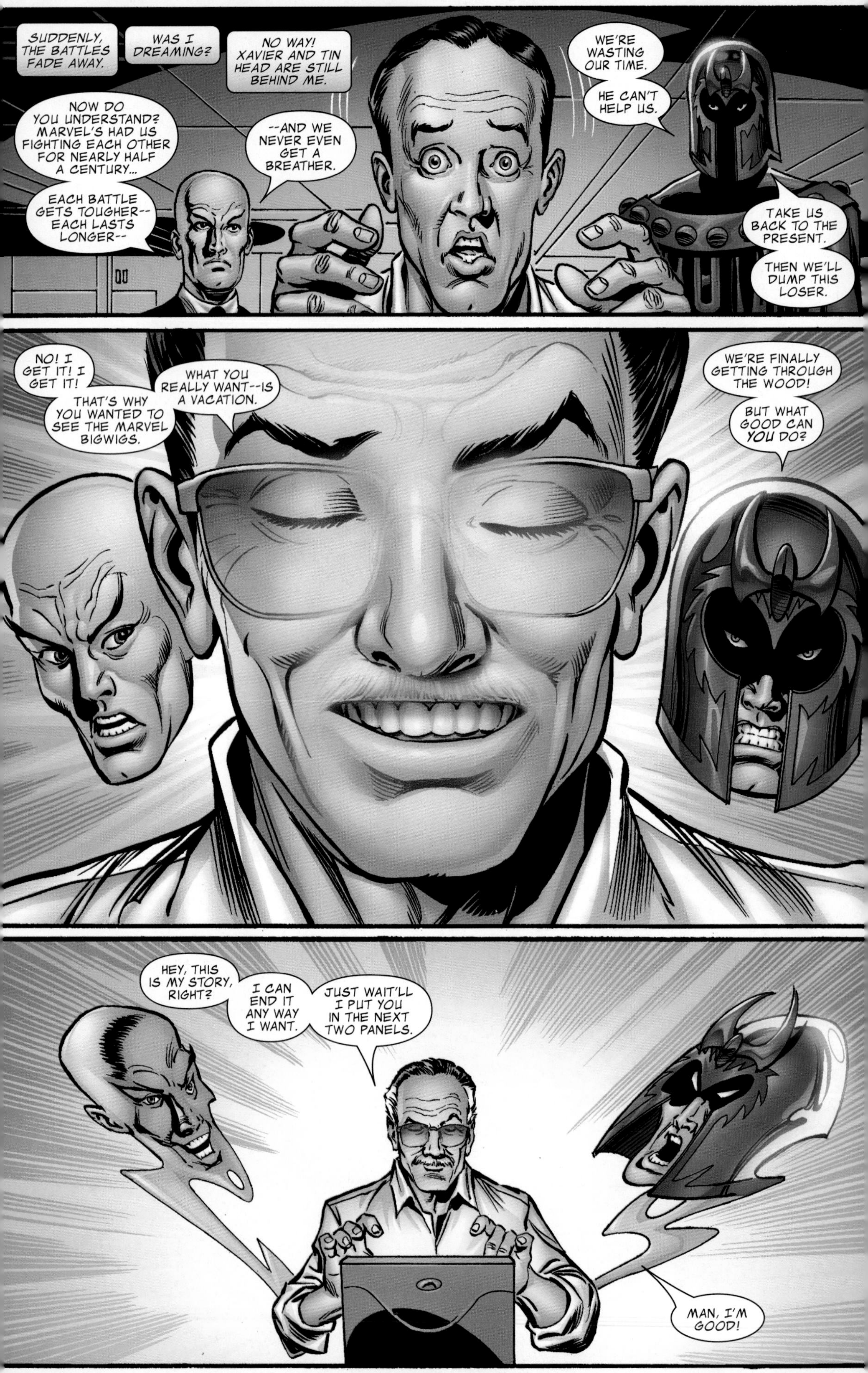
SUDDENLY, THE BATTLES FADE AWAY.
WAS I DREAMING?
NO WAY! XAVIER AND TIN HEAD ARE STILL BEHIND ME.
NOW DO YOU UNDERSTAND? MARVEL'S HAD US FIGHTING EACH OTHER FOR NEARLY HALF A CENTURY...
EACH BATTLE GETS TOUGHER-- EACH LASTS LONGER--
--AND WE NEVER EVEN GET A BREATHER.
WE'RE WASTING OUR TIME.
HE CAN'T HELP US.
TAKE US BACK TO THE PRESENT.
THEN WE'LL DUMP THIS LOSER.
NO! I GET IT! I GET IT!
THAT'S WHY YOU WANTED TO SEE THE MARVEL BIGWIGS.
WHAT YOU REALLY WANT--IS A VACATION.
WE'RE FINALLY GETTING THROUGH THE WOOD!
BUT WHAT GOOD CAN YOU DO?
HEY, THIS IS MY STORY, RIGHT?
I CAN END IT ANY WAY I WANT.
JUST WAIT'LL I PUT YOU IN THE NEXT TWO PANELS.
MAN, I'M GOOD!

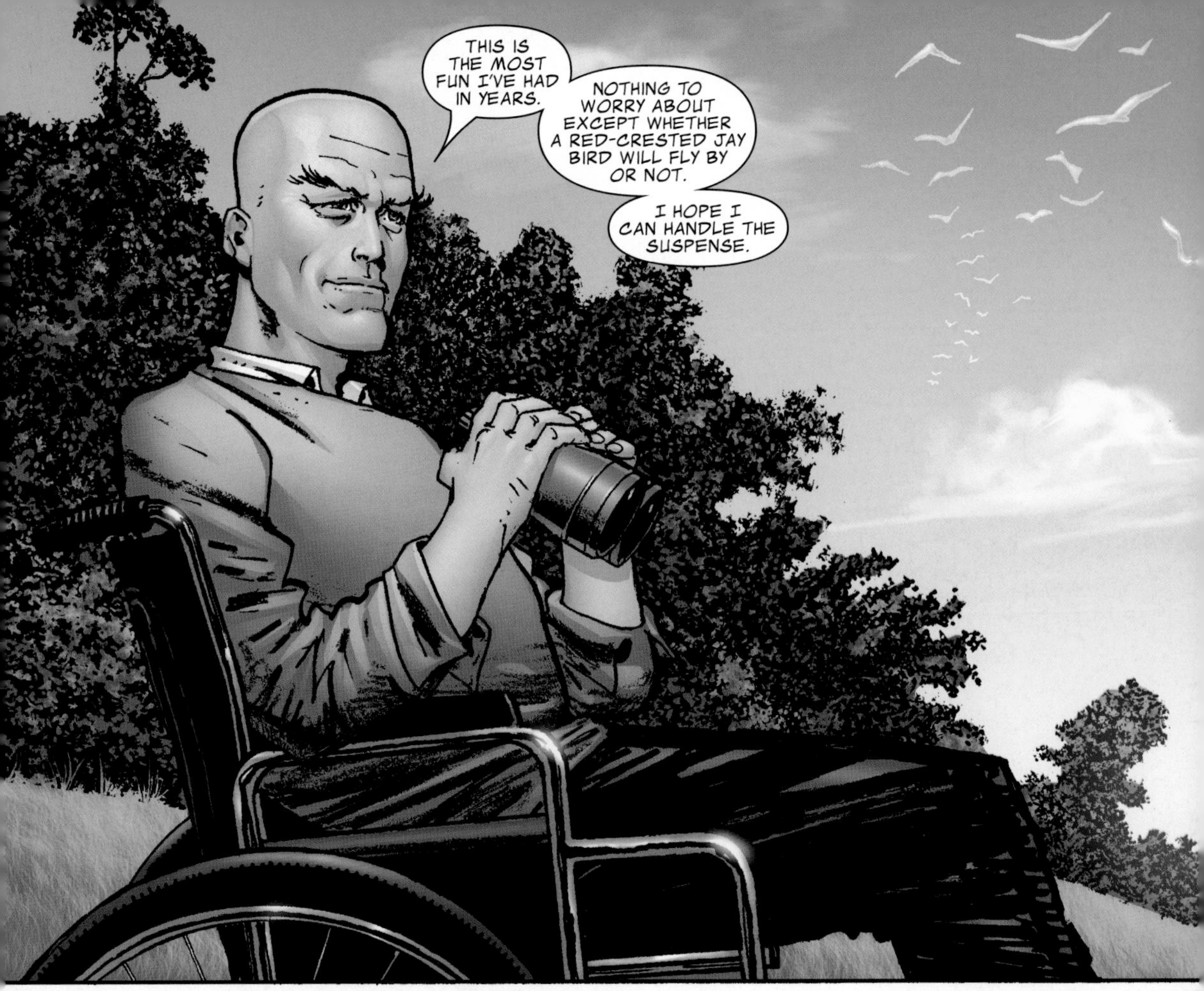
THIS IS THE MOST FUN I'VE HAD IN YEARS.
NOTHING TO WORRY ABOUT EXCEPT WHETHER A RED-CRESTED JAY BIRD WILL FLY BY OR NOT.
I HOPE I CAN HANDLE THE SUSPENSE.

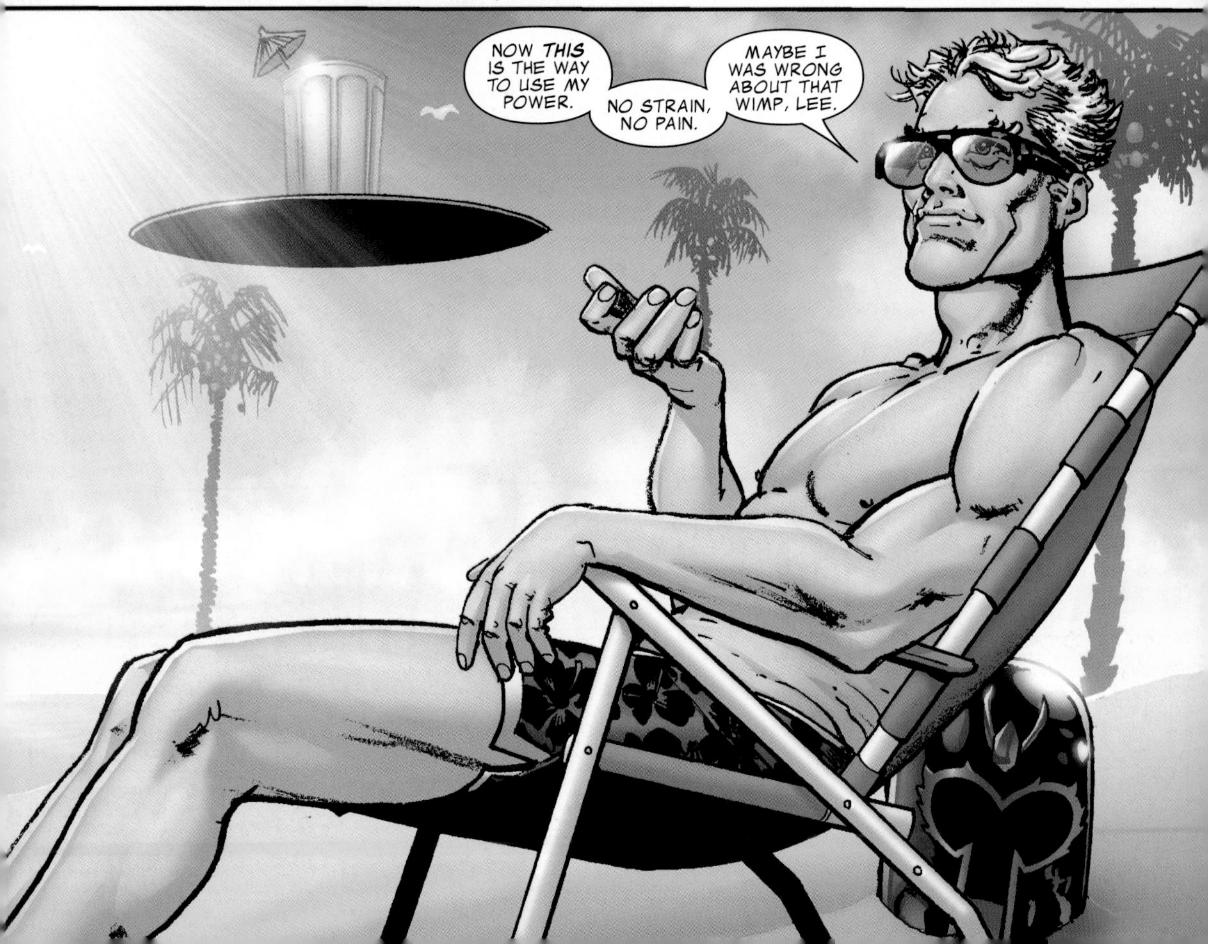
NOW *THIS* IS THE WAY TO USE MY POWER.
NO STRAIN, NO PAIN.
MAYBE I WAS WRONG ABOUT THAT WIMP, LEE.

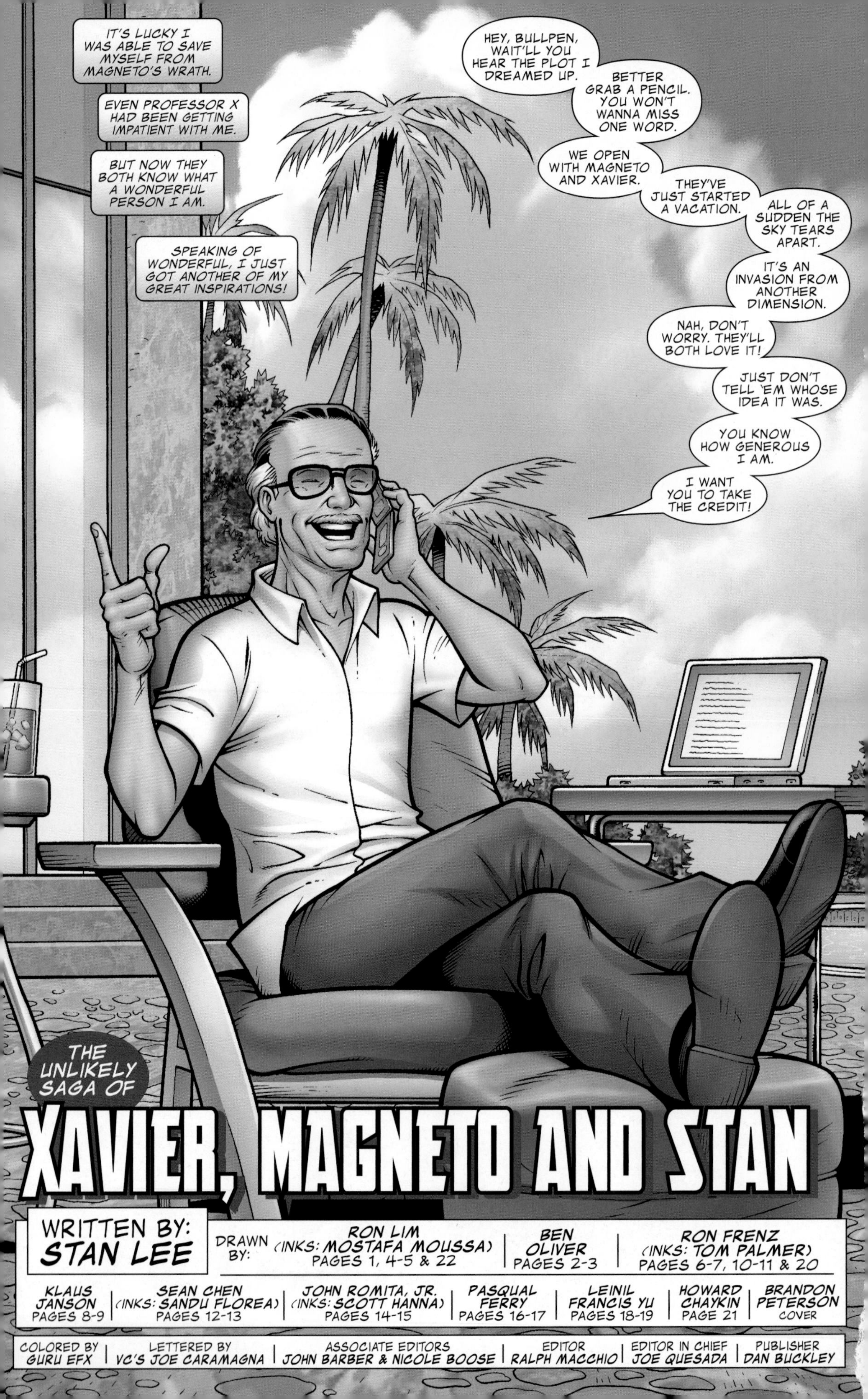
IT'S LUCKY I WAS ABLE TO SAVE MYSELF FROM MAGNETO'S WRATH.
EVEN PROFESSOR X HAD BEEN GETTING IMPATIENT WITH ME.
BUT NOW THEY BOTH KNOW WHAT A WONDERFUL PERSON I AM.
SPEAKING OF WONDERFUL, I JUST GOT ANOTHER OF MY GREAT INSPIRATIONS!
HEY, BULLPEN, WAIT'LL YOU HEAR THE PLOT I DREAMED UP.
BETTER GRAB A PENCIL. YOU WON'T WANNA MISS ONE WORD.
WE OPEN WITH MAGNETO AND XAVIER.
THEY'VE JUST STARTED A VACATION.
ALL OF A SUDDEN THE SKY TEARS APART.
IT'S AN INVASION FROM ANOTHER DIMENSION.
NAH, DON'T WORRY. THEY'LL BOTH LOVE IT!
JUST DON'T TELL 'EM WHOSE IDEA IT WAS.
YOU KNOW HOW GENEROUS I AM.
I WANT YOU TO TAKE THE CREDIT!
THE UNLIKELY SAGA OF
XAVIER, MAGNETO AND STAN
WRITTEN BY: STAN LEE
DRAWN BY: RON LIM (INKS: MOSTAFA MOUSSA) PAGES 1, 4-5 & 22
BEN OLIVER PAGES 2-3
RON FRENZ (INKS: TOM PALMER) PAGES 6-7, 10-11 & 20
KLAUS JANSON PAGES 8-9
SEAN CHEN (INKS: SANDU FLOREA) PAGES 12-13
JOHN ROMITA, JR. (INKS: SCOTT HANNA) PAGES 14-15
PASQUAL FERRY PAGES 16-17
LEINIL FRANCIS YU PAGES 18-19
HOWARD CHAYKIN PAGE 21
BRANDON PETERSON COVER
COLORED BY GURU EFX
LETTERED BY VC'S JOE CARAMAGNA
ASSOCIATE EDITORS JOHN BARBER & NICOLE BOOSE
EDITOR RALPH MACCHIO
EDITOR IN CHIEF JOE QUESADA
PUBLISHER DAN BUCKLEY